Funding for Museums, Archives and Special Collections

T5-AEW-622

Edited by Denise Wallen and Karen Cantrell

ORYX PRESS
1988

The rare Arabian Oryx is believed to have inspired the myth of the unicorn. This desert antelope became virtually extinct in the early 1960s. At that time several groups of international conservationists arranged to have 9 animals sent to the Phoenix Zoo to be the nucleus of a captive breeding herd. Today the Oryx population is nearly 800, and over 400 have been returned to reserves in the Middle East.

Library of Congress Cataloging-in-Publication Data

Funding for museums, archives and special collections / edited by
    Denise Wallen and Karen Cantrell.
        p. cm.
    Bibliography: p.
    Includes indexes.
    ISBN 0-89774-347-4
    1. Museum finance—United States—Handbooks, manuals, etc.
2. Endowments—United States—Directories. I. Wallen, Denise.
II. Cantrell, Karen.
AM122.F86 1988
069'.068'1—dc19   88-21081

Table of Contents

Acknowledgements

There are many people whose help we have valued in the preparation of this directory and whom we wish to thank. Our colleagues at The University of New Mexico are continuously supportive. We would like to thank the reference librarians at the university's Zimmerman Library, especially Barbara Rosen, Reference Library Specialist. We also offer thanks to the many association, corporation, federal, foundation, library, and museum program officers and staff assistants who patiently answered our many questions and provided us with the information necessary to compile this directory. Finally, special thanks to Sue Johnson, our editor at The Oryx Press.

Introduction

Funding for Museums, Archives and Special Collections is designed to facilitate the search for financial support for museums and museum activities and programs. A museum, as defined by the American Association of Museums, is considered to be any "...nonprofit institution essentially educational or aesthetic in purpose with professional staff, which owns or utilizes tangible objects, cares for them, and exhibits them to the public on some schedule." Thus, this directory includes funding for aquariums; archives; art, history, natural history, science, and science/technology museums; botanical gardens; historic sites and museum villages; planetariums; special collections; and zoos. The programs listed support a wide variety of activities or needs including administration and operations, acquisitions and collections management, conservation, education, endowment and capital campaigns, exhibitions, historic preservation, internships, outreach programs, and renovation.

The directory also includes sources of support for individuals who wish to work, study, or conduct research in museums or special collections. Museum professionals, scholars, and advanced students who wish, for example, to travel to collections, conduct research on collections held in museums or archives, undertake advanced training in museology or collections conservation, compete for specialized curatorial positions, or prepare scholarly publications, including catalogues, will find fellowship or grant support for their activities in this directory. Available support cuts across many disciplines, from art history to zoology.

Listing over 500 sources of support for museums or individuals wishing to work or conduct research in museums, this directory is designed to provide sufficient detail to steer applicants in the right direction in their search for funding. The programs, arranged alphabetically by sponsor, include support offered by private and corporate foundations, corporate direct giving, government agencies, associations and organizations, and professional societies. Each funding program profile includes available information essential to securing support: address, telephone number, program purpose and activities, samples of previously funded projects, eligibility and limitations, fiscal information, application information, deadlines, and any useful additional information. Applicants should, however, confirm all profile contents prior to proposal development. This means that current funding priorities, the availability of funding, and deadlines should be confirmed with the sponsor.

To facilitate the identification of appropriate sources of support, a number of useful indexes have been designed and included in the directory. A subject index of keyword terms allows the user to locate sources of funding in a particular discipline or area of interest, e.g., African art, art history, conservation, Middle Eastern studies, or zoology; to identify funding mechanisms such as fellowships, travel grants, or publication support; and to identify specific types of support, including building funds, capital support, education, exhibitions, general/operating support, or renovation support. A geographic restriction index is included for swift location of funding sources that focus or limit their giving to specific states or, in the case of corporate direct-giving programs and corporate foundations, in company operating areas. This specially designed index serves as a valuable short-cut in the identification of available funding sources for museums, archives, and special collections in each of the fifty states, the District of Columbia, and U.S. Territories. This index should *always* be consulted; many corporations, corporate foundations, and private foundations limit their giving programs to specific geographic areas. Finally, a sponsor type index is included so the user may properly discern corporate and private foundations, associations and organizations, and government agencies.

How to Use This Directory

Funding for Museums, Archives and Special Collections is composed of a Program Profiles Section, a Subject Index, a Geographic Restriction Index, a Sponsor Type Index, a Listing of Sponsoring Organizations, and a Bibliography.

PROGRAM PROFILES SECTION

Each entry in this section is composed of all or some of the following elements: accession number; sponsoring organization name; department or division name; street address with city, state, zip, country, and telephone number; the program title; for federal programs, the *Catalog of Federal Domestic Assistance* program identification number; a program description which briefly details the purpose of the program; a sample grants statement which lists programs recently funded by the sponsor; a statement of program eligibility/limitations describing any special requirements or restrictions for each program; fiscal information; application information; deadline information; and a statement of any additional, useful information that does not fit into one of the listed categories (the illustrated entry does not contain this element).

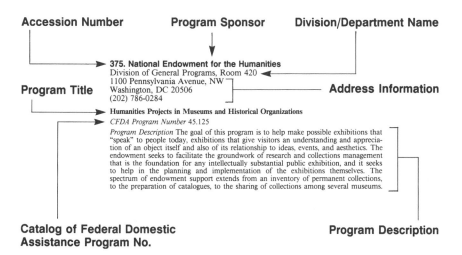

Accession Number   **Program Sponsor**   **Division/Department Name**

375. National Endowment for the Humanities
Division of General Programs, Room 420
1100 Pennsylvania Avenue, NW
Washington, DC 20506
(202) 786-0284

Program Title   **Address Information**

Humanities Projects in Museums and Historical Organizations

CFDA Program Number 45.125

Program Description The goal of this program is to help make possible exhibitions that "speak" to people today, exhibitions that give visitors an understanding and appreciation of an object itself and also of its relationship to ideas, events, and aesthetics. The endowment seeks to facilitate the groundwork of research and collections management that is the foundation for any intellectually substantial public exhibition, and it seeks to help in the planning and implementation of the exhibitions themselves. The spectrum of endowment support extends from an inventory of permanent collections, to the preparation of catalogues, to the sharing of collections among several museums.

Catalog of Federal Domestic
Assistance Program No.

Program Description

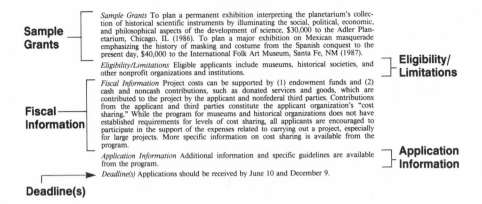

SUBJECT INDEX

The most effective way to access specific funding programs is by searching the Subject Index. Index terms have been assigned to each program. All subject terms are displayed with the applicable program and the program's accession number listed alphabetically under each term.

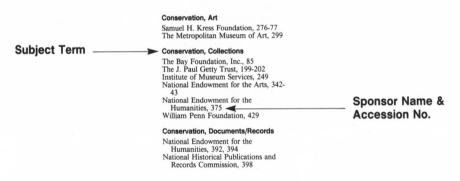

GEOGRAPHIC RESTRICTION INDEX

In order to identify funding programs which may be focused or limited to a specific geographic area, the geographic restriction index should be consulted. This index is divided into five restriction types:

- **Company Operating Areas (no state preference)**
  These awards are made by program sponsors who limit funding to areas in which their company has facilities or operations. The program sponsors do not specify the states in which they do business in their grant materials.

- **Company Operating Areas (with state preference)**
  These awards are made by program sponsors who limit their funding to areas in which their company has facilities or operations. All awards are made in company operating areas within the states specified.

- **International/National (no state preference)**
  These programs are funded by sponsors on a national and/or international basis.

- **International/National (with state preference)**
  These programs are funded by sponsors who prefer to concentrate their grantmaking activities in certain states, but will also consider requests from other areas.

- **State**
  These awards are made by program sponsors to recipients within specific states.

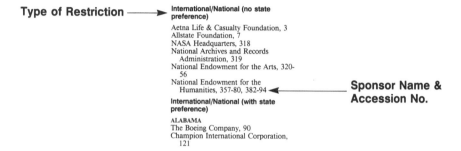

SPONSOR TYPE INDEX

This index is organized into six different sponsor types with the name of the program sponsor and the program's accession number listed under each type. The six sponsor types are: Corporation; Federal; Foundation; Museum/Library; Nonprofit Organization; and University.

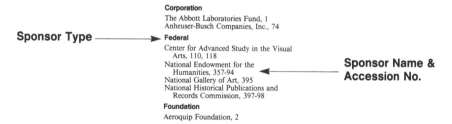

LISTING OF SPONSORING ORGANIZATIONS

This index alphabetically lists all sponsors with address.

Program Profiles

1. The Abbott Laboratories Fund

Abbott Laboratories
Abbott Park
North Chicago, IL 60064
(312) 937-7075

Contributions Program

Program Description Fund contributions are directed towards those areas in which Abbott has an immediate or long-range interest and relevant expertise. The primary areas of the fund's interest are in the fields of education and human health and welfare. In addition, support of appropriate programs in culture, the arts and civic activities will continue to to be a portion of Abbott's program. In the areas of culture, art, and civic activities, the fund may consider support for specific projects having unusual needs which are related to Abbott's overall interests and areas of activities. These would include community improvement projects in areas having a high concentration of employees and organizations providing cultural enrichment in such communities.

Eligibility/Limitations Grants will be made only to associations and organizations and not directly to individuals. Grantees must be able to provide evidence of nonprofit, tax-exempt status. Contributions will not be made for social or fund-raising events. The fund's general policy will be to give preference to requests for one-time contributions and for programmatic and operating purposes. However, grants extending over a defined period of years or directed towards the support of specific building or other capital projects will be considered on an exception basis.

Fiscal Information The contributions program and policies of the fund are administered by its board of directors through its policy committee and a contributions committee. The board of directors establishes annual budgets and the allocation of those budgets to the primary areas of the fund's interest. The contributions committee, under the guidance of such policies, considers requests for support directed to the fund and will be responsible for recommending specific recipients of fund support.

Application Information Requests for support from the Abbott Laboratories Fund should be directed in writing to the president of the fund at the address listed above. Application forms are not required.

Deadline(s) No deadlines are announced.

2. Aeroquip Foundation

300 South East Avenue
Jackson, MI 49203-1972
(517) 787-8121

Grants

Program Description The Aeroquip Foundation was established in 1962. Its only contributor is Aeroquip Corporation of Jackson, Michigan. The objectives of the foundation are to fulfill the philanthropic obligations of Aeroquip corporation to those communities where the corporation has its manufacturing plants by supporting charitable and educational organizations.

Sample Grants In support of the Ella Sharp Museum Expansion Project, $33,300 to the Ella Sharp Museum, Jackson, MI (1986).

Eligibility/Limitations The foundation does not make grants to individuals for special research projects, nor for sectarian or religious purposes. It is the policy of the foundation to make grants for operating funds only to United Funds, regional funds supporting independent colleges, junior achievement groups, and certain cultural organizations. The applying organization must be tax-exempt.

Fiscal Information Grants awarded in 1986 totaled over $340,000.

Application Information Requests should be in writing and submitted through the local Aeroquip Corporation plant manager and include: a completed Aeroquip Foundation Grant Application form; letter of recommendation from the local plant manager or other executive; evidence of tax-exempt status, with a copy of the Internal Revenue Service ruling letter; a detailed budget justifying the amount requested; and verification that the request is made by action of the organization's governing body.

Deadline(s) Proposals may be submitted at any time, preferably between May and December.

3. Aetna Life & Casualty Foundation
Corporate Public Involvement Department
151 Farmington Avenue
Hartford, CT 06156
(203) 273-3340

Contributions Program

Program Description The Aetna Life and Casualty Company and Aetna Life & Casualty Foundation, Inc., are able to help communities meet their needs through grants and investment programs, partnerships with community organizations and encouragement of employees' volunteer activities. The foundation's national grants program focuses on organizations which pursue innovative work in education and youth employment, urban revitalization, civil justice reform, leadership development, and arts and culture. The foundation's priorities target the young and disadvantaged, the needs of urban communities, and programs that help disadvantaged persons attain economic and social self-sufficiency. In addition, the foundation looks for programs that have measurable results and offer opportunities to leverage their resources with those of other funders.

Sample Grants To the Rochester Museum Science Center, Rochester, NY, $2,000 (1985). To the Mint Museum, Charlotte, NC, $10,000 (1985). To the Friends of the Barnet Park Zoo, Syracuse, NY, $10,000 (1985). To the Clarke Memorial Museum, Eureka, CA, $5,000 (1985).

Eligibility/Limitations The foundation will not make grants to: individuals; organizations not designated 501(c)(3) tax-exempt public charities by the Internal Revenue Service; capital or endowment campaigns; fund-raising dinners or special events; or the sponsorship of conferences.

Fiscal Information The foundation awarded over $6.7 million in grants in 1985. The company made contributions separate from the foundation in 1985 totaling over $1.9 million.

Application Information The foundation requires that all grant applicants submit a preliminary proposal. The proposal must include: a description of the organization, its history and purpose; documentation of 501(c)(3) public charity status; a description of the project for which funds are requested; a summary of the program or organization budget; and the amount requested. The foundation staff will review this information and determine if the organization and its project are consistent with foundation priorities. Once the foundation staff gives a positive response, a formal proposal will be requested.

Deadline(s) The foundation staff will acknowledge receipt of a proposal within three weeks.

Additional Information In addition to a national grants program, the foundation also operates local grants programs through selected Aetna field offices across the country. If the foundation staff thinks an organization's needs may be more appropriately served by manager-referred programs, proposals may be referred to the nearest field office for review.

4. The Ahmanson Foundation
9215 Wilshire Boulevard
Beverly Hills, CA 90210
(213) 278-0770

Program Description The foundation emphasizes support of the arts and humanities, education, medicine and health, and support for a broad range of social welfare programs.

Eligibility/Limitations Grants are provided only to nonprofit organizations classified as tax-exempt under Section 501(c)(3) of the Internal Revenue Code of 1954 and treated as other than a private foundation under Section 509(a) of the code. Grants are made primarily to organizations in Southern California with an emphasis on the Los Angeles area. The foundation occasionally makes a few selected grants to organizations located outside of this geographic area; proposals are invited. The foundation does not make grants to individuals, nor for continuing support, annual campaigns, deficit financing, professorships, internships, individual scholarships, fellowships or exchange programs, film productions, or for loans.

Fiscal Information The foundation offers support for building funds, capital campaigns, endowment funds, equipment, matching funds, renovation projects, scholarship funds to institutions, and special projects.

Application Information Organizations seeking funding should initially submit a brief proposal letter which describes the goals and activities of the organization and its specific need for funding. The proposal letter should include: brief budgetary information related to the request, the funding plan, a financial statement, and other commitments received for support. If the proposal is within the scope of the foundation's activities and resources permit consideration of the request, a review will be made. If necessary, additional information will be requested.

Deadline(s) The foundation has no application deadlines.

5. Alcoa Foundation
1501 Alcoa Building
Pittsburgh, PA 15219
(412) 553-2348

Grants

Program Description The Alcoa Foundation was established in 1952 in order to help people and programs in communities where Aluminum Company of America (Alcoa) operates facilities, and contribute to worthwhile projects and organizations that benefit the public at large. Grants are made for educational, cultural, health and welfare, civic and community development, and youth organization purposes at the discretion of the foundation directors.

Sample Grants For catalogue production for exhibit of five artists, grant awarded to North Central Washington Museum Association, Wenatchee, WA (1987). For quadrangle construction project, grant awarded to Smithsonian Institution, Washington, DC (1987).

Eligibility/Limitations Priority consideration is given to programs and activities or organizations and educational institutions in or near communities where Alcoa plants or offices are located. Attention also is given to certain national and international organizations. Only those organizations classified as "public" charities and tax-exempt under Section 501(c)(3) of the Internal Revenue Code will be considered. In general, the foundation does not consider the following for funding: organizations and causes in states or countries where Alcoa does not have a facility; individuals; endowment funds; trips or tours; tickets or tables for benefit purposes; or advertising.

Fiscal Information In 1987, Alcoa awarded grants in support of cultural activities totaling over $1.3 million.

Application Information Address grant requests to a specific project or need. All requests for funding must be in writing. The foundation prefers that you do not send a letter of inquiry; include a proposal with your initial letter. All requests for funding will be acknowledged upon receipt. The foundation does not have a special application form; requests should be in letter format, including or attaching the following: a description of the project; its purpose and objective; in the case of research, the procedure to be followed; an itemized budget for the project, including income and expenses; list of other corporate and foundation donors; copy of 501(c)(3) tax-exempt declaration ruling from the Internal Revenue Service; audited financial statement; and the amount of money requested.

Deadline(s) Grant applications are accepted year-round, and there is no deadline for submitting a request.

6. The George I. Alden Trust

370 Main Street
Worcester, MA 01608
(617) 757-9243

Grants

Program Description The George I. Alden Trust has education as its primary purpose. While its major focus is on higher education, it supports worthy projects in secondary education as well. Over the years, the trustees have broadly interpreted the founder's interest in career-related education for serious-minded youth. Thus scholarship support of students has been of importance as well as laboratory or other equipment, and building programs where relevant. The trust is especially supportive of institutions that can demonstrate a strong combination of educational excellence with efficient and economical administration.

Sample Grants For the building fund of the Fitchburg Art Museum, Fitchburg, MA, $5,000 (1986). For the capital campaign of the Higgins Armory Museum, Worcester, MA, $50,000 (1986). Toward support of "The Thinking Gallery," New England Aquarium, Boston, MA, $5,000 (1986). Toward purchase of new quarters for the Worcester Historical Museum, Worcester, MA, $50,000, with $100,000 payable in the future (1986).

Eligibility/Limitations Grants are awarded largely in the Northeast, with a special interest in Worcester institutions; but the quality of a proposed program and institution is a major factor in any grant decision. Applications are accepted from private institutions. Signature by the chief executive officer of the institution is required. No grants are made to individuals or tax supported institutions.

Fiscal Information As of December 31, 1986 the trust had approved grants amounting to over $1.4 million to be paid during the next four years subject to satisfaction by the intended recipients of prior conditions before payment.

Application Information Applications should be made in a reasonably brief narrative form with an appropriate budget. The purposes to be achieved, reasons why the proposing institution is well fitted to achieve them, and how these purposes integrate with the existing activities of the institution are of interest. If not previously provided, other useful information includes evidence of tax-exempt status under Section 501(c)(3) of the Internal Revenue Code and the organization's most recent annual report, including audited financial report.

Deadline(s) Applications for support are accepted throughout the year, and are reviewed bimonthly.

7. Allstate Foundation
Executive Director
Allstate Plaza
Northbrook, IL 60062
(312) 291-5502

Grants

Program Description The Allstate Foundation is dedicated to supporting well-managed organizations that are responsive to changing social needs. The foundation is particularly interested in those organizations that are dedicated to the principles of self-help and self-motivation. These organizations should make significant contributions toward improving the quality of community life, with specific emphasis on the urban community. The foundation believes its most important responsibility is to provide a comprehensive program that will give support to general welfare, youth, urban, civic, cultural, educational, health, safety, and other charitable organizations. Special consideration will be given to programs and organizations that foster: improvement of economic conditions and the general quality of life; improvement of health care; improvement of the overall quality of higher education; and greater accessibility to cultural programs.

Eligibility/Limitations Grants will not be awarded to individuals or to tax-exempt organizations outside the United States.

Application Information Proposals should be submitted in letter form and should contain the following information: a description of the organization, including a statement of purpose and objectives; specific reason for the grant request and amount of support required; audited financial report, budget and sources of income for most recently completed year; donors' list, complete or representative, showing corporate and foundation contributions to the organization during the past twelve months; and copies of tax-exempt status under Section 501(c)(3) and 509(a) of the Internal Revenue Code.

Deadline(s) Allow thirty to ninety days for review and response.

8. The American Academy and Institute of Arts and Letters
633 West 155th Street
New York, NY 10032-7599
(212) 368-5900

Hassam and Speicher Purchase Fund

Program Description The American Academy and Institute of Arts and Letters is an organization whose function is to foster, assist, and sustain an interest in literature, music, and the fine arts in our society. This is done primarily by giving awards and prizes, but the program also includes exhibitions of art and manuscripts, readings and performances of new work, and the purchase of works of art and their distribution to museums. Childe Hassam, a founding member of the institute, bequeathed to the academy in 1946 a large collection of his paintings, watercolors, pastels, and etchings, with the request that, as they were sold, the accumulated income from the sales be used to purchase works by living contemporary American painters for presentation to museums in the United States. A similar bequest was provided in the will of Eugene Speicher, a former member of the academy, who died in 1962.

Application Information Additional information is available from the organization.

9. American Academy in Rome
41 East 65th Street
New York, NY 10021
(212) 517-4200

Andrew W. Mellon Fellowships in the Humanities

Program Description One research fellowship is available in each of the following fields: classics, art history, and Medieval or Renaissance studies. Fellows for these one-year appointments are asked to spend part of their time contributing to the academic programs of the academy's School of Classical Studies.

Eligibility/Limitations Applicants must hold the Ph.D. and, at the time of appointment, a position of assistant professor, or have been appointed associate professor within the previous two years. Winners who accept this fellowship may not hold another fellowship concurrently. Fellows may not hold a regular job in Rome during their fellowship residency. Extended travel away from the academy is not accepted during the fellowship residency.

Fiscal Information The fellowship includes one year of residence at the academy, an annual stipend of $17,000, and a travel allowance of $800.   ·

Application Information Program information forms are available on request. When requesting a fellowship application, specify field. An application fee of $25 must accompany each application submitted.

Deadline(s) Applications must be postmarked or filed by November 15.

10. American Academy in Rome
41 East 65th Street
New York, NY 10021
(212) 517-4200

Fellowships in Classical Studies, Post Classical Humanistic Studies and Art History (Predoctoral)

Program Description These fellowships offer predoctoral study in classical studies, including Greek and Latin literature, archaeology, and ancient history. Post classical fields include political, economic, cultural, and Church history, and the history of literature and musicology from A.D.300 to A.D.1800.

Eligibility/Limitations Applicants in the scholarly fields should have completed all work for the Ph.D. and have done approximately one year's work on a dissertation. Winners who accept this fellowship may not hold another fellowship concurrently. Fellows may not hold a regular job in Rome during their fellowship residency. Extended travel away from the academy is not accepted during the fellowship residency.

Fiscal Information The fellowship includes one year of residence at the academy, a monthly stipend of $450, and a travel allowance of $800.

Application Information Program information forms are available on request. When requesting a fellowship application, specify field. An application fee of $25 must accompany each application submitted.

Deadline(s) Applications must be postmarked or filed by November 15.

11. American Academy in Rome
41 East 65th Street
New York, NY 10021
(212) 517-4200

National Endowment for the Humanities Postdoctoral Fellowships in Humanistic Studies

Program Description These fellowships offer postdoctoral study in classical studies, including Greek and Latin literature, archaeology, and ancient history. Post classical fields include political, economic, cultural, and Church history, and the history of literature and musicology from A.D.300 to A.D.1800.

Eligibility/Limitations Applicants for these fellowships must have the Ph.D. at the time of application. Fellows may not hold a regular job in Rome during their fellowship residency. Extended travel away from the academy is not accepted during the fellowship residency.

Fiscal Information The fellowship includes one year of residence at the academy, a one-year stipend of $15,000, and a travel allowance of $800.

Application Information Program information forms are available on request. When requesting a fellowship application, specify field. An application fee of $25 must accompany each application submitted.

Deadline(s) Applications must be postmarked or filed by November 15.

12. American Academy in Rome
41 East 65th Street
New York, NY 10021
(212) 517-4200

National Gallery of Art Predoctoral Fellowship in Art History

Program Description This one-year predoctoral fellowship allows an art history student to live and study at the American Academy in Rome.

Eligibility/Limitations Predoctoral candidates in art history may be nominated for this fellowship.

Fiscal Information The fellow receives a cash award from the National Gallery. From this award the fellow must cover travel expenses and must contribute to the cost of study, room, and board at the academy.

Application Information Application for this fellowship must be made through chairpersons of graduate art history departments in American universities who should act as sponsors for applicants from their respective schools. For additional information write to the National Gallery of Art, 6th and Constitution Avenue, NW, Washington, DC 20565, Attn: Prof. Henry Millon.

13. American Academy in Rome
41 East 65th Street
New York, NY 10021
(212) 517-4200

Samuel H. Kress Foundation Fellowships in Art History, Classical Art and Archaeology (Predoctoral)

Program Description These fellowships support predoctoral studies in classical art and archaeology. The fellowships include two years of residence at the American Academy in Rome.

Eligibility/Limitations Applicants for these fellowships must have completed all Ph.D. course work. Winners who accept the fellowship may not hold another fellowship concurrently. Fellows may not hold a regular job in Rome during their fellowship residency. Extended travel away from the academy is not accepted during the fellowship.

Fiscal Information The fellowship includes two years of residence at the academy, a monthly stipend of $450 (24 months), and a travel allowance of $800.

Application Information Program information forms are available on request. When requesting a fellowship application, specify field. An application fee of $25 must accompany each application submitted.

Deadline(s) Applications must be postmarked or filed by November 15.

14. American Antiquarian Society
185 Salisbury Street
Worcester, MA 01609-1634
(617) 752-5813 or (617) 755-5221

AAS-Northeast Modern Language Association Fellowship

Program Description The American Antiquarian Society, in order to encourage imaginative and productive research in its unparalleled library collections in early American history and culture, awards to qualified scholars a number of short- and long-term visiting research fellowships. The AAS-Northeast Modern Language Association Fellowship provides support for research at AAS in American literary studies through 1876.

Eligibility/Limitations Individuals, including foreign nationals, are eligible to apply. Degree candidates are not eligible in this category. Membership in NEMLA is not required for application, but is mandatory upon taking up a fellowship award. Recipients are expected to be in regular and continuous residence at the society's library during the period of the grant.

Fiscal Information Either a single two-month fellowship will be awarded, or two one-month fellowships. The stipend is $750 per month.

Application Information Application materials are available from the Associate Director for Research and Publication.

Deadline(s) Completed applications must be received by January 31.

Additional Information AAS and The Newberry Library in Chicago encourage scholars whose research can be strengthened and enriched through residence at both libraries to make application jointly to both institutions' short-term fellowship programs. Scholars seeking short-term fellowships at both institutions may make application using either the AAS or the Newberry form. Applicants for joint consideration must hold the Ph.D. or have completed all requirements for it except the dissertation. Each library's selection committee will judge joint applications independently. Applicants must meet each institution's deadlines in order to be considered for awards by both libraries.

15. American Antiquarian Society
185 Salisbury Street
Worcester, MA 01609-1634
(617) 752-5813 or (617) 755-5221

Albert Boni Fellowship

Program Description The American Antiquarian Society, in order to encourage imaginative and productive research in its unparalleled library collections in early American history and culture, awards to qualified scholars a number of short- and long-term visiting research fellowships. The Albert Boni Fellowship is awarded to a qualified scholar working in the general fields of early American bibliography or printing or publishing history. This fellowship is attached to the society's program in the History of the Book in American Culture.

Eligibility/Limitations Foreign nationals and individuals working on dissertations are eligible to apply.

Fiscal Information The award enables the recipient to work in the society's library from one to two months. The monthly stipend is $750.

Application Information Application materials are available from the Associate Director for Research and Publication.

Deadline(s) Completed applications must be received by January 31.

Additional Information AAS and The Newberry Library in Chicago encourage scholars whose research can be strengthened and enriched through residence at both libraries to make application jointly to both institutions' short-term fellowship programs. Scholars seeking short-term fellowships at both institutions may make application using either the AAS or the Newberry form. Applicants for joint consideration must hold the Ph.D. or have completed all requirements for it except the dissertation. Each library's selection committee will judge joint applications independently. Applicants must meet each institution's deadlines in order to be considered for awards by both libraries.

16. American Antiquarian Society
185 Salisbury Street
Worcester, MA 01609-1634
(617) 752-5813 or (617) 755-5221

Frances Hiatt Fellowships

Program Description The American Antiquarian Society, in order to encourage imaginative and productive research in its unparalleled library collections in early American history and culture, awards to qualified scholars a number of short- and long-term visiting research fellowships. The Frances Hiatt Fellowships provide short-term support to graduate students engaged in research for doctoral dissertations in any field of American history and culture.

Eligibility/Limitations Recipients are expected to be in regular and continuous residence at the society's library during the period of the grant.

Fiscal Information The awards carry stipends of $750 per month for one or two months' study at the society.

Application Information Application materials are available from the Associate Director for Research and Publication.

Deadline(s) Completed applications must be received by January 31.

Additional Information AAS and The Newberry Library in Chicago encourage scholars whose research can be strengthened and enriched through residence at both libraries to make application jointly to both institutions' short-term fellowship programs. Scholars seeking short-term fellowships at both institutions may make application using either the AAS or the Newberry form. Applicants for joint consideration must hold the Ph.D. or have completed all requirements for it except the dissertation. Each library's selection committee will judge joint applications independently. Applicants must meet each institution's deadlines in order to be considered for awards by both libraries.

17. American Antiquarian Society
185 Salisbury Street
Worcester, MA 01609-1634
(617) 752-5813 or (617) 755-5221

Kate B. and Hall J. Peterson Fellowships

Program Description The American Antiquarian Society, in order to encourage imaginative and productive research in its unparalleled library collections in early American history and culture, awards to qualified scholars a number of short- and long-term visiting research fellowships. Peterson Fellowships provide short-term support of scholarly research and writing in any field of early American history and culture through 1876.

Eligibility/Limitations Individuals, including foreign nationals and persons at work on dissertations, are eligible to apply. Recipients are expected to be in regular and continuous residence at the society's library during the period of the grant.

Fiscal Information Fellowships vary in duration from one to three months and carry monthly stipends of $750.

Application Information Application materials are available from the Associate Director for Research and Publication.

Deadline(s) Completed applications must be received by January 31.

Additional Information AAS and The Newberry Library in Chicago encourage scholars whose research can be strengthened and enriched through residence at both libraries to make application jointly to both institutions' short-term fellowship programs. Scholars seeking short-term fellowships at both institutions may make application using either the AAS or the Newberry form. Applicants for joint consideration must hold the Ph.D.

or have completed all requirements for it except the dissertation. Each library's selection committee will judge joint applications independently. Applicants must meet each institution's deadlines in order to be considered for awards by both libraries.

18. American Antiquarian Society
185 Salisbury Street
Worcester, MA 01609-1634
(617) 752-5813 or (617) 755-5221

National Endowment for the Humanities Fellowships

Program Description The American Antiquarian Society, in order to encourage imaginative and productive research in its unparalleled library collections in early American history and culture, awards to qualified scholars a number of short- and long-term visiting research fellowships. These fellowships offer long-term support of scholarly research and writing in any field of early American history and culture.

Eligibility/Limitations Fellowships are not awarded to degree candidates or for study leading to advanced degrees, nor are they granted to foreign nationals unless they have been residents in the United States for at least three years preceding the award. NEH fellows must devote full time to their study and may not accept teaching assignments or undertake any other major activities during the tenure of the award. Also, they may not hold any other major fellowships, except sabbaticals or other grants from their own institutions. Fellows are expected to be in regular and continuous residence at the society's library during the period of the grant.

Fiscal Information At least two fellowships are available, tenable for from six to twelve months; the maximum available stipend is $27,500.

Application Information Application materials are available from the Associate Director for Research and Publication.

Deadline(s) Completed applications must be received by January 31.

Additional Information AAS and The Newberry Library in Chicago encourage scholars whose research can be strengthened and enriched through residence at both libraries to make application jointly to both institutions' short-term fellowship programs. Scholars seeking short-term fellowships at both institutions may make application using either the AAS or the Newberry form. Applicants for joint consideration must hold the Ph.D. or have completed all requirements for it except the dissertation. Each library's selection committee will judge joint applications independently. Applicants must meet each institution's deadlines in order to be considered for awards by both libraries.

19. American Antiquarian Society
185 Salisbury Street
Worcester, MA 01609-1634
(617) 752-5813 or (617) 755-5221

Research Associates

Program Description Scholars who hold sabbaticals or fellowships from other grant-making agencies and who wish to spend at least four weeks researching in the society's collections may make application to be designated a Research Associate. Research Associates may be granted the privileges accorded the society's own fellows, including access to a carrel and participating in the society's seminars and colloquia.

Fiscal Information Research Associates will be paid no stipend by AAS.

Application Information Scholars interested in applying should write the Associate Director for Research and Publication, enclosing a current curriculum vitae, listing the names of two scholarly references, and giving particulars of the sabbatical or fellowship held or to be held, the subject of research, and the dates of proposed residence at the society

Deadline(s) Applications for designation as a Research Associate may be made at any time.

20. American Association of University Women Educational Foundation
2401 Virginia Avenue, NW
Washington, DC 20037
(202) 728-7630

American Fellowships—Dissertation Fellowships

Program Description Dissertation Fellowships are available to women in any field who will complete all required course work and examinations for the doctorate, except the dissertation defense, by November 30. It is expected that the fellowship will be used for the final year of doctoral work and that the degree will be received at the end of the fellowship year.

Sample Grants Support for a chronological and typological study of terra-cotta figurines from Karanis (1982-1983). Support for a study of liturgical manuscripts made in Toledo at the end of the fifteenth century (1982-1983).

Eligibility/Limitations Women who are citizens of the United States or hold permanent resident status are eligible to apply for the final year of doctoral work. There is no restriction as to place of study.

Fiscal Information Awards are $10,000 for a twelve-month period beginning July 1. Fellows are expected to devote full time to their projects during the fellowship year.

Application Information Application forms are available to individuals only from the AAUW Educational Foundation Programs Office by written request from August 1 to November 1. No telephone requests will be honored.

Deadline(s) Final date for postmark of completed applications is November 15.

21. American Association of University Women Educational Foundation
2401 Virginia Avenue, NW
Washington, DC 20037
(202) 728-7630

American Fellowships—Postdoctoral

Program Description Postdoctoral fellowships are available to women who hold a doctoral degree and wish to pursue research. These awards are limited to five restricted, endowed fellowships including: the Founders Fellowship for a distinguished scholar's postdoctoral research in any field; the Alice Palmer Fellowship for postdoctoral research in any field; the Irene C. Cuneo Fellowship for postdoctoral research in any field; and the Leona Beckman Fellowship for postdoctoral research in the theory, criticism, or history of the arts.

Sample Grants Support for a study of the interrelations of Netherlandish and Bohemian painting, 1350-1420 (1983-1984).

Eligibility/Limitations Women who are citizens of the United States or hold permanent resident status and who have achieved distinction or promise of distinction in their fields are eligible to apply. There are no restrictions as to an applicant's age or place of study. Postdoctoral fellowships are not awarded for revision of the dissertation nor for tuition for additional course work. Preference is given to women who have held the doctorate at least three years. Fellows are expected to devote full time to their projects during the fellowship year.

Fiscal Information Postdoctoral fellowships carry an award of $15,000 for a twelve month period of research except for the Founders Fellowship which carries an award of $20,000.

Application Information Application forms are available to individuals between August 1 and November 1 only from the AAUW Educational Foundation Programs Office by written request. No telephone requests will be honored.

Deadline(s) The final date for postmark of completed applications is November 15.

Additional Information Additional research and project grants for AAUW members are available. Contact the Programs Office for additional information.

22. American Association of University Women Educational Foundation
2401 Virginia Avenue, NW
Washington, DC 20037
(202) 728-7630

Research and Project Grants

Program Description The AAUW Educational Foundation's Research and Project (R&P) Grants offer women the opportunity to foster equity and positive societal change through projects, research, or study. Individual grants are available to women to conduct research in the public interest, implement community service projects or prepare literary works for publication. Public service grants support AAUW branch and division projects that address specific community needs or provide information to educate and benefit the public. Issue focus grants offer assistance to encourage the participation in several topics, including support for public education to promote community collaboration that will achieve excellence and equity in the elementary and secondary public school systems. Short-term project grants provide funds for community service projects or public interest research.

Eligibility/Limitations Any woman holding a baccalaureate degree is eligible to apply for an R&P Grant. Members of the boards, standing committees, panels, task forces, and staff of the AAUW, AAUW Educational Foundation, and AAUW Legal Advocacy Fund are ineligible to apply. All R&P applications must be consistent with the mission of the AAUW Educational Foundation.

Fiscal Information R&P Grants are intended as seed money, and as such, may not provide full funding for a proposed activity. Individual grants range from $500 to $2,500; public service grants range from $500 to $5,000; issue focus grants range from $500 to $5,000; and short-term project grants range from $500 to $3,000.

Application Information Application forms and additional information are available from the foundation.

Deadline(s) Application forms for individual, public service, and issue focus grants are available from September 1 through January 15; postmark deadline for completed grant applications is February 1. Short-term project grant applications are available from April 1 to August 15; postmark deadline for completed applications is September 1.

23. American Council of Learned Societies
228 East 45th Street
New York, NY 10017
(212) 697-1505

China Conference Travel Grants

Program Description Partial support is offered to United States scholars attending research conferences in the People's Republic of China. Eligible scholars must, as shown in their training, teaching, and research interests, be specialists in some aspect of the study of China.

Eligibility/Limitations Applicants must hold the Ph.D. and they must have been invited to present to the conference the results of their recent research. Eligible conferences must be concerned with the humanities or social sciences, and preference will be given to conferences concerned with some aspect of China area studies. Support is not available for travel to the PRC to lecture, teach, or consult, to inform Chinese scholars of the state of scholarship in the U.S. on any topic, or to examine the state of scholarship in the PRC on any topic.

Fiscal Information Partial support is offered.

Application Information To request application forms write to the China Conference Travel Grants Program of the ACLS, stating: date of receipt of the doctorate; academic position; research interests; evaluation of your Chinese language ability; name, location, and date of the conference; and title of the paper to be delivered.

Deadline(s) Completed applications are evaluated in accordance with the following deadlines: October 1 for conferences December-February; January 1 for conferences March-May; April 1 for conferences June-August; and July 1 for conferences September-November.

24. American Council of Learned Societies
228 East 45th Street
New York, NY 10017
(212) 697-1505

Dissertation Fellowships

Program Description Fellowships are offered for research and training in the social sciences and humanities relating to Albania, Bulgaria, Czechoslovakia, the German Democratic Republic, Hungary, Poland, Romania, and Yugoslavia. In awarding these grants, consideration is given to the scholarly merit of the proposal, its importance to the development of East European studies, and the scholarly potential, accomplishments, and financial need of the applicant. The fellowships are not intended to support research within Eastern Europe.

Eligibility/Limitations Doctoral candidates may apply for support of dissertation research and writing to be undertaken at any university or institution outside of Eastern Europe.

Fiscal Information The maximum stipend will be $12,000 plus expenses per year. Reapplication for a second year, if necessary, is encouraged.

Application Information General inquiries and requests for application forms should be addressed to the Office of Fellowships and Grants. In requesting application forms the prospective applicant should state the highest academic degree held and the date the degree was received, country of citizenship or permanent legal residence, academic or other position, field of specialization, proposed subject of research or study, and the period of time for which support is requested.

Deadline(s) The deadline for receipt of applications is November 15.

25. American Council of Learned Societies
228 East 45th Street
New York, NY 10017
(212) 697-1505

Fellowships

Program Description The general programs of the American Council of Learned Societies support postdoctoral research in the humanities. The following fields of specialization are included: philosophy (including the philosophy of law and science), aesthetics, philology, languages, literature and linguistics, archaeology, art history and musicology, history (including the history of science, law, and religions), cultural anthropology, and folklore. Proposals with a predominantly humanistic emphasis in economics, geography, political science, psychology, sociology, and the natural sciences will also be considered.

Sample Grants Support for study of early Christian and Medieval art in the cathedral treasury of Monza to the Curator of Medieval Art, The Metropolitan Museum of Art (1985-1986).

Eligibility/Limitations Fellows must devote a minimum of six continuous months (to a maximum of twelve) to full time work on their projects. Applicants must be citizens and permanent residents of the United States, hold the doctorate or its equivalent (scholarly maturity as demonstrated by professional experience and publications) as of the deadline that has been set. The awards should be of particular interest to scholars

W/C

whose teaching loads restrict time for research, those whose normal places of work are remote from repositories of research materials, and those independent scholars who have no institutional support for their research and writing.

Fiscal Information Awards do not exceed $15,000 and are intended primarily as salary replacement for the provision of free time for research. The ACLS Fellowship stipend, plus any sabbatical salary and minor grants, may not exceed the candidate's normal salary for the period.

Application Information General inquiries and requests for application forms should be addressed to the Office of Fellowships and Grants. In requesting application forms the prospective applicant should state the highest academic degree held and the date the degree was received, country of citizenship or permanent legal residence, academic or other position, field of specialization, proposed subject of research or study, and the period of time for which support is requested.

Deadline(s) The deadline for receipt of applications is September 30.

26. American Council of Learned Societies
228 East 45th Street
New York, NY 10017
(212) 697-1505

Fellowships for Advanced Graduate Training

Program Description Fellowships are offered for research and training in the social sciences and humanities relating to Albania, Bulgaria, Czechoslovakia, the German Democratic Republic, Hungary, Poland, Romania, and Yugoslavia. In awarding these grants, consideration is given to the scholarly merit of the proposal, its importance to the development of East European studies, and the scholarly potential, accomplishments, and financial need of the applicant. The fellowships are not intended to support research within Eastern Europe.

Eligibility/Limitations Graduate students currently enrolled in a degree program who will have completed at least two academic years of work toward the doctorate by June 30 are eligible to apply. The work to be supported must be done at a university or research institute outside of Eastern Europe, except that brief trips to Eastern Europe of up to two months, especially for advanced language training, may be supported when they are part of a coherent overall program.

Fiscal Information The fellowship carries a stipend of up to $10,000 plus expenses for a program of course work and training in any aspect of East European studies or in any discipline in which the applicant is preparing to qualify for writing a dissertation on Eastern Europe.

Application Information General inquiries and requests for application forms should be addressed to the Office of Fellowships and Grants. In requesting application forms the prospective applicant should state the highest academic degree held and the date the degree was received, country of citizenship or permanent legal residence, academic or other position, field of specialization, proposed subject of research or study, and the period of time for which support is requested.

Deadline(s) The deadline for receipt of applications is November 15.

27. American Council of Learned Societies
228 East 45th Street
New York, NY 10017
(212) 697-1505

Fellowships for Dissertation Research Abroad

Program Description These fellowships are offered to enable doctoral degree candidates to undertake a period of dissertation research outside the United States in any country with the exception of the People's Republic of China. The dissertation must be related to China, although it may be comparative in nature, and the research may be in any discipline of the humanities and social sciences or interdisciplinary.

Eligibility/Limitations Applicants must be regular Ph.D. candidates who expect to complete all requirements for the doctorate except the dissertation by June 30 of the award year. There are no citizenship restrictions, but foreign nationals must be enrolled as full-time Ph.D. candidates in U.S. institutions.

Fiscal Information Stipends include funds up to $20,000 for full-year programs for maintenance, transportation, and research expenses.

Application Information General inquiries and requests for application forms should be addressed to the Office of Fellowships and Grants. In requesting application forms the prospective applicant should state the highest academic degree held and the date the degree was received, country of citizenship or permanent legal residence, academic or other position, field of specialization, proposed subject of research or study, and the period of time for which support is requested.

Deadline(s) Applications must be received by November 15.

28. American Council of Learned Societies
228 East 45th Street
New York, NY 10017
(212) 697-1505

Fellowships for Postdoctoral Research

Program Description Grants are offered to support original research on Chinese culture or society, including research designed to synthesize or reinterpret the applicant's past research in order to produce an original overview of scholarship on any topic or problem of importance in the study of China. Awards will be made on the basis of the quality and scholarly importance of the proposed research, its importance to the development of scholarship on China, and its contribution to knowledge of other areas or disciplines. This program is not intended to support research within the People's Republic of China.

Eligibility/Limitations Applicants for postdoctoral research or study must be citizens and permanent residents of the United States and hold the doctorate or expect to receive it in the current academic year.

Fiscal Information Fellowships are generally awarded for six months to one year of full-time research. Stipends, which are adjusted according to need, are generally set at one-half the applicant's academic salary, not including fringe benefits, less other outside support, up to a maximum of $25,000. Normally the cost of travel to Asia for less than six months of research cannot be covered.

Application Information General inquiries and requests for application forms should be addressed to the Office of Fellowships and Grants. In requesting application forms the prospective applicant should state the highest academic degree held and the date the degree was received, country of citizenship or permanent legal residence, academic or other position, field of specialization, proposed subject of research or study, and the period of time for which support is requested.

Deadline(s) Applications must be received by November 15.

29. American Council of Learned Societies
228 East 45th Street
New York, NY 10017
(212) 697-1505

Fellowships for Recent Recipients of the Ph.D.

Program Description The general programs of the American Council of Learned Societies support postdoctoral research in the humanities. The following fields of specialization are included: philosophy (including the philosophy of law and science), aesthetics, philology, languages, literature and linguistics, archaeology, art history and musicology, history (including the history of science, law, and religions), cultural anthropology, and folklore. Proposals with a predominantly humanistic emphasis in economics, geography, political science, psychology, sociology, and the natural sciences will also be considered.

Eligibility/Limitations These awards are limited to scholars whose Ph.D. degree has been conferred in the year of and not more than two calendar years prior to the competition to engage in research. Proposals for dissertation revision as well as those for work on other projects are appropriate. Fellows must devote a minimum of six continuous months (to a maximum of twelve) to full-time work on their proposals. Applicants must be citizens and permanent residents of the United States.

Fiscal Information Fellowships do not exceed $10,000 and are intended primarily as salary replacement for the provision of free time for research. The stipend, plus any sabbatical salary and minor grants, may not exceed the candidate's normal salary for the period.

Application Information General inquiries and requests for application forms should be addressed to the Office of Fellowships and Grants. In requesting application forms the prospective applicant should state the highest academic degree held and the date the degree was received, country of citizenship or permanent legal residence, academic or other position, field of specialization, proposed subject of research or study, and the period of time for which support is requested.

Deadline(s) The deadline for receipt of applications is September 30.

30. American Council of Learned Societies
228 East 45th Street
New York, NY 10017
(212) 697-1505

Fellowships for Tenured Scholars

Program Description Fellowships are offered for research and training in the social sciences and humanities relating to Albania, Bulgaria, Czechoslovakia, the German Democratic Republic, Hungary, Poland, Romania, and Yugoslavia. In awarding these grants, consideration is given to the scholarly merit of the proposal, its importance to the development of East European studies, and the scholarly potential, accomplishments, and financial need of the applicant. The fellowships are not intended to support research within East Europe.

Eligibility/Limitations Tenured scholars may apply for fellowships to undertake a period of at least six consecutive months of full-time research.

Fiscal Information Awards range up to $25,000 maximum. The fellowships are intended primarily as salary replacement to provide time free for research; the funds may be used to supplement sabbatical salaries or awards from other sources, provided they would intensify or extend the contemplated research.

Application Information General inquiries and requests for application forms should be addressed to the Office of Fellowships and Grants. In requesting application forms the prospective applicant should state the highest academic degree held and the date the degree was received, country of citizenship or permanent legal residence, academic or other position, field of specialization, proposed subject of research or study, and the period of time for which support is requested.

Deadline(s) The deadline for receipt of applications is November 15.

31. American Council of Learned Societies
228 East 45th Street
New York, NY 10017
(212) 697-1505

Fellowships for Untenured Scholars

Program Description Fellowships are offered for research and training in the social sciences and humanities relating to Albania, Bulgaria, Czechoslovakia, the German Democratic Republic, Hungary, Poland, Romania, and Yugoslavia. In awarding these grants, consideration is given to the scholarly merit of the proposal, its importance to the development of East European studies, and the scholarly potential, accomplishments, and financial need of the applicant. The fellowships are not intended to support research within East Europe.

Eligibility/Limitations Untenured scholars or younger independent scholars without academic appointment may apply for support of a coherent research program designed to fit their needs and interests. Scholars may apply for support to expand and revise their dissertations.

Fiscal Information Awards range up to $25,000 maximum and may be expended over one to three years. The stipend can be used for research-related expenses as well as funding for time off for research.

Application Information General inquiries and requests for application forms should be addressed to the Office of Fellowships and Grants. In requesting application forms the prospective applicant should state the highest academic degree held and the date the degree was received, country of citizenship or permanent legal residence, academic or other position, field of specialization, proposed subject of research or study, and the period of time for which support is requested.

Deadline(s) The deadline for receipt of applications is November 15.

32. American Council of Learned Societies
228 East 45th Street
New York, NY 10017
(212) 697-1505

Grants for Travel to International Meetings Abroad

Program Description The ACLS, in cooperation with its constituent societies, administers a program of travel grants, awarded on a competitive basis to enable scholars in the humanities and humanities-related disciplines to participate in international scholarly meetings outside North America.

Eligibility/Limitations Persons having a major, official role in a meeting are eligible to apply, but preference is given to those who are to present scholarly papers. Applications are encouraged from scholars who are still young in the professions, e.g. in untenured ranks, and from those who have not held ACLS travel grants in the past. All applicants must hold the Ph.D. degree or its equivalent and must be citizens or permanent residents of the United States. Applications may not be submitted by scholars who were awarded travel grants in competitions taking place in either the current or the two preceding calendar years.

Fiscal Information Financial assistance will approximate an amount not less than one-half of the most economical airfare available between major commercial airports. The use of U.S. flag carriers is required. Travel grant stipends are expendable for travel only and cannot be applied to per diem expenses. Funds are paid to an awardee only after the meeting has taken place and on receipt of travel documentation and a substantive report.

Application Information Address inquiries to the Travel Grant Office of the ACLS setting forth the name, dates, place, and sponsorship of the meeting, as well as a brief description of the nature of the applicant's scholarly interests and proposed role in the meeting.

Deadline(s) Grant application deadlines are October 1 for meetings January-June, and March 1 for meetings July-December. Since all applications for any one period are competitive and must be judged comparatively, late applications and requests for early consideration cannot be accepted.

33. American Council of Learned Societies
228 East 45th Street
New York, NY 10017
(212) 697-1505

Grants-in-Aid

Program Description The general programs of the American Council of Learned Societies support postdoctoral research in the humanities. The following fields of specialization are included: philosophy (including the philosophy of law and science), aesthetics, philology, languages, literature and linguistics, archaeology, art history and musicology, history (including the history of science, law, and religions), cultural anthropology, and folklore. Proposals with a predominantly humanistic emphasis in economics, geography, political science, psychology, sociology, and the natural sciences will also be considered. ACLS Grants-in-Aid are designed to assist scholars with the expenses of specific programs of research in progress.

Sample Grants Support for study of Bronze-Age artifacts from Gordion (1982-1983). Support for study of the Attic black-figure pottery from Corinth (1983-1984). Support for study of the Ter Borch family collection of drawings in the Rijksmuseum (1982-1983).

Eligibility/Limitations Applicants must be citizens and permanent residents of the United States and hold the doctorate or its equivalent.

Fiscal Information Stipends will not exceed $3,000 and should be expended within one year after acceptance. Awards for living expenses at home to relieve the applicant of the necessity of teaching beyond the conventional academic year will be made only in exceptional cases. Allowable expenses may include personal travel and maintenance away from home while gaining access to materials, research or clerical assistance, and reproduction or purchase of materials. Grants are not ordinarily made for the purchase of personal computers, books, or other non-expendable materials.

Application Information General inquiries and requests for application forms should be addressed to the Office of Fellowships and Grants. In requesting application forms the prospective applicant should state the highest academic degree held and the date the degree was received, country of citizenship or permanent legal residence, academic or other position, field of specialization, proposed subject of research or study, and the period of time for which support is requested.

Deadline(s) The deadline for receipt of applications is December 15.

34. American Council of Learned Societies
228 East 45th Street
New York, NY 10017
(212) 697-1505

Mellon Research and Training Fellowships for Young China Scholars

Program Description These fellowships are designed to facilitate the development and enrichment of young China scholars by allowing them to engage in programs of research or study. Study and training programs, of any topic, subject, discipline, or methodology, should be designed to enhance the applicant's scholarly capacity and must be undertaken with the close supervision of expert scholars.

Eligibility/Limitations Applicants must have received their doctorates within the last five years. Doctoral candidates who expect to receive their degrees by June 30 of the award year are also eligible to apply. While research funds may be used to expand the dissertation significantly, preference will be given to scholars beginning new research projects.

Fiscal Information Stipends range up to $20,000 for full-year programs.

Application Information General inquiries and requests for application forms should be addressed to the Office of Fellowships and Grants. In requesting application forms the prospective applicant should state the highest academic degree held and the date the degree was received, country of citizenship or permanent legal residence, academic or other position, field of specialization, proposed subject of research or study, and the period of time for which support is requested.

Deadline(s) The deadline for receipt of applications is November 15.

35. American Express Foundation
American Express Plaza, 19th Floor
New York, NY 10004
(212) 640-5661

Philanthropic Program

Program Description The foundation concentrates its efforts on those areas where real and lasting impact can be attained, harnessing talent and resources from the company to evaluate and address local needs. The Philanthropic Program is committed to developing public-private partnerships, both in the U.S. and internationally, with a special emphasis on (1) education, employment and training and (2) cultural diversity and national heritage. Within the cultural diversity and national heritage area the foundation seeks to promote: an understanding of diverse cultures and artistic accomplishment through support for visual and performing arts institutions; preservation of the world's cultural, architectural and natural heritage; and traveling and in-place exhibitions.

Sample Grants For support of an exhibition on Silk Roads/China Ships, $50,000 to the American Museum of Natural History (1984). For partial support of an exhibit on Archaeology from Beneath the Sea, $10,000 to American Friends of the Israel Museum, New York, NY (1985). For an antiques show, $40,000 to the Museum of American Folk Art, New York, NY (1985). For an inaugural exhibition, $75,000 to the Fort Lauderdale Museum of Art, Fort Lauderdale, FL (1985).

Eligibility/Limitations Applicant organizations must be recognized by the Internal Revenue Service as having 501(c)(3) charitable status. The foundation does not award grants to individuals or for religious, veterans, labor or fraternal organizations, or to political candidates.

Fiscal Information 1987 grants by the program totaled $17.3 million, with $5.7 million distributed in cultural diversity and natural heritage areas.

Application Information Applicants may request an application form or receive more information by contacting the foundation.

Deadline(s) Applications are accepted at any time.

36. American Historical Association
400 A Street SE
Washington, DC 20003
(202) 544-2422

The Albert J. Beveridge Grant for Research in the History of the Western Hemisphere

Program Description The American Historical Association announces the availability of modest grants to support research in the history of the Western hemisphere (United States, Canada, and Latin America). The grants are intended to further research in progress and may be used for travel to a library or archive, for microfilms, photographs, xeroxing—a list of purposes that is meant to be merely illustrative, not exhaustive. Preference will be given to those with specific research needs, such as the completion of a project or completion of a discrete segment thereof.

Eligibility/Limitations Only members of the association are eligible.

Fiscal Information The grants will be awarded annually and individual grants will not exceed $1,000.

Application Information Application forms and guidelines are available from the Beveridge Research Grants Program at the address listed above.

Deadline(s) The deadline for receipt of applications is February 1.

37. American Historical Association
400 A Street SE
Washington, DC 20003
(202) 544-2422

The J. Franklin Jameson Fellowship in American History

Program Description The J. Franklin Jameson Fellowship in American History is offered annually by the Library of Congress and the American Historical Association to support significant scholarly research for one semester in the collections of the Library of Congress by young historians. The applicant's project in American history must be one for which the general and special collections of the Library of Congress offer unique research support.

Eligibility/Limitations At the time of application, applicants must hold the Ph.D. degree or equivalent, must have received this degree within the last five years, and must not have published or had accepted for publication a book-length historical work. The fellowship will not be awarded to permit completion of a doctoral dissertation.

Fiscal Information The total stipend may vary from year to year. For 1988-1989 the amount is $9,000. This amount will not be prorated according to the proposed length of tenure of the fellowship.

Application Information Applications must include a vita, a statement concerning the proposed project and its relationship to the Library of Congress holdings, a tentative schedule for tenure of the fellowship, and the names and addresses of three persons qualified to judge the project and the applicant's fitness to undertake it. Applications should be sent to the J. Franklin Jameson Fellowship at the address listed above.

Deadline(s) Applicants must be postmarked no later than March 1 and received not later than March 15.

38. American Historical Association
400 A Street SE
Washington, DC 20003
(202) 544-2422

The Michael Kraus Research Grant in History

Program Description The American Historical Association announces the availability of this grant to recognize the most deserving proposal relating to work in progress on a research project in American colonial history, with particular reference to the intercultural aspects of American and European relations. The grants are intended to further research in progress and may be used for travel to a library or archive, for microfilms, photographs, xeroxing—a list of purposes that is meant to be merely illustrative, not exhaustive. Preference will be given to those with specific research needs, such as the completion of a project or completion of a discrete segment thereof.

Eligibility/Limitations Only members of the association are eligible.

Fiscal Information The grant will be awarded annually and will not exceed $800.

Application Information Application forms and guidelines are available from the Kraus Research Grant Program at the address listed above.

Deadline(s) The deadline for receipt of applications is February 1.

39. American Institute of Indian Studies
1130 East 59th Street
Chicago, IL 60637
(312) 702-8638

Fellowships for Scholarly Development

Program Description The American Institute of Indian Studies (AIIS) is a cooperative, nonprofit organization of forty American colleges and universities with a special interest in Indian studies. It is designed to support the advancement of knowledge and understanding of India primarily through research conducted in that country by American scholars. The AIIS offers a variety of fellowships for research in India. Fellowships for scholarly development are awarded to established scholars who have not previously specialized in Indian studies, and to established professionals who have not previously worked or studied in India. Proposals in this category should have a substantial research or project component and the anticipated results should be clearly defined.

Eligibility/Limitations U.S. citizens are eligible for AIIS grants. Resident aliens who are engaged in research or teaching at American colleges or universities are also eligible. No individual will be awarded grants in this category more than once.

Fiscal Information Award periods are short-term (up to four months) and long-term (six to ten months).

Application Information Application forms and additional information are available from AIIS.

Deadline(s) The deadline for submitting applications is July 1.

40. American Institute of Indian Studies
1130 East 59th Street
Chicago, IL 60637
(312) 702-8638

Junior Fellowships

Program Description The American Institute of Indian Studies (AIIS) is a cooperative, nonprofit organization of forty American colleges and universities with a special interest in Indian studies. It is designed to support the advancement of knowledge and understanding of India primarily through research conducted in that country by American scholars. The AIIS offers a variety of fellowships for research in India. Junior fellowships are awarded to graduate students specializing in Indian aspects of academic disciplines.

Eligibility/Limitations Graduate students specializing in Indian aspects of academic disciplines for dissertation research are eligible to apply. Junior Fellows will have formal affiliation with Indian universities and Indian research supervisors.

Fiscal Information Awards are for a period of nine to twelve months.

Application Information Application forms and additional information are available from AIIS.

Deadline(s) The deadline for submitting applications is July 1.

41. American Institute of Indian Studies
1130 East 59th Street
Chicago, IL 60637
(312) 702-8638

Senior Research Fellowships

Program Description The American Institute of Indian Studies (AIIS) is a cooperative, nonprofit organization of forty American colleges and universities with a special interest in Indian studies. It is designed to support the advancement of knowledge and understanding of India primarily through research conducted in that country by American scholars. The AIIS offers a variety of fellowships for research in India. Senior Research Fellowships are awarded to academic specialists in Indian studies.

Eligibility/Limitations Applicants must possess the Ph.D. or its equivalent. While in India, each Senior Research Fellow will be formally affiliated with an Indian university.

Fiscal Information Award periods range from six to ten months.

Application Information Application forms and additional information are available from AIIS.

Deadline(s) The deadline for submitting applications is July 1.

42. American Institute of Indian Studies
1130 East 59th Street
Chicago, IL 60637
(312) 702-8638

Short-Term Fellowships

Program Description The American Institute of Indian Studies (AIIS) is a cooperative, nonprofit organization of forty American colleges and universities with a special interest in Indian studies. It is designed to support the advancement of knowledge and understanding of India primarily through research conducted in that country by American scholars. The AIIS offers a variety of fellowships for research in India. Short-Term Fellowships are awarded to academic specialists in Indian studies.

Eligibility/Limitations Applicants must possess the Ph.D. or its equivalent. While in India, Short-Term Fellows will be formally affiliated with an Indian university.

Fiscal Information Award periods are for up to four months.

Application Information Application forms and additional information are available from AIIS.

Deadline(s) The deadline for submitting applications is July 1.

43. American Institute of Indian Studies
1130 East 59th Street
Chicago, IL 60637
(312) 702-8638

Translation Projects

Program Description The American Institute of Indian Studies (AIIS) is a cooperative, nonprofit organization of forty American colleges and universities with a special interest in Indian studies. It is designed to support the advancement of knowledge and understanding of India primarily through research conducted in that country by American scholars. The AIIS, the Smithsonian Institution, and the National Endowment for the Humanities have established a cooperative program to support translations of Indian texts into English.

Application Information Application forms and additional information are available from AIIS. Please indicate your interest in this grant when requesting application materials.

Deadline(s) The deadline for submitting applications is July 1.

44. American Institute of Pakistan Studies
Villanova University
138 Tolentine Hall
Villanova, PA 19085
(215) 645-4738 or -4791

Fellowships

Program Description Fellowships are awarded to support research on Pakistan by scholars and advanced graduate students engaged in research on Pakistan in ancient, medieval, and modern times, in any field of the humanities or social sciences. Topics by specialists in other countries or areas which include research on Pakistan in a comparative perspective are also encouraged. Such topics as rural development, agriculture, local government, economic problems, and demography as well as broader historical and cultural subjects, are suggestive of suitable projects. Acceptable subjects are not, however, limited to these.

Eligibility/Limitations Applicants must be citizens of the United States. Fellowships are offered in several categories including predoctoral research and postdoctoral study. Graduate student applicants must have fulfilled all residence, language, and preliminary examination requirements for the doctorate. In addition, their dissertation projects must have the approval of their faculty. Postdoctoral applicants are expected to be members in good standing of educational or research institutions in the United States and to submit a suitable research project or program of study.

Fiscal Information Because major support for the institute's activities is derived from Pakistani currency, support is provided in terms of air transportation, maintenance, and travel allowances in Pakistan, paid in local currency. The amount paid for maintenance will depend upon whether the fellow is a predoctoral or a postdoctoral fellow. A rental allowance is also provided. A small contribution is made toward excess baggage, research materials in Pakistan, and internal travel. International travel is paid only for the fellow and not for dependents. Grantees who are not affiliated with supporting institutions are required to pay an administrative fee in United States currency to partially defray the costs of processing their applications. All awards are subject to confirmation by the government of Pakistan.

Application Information Packets of application materials for grants are available from the director of the institute.

Deadline(s) Application for grants should not be made later than January 1

Additional Information Special Project Grants in archaeology, anthropology, and other social sciences funded by the Smithsonian Institution are available. In addition to normal review procedures, these grants are subject to additional approval by the Smithsonian Institution. The deadline for these grants is January 1.

45. American Jewish Archives
Administrative Director
3101 Clifton Avenue
Cincinnati, OH 45220
(513) 221-1875

The Bernard and Audre Rapoport Fellowships in American Jewish Studies

Program Description These fellowships are available for research or writing at the American Jewish Archives.

Eligibility/Limitations Postdoctoral scholars are eligible to apply.

Fiscal Information The stipend is $4,000 for two months' active research or writing at the archives.

Application Information Applicants must provide current curriculum vitae, evidence of published research, and two recommendations from academic colleagues. These will constitute the application forms.

Deadline(s) The application deadline is April 1.

46. American Jewish Archives
Administrative Director
3101 Clifton Avenue
Cincinnati, OH 45220
(513) 221-1875

The Loewenstein-Wiener Summer Fellowship Awards in American Jewish Studies

Program Description These fellowships are available for one month of research or writing at the American Jewish Archives during the stipend year.

Eligibility/Limitations ABDs or postdoctoral scholars are eligible to apply.

Fiscal Information The stipend is $1,000 for ABDs and $2,000 for postdoctoral scholars.

Application Information Applicants must provide a current curriculum vitae and evidence of published research, where possible. ABDs must provide three faculty recommendations (including dissertation supervisor's) and postdoctoral scholars must provide two recommendations from academic colleagues. These will constitute application forms.

Deadline(s) The deadline for applications is April 1.

47. American Jewish Archives
Administrative Director
3101 Clifton Avenue
Cincinnati, OH 45220
(513) 221-1875

The Marguerite R. Jacobs Memorial Postdoctoral Award in American Jewish Studies

Program Description This fellowship supports research and writing at the American Jewish Archives.

Eligibility/Limitations Postdoctoral scholars are eligible to apply.

Fiscal Information The stipend is $2,000 for one month of active research at the archives.

Application Information Applicants must provide a current curriculum vitae, evidence of published research, where possible, and two recommendations from academic colleagues. These will constitute the application forms.

Deadline(s) The application deadline is April 1.

48. American Jewish Archives
Administrative Director
3101 Clifton Avenue
Cincinnati, OH 45220
(513) 221-1875

The Rabbi Levi A. Olan Memorial Fellowship in American Jewish Studies

Program Description This fellowship is available for one month of research or writing at the American Jewish Archives.

Eligibility/Limitations Doctoral candidates who have completed all requirements for the degree except the dissertation are eligible to apply.

Fiscal Information The stipend is $1,000 for one month of research or writing at the archives.

Application Information Applicants must provide three faculty recommendations (including dissertation supervisor's). These will constitute the application forms.

Deadline(s) The deadline for submitting applications is April 1.

49. American Jewish Archives
Administrative Director
3101 Clifton Avenue
Cincinnati, OH 45220
(513) 221-1875

The Rabbi Theodore S. Levy Tribute Fellowship in American Jewish Studies

Program Description The fellowship supports one month of research or writing at the American Jewish Archives.

Eligibility/Limitations This fellowship is available to doctoral candidates who have completed all requirements for the Ph.D. except the dissertation.

Fiscal Information The stipend is $1,000 for one month's active research at the archives.

Application Information Applicants must provide three faculty recommendations (including the dissertation supervisor's). These will constitute the application forms.

Deadline(s) The application deadline is April 1.

50. American Museum of Natural History
Office of Grants and Fellowships
Central Park West at 79th Street
New York, NY 10024
(212) 873-1300 ext. 517

Collection Study Grants

Program Description These grants provide financial assistance to enable predoctoral and recent postdoctoral investigators to study any of the scientific collections at the American Museum. These collections represent the fields of vertebrate zoology, invertebrate zoology, paleozoology, anthropology, and mineral sciences.

Eligibility/Limitations Predoctoral and recent postdoctoral investigators are eligible to apply. Grants are not available to investigators residing within daily commuting distance of the American Museum. Only one Collection Study Grant will be awarded to an individual.

Fiscal Information The awards partially support travel and subsistence while visiting the American Museum; the visit is expected to be four days or longer in duration. The maximum amount of the award is $400.

Application Information Applicants for Collection Study Grants should first contact the appropriate museum department to discuss the feasibility of the proposed visit. Approval by the department chairman is required. These grants require a special application form which must be requested by name from the Office of Grants and Fellowships.

Deadline(s) Applicants may submit their forms at any time during the year and may expect a decision within two months of submission.

Additional Information Applicants requiring larger grants for collection study may apply instead to one of the other grant programs offered by the museum.

51. American Museum of Natural History
Office of Grants and Fellowships
Central Park West at 79th Street
New York, NY 10024
(212) 873-1300 ext. 517

Curatorial Fellowships

Program Description These fellowships bring to the museum individuals holding the doctoral degree or its equivalent to assume all the duties, responsibilities, and activities of members of the curatorial staff for a limited term. Appointees are expected to engage in an active research program and to participate in exhibition planning, educational activities, management of collections, and administration of their department to varying degrees.

Eligibility/Limitations Fellowships are available to individuals holding the doctoral degree or its equivalent.

Fiscal Information Fellowship appointments are non-tenured, may not exceed a five-year period, and are renewable annually. Limited support for relocation, research, and publication costs is generally offered.

Application Information Museum departments compete for curatorial fellowship positions, and once a position is awarded, the department receiving it recruits for candidates as it would for a tenure track curatorship. Hence announcements stating qualifications and application procedures for a curatorial fellowship opening will appear in journals appropriate to the field.

Deadline(s) Application deadlines appear in announcements for fellowship openings.

52. American Museum of Natural History
Office of Grants and Fellowships
Central Park West at 79th Street
New York, NY 10024
(212) 873-1300 ext. 517

Frank M. Chapman Memorial Grants

Program Description The Frank M. Chapman Memorial Grants support and foster research in ornithology, both neontological and paleontological, from a broad and international point of view. Research projects need not be carried out at the American Museum.

Eligibility/Limitations Advanced graduate students and postdoctoral researchers who are commencing their careers are eligible to apply.

Fiscal Information Awards range from $200-$1,000 and average $550.

Application Information Application forms and additional information are available from the museum.

Deadline(s) Applications must be postmarked on the prescribed form by January 15.

53. American Museum of Natural History
Office of Grants and Fellowships
Central Park West at 79th Street
New York, NY 10024
(212) 873-1300 ext. 517

Research and Museum Fellowships

Program Description These fellowships provide support to recent postdoctoral investigators, established scientists and other scholars to carry out a specific project within a limited time period. The project must fit into the areas of vertebrate zoology, invertebrate zoology, paleozoology, anthropology, mineral sciences, astronomy, or museum education. The program is designed to advance the training of the participant by having her/him pursue a project in association with museum professionals in a museum setting.

Eligibility/Limitations Fellowships are available to candidates with a doctoral degree or its equivalent.

Fiscal Information These awards offer salary or stipend and modest expenses to a scholar while in residence at the American Museum or one of its field stations, to carry out a specific project within a prescribed time period. The period is usually for one year, but may be more or less in accordance with the nature of the project.

Application Information Interested researchers should obtain a special Research-Museum Fellowship application form from the Office of Grants and Fellowships.

Deadline(s) Applications must be postmarked by January 15.

54. American Museum of Natural History
Office of Grants and Fellowships
Central Park West at 79th Street
New York, NY 10024
(212) 873-1300 ext. 517

Theodore Roosevelt Memorial Grants

Program Description These grants offer financial support to individuals for research on the fauna of North America and adjoining regions in any phase of wildlife conservation or natural history related to the activities of the American Museum.

Eligibility/Limitations Grants are intended principally to assist advanced predoctoral candidates and postdoctoral researchers, although there are no formal educational restrictions for application. Research projects need not be carried out at the American Museum.

Fiscal Information Awards range from $200 to $1,000 and average $550.

Application Information Application forms are available from the Office of Grants and Fellowships.

Deadline(s) Applications on prescribed forms must be postmarked by February 15.

55. The American Numismatic Society
Broadway at 155th Street
New York, NY 10032
(212) 234-3139

Graduate Fellowships

Program Description Each year the American Numismatic Society awards a fellowship in support of a doctoral dissertation which employs numismatic evidence. Applicants may be from the fields of classical studies, history, archaeology, art history, economic history, or related disciplines.

Eligibility/Limitations Applicants must be graduate students who have completed the general examinations (or the equivalent) for the doctorate, be writing a dissertation in which the use of numismatic evidence plays a significant part, and have attended one of the American Numismatic Society's Graduate Seminars prior to the time of application.

Fiscal Information One award of $3,500 is granted annually.

Application Information Information and application materials may be obtained from the society.

Deadline(s) Applications must be completed by March 1.

56. American Oriental Society
329 Sterling Memorial Library, Yale Station
New Haven, CT 06520
(203) 436-1040

The American Oriental Society Fellowship for the Study of Chinese Painting

Program Description This award is granted to a student for the study of the history of Chinese painting.

Eligibility/Limitations Applicants should have completed all requirements for a Ph.D. in the study of Chinese painting, except for research travel, the written dissertation, and its defense. Applicants should have completed three years of study of the Chinese language or its equivalent and should be able to demonstrate that they have already committed themselves to the serious study of this important area of oriental art.

Fiscal Information One award in the amount of $6,000 is granted annually. The fellowship covers a period of 12 months, extending from July 1 of the year of the award until June 30 of the following year; stipends are dispensed in monthly payments during this period. In exceptional circumstances payments may be combined to cover the initial costs of travel or research materials.

Application Information All inquiries and applications should be sent to the secretary of the society. Please specify the fellowship for which you are applying.

Deadline(s) The closing date for application is February 1.

57. American Oriental Society
329 Sterling Memorial Library, Yale Station
New Haven, CT 06520
(203) 436-1040

The Louise Wallace Hackney Fellowship for the Study of Chinese Art

Program Description This award is conceived to permit the study of Chinese art, with special relation to painting and its reflection of Chinese culture, and to permit the translation into English of works upon the said subject for the purpose of furthering a better understanding of Chinese painting in the United States. The aim of the Hackney Fellowship is to remind scholars that Chinese art, like all art, is not a disembodied creation, but the outgrowth of the life and culture from which it has sprung, and it is requested that scholars give special attention to this approach in their study.

Eligibility/Limitations This award is open only to individuals who are citizens of the United States. It is possible to apply for renewal of this grant. Applicants should have completed three years of study of the Chinese language or its equivalent and should be able to demonstrate that they have already committed themselves to the serious study of this important area of oriental art. The award is open to postdoctoral as well as doctoral students. In no case shall a fellowship be awarded to scholars of well recognized standing, but shall be given to men or women who show aptitude or promise in the field of Chinese art.

Fiscal Information The award is in the amount of $7,000 for a period of twelve months, extending from July 1 of the year of the award until June 30 of the following year; stipends are dispensed in monthly payments during this period. The fellowships permit travel by those to whom the award is given, if such travel is possible. In exceptional circumstances payments may be combined to cover the initial costs of travel or research materials.

Application Information All inquiries and applications should be sent to the secretary of the society. Please specify the fellowship for which you are applying.

Deadline(s) The closing date for application is February 1.

58. American Philosophical Society
104 South Fifth Street
Philadelphia, PA 19106
(215) 627-0706

Research Grants

Program Description The American Philosophical Society makes grants toward the cost of scholarly research in all areas of knowledge except those in which support by government or corporate enterprise is more appropriate and regularly available. "Scholarly research," as the term is used here, covers most kinds of scholarly inquiry by individuals. It does not include journalistic or other writing for general readership; the preparation of textbooks, casebooks, anthologies, or other materials for classroom use by students; or the work of creative and performing artists.

Sample Grants Support for research on Attic red-figure vases in the University Museum, University of Pennsylvania (1983).

Eligibility/Limitations Applicants are normally expected to have a doctorate, but applications will be considered from persons who display equivalent scholarly preparation and achievement. Grants are rarely made to persons who have held the doctorate less than a year; and never for predoctoral study or research. Applications may be made by residents of the United States, by American citizens on the staffs of foreign institutions, and by foreign nationals whose research can only or best be carried out in the United States. Applicants expecting to use materials or conduct interviews in a foreign language must possess the necessary competence in the language or languages involved. It is the society's long-standing practice to encourage research by younger and less well-established scholars.

Fiscal Information The maximum grant that will be made is $3,500, and this amount will be approved only in exceptional cases. The maximum grant for a full professor is

$2,500. The grant will pay for: living costs while away from home; microfilms, photostats, photographs and the like, which will shorten the grantee's stay away from home, or enable him to do his work more efficiently and accurately; consumable supplies; and necessary foreign and domestic travel.

Application Information To request application forms, briefly describe your project and proposed budget in a letter to the Committee on Research.

Deadline(s) Deadlines are December 1, February 1, April 1, August 1, and October 1.

59. The American Research Center in Egypt
New York University
50 Washington Square South
New York, NY 10003
(212) 998-8890

ARCE Fellowships

Program Description The American Research Center in Egypt, Inc., founded in 1948, promotes research on Egypt and in Egypt from earliest times to the present. The broad aims of ARCE are to obtain a fresh and more profound knowledge of Egypt and the Near East through scholarly research; train American specialists in Near Eastern studies in academic disciplines which require familiarity with Egypt; disseminate knowledge of Egypt and thus understanding of the whole Near East; and promote American-Egyptian cultural relations. In pursuit of these goals, ARCE supports a Research Fellowship Program to enable American scholars and students to conduct research in all periods and in all phases of Egyptian civilization.

Eligibility/Limitations Awards are open to all qualified candidates without regard to sex, race, or religion. Because under certain circumstances non-U.S. nationality results in funding problems, it is advisable to contact the U.S. office for further clarification if there is a doubt about status.

Fiscal Information Most fellows receive a monthly stipend commensurate with academic status and number of accompanying dependents plus round-trip air transportation for recipients only. Monthly stipends range from $1,000 to $2,750 commensurate with academic status. Stipends are normally for from three to twelve months' duration.

Application Information Contact the center for information, applications, and brochures.

Deadline(s) Applications, letters of recommendation, and filing fees must be received by November 30.

60. American Research Institute in Turkey
Oriental Institute
1155 East 58th Street
Chicago, IL 60637
(312) 962-9514

Fellowships

Program Description These awards support scholars and advanced graduate students engaged in research in Turkey in ancient, medieval, or modern times, in any field of the humanities and social sciences.

Eligibility/Limitations Student applicants must have fulfilled all requirements for the doctorate except the dissertation. Applicants are expected to be members in good standing of educational institutions in the United States or Canada.

Fiscal Information While grants for travel and maintenance for up to one year will be considered, preference will be given to projects of shorter duration (generally no less than two months). Grants are made only for research to be carried out in Turkey and to defray costs of transportation to and from Turkey.

Application Information In order to be considered, applicants must follow the form and specifications given on an instruction sheet available from the institute.

Deadline(s) Completed application forms and letters of recommendation must be submitted before November 15.

Additional Information Turkish law requires all foreigners to obtain permission for any research to be carried out in Turkey prior to entering the country. ARIT fellowship applicants are personally responsible for obtaining their own research permission. Forms should be obtained from the Cultural Office, Turkish Embassy, 1606 23rd Street NW, Washington, DC 20008. Since replies for permission may take as long as six months, applicants are urged to apply well in advance of the time they expect to carry out the research. ARIT reserves the right to withhold payment of fellowship stipends if appropriate research permission has not been obtained.

61. American School of Classical Studies at Athens
41 East 72nd Street
New York, NY 10021
(212) 861-0302

Fellowships for Regular Members

Program Description The school aims to give qualified members the opportunity to study the antiquities and the art, the topography, history, language, and literature of Greece in all periods; to pursue and aid original research in these fields; and to conduct and sponsor excavation and exploration. The school does not limit its activities to the Classical period but encourages the study of Greece from earliest prehistoric to post-Byzantine times. Four fellowships are normally available: the John Williams White and Heinrich Schliemann Fellowships in Archaeology, the Thomas Day Seymour Fellowship in History and Literature, and the James Rignall Wheeler Fellowship (unrestricted).

Eligibility/Limitations Applicants must be regular members of the school. Admission to regular membership is granted annually to graduate students in Classical Studies (literature, archaeology, history) in the United States or Canada who will preferably have taken at least one year of graduate work but will not have completed the Ph.D. Transcripts, recommendations, and examinations in Greek language, history, and archaeology or literature are required for admission to membership.

Fiscal Information Stipends are $4,000 plus room and board.

Application Information For information on these fellowships contact Prof. Geraldine C. Gesell, University of Tennessee, Department of Classics, Knoxville, TN 37996.

Deadline(s) Applications must be received by January 5.

62. American School of Classical Studies at Athens
41 East 72nd Street
New York, NY 10021
(212) 861-0302

Gennadeion-Dumbarton Oaks Fellowship

Program Description This award is available for a graduate student writing a dissertation on some aspect of post-Classical Greece, or a recent Ph.D. in that field who is completing a project such as the revision of a dissertation for publication.

Eligibility/Limitations The applicant must propose a project which necessitates use of the Gennadius Library.

Fiscal Information This fellowship carries a stipend of $4,000 plus room and board.

Application Information Applicants must submit a full curriculum vitae, a project description, and three supporting letters from qualified scholars. Application is made to the Chairman of the Committee on the Gennadius Library. Address inquiries to Prof. Angeliki Laiou, Harvard University, Department of History, Cambridge, MA 02138.

Deadline(s) Application should be made before January 15.

63. American Schools of Oriental Research
4243 Spruce Street
Philadelphia, PA 19104
(215) 222-4643

Annual Professorships

Program Description These awards support postdoctoral study of the Middle East at The Albright Institute for Archaeological Research, Jerusalem; The American Center of Oriental Research, Amman; and the Cyprus American Archaeological Research Institute.

Eligibility/Limitations These awards are open to postdoctoral scholars from any country. Applicants must be or must become individual professional members of ASOR. Applicants must be affiliated with an institution that is a member of the ASOR corporation or must have been an individual professional member for more than two years.

Fiscal Information Annual professorships carry no stipend. These awards provide room-and-board benefits for nine to twelve months for the professor and spouse. ACOR and CAARI cannot accommodate dependent children.

Application Information Prospective applicants are encouraged to consult with the ASOR administrative director about application procedures, the competitiveness of their applications, or any other questions they might have about the program.

Deadline(s) Application deadline is November 2.

64. American Schools of Oriental Research
4243 Spruce Street
Philadelphia, PA 19104
(215) 222-4643

The George A. Barton Fellowship

Program Description This fellowship supports study or research at the Albright Institute for Archaeological Research in Jerusalem.

Eligibility/Limitations This fellowship is open to qualified scholars from any country. Seminarians, predoctoral students, and recent postdoctoral scholars are eligible.

Fiscal Information The fellowship carries a stipend of $5,000 for a one to five month research period. Three thousand dollars will be paid directly to the Albright Institute for room and half board; a stipend of $2,000 will be paid directly to the recipient. Residence at the Albright Institute is required.

Application Information Prospective applicants are encouraged to consult with the ASOR administrative director about application procedures, the competitiveness of their applications, or any other questions they might have about the program.

Deadline(s) Deadline for receipt of applications is November 2.

65. American Schools of Oriental Research
ASOR NEH Postdoctoral Fellowships
4243 Spruce Street
Philadelphia, PA 19104
(215) 222-4643

ASOR/NEH Postdoctoral Fellowships

Program Description The National Endowment for the Humanities (NEH) and the American Schools of Oriental Research (ASOR) are offering postdoctoral fellowships at the Albright Institute of Archaeological Research in Jerusalem, and at the American Center of Oriental Research in Amman. Research should contribute to the understanding of the cultures and peoples of the Middle East. Projects may be humanistically oriented, ancient or modern, in the fields of: archaeology, anthropology, ancient history, philology, epigraphy, biblical studies, religion, art history, military history, economics, topography, geography or related disciplines.

Eligibility/Limitations Any U.S. citizen or alien residing in the U.S. continuously since 1983, holding a Ph.D. degree as of January 1, 1988, may apply. Established researchers without the Ph.D. may also apply.

Fiscal Information Fellowships can be held for a maximum of twelve months, with a stipend of $27,500, or a minimum of six months, with a stipend of $13,750. Fellowship tenure in Jerusalem or Amman is expected to be continuous.

Application Information Complete eligibility information and application procedures for the ASOR/NEH fellowships are available from the administrative director of ASOR.

Deadline(s) Deadline for completed applications and all support materials is November 2.

66. American Schools of Oriental Research
Mesopotamian Fellowship
4243 Spruce Street
Philadelphia, PA 19104
(215) 222-4643

Mesopotamian Fellowships

Program Description This award encourages scholars to undertake study and research about ancient Mesopotamian civilization or culture, preferably in Iraq or immediately adjacent sections of bordering countries (ancient Mesopotamia).

Eligibility/Limitations This fellowship is open to qualified scholars from any country. Seminarians, predoctoral students, and recent postdoctoral scholars are eligible. Applicants must be or become individual professional members of ASOR. Applicants must be affiliated with an institution that is a member of the ASOR corporation or must have been an individual professional member for more than two years.

Fiscal Information The award carries a stipend of $5,000 for three to six months of study or research.

Application Information Prospective applicants are encouraged to consult with the ASOR administrative director about application procedures, the competitiveness of their applications, or any other questions they might have about the program.

Deadline(s) Deadline for receipt of applications is November 2.

67. American Schools of Oriental Research
Pacific Scientific Company Fellowship, CAARI
4243 Spruce Street
Philadelphia, PA 19104
(215) 222-4643

Pacific Scientific Company Fellowship, CAARI

Program Description These fellowships are available at the Cyprus American Archaeological Research Institute (CAARI) for research positions in Cypriot art or archaeology.

Eligibility/Limitations The positions available vary from year to year, but typically include support at the predoctoral and postdoctoral researcher levels.

Fiscal Information Stipends are $2,500 for a three month research period.

Application Information Applications and additional information are available from ASOR.

Deadline(s) Deadline for application is November 2.

68. American Schools of Oriental Research
Samuel H. Kress Foundation Fellowship
4243 Spruce Street
Philadelphia, PA 19104
(215) 222-4643

Samuel H. Kress Foundation Fellowship

Program Description The Samuel H. Kress Foundation Fellowship supports dissertation research in the field of art history or architecture for ten months at the Albright Institute of Archaeological Research (AIAR).

Eligibility/Limitations Applicants must be well advanced in their dissertation research and demonstrate the importance of continuing research in Jerusalem.

Fiscal Information The fellowship will provide $8,500 to the successful applicant to be divided as follows: a payment of $5,800 will be made to AIAR for room and half-board; a stipend of $2,700 will be paid to the recipient. Residence at AIAR is mandatory and should be continuous.

Application Information Additional information is available from ASOR.

Deadline(s) The deadline for applications is November 2.

69. American Schools of Oriental Research
Shell Fellowship
4243 Spruce Street
Philadelphia, PA 19104
(215) 222-4643

Shell Fellowship

Program Description This award supports study or research at the American Center of Oriental Research in Amman (ACOR).

Eligibility/Limitations Seminarians, predoctoral students, and recent postdoctoral scholars are eligible.

Fiscal Information The fellowship carries a stipend of $6,000 for six to nine months of research or study. Recipients are expected to reside at ACOR and fellowship time should be continuous.

Application Information Prospective applicants are encouraged to consult with the ASOR administrative director about application procedures, the competitiveness of their applications, or any other questions they might have about the program.

Deadline(s) Deadline for receipt of applications is November 2.

70. American Schools of Oriental Research
Teagle Fellowship
4243 Spruce Street
Philadelphia, PA 19104
(215) 222-4643

Teagle Fellowship

Program Description The Teagle Foundation, Inc., has established a fellowship to support research in Middle Eastern studies in the areas of anthropology, archaeology, religion (Old and New Testament, Islam), art history, the social sciences and humanities.

Eligibility/Limitations Predoctoral scholars are eligible to apply.

Fiscal Information The fellowship will provide $10,000 for research in Jordan at the American Center of Oriental Research (ACOR), for a minimum of six months and a maximum of nine months. Four thousand dollars of the fellowship will be paid directly to ACOR for room and board. The remaining $6,000 will be paid to the recipient prior to the beginning of the grant period. Fellowship time should be continuous.

Application Information Application information is available from the school.

Deadline(s) The deadline for applications is November 2.

71. American Schools of Oriental Research
William Foxwell Albright Fellowship
4243 Spruce Street
Philadelphia, PA 19104
(215) 222-4643

William Foxwell Albright Fellowship

Program Description This award encourages scholars to undertake study and research at large in the Middle East or eastern Mediterranean. The program encourages study of the Middle East, from prehistoric times to the modern era. Study or research in humanistic disciplines such as anthropology, archaeology, biblical studies, epigraphy, history, history of art and architecture, literature, philology, prehistory, and topography is supported.

Eligibility/Limitations This fellowship is open to qualified students and scholars from any country. Seminarians, predoctoral students, and recent postdoctoral scholars are eligible to apply, but must be affiliated with an institution that is a member of the ASOR corporation or must have been an individual professional member for more than two years. The award can be used in any country of the Middle East or eastern Mediterranean; if it is used in a country where there is an ASOR institute, the fellow is expected to live at the institute and participate actively in its formal and informal activities.

Fiscal Information One fellowship of $5,000 is awarded for a one to four month period of research or study.

Application Information Prospective applicants are encouraged to consult with the ASOR administrative director about application procedures, the competitiveness of their applications, or any other questions they might have about the program.

Deadline(s) The deadline for application is November 2.

72. Ameritech Foundation
30 South Wacker Drive, 34th Floor
Chicago, IL 60606
(312) 750-5223

Grants

Program Description The Ameritech Foundation serves as the philanthropic organization for Ameritech—the parent company of the Bell companies serving Illinois, Indiana, Michigan, Ohio, and Wisconsin and several other communications-related companies—contributing to the attainment of corporate goals by designing and executing programs which match Ameritech's interests to community and social needs. The foundation concentrates on providing grants to recognized institutions which address three issues: research and programs designed to determine ways that communications can contribute to the long-term betterment of society and quality of life; programs and activities that stimulate and improve the economic vitality of the Great Lakes area, including grants to major educational and cultural organizations; and research and development aimed at reshaping policy into forms more relevant to the current and future nature of the communications industry.

Sample Grants For general operating support, $1,000 to the Adler Planetarium, Chicago, IL (1986). To underwrite a special exhibition, "Blood of Kings, New Interpretation of Maya Art," $37,500 to the Cleveland Museum of Art, Cleveland, OH (1986). The first payment of a two-year $75,000 pledge to the campaign for the Field Museum of Natural History, $37,500 to the Field Museum of Natural History, Chicago, IL (1986). Final payment of a two-year $100,000 pledge toward construction of the Museum's Crown Space Center, $50,000 to the Museum of Science and Industry, Chicago, IL (1986).

Eligibility/Limitations Applicant organizations must be tax-exempt under Section 501(c)(3) of the Internal Revenue Code. The foundation limits its contributions to significant organizations that are regional or national in orientation or impact. The foundation also recognizes its obligation to Chicago as Ameritech's headquarters city and may elect to contribute to selected local organizations. The foundation does not make direct contributions to individuals, to individual community organizations, or to local chapters of national organizations.

Fiscal Information The foundation awarded 82 grants totaling $1.6 million in 1986.

Application Information Organizations which qualify under the foundation's guidelines should provide a brief letter of inquiry before a formal proposal is submitted. It should include: a description of the organization, its history and purpose; an overview of the proposed project for which funding is requested; a summary of the program's budget; an indication of the level of support requested; a list of sources and amounts of other funding obtained, pledged, or requested for this purpose; the population and geographic area served; and documentation of 501(c)(3) public charity status. If the initial review is favorable, a formal proposal will be requested. Preliminary inquiries by telephone or personal visits are discouraged. Proposals should be directed to Michael E. Kuhlin, Executive Director of the foundation.

Deadline(s) There is no deadline for submitting proposals.

73. Amoco Foundation
200 East Randolph Drive
Chicago, IL 60601
(312) 856-6306

Grants

Program Description Since Amoco Foundation was organized in 1952, it has maintained a commitment to improve the social and economic development in areas where Amoco Corporation operates. The foundation also emphasizes and promotes excellence in education. Since 1980, Amoco has made a major commitment to urban neighborhood organizations working in areas of housing, jobs, energy, and education to help residents stabilize and improve their communities. With operations in more than forty countries, Amoco strives to be an ambassador of goodwill in foreign lands. In support of this policy, the Amoco Foundation makes grants overseas to hospitals, schools, museums, and other institutions in areas where the company has operations. Local and national groups that are dedicated to improving conditions for the citizens in the host country also receive foundation support.

Eligibility/Limitations Amoco Foundation makes its domestic contributions only to organizations exempt from federal income tax under Section 501(c)(3) of the Internal Revenue Code, and that are not private foundations as defined in Section 509(a) of the code. It does not normally make grants to organizations that already receive operating support through United Ways, to primary and secondary schools, or to religious, fraternal, social or athletic organizations. Endowment grants are not provided for any purpose.

Fiscal Information The foundation made grants in 1986 totaling nearly $24 million, including over $1.3 million to culture and the arts.

Application Information All requests for grants or other information about the foundation should be directed to the address listed above. Requests for funding must be submitted in writing and should include: a brief description of the organization; a specific purpose for requesting the grant and the benefits it is expected to make possible; the amount of the grant requested and plans to evaluate its effectiveness; budget information including an annual report and a copy of the latest IRS Form 990 report; and a copy of letter(s) from the Internal Revenue Service declaring that the organization is exempt from federal income taxes under Section 501(c)(3) and is not a private foundation under Section 509(a) of the Internal Revenue Code.

Deadline(s) Application deadlines are not announced.

74. Anheuser-Busch Companies, Inc.
Executive Offices
One Busch Place
Saint Louis, MO 63118-1852
(314) 577-7368

Contributions Program

Program Description The company, through a foundation and a charitable trust, as well as through corporate funds, supports charitable organizations active in the fields of education, health care, programs for minorities and youth, cultural enrichment, and environmental protection.

Eligibility/Limitations Support is restricted almost entirely to causes that are located in cities where the company has manufacturing facilities. The company does not contribute to individuals or to groups that are not designated tax-exempt by the Internal Revenue Service.

Fiscal Information In 1986, contributions totaled approximately $16 million.

Application Information A grant application form and application guidelines are available from the contributions administrator of the company.

75. ARCO Foundation
Public Affairs
515 South Flower Street
Los Angeles, CA 90071
(213) 486-3342

Direct Grants

Program Description The ARCO Foundation awards most of its grants in geographic areas where ARCO has major operations and large numbers of employees. The foundation's target priorities are education, community programs, humanities and the arts, public information programs, and environmental programs. In the area of humanities and the arts, the ARCO Foundation supports a wide variety of arts organizations that enrich communities where ARCO does business. The foundation concentrates on programs that give underserved groups access to the arts and cultural experiences that they would not otherwise have. This focus not only makes arts experiences more meaningful to more people but serves to promote intercultural understanding.

Sample Grants For "Spiritualism in Art: Abstract Painting 1890-1986," $100,000 to the Los Angeles County Museum of Art, Los Angeles, CA (1986). For expansion and renovation of facilities, $52,500 to the Museum of Modern Art, New York (1986). For science and industry programs for youth, $50,000 to the California Foundation, Los Angeles, CA (1986). For a planning grant, $7,500 to the California Museum of Latino History, Los Angeles, CA (1986). For a community outreach program, $5,000 to the Afro-American Historical and Cultural Museum, Philadelphia, PA (1986).

Eligibility/Limitations Eligible organizations must be nonprofit, tax-exempt public charities as defined in Sections 501(c)(3) and 509(a) of the Internal Revenue Code. The foundation considers funding of the following: quality arts organizations, such as symphony or chamber orchestras, noncommercial theater groups, major dance companies and museums; outreach activities that offer exposure to the arts for underserved neighborhoods, diverse ethnic groups, young people or senior citizens; community organizations that provide quality arts and cultural experiences for grassroots neighborhood organizations; arts and humanities service organizations; and programs that help arts organizations widen their base of private donors, increase the level of individual contribution and strengthen volunteer participation and board leadership. The foundation generally does not consider the following: endowment grants; university art museums; individual artists; film and video projects; building programs; or fundraising dinners or similar activities.

Fiscal Information The foundation awarded direct grants totaling over $1.9 million to arts organizations in 1986.

Application Information Qualified applicants should submit a concise proposal, not more than two double-spaced typewritten pages. The proposal should contain the following information: a brief description of the organization, including its purpose and an explanation of how it meets the ARCO Foundation's stated guidelines and priorities; a statement of need for the proposed project; the amount of time needed to complete the project; the total cost of the project, other sources of funding, and the amount requested from the ARCO Foundation; and a statement describing community support for or involvement in the project and organization. In addition, the following support data should be submitted: a current budget and the most recent audited financial statement, an annual report, and a copy of the IRS letter of designation as a publicly supported, tax-exempt organization; a copy of the organization's most recent Form 990-A submitted to the IRS; and a list of the organization's board of directors, including their outside affiliations.

Deadline(s) Applications may be submitted at any time. Proposals are accumulated by category and judged with similar requests on a periodic basis.

Additional Information Local and regional organizations must initiate their requests through regional ARCO public affairs offices. Contact the foundation office for a list of regional public affairs offices.

76. Asian Cultural Council
280 Madison Avenue
New York, NY 10016
(212) 684-5450

Art History, Curatorial, and Conservation Fellowships

Program Description The Asian Cultural Council supports cultural exchange between Asia and the United States in the performing and visual arts. The council, with financial assistance from the Henry Luce Foundation, has established a fellowship program for American scholars, curators, and conservators of Asian art to conduct research and travel in East and Southeast Asia, including China, Hong Kong, Indonesia, Korea, Malaysia, the Philippines, Singapore, Thailand, and Vietnam.

Eligibility/Limitations Eligible for support are individual research projects, visits to Asian institutions in connection with proposed exhibitions of Asian art in the United States, and observation tours to collections, sites, and conservation facilities in Asia.

Fiscal Information Grants provide travel, research, and related costs and range in duration from one to three months. Total appropriations for fellowship grants in 1985 were $415,842.

Application Information Individuals wishing to inquire about the possibility of grant support should send a brief description of the activity for which assistance is being sought to the council. If the proposed activity falls within the council's guidelines, application materials requesting more detailed information will be provided by the ACC.

Deadline(s) Completed applications must be submitted at least six months prior to the planned date of project implementation.

77. Asian Cultural Council
280 Madison Avenue
New York, NY 10016
(212) 684-5450

Fellowship Grants

Program Description The Asian Cultural Council supports cultural exchange in the visual and performing arts between Asia and the United States. The emphasis of the ACC's programs is on providing fellowship grants to Asian artists, scholars, students, and specialists for study, research, and travel in the United States. A limited number of grants are also awarded to Americans for similar activities in Asia. The council's geographic purview extends from Afghanistan eastward through Japan, and its disciplinary range includes both traditional and contemporary arts. Grants are made in the following fields: archaeology, architecture, art history, conservation, crafts, dance, design, film, museology, music, painting, photography, printmaking, sculpture, and theater.

Sample Grants To pursue graduate studies in Indian art history leading to the Ph.D. degree, support to the director of archaeology and museums, Government of Madhya Pradesh, India (1985).

Eligibility/Limitations Asians in the visual and performing arts seeking grant assistance to conduct research, study, receive specialized training, undertake observation tours, or pursue creative activity in the U.S. are eligible to apply for fellowship support from the council. Americans seeking aid to undertake similar activity in Asia are also eligible to apply, although most of the ACC's fellowships are awarded to Asian candidates.

Fiscal Information Fellowships are generally awarded for periods ranging from three to twelve months. Full fellowship grants provide for round-trip international air transportation, per diem, domestic travel, maintenance, medical insurance allowances, and a miscellaneous expense allocation for books, supplies, and other grant-related costs. The council also makes partial fellowship grants. Fellowships are not awarded for: lecture programs, personal exhibitions, or individual performance tours; undergraduate study; or activities conducted by individuals in their home countries.

Application Information Individuals wishing to inquire about the possibility of grant support should send a brief description of the activity for which assistance is being sought to the council. If the proposed activity falls within the council's guidelines, application materials requesting more detailed information will be provided by the ACC.

Deadline(s) Completed applications must be submitted at least six months prior to the planned date of project implementation.

78. Asian Cultural Council
280 Madison Avenue
New York, NY 10016
(212) 684-5450

Humanities Fellowships

Program Description The Asian Cultural Council supports cultural exchange between Asia and the United States in the performing and visual arts. A fellowship program, made possible by a Challenge Grant from the National Endowment for the Humanities, will assist American scholars, doctoral students, and specialists in the humanities to undertake research, training, and study in Asia in the following fields: archaeology; conservation; museology; and the theory, history, and criticism of architecture, art, dance, design, film, music, photography, and theater. It will also allow the council to support American and Asian scholars participating in conferences, exhibitions, visiting professorships, and similar projects.

Eligibility/Limitations American scholars, doctoral students, and specialists in the humanities are eligible to apply.

Fiscal Information Grants provide for international travel, maintenance, per diem, and related research expenses and range in duration from one to twelve months.

Application Information Individuals wishing to inquire about the possibility of grant support should send a brief description of the activity for which assistance is being sought to the council. If the proposed activity falls within the council's guidelines, application materials requesting more detailed information will be provided by the ACC.

Deadline(s) Completed applications must be submitted at least six months prior to the planned date of project implementation.

79. Asian Cultural Council
280 Madison Avenue
New York, NY 10016
(212) 684-5450

Japan-United States Arts Program

Program Description The Asian Cultural Council supports cultural exchange in the visual and performing arts between Asia and the United States. The Japan-United States Arts Program of the council promotes cultural exchange specifically between Japan and the United States. Both short-term and long-term individual fellowship grants are awarded to enable Japanese artists, scholars, and arts specialists to visit the United States for research, observation, and creative work and to enable American artists, scholars, and arts specialists to conduct similar activities in Japan. Project grants are awarded for international exchange projects between Japan and the United States for activities pertaining to Japanese art and culture, including exhibition, performances, and similar events. Fields of award include architecture, art criticism, art history, crafts, dance, design, film, literature, museology, music, painting, photography, printmaking, sculpture, and theater.

Sample Grants To study the conservation of woodblock prints in Japan, support to the assistant conservator of prints and drawings, The Metropolitan Museum of Art, New York (1985). To survey collections of Asian ceramics in American museums, support to the curator, Museum of Oriental Ceramics, Osaka, Japan (1985).

Eligibility/Limitations Individuals and institutions are eligible to apply to the program.

Fiscal Information Short-term exchange fellowships range from one to six months in duration; long-term exchange fellowships range from six to twelve months in duration. Fellowship grants provide for round-trip international air transportation, per diem, domestic travel, maintenance, medical insurance allowances in the host country for the duration of the grant period, and a miscellaneous expense allocation for books, supplies, and other grant-related costs.

Application Information Individuals and institutions wishing to inquire about the possibility of grant support should send a brief description of the activity for which assistance is being sought to the council. If the proposed activity falls within the council's guidelines, application materials requesting more detailed information will be provided by the ACC.

Deadline(s) Completed applications must be submitted at least six months prior to the planned date of project implementation.

80. Asian Cultural Council
280 Madison Avenue
New York, NY 10016
(212) 684-5450

Project Grants

Program Description The Asian Cultural Council supports cultural exchange between Asia and the United States in the performing and visual arts. The council's geographic purview extends from Afghanistan eastward through Japan, and its disciplinary range includes both traditional and contemporary arts. Grants are made in the following fields: archaeology, architecture, art history, conservation, crafts, dance, design, film, museology, music, painting, photography, printmaking, sculpture, and theater. Arts organizations and educational institutions may apply to the council for support for projects of exceptional importance involving cultural exchange between Asia and the United States.

Sample Grants To support curatorial travel involved in planning an exhibition of the work of Ito Jakuchu, scheduled to open at the Asia Society, $6,000 to the Asia Society, New York (1985). To support the catalogue of the exhibition "Tales of Japan: Scrolls and Prints from the New York Public Library," $5,000 to the New York Public Library (1985). To provide support for the exhibition "Art in Action" held at the museum, $8,000 to Sogetsu Museum, Tokyo, Japan (1985).

Eligibility/Limitations Arts organizations and educational institutions may apply for project grants.

Fiscal Information Because the council's program resources are concentrated on fellowship awards to individuals, ACC grants are usually modest in size. The council is unable to consider proposals for publications, capital campaigns, and general program and administrative costs.

Application Information Organizations and institutions wishing to inquire about the possibility of grant support should send a brief description of the activity for which assistance is being sought to the council. If the proposed activity falls within the council's guidelines, application materials requesting more detailed information will be provided by the ACC.

Deadline(s) Completed applications must be submitted at least six months prior to the planned date of project implementation.

81. Asian Cultural Council
280 Madison Avenue
New York, NY 10016
(212) 684-5450

The Samuel H. Kress Foundation Fellowships

Program Description The Asian Cultural Council supports cultural exchange between Asia and the United States in the performing and visual arts. The past two decades have seen a dramatic rise in interest in Asian art history at universities across the United States. In response to the need to expand sources of support for American doctoral candidates in the field, the Samuel H. Kress Foundation has made a five-year grant to the Asian Cultural Council to fund fellowships for American art history students conducting dissertation research in Asia.

Eligibility/Limitations Applicants must be American doctoral candidates in art history.

Fiscal Information Fellowships are generally awarded for periods ranging from three to twelve months. Full fellowship grants provide for round-trip international air transportation, per diem, domestic travel, maintenance, medical insurance allowances, and a miscellaneous expense allocation for books, supplies, and other grant-related costs.

Application Information Individuals wishing to inquire about the possibility of grant support should send a brief description of the activity for which assistance is being sought to the council. If the proposed activity falls within the council's guidelines, application materials requesting more detailed information will be provided by the ACC.

Deadline(s) Completed applications must be submitted at least six months prior to the planned date of project implementation.

82. The Vincent Astor Foundation
405 Park Avenue
New York, NY 10022
(212) 758-4110

Grants

Program Description The foundation gives almost without exception to organizations located in New York City. Grants are made for neighborhood revitalization projects, parks and landmark preservation, community-based programs involving children or the elderly, to a limited number of educational programs, and to certain cultural institutions.

Sample Grants For the renovation of the galleries in the museum's West Wing, $200,000 (with an unpaid balance of $800,000) to The Brooklyn Museum (1986). Toward the museum's endowment—income to be used first to meet the direct costs attributable to the Astor Chinese Garden Court; additional income to be used for acquisition of Far Eastern art, $1 million to The Metropolitan Museum of Art, New York (1986). Toward the renovation of the museum's Chinese Sculpture Hall,

$300,000 to The Metropolitan Museum of Art, New York (1986). Toward the purchase of an 8th-century Korean bronze statue of Buddha, $100,000 to The Metropolitan Museum of Art, New York (1986). Toward the renovation of the Elephant House at the Bronx Zoo, $1 million to the New York Zoological Society (1986). To secure the Jasper Ward House, which is currently under renovation, $10,000 to the South Street Seaport Museum, New York (1986).

Eligibility/Limitations As a rule the foundation does not give to programs involving the performing arts, mental health, medicine, research, or advocacy. The foundation does not make grants to individuals or loans for any purpose.

Fiscal Information The foundation's grants budget is approximately $1 to $1.5 million a year, depending on market conditions, and most grants range from $10,000 to $25,000, although a few grants are somewhat smaller.

Application Information The foundation has no application form but prefers at the initial stage a brief letter of inquiry addressed to the director which describes the proposed project, the sponsoring agency, and the estimated budget. If the request falls within the foundation's guidelines and appears to have a reasonable chance for funding, a meeting will be arranged and the foundation will request a more detailed proposal.

Deadline(s) Foundation trustees meet to consider grant applications three times a year, in May, October, and December. There are no formal deadlines by which applications must be submitted.

83. AT&T Foundation
Secretary
550 Madison Avenue, Room 2700
New York, NY 10022

Grants

Program Description AT&T Foundation is the principal source of philanthropic activity by AT&T and its subsidiaries. The foundation's scope is national, emphasizing support for higher education, health care, social action and the arts. Grants in the arts and culture category support nationally-known cultural organizations and projects of national or regional scope in areas where AT&T has a major presence. Its primary interest is in the performing arts. The foundation has a particular interest in projects including: special performances, new productions, presentations or commissions of new works, special exhibitions, and major institutional development or expansion programs for which there is a demonstrated need.

Sample Grants To the Iowa Historical Museum Foundation, $60,000 (1985). To the Metropolitan Museum of Art, New York, $150,000 (1984). To the Children's Museum of Indianapolis Inc., $25,000 (1985).

Eligibility/Limitations To qualify for consideration, organizations must have been classified as tax-exempt under Section 501(3)(c) of the Internal Revenue Code and must have been professionally managed for at least five years and compensate both artistic and managerial personnel. Eligible organizations include museums and private non-academic libraries. The foundation does not award grants to individuals. The program will not support competitions, training or scholarships, restorations or historic villages, endowment for unrestricted purposes, or projects in the early stages of research and planning.

Fiscal Information In 1985, the foundation awarded over $3.3 million in support in the arts and culture category.

Application Information If you wish to determine foundation interest in receiving a proposal, please write to the contributions coordinator at the above address. Letters of inquiry should contain no more than three pages with the following information: a description of the institution or organization; a statement relating its purpose to the general interests and specific priorities of the foundation; a summary of the purpose for which the grant is sought and evidence of need for the activity; an overall operating budget for the current fiscal year showing anticipated sources of revenue and expenses; and (if project support is sought) a detailed budget of the project.

Deadline(s) No deadlines are announced.

84. Mary Reynolds Babcock Foundation
102 Reynolda Village
Winston-Salem, NC 27106-5123
(919) 748-9222

Grants

Program Description The Mary Reynolds Babcock Foundation was created in 1953 by a $12 million bequest of Mary Reynolds Babcock, daughter of R.J. Reynolds. The foundation has awarded over $55 million in grants, primarily in education, social services, the environment, the arts, and public policy. The foundation provides support for programs to support active citizen participation in the following areas: environmental protection, development of public policy, education, well-being of children and adolescents, philanthropy, the arts, grassroots organizing, rural issues, and women's concerns. The majority (seventy-five percent) of grants are made to organizations working in North Carolina and the Southeast.

Sample Grants For general support, $30,000, second year of a three-year grant, to Reynolda House Museum of American Art, Winston-Salem, NC (1986).

Eligibility/Limitations Tax-exempt organizations are eligible to apply. The foundation does not make grants to individuals, for construction or restoration projects, international programs, film or video production, or activities of tax-supported educational institutions outside North Carolina.

Fiscal Information During 1986 the foundation board reviewed more than 600 proposals and made 84 grants averaging around $32,000. In addition, under board guidelines, the staff made thirty-one emergency, or interim, grants averaging approximately $2,500.

Application Information Applicants are encouraged to approach the foundation well ahead of the announced deadlines to explore the possibility of foundation interest in proposed programs. This may be done by telephone, by letter, or in person. Additional information and application guidelines are available from the foundation.

Deadline(s) Application deadlines are March 1 and September 1.

Additional Information The foundation will consider exceptions to their general guidelines.

85. The Bay Foundation, Inc.
14 Wall Street, Suite 1600
New York, NY 10005
(212) 815-7500

Grants

Program Description The foundation's current areas of interest are: museum collections care and conservation; veterinary science and species preservation; and children's education and service programs.

Sample Grants For a collections conservation project, $4,000 to C.M. Russell Museum, Great Falls, MT (1986). For marine research specimens facilities, $15,000 to the New England Aquarium, Boston, MA (1986). For a reproduction laboratory, $5,000 to the San Diego Zoo, San Diego, CA (1986).

Eligibility/Limitations No grants are made to individuals, building campaigns, the performing arts, or to other publicly supported charities.

Fiscal Information Typical first time grants are in the $2,000 to $6,000 range. Support for any one institution will generally be limited to not more than three years in any one five year period.

Application Information There is no application form. Letters of solicitation may be written at any time to the executive director and should include: a brief description of the applicant organization; a description of the program for which funding is being sought, including objectives and budget; additional sources of support; and tax-exempt certification.

Deadline(s) The foundation's directors meet twice a year, usually in March and October. The fall meeting sets the larger part of the grants budget for the following year; no commitments can be made between these meetings.

86. Best Products Foundation
1616 P Street, NW, Suite 100
Washington, DC 20036
(202) 328-5188

Grants

Program Description The Best Products Foundation supports selected activities in the following areas of foundation priorities: arts and culture, civic organizations, education, and health and welfare.

Sample Grants For support of a music series, $14,000 to the Virginia Museum, Richmond, VA (1986).

Eligibility/Limitations The foundation supports activities in the form of challenge, matching, one-time and multi-year grants to organizations located in the geographic areas where its sponsor, Best Products Co., Inc., has facilities. The foundation makes grants only to organizations which are ruled tax-exempt by the IRS.

Fiscal Information The foundation does not normally provide support for building funds; annual support; organizations deriving major support from any governmental unit; "goodwill" or journal advertisements; secondary or elementary educational institutions; national organizations; or publications, conferences, seminars or research.

Application Information An organization wishing to apply should send an initial letter of inquiry to the foundation describing the organization, the proposed program, and budget needs. If the program fits the foundation's program priorities, a detailed proposal will be requested.

Deadline(s) The foundation board meets four times a year to consider applications.

87. The William Bingham Foundation
1250 Leader Building
Cleveland, OH 44114
(216) 781-3270

Grants

Program Description The foundation currently contributes to a wide range of organizations in the areas of education, the arts, health, and welfare, reflecting the diverse interests of the trustees. Programs relating to environmental preservation and conflict resolution, including nuclear arms control, have been significant interests of the foundation, with emphasis on programs with practical application in these areas.

Sample Grants For support of the Northeast Ohio Art Museum, $15,000 to the Cleveland Artists Foundation, Cleveland, OH (1986). For maintenance of the exhibition "The Atom: Peril and Promise" on its national tour, $11,820 to Cleveland Health Education Museum, Cleveland, OH (1986). For partial support of the museum's Archaeology Field School, $5,000 to the Cleveland Museum of Natural History, Cleveland, OH (1986). For general operating support of the museum, $10,000 to The Peace Museum, Chicago, IL (1986).

Eligibility/Limitations Grants are made primarily to tax-exempt organizations in the eastern U.S. Grants are not made to individuals.

Fiscal Information Grants paid in 1986 totaled over $800,000.

Application Information To apply for a grant, submit to the executive director a letter not to exceed two pages, outlining the nature of the project, budget requirements, and the contribution requested. If the project coincides with the foundation's interests, a trustee or the executive director may request a meeting with the applicant and preparation of a complete grant proposal. Complete proposals should be submitted only at the request of the foundation.

Deadline(s) The query letter may be submitted at any time throughout the year. When the foundation requests a complete grant proposal, the proposal will be due two months before the next semi-annual meeting of the board of trustees, usually held in May and October.

88. Blandin Foundation
100 Pokegama Avenue North
Grand Rapids, MN 55744
(218) 326-0523

Grants

Program Description The Blandin Foundation supports projects in the following areas: economic development; education; health and human services; and the arts and humanities.

Sample Grants A sustaining contribution to the Minnesota Museum of Art, St. Paul, MN, $5,000 (1986). To develop a promotional campaign to raise endowment funds, $2,500 to the North Country Museum of Arts, Park Rapids, MN (1986). For restorative work on its permanent collection of paintings and to build an exhibit case for its Nigerian objects, $5,500 to North Country Museum of Arts, Park Rapids, MN (1986). A three year grant to Tweed Museum of Art to support a series of exhibitions of rural artists in cooperation with other museums, $110,000 to the University of Minnesota, Duluth, MN (1986).

Eligibility/Limitations The foundation gives to organizations in Minnesota and restricts its support to organizations with a nonprofit 501(c)(3) tax-exempt status from the Internal Revenue Service. Governmental units are eligible to receive foundation support provided the purpose of the grant request goes beyond the limits of expected governmental services. Grants are not made to individuals, except for educational awards.

Fiscal Information The foundation does not support capital campaigns for construction, renovation, or purchase of equipment or endowments beyond the home community of Grand Rapids/Itasca County; publications, films or videos, except for those reflecting unique subjects of special interest to the region and state; travel grants for individuals or groups; or ordinary governmental services.

Application Information The foundation requests that prospective applicants make a preliminary inquiry to staff concerning the nature of the proposed grant request. This preliminary inquiry can be accomplished in a short letter of inquiry, by a telephone call, or in an appointment to meet with a staff member. Depending upon the outcome of the preliminary inquiry, a fully developed application may be requested.

Deadline(s) The board of trustees of the foundation meets four times each year to review and authorize grants. Applications must be received by the following dates to be considered at the next quarterly meeting: February 1 for review in May; May 1 for review in August; August 1 for review in November; November 1 for review in February.

89. Bodman Foundation
767 Third Avenue
New York, NY 10017
(212) 418-0500

Grants

Program Description The foundation's stated purpose is the distribution of funds in the religious, educational and charitable fields "for the moral, ethical, and physical well-being and progress of mankind." Grants are awarded in the following areas: social services; medical and health related; cultural and educational; and religious.

Sample Grants A $70,000 grant pledge, to be paid equally in 1984 and 1985, to be used toward the $10 million Conservatory campaign, with an additional $5,000 grant voted in 1984 towards the Fragrance Garden for the Blind's current operating cost, to the Brooklyn Botanic Garden, New York (1985). Toward the cost of construction of the aquarium's proposed Discovery Cove, $100,000 to New York Zoological Society, Bronx, NY (1985).

Eligibility/Limitations Grant aid may be extended, from time to time, to colleges and universities, performing arts groups, and museums. For the most part, the foundation's program continues to be locally oriented. Grants are awarded in support of duly incorporated and tax-exempt agencies and institutions under the regulations of the IRS. Under current guidelines, grants for conferences, travel, films, and publications are usually precluded. The foundation does not make loans, nor does it make grants to individuals.

Fiscal Information In 1985, $2.5 million was awarded in grants; seventeen percent of this total was awarded in the culture and education category.

Application Information The foundation has no standard application form. A request for funding assistance must be made in writing. Grant proposals, one copy only, should be forwarded with a cover letter, together with supporting documents and information. Organizations with which the foundation may not be familiar should include a statement of history and objectives, a list of board members and key personnel, the scope of current activities, a description of the project or purposes for which funds are sought, and financial data (including budgets and audited financial statements) as to both the organization and the proposal itself, as well as evidence of tax-exemption and classification by the IRS.

Deadline(s) Applications may be submitted at any time during the year.

90. The Boeing Company
Public and Community Affairs
Mail Stop: P.O. Box 3707
Seattle, WA 98124-2207
(206) 655-6679

Grants

Program Description The Boeing Company contributes in four major categories: education, health and human services, culture and the arts, and civic and community activities.

Eligibility/Limitations Applicant organizations must be exempt from federal income tax under Section 501(c)(3) of the Internal Revenue Code.

Fiscal Information In 1986, the company contributed $14 million in cash and in-kind donations to about 1,000 organizations.

Application Information The company does not have a formal application form. Requests for funding should be made by letter and should include the following information: brief description of the organization, including its legal name, its primary purpose and history, the amount of grant request and how it will be used, clear statement of the purpose of the organization's program(s), including the benefits it is expected to provide, and the official contact person; attached additional information such as an annual report or financial statement, budget for the proposed project and other factual information related to the organization or the request that may be useful for evaluation (e.g., list of support from other donors); and documentation affirming that the organization is exempt from federal income tax under Section 501(c)(3) of the Internal Revenue Code.

Deadline(s) Applications are accepted throughout the year.

91. Boettcher Foundation
1670 Broadway, Suite 3301
Denver, CO 80202
(303) 831-1937

Grants

Program Description The purposes of the foundation are general, as established by charter, and are limited to the well-being of mankind within the State of Colorado. Full powers have been lodged in the trustees of the foundation to accomplish these purposes which are principally educational, charitable, scientific, or religious, or broadly speaking any objects or purposes which are deemed charitable under prevailing law. Within the framework of the foundation's charter and prevailing law, the trustees have established policies over the years to meet the broad charitable needs of these changing times as they interpret them. Current program areas of interest to the foundation are: education; community and social services; hospital and health services; and civic and cultural programs.

Sample Grants Toward restoration projects, $1,000 to Denver Firefighters Museum, Inc., Denver, CO (1986). In support of permanent endowment, $1 million to Denver Art Museum, Denver, CO (1986). In support of permanent endowment, $1 million to Denver Botanic Gardens, Denver, CO (1986).

Eligibility/Limitations Giving is strictly limited to tax-exempt organizations in Colorado; the expenditure of a grant must either directly or indirectly take place within the state.

Fiscal Information During 1986 the trustees of the foundation distributed a total of over $4.3 million in grants. In addition, at year-end there were unconditional grant commitments of over $2.5 million and conditionally committed grants of over $6 million for a total of over $8.5 million of grants approved but unpaid.

Application Information There are no forms for making application to the trustees for grants. A brief letter will suffice and should be submitted preliminary to formal application, if the applicant feels that the project involved is within the scope of the foundation's activities. This letter should describe concisely the project and its intended purpose and will serve to initiate a request for formal application from the foundation if the application is determined to be within the current scope of its operations.

Deadline(s) No deadlines are announced. Applicants should allow two or three months for an application to be processed although a more prompt answer will be given whenever feasible.

92. Borg-Warner Foundation
Corporate Contributions
200 South Michigan Avenue
Chicago, IL 60604
(312) 322-8657

Contributions

Program Description The mission of the Borg-Warner Foundation is to strengthen the individual's capacity to participate in and contribute to society and to serve as one mechanism through which the corporation carries out its citizenship responsibilities. To carry out this mission the foundation seeks to promote opportunities that encourage and enable: individuals to expand their personal horizons; community systems to function effectively; and partnerships among individuals and institutions. Foundation contributions are viewed as an investment in overall community well-being. Through donations, the foundation strives to: respond to a wide spectrum of quality of life issues; serve as a catalyst for innovation; take risks in supporting valuable ideas; and build on community strengths.

Sample Grants Grant in the amount of $15,000 in support of the Brookfield Zoo, Chicago, IL (1986). Grant in the amount of $100,000 in support of the Field Museum of Natural History, Chicago, IL (1986). Grant in the amount of $5,000 in support of the Mexican Fine Arts Center Museum, Chicago, IL (1986). Grant in the amount of $25,000 in support of the Museum of Contemporary Art, Chicago, IL (1986).

Eligibility/Limitations In general contributions are confined to tax-exempt organizations in the Chicago area. The foundation will consider providing seed money, capital support, endowment funds, challenge grants, support for general operations, and special project funding. Grants are not given to foreign-based institutions; testimonial dinners, fund-raising events, or advertising; medical or academic research; or to individuals.

Fiscal Information 1986 contributions totaled over $2.5 million.

Application Information There is no grant application form. The foundation requests that you submit a cover letter summarizing: why financial aid is requested; the amount of money sought; and the name, daytime phone number and relationship to the organization of an individual who may be contacted regarding the request. Applicants must submit a funding proposal—preferably no more than ten pages long—including the following information about the applicant organization: purpose and history; objectives for the coming year and the activities necessary to carry them out; who is served; the membership of each of the governing boards; projected income and expenses for the current fiscal year, with an audited financial statement from the previous year; size and source of corporate and foundation grants; proof of tax-exempt status; documentation of the needs to be met or problems to be solved; and a statement of the agency's qualifications for getting the job done. If the applicant is seeking support for a specific project, include a specific budget and program description for this project in addition to the above information.

Deadline(s) Requests are accepted throughout the year.

93. The Boston Foundation
One Boston Place
Boston, MA 02109
(617) 723-7415

Grants

Program Description The Boston Foundation will consider any proposal for a program that seeks to meet in a significant way health, human service, educational, housing, environmental, or cultural needs in the Greater Boston community. The foundation favors: programs that will serve a broad sector of the community and that will assist those who are not being adequately served by existing community resources; demonstration projects that propose practical approaches to specific community problems; programs that help coordinate community services; programs that will provide leverage for generating additional funds and community support; and building, renovation, and energy conservation projects that will improve the delivery of basic services.

Sample Grants Grant in the amount of $20,000 in support of the Children's Discovery Museum, Inc. (1987). Grant in the amount of $43,462 in support of the Children's Museum (1987). Towards 1986-1987 operating budget, grants in the amount of $25,000 to the Museum of Afro-American History (1987). Grant in the amount of $116,000 in support of the Museum of Science (1987). Grant in the amount of $100,000 for a matching grant in support of the New England Aquarium Education Fund (1987).

Eligibility/Limitations Grants are made only to tax-exempt organizations as defined by Section 501(c)(3) of the Internal Revenue Code. In general, grants are not made from undesignated funds for: general operating expenses; medical, scientific, or academic research; scholarships, fellowships, or loans; the writing, publication, or distribution of books or articles; conferences or symposiums; travel; the production or distribution of films, radio, or television programs; audio and/or video equipment; or capital campaigns of institutions that have nationwide support. In addition, grants are not made from undesignated funds to: individuals; organizations outside the Boston geographic area; or to national or international organizations.

Fiscal Information Grants paid in 1987 totaled more than $12.8 million.

Application Information A formal written proposal should include: a cover letter, signed by the organization's president and executive director, outlining a brief summary of the request and the amount requested; a report on the expenditure of any previous grant; a copy of the most recent 501(c)(3) IRS ruling; a description of the organization's background, history, purpose, current programs, and the people it serves; a list of board members, officers, and staff; financial statements from the last three years of operation, including the organization's most recent audit and the current operating budget; project description and an estimate of the number of people to be served; specific plans for evaluating the project; project budget; the amount requested; the amount raised or expected from other sources; an explanation of how the project is to be funded; a contact person; and a telephone number.

Deadline(s) The foundation considers grant proposals four times a year, generally in March, June, September, and December. A minimum of ten weeks before scheduled meetings is required to process proposals. A longer advance period may be necessary in the case of a proposal that requires an unusual amount of preliminary investigation.

94. The Boston Globe Foundation
135 Morrissey Boulevard
Boston, MA 02107
(617) 929-2895

Grants

Program Description The Boston Globe Foundation makes grants to nonprofit organizations from funds made available by Affiliated Publications, Inc. The foundation has seven areas of giving: community services, culture and the arts, education, science and the environment, hospitals and health care, summer camps, and media business.

Sample Grants Annual payment toward multiple year $30,000 grant in support of newspaper archival preservation program, $6,000 to American Antiquarian Society, Worcester, MA (1986). Final payment of $25,000 pledge towards capital campaign, $12,500 to Children's Museum, Boston (1986). First payment toward two-year $20,000 grant to design and construct an exhibit which will graphically depict Boston Harbor's plant and animal life—as it is and as it could be if the harbor is pollution-free, $10,000 to New England Aquarium, Boston (1986).

Eligibility/Limitations The foundation approves grants for operating expenses, special projects, and capital drives to agencies located within the Greater Boston area. Gifts are made to regional or national groups, but the main purpose of the foundation is to service and assist communities in the Boston area.

Fiscal Information The foundation completed its fifth year of operation in 1986 with total contributions in excess of $3.1 million.

Application Information Application guidelines and required application forms are available from the foundation and will be supplied upon request. Foundation staff review all proposals, investigate agencies, evaluate the budgetary requirements, and then make recommendations to the board of directors of the foundation.

Deadline(s) Requests for grants may be submitted at any time. Allow three to four months to process a proposal.

95. BP America Inc.
200 Public Square
Cleveland, OH 44114-2376
(216) 586-4141

Corporate Contributions

Program Description BP America awards financial support on two levels. Corporate Initiatives grants support organizations and programs which address three areas of national concern: education, urban planning and economic redevelopment, and energy and natural resources. Local and regional grants support education, the arts, health and human services, and civic organizations. These grants are made after review with local representatives of BP America business units. The grants support colleges, museums, human service organizations, and other civic programs and institutions.

Sample Grants To the Children's Museum of Utah, Salt Lake City, $7,500 (1986). To the Cleveland Museum of Natural History, Cleveland, OH, $25,000 (1986). To the Houston Museum of Natural Science, Houston, TX $25,000 (1986). To the Hansen Planetarium, Salt Lake City, UT, $1,000 (1986). To the University of Alaska Museum, Fairbanks, AK $20,000 (1986). To the Cleveland Metroparks Zoo, Cleveland, OH, $95,000 (1986).

Eligibility/Limitations The company gives support for general operations and for specific purposes, usually to organizations in existence for at least a year. The institution or program should seek to fill a specific, demonstrable community need. Grants are made only to organizations who receive tax-exempt status from the Internal Revenue Service and conform to the requirements of the Tax Reform Act of 1969. Grants are not made to individuals or for religious purposes.

Fiscal Information Contributions in 1986 totaled over $13 million, including over $1 million to culture and the arts.

Application Information There is no application form. The company asks that all proposals be submitted as typewritten letters. Guidelines for proposals are available from the company. Preliminary inquiries may be made in writing or by telephone.

Deadline(s) Applications are accepted at any time. Contribution decisions are made several times each year. The review process normally takes up to twelve weeks.

96. The Bristol-Myers Fund, Inc.

345 Park Avenue
New York, NY 10154
(212) 546-4331

Contributions

Program Description Bristol-Myers recognizes that in addition to its primary objectives as a business enterprise, it also has a responsibility to contribute material support to nonprofit institutions via The Bristol-Myers Fund, Inc. These institutions include scientific, medical, educational, charitable and cultural organizations, as well as the local communities around the nation where the company maintains facilities and where its employees and their families live. The company has identified five broad areas as being particularly appropriate for support: medical research and health; education; civic and community services; cultural activities; and international affairs. Within the scope of cultural activities, the fund provides support to prominent cultural institutions. This support is directed particularly to nationally recognized performing arts centers and major natural history, science, and art museums, but the fund will also consider requests from cultural institutions having a broad appeal in communities where the company has operations.

Eligibility/Limitations The fund will consider requests for support only from tax-exempt organizations which satisfy the requirements of Section 501(c)(3) of the Internal Revenue Code. The fund will not support individuals, organizations receiving support through the United Way or other federated campaigns, endowments, or courtesy advertising.

Application Information Any nonprofit organization which conforms to giving guidelines should submit a written request containing the following information: a brief statement of history, goals and accomplishments to date; statement of purpose for which the grant is requested; and amount requested with list of current funding sources. Attachments should include: current annual report and list of board members; copy of IRS tax-exemption letter 501(c)(3); copy of organization's most recent Form 990 Income Tax Return; and current year's operating budget and copy of the organization's most recent audited financial statements.

Deadline(s) The board meets in December, and as needed, to consider requests. Applications should reach the fund from February through September.

97. The Brown Foundation, Inc.
2118 Welch Avenue, P.O. Box 13646
Houston, TX 77219
(713) 523-6867

Grants

Program Description Foundation funds are used principally for the support, encouragement, and assistance to arts and education.

Eligibility/Limitations Organizations eligible to apply must be tax-exempt as described in Section 509(a)(1), (2), or (3) of the Internal Revenue Code.

Application Information The foundation publishes guidelines for grant proposals. Each proposal should include the following background information: name, address, and telephone number of the organization requesting funds; purpose and summary of organization's activities; evidence of tax-exempt status; and a list of officers and board of directors or trustees of the organization. Support information should include: audited financial statements for the most recent year; interim statement of income and expenses from time of last audit to present; current operating budget for the organization; and projected operating budget for year(s) in which funding is requested. A summary of the proposed project should include: nature of project; specific goal or objective of the project; justification for need; plans for administration and operation of proposed activity; plans for evaluating the impact or success of project; dates of implementation and conclusion; plans for financing project including an itemized budget, funds on hand or pledged, and other sources of funding; and the specific amount requested from the foundation. A letter of approval from the chief administrator, if the request is signed by a division or department head, should also be included.

Deadline(s) Requests are handled on a weekly basis. When a request is received from a qualified organization it is submitted to the executive committee, consisting of members of the board of trustees, for appropriate action. Trustee meetings are held quarterly.

98. John Carter Brown Library
Brown University
Box 1894
Providence, RI 02912
(401) 863-2725

John Carter Brown Library Fellowships

Program Description The John Carter Brown Library is an outstanding collection of primary materials relating to virtually all aspects of the discovery, exploration, and development of the New World. Collections range from the late fifteenth century to about 1830, when direct European involvement in American affairs came to an end. Regular library fellowships are available for research in the collections of the library for periods of one to four months.

Eligibility/Limitations Fellowships are open to Americans and foreign nationals who are engaged in predoctoral, postdoctoral, or independent research. Fellows are expected to be in regular residence at the library and to participate in the intellectual life of Brown University. Therefore, preference may be given to applicants able to take up the fellowship during the course of the academic year.

Fiscal Information Fellowships range from one to four months with a monthly stipend of $800. (Foreign nationals are advised that the monthly stipend may not be sufficient to cover all of a fellow's travel and living expenses.) One appointment each year, for up to three months, will be reserved for the recipient of the Jeannette D. Black Memorial Fellowship. This fellowship is awarded to a scholar with a particular interest in research on the history of cartography or to one who intends to make considerable use of early maps in his or her research.

Application Information Application forms are available on request.

Deadline(s) Applications should be postmarked no later than January 15.

99. John Carter Brown Library
Brown University
Box 1894
Providence, RI 02912
(401) 863-2725

National Endowment for the Humanities Fellowships

Program Description Long-term fellowships funded by the National Endowment for the Humanities are available in support of research appropriate to the holdings of the John Carter Brown Library.

Eligibility/Limitations Applicants must hold a doctorate and be American citizens or have been resident in the U.S. for the three years immediately preceding the term of the fellowship.

Fiscal Information Fellowships consist of either two six-month awards, carrying a stipend of $13,750 each, or a single twelve-month award with a stipend of $27,500. Fellows are expected to be in regular residence at the library and to participate in the intellectual life of Brown University. Therefore, preference may be given to applicants able to take up the fellowship during the course of the academic year.

Application Information Application forms may be obtained from the director of the library.

Deadline(s) Applications should be postmarked no later than January 15.

100. Mary Ingraham Bunting Institute of Radcliffe College
10 Garden Street
Cambridge, MA 02138
(617) 495-8212

Berkshire Summer Fellowship

Program Description This fellowship is designed to support women historians at the postdoctoral level.

Eligibility/Limitations Women historians at the postdoctoral level are eligible to apply.

Fiscal Information The fellowship carries a stipend of $2,500.

Application Information For information and application contact the fellowship program of the Bunting Institute.

Deadline(s) The deadline for receipt of application is October 1.

101. Mary Ingraham Bunting Institute of Radcliffe College
10 Garden Street
Cambridge, MA 02138
(617) 495-8212

The Bunting Fellowship Program

Program Description These fellowships are designed to support women who wish to pursue independent study in academic and professional fields, in creative writing, in the visual and performing arts, and in music, and thereby advance their careers.

Eligibility/Limitations Women scholars, professionals, creative writers, poets, visual and performing artists, and musicians at various levels of career development are eligible to apply. The applicant must have received the doctorate at least two years prior to appointment, or have equivalent professional experience for non-academic applicants.

Fiscal Information Award of the fellowship carries a stipend of $17,600 for a one-year appointment, office or studio space, auditing privileges, and access to libraries and other resources of Radcliffe College and Harvard University. Residence in the Boston area is required during the fellowship appointment.

Application Information For information and application forms contact the Fellowship Program of The Bunting Institute.

Deadline(s) Applications and recommendations must be postmarked by October 1.

Additional Information Affiliation with the institute is also available. Affiliation appointment is without stipend for one or two semesters with office/studio space and other resources available to all fellows.

102. Mary Ingraham Bunting Institute of Radcliffe College
10 Garden Street
Cambridge, MA 02138
(617) 495-8212

The Science Scholars Fellowship Program

Program Description These fellowships are designed to support women scientists who wish to pursue independent study in the following science fields: physical and mathematical, environmental, engineering, biological, and psychological.

Eligibility/Limitations Women scientists at any level in their careers who have received the doctorate at least two years prior to appointment are eligible to apply.

Fiscal Information Award of the fellowship carries a stipend of $20,000 plus research expenses. Two-year appointments are awarded to recipients affiliated with a laboratory; one-year appointments are awarded to recipients who do not require a laboratory affiliation. Office space, auditing privileges, and access to libraries and other resources of Radcliffe College and Harvard University are provided. Residence in the Boston area is required during the fellowship appointment.

Application Information For information and application forms contact the Fellowship Program of The Bunting Institute.

Deadline(s) Applications and recommendations must be postmarked by October 1.

103. Burlington Northern Foundation
999 Third Avenue
Seattle, WA 98104-4097
(206) 467-3895

Grants

Program Description The Burlington Northern Foundation is the major channel of philanthropy for Burlington Northern Inc. and its subsidiaries. The foundation administers a consistent contributions program in recognition of the company's responsibilities to support and improve the general welfare and quality of life in the communities it serves.

Eligibility/Limitations Contributions are limited to nonprofit, tax-exempt organizations which have obtained IRS status under Section 501(c)(3). Generally, contributions will be considered for educational institutions, youth organizations, hospital and medical facilities, cultural organizations, civic services, and human service organizations. Contributions will not be made to individuals, for general endowment funds, or for fundraising events.

Application Information For further information and an application form, write to the foundation. Do not send additional information at this time. Please make first contacts with the foundation by mail.

Deadline(s) Applications are reviewed as quickly as possible, normally within four months.

104. Burroughs Corporation
Corporate Contributions and Community Relations Programs, Public Affairs
  Department
One Burroughs Place
Detroit, MI 48232

Contributions Program

Program Description The Burroughs Contributions Program provides support in the areas of health and welfare, education, civic and community service, culture and the arts, and to those organizations that improve the business climate in the areas where company activities are located. Within the category of culture and the arts, community cultural institutions that promote a greater appreciation of culture and the arts are supported.

Eligibility/Limitations The corporation supports nonprofit organizations that qualify for contribution deductions under Section 501(c)(3) of the U.S. Internal Revenue Code or qualify for taxable deductions under a specific country's tax laws.

Fiscal Information The corporation will support the following types of grants: undesignated funds given for use in general support of a nonprofit organization; funds designated for implementation of a specific program by a nonprofit organization; funds designated for purchase of equipment primarily for instructional and research purposes; and, on a limited basis, support to building funds will be considered.

Application Information All requests must be in writing, signed by an authorized official of the organization and accompanied by the following information: background of the organization; present structure of the organization, including the board of control; fund-raising efforts; and budget.

Deadline(s) Requests for contributions should be sent before September 30. Requests for equipment contributions should be sent before June 30.

105. Cabot Corporation Foundation
950 Winter Street, P.O. Box 9073
Waltham, MA 02254-9073
(617) 890-0200

Grants

Program Description Cabot Corporation makes contributions through the Cabot Corporation Foundation and the company's operating divisions. Cabot extends support to a wide array of programs and organizations that pertain to education, community support, cultural advancement, public policy and international affairs. Within the cultural advancement area, Cabot provides limited support to cultural organizations, concentrating its giving in the following areas: museums, especially museums that consider science education to be a top priority; and community arts organizations.

Sample Grants For construction of an education center, $2,500 to the Carson County Square House Museum, TX (1986). For general support and Boston Artists (1945-1985), $2,900 to DeCordova and Dana Museum and Park, Lincoln, MA (1986). For a capital campaign (part of four-year pledge), $5,000 to the New England Aquarium, Boston, MA (1986).

Eligibility/Limitations The foundation supports only nonprofit organizations holding active 501(c)(3) status under the IRS Code. Cabot does not make contributions to individuals, political organizations, religious institutions (except for projects conducted by religious groups that are open to individuals without regard to religious preference), advertising, dinner-table sponsorship, or fraternal organizations.

Fiscal Information Cabot Corporation Foundation grants totaled over $1.2 million in 1986, including $90,100 in the cultural activities category.

Application Information Organizations with programs falling within Cabot's guidelines should submit a concisely written proposal containing: a statement of the proposed project, not more than two pages, which addresses the purpose of the project, its uniqueness, its long-term goals and more specific short-term objectives, the estimated time required for project completion, and the way results can be measured; brief background information about the organization, its board of directors, and the qualifications of those who lead the proposed effort; evidence of the organization's tax-exempt status; the total cost, present and potential sources of funding, and the amount requested from Cabot; and the latest audited financial statement (in cases where the organization's total budget exceeds $100,000). Proposals should be submitted either to the executive director at the foundation headquarters, or to the appropriate individual Cabot facility.

Deadline(s) Funding decisions are made four times a year—in December, March, June and September—by the foundation's board of directors. Applications received less than a month in advance of a directors' meeting will not be considered until the next quarterly meeting.

106. The Morris and Gwendolyn Cafritz Foundation
1825 K Street, NW
Washington, DC 20006
(202) 223-3100

Grants

Program Description The Morris and Gwendolyn Cafritz Foundation was incorporated under the laws of the District of Columbia in 1948. The foundation makes grants to charitable, educational, and cultural organizations operating within the Washington metropolitan area, with programs of direct assistance to the District of Columbia. Grants are awarded in the following general areas: arts and humanities, community services, education, and health.

Sample Grants Additional funds to purchase a work of art, $1.2 million to the National Gallery of Art, Washington, DC (1987). To underwrite "Washingtoniana II", a guide to the architecture, design, and engineering collections of the Washington, DC metropolitan area, $252,341 to The Library of Congress, Washington, DC (1987). For a $50,000 challenge grant matched two-to-one by new and increased contributions from other sources and $100,000 to support "The Pastoral Landscape," a joint exhibition with the National Gallery of Art, $150,000 to The Phillips Collection, Washington, DC (1987). To help open the museum on Sundays and to support the annual open house "Celebration of Textiles," $30,000 to the Textile Museum, Washington, DC (1987).

Eligibility/Limitations Grants are made only to tax-exempt organizations *in the District of Columbia.* Grants generally are made only on a specific project basis and are not made to private foundations, for capital purposes, for research, or to individuals.

Fiscal Information Grants authorized May 1986 to April 1987 totaled over $6 million, including over $4 million in support in the area of arts and humanities.

Application Information Requests for grants need not be formal or expensive and there is no application form. Each grant request should set forth briefly at the outset (1) the purpose of the project, (2) the amount requested and (3) proof of tax-exemption. The application should also include: background of the sponsoring organization; the need for the project in the community; a complete budget for the project; a statement of whether aid has been sought during the preceding three years from other foundations and sources and, if so, the names of such foundations and sources and the amount received from each, if any; a statement of whether aid is presently sought from other foundations and sources or whether such solicitation is contemplated and, if so, naming them; the organization's latest audited balance sheet; and the organization's audited detailed income statement.

Deadline(s) Grant applications are acted upon in January, May, and October of each year; the closing dates for receipt of applications for these respective action dates are November 1, March 1, and July 1.

107. The Louis Calder Foundation
230 Park Avenue
New York, NY 10169

Grants

Program Description The present policy of the foundation is to support mainly those programs deemed best calculated to promote health, education, and welfare through grants to established organizations with programs and projects in or beneficial to the people of the New York metropolitan area. Current funding priorities are grants for health and welfare programs, educational and cultural projects, and medical research.

Sample Grants To support educational programs for young people in the City of New York, $20,000 to The Brooklyn Children's Museum Corporation (1986). To support various educational programs of the Junior Museum, $10,000 to Metropolitan Museum of Art (1986). To support their Education Department's programs for children, $25,000 to New York Zoological Society (1986). To support current programs and activities, $15,000 to Staten Island Children's Museum (1986). To support the Artreach program during the 1986-87 school year, $15,000 to Whitney Museum of American Art (1986).

Eligibility/Limitations Grants are not made to individuals, "private foundations," governmental organizations, or publicly operated educational and medical institutions. Grants for endowment, building funds and capital development, and grants payable over a period of years are made only occasionally.

Fiscal Information Foundation grants paid for the year ended October 31, 1986, totaled over $4.1 million, including over $850,000 paid to libraries and cultural organizations. The foundation encourages applicants to submit proposals on a challenge, matching grant basis, particularly in the case of proposed funding in excess of $50,000.

Application Information The foundation has no formal application form. A one- to three-page letter will ordinarily suffice, and should include a concise statement of the purpose of the grant and the amount of the funding requested. The letter should be accompanied by: a copy of Internal Revenue Service "Letter of Determination" confirming applicant's tax status as an "exempt organization:" including, when applicable, "not a private foundation;" where the applicant is not widely known, a brief description of the nature, history, and activities of the applicant organization; a current list of the applicant organization's members, trustees, directors and/or officers; a copy of the applicant organization's latest audited financial report or a summary thereof, if included in an official publication of the applicant organization; a detailed budget for the project, program, or organization, as applicable; and a statement of other foundations currently contributing to applicant or to the project and the amounts of their commitments.

Deadline(s) The trustees have no set schedule of meetings. The timing of a review of, and decision among, pending proposals depends upon their number and nature, the fiscal year and the availability of funds. The foundation's fiscal year ends on October 31 and applications for funding should be sent to the foundation office between November 1 and March 31 in order to receive consideration during the then current fiscal year. It is contemplated that all decisions upon pending proposals will be completed by the following July 31.

108. Amon G. Carter Foundation
1212 InterFirst Bank Building, P.O. Box 1036
Fort Worth, TX 76101
(817) 332-2783

Grants

Program Description The foundation's purpose is "to support benevolent, charitable, educational, or missionary undertakings, the purpose for which is religious, charitable, literary, or educational." Primary fields of interest include education, health, social services, programs that benefit youth and the elderly, civic and community endeavors that enhance the quality of life, visual arts, and performing arts. Grants are basically directed to the Fort Worth/Tarrant County area. Grants in other fields and geographic areas are considered based on the individual merit of the program. These grants are usually initiated within the board of directors.

Eligibility/Limitations Applying organizations must qualify for exemption under Section 501(c)(3), or other appropriate section, of the Internal Revenue Code. Special consideration must be given by the board of directors should an applying organization not be exempt as a private foundation within the meaning of Section 509(a) of the code.

Fiscal Information Present board policy targets projected grant funds of fifty percent to Amon Carter Museum for support and acquisitions and fifty percent to general grants.

Application Information Contact the foundation for grant policy and guidelines statement.

Deadline(s) No deadlines are announced.

109. Caterpillar Foundation
Corporate Support Programs
100 NE Adams
Peoria, IL 61629-1480
(309) 675-46433

Caterpillar Corporate Support Programs

Program Description Because of the company's presence in certain communities, there is a benefit to investing in programs and organizations that add to the quality of life and economic development in those communities. The company also recognizes its responsibility as a corporate citizen to be supportive of worthwhile activities in the following areas: health and welfare, education, culture, civic concerns, and public policy. Support for culture consists of operating, capital, and matching gift grants. The arts are recognized as an important dimension in Caterpillar communities.

Eligibility/Limitations Caterpillar considers grants for annual operating support, special projects, and capital development needs. Grants are generally confined to communities where Caterpillar has a presence; however, the Educational Matching Gifts Program is national in scope. In general, Caterpillar will not make grants to support: individuals, fraternal organizations, religious organizations whose services are limited to any one sectarian group, political activity, tickets or advertising for fund-raising benefits, or general operations or ongoing programs of agencies funded by the United Way.

Fiscal Information Caterpillar made grants of over $2.7 million during the year ended December 31, 1986, including over $320,000 in the culture category.

Application Information Organizations applying for grants from Caterpillar should submit the following: a short cover letter or proposal describing the organization, the need for funds, and the plans for their use; an operating budget for the current year showing breakdown of anticipated expenses and sources of income; a copy of the most recent audited financial statement; a list of members of the governing board; and a 501(c)(3) letter indicating IRS qualified tax-exempt status. Requests for further information on Caterpillar corporate support programs should be sent to the Corporate Support Programs Manager.

Deadline(s) Applications are accepted throughout the year.

110. Center for Advanced Study in the Visual Arts
National Gallery of Art
Washington, DC 20565
(202) 842-6480

Associate Appointments

Program Description The Center for Advanced Study in the Visual Arts, a part of the National Gallery of Art, was founded in 1979 to facilitate study of the history, theory, and criticism of art, architecture, and urbanism. Scholars in the history, theory, and criticism of the visual arts (painting, sculpture, architecture, landscape architecture, urbanism, graphics, film, photography, decorative arts, industrial design, etc.) of any geographical area and of any period are supported. Applications are also solicited from scholars in other disciplines whose work examines physical objects or has the implication for the analysis and criticism of physical form. The notable resources represented by the collections of the gallery, the library, and the photographic archives will be available to associates as will the Library of Congress and other specialized libraries and collections in Washington. Lectures, colloquia, and informal discussions will complement the fellowship program.

Eligibility/Limitations Associates are limited to those who have held the Ph.D. for five years or more or who possess a record of professional accomplishment at the time of application. Associateships are awarded without regard to the age or nationality of the applicant.

Fiscal Information The center will consider appointment of associates who have obtained awards from other granting institutions and would like to be affiliated with the center. Appointments to associate status will be considered for periods from one month to an academic year.

Application Information Descriptive brochure and application forms are available on request.

Deadline(s) For appointments of up to sixty days, the deadline for application is March 21 for the award period September-February and September 21 for the award period March-August. For appointments over sixty days, the deadline for application is October 15.

111. Center for Advanced Study in the Visual Arts
National Gallery of Art
Washington, DC 20565
(202) 842-6480

Predoctoral Program: The Chester Dale Fellowships

Program Description The National Gallery of Art, Center for Advanced Study in the Visual Arts, announces its annual program of predoctoral fellowships for productive scholarly work in the history of art, architecture, and urban form in the western world. The Chester Dale Fellowships are intended for the advancement or completion of a doctoral dissertation, either in the U.S. or abroad. The Dale Fellowships may be used entirely at one place of research, for travel, or for a combination of the two; they carry no stipulation for the candidate's residence at the National Gallery of Art, Center for Advanced Study in the Visual Arts, although such use is possible.

Eligibility/Limitations Applicants must have completed their residence requirements and coursework for the Ph.D. and general or preliminary examinations before the date of application, and have devoted at least one-half year's full-time research to their proposed dissertation topic before the commencement of the fellowship. Candidates may begin fellowships in the fourth year of their graduate studies. Applicants must be either U.S. citizens or enrolled in a university in the U.S.

Fiscal Information The Dale Fellowship carries a stipend of $10,000 for one year.

Application Information Applications may be made only through the chairpersons of graduate departments of art history who should act as sponsors for applicants from their respective schools. The candidate must assemble the following material (in quintuplicate) for transmittal by the chairperson: a title for the dissertation, a description of the dissertation project, and a report on the preparatory research; a tentative schedule of work to be accomplished during the grant; a short personal biography with current and permanent addresses and telephone numbers; a curriculum vitae and four offprints of each published work, or typescripts of work accepted for publication (with indication of place of publication); a list of other applications for fellowships for the same period; official transcripts of both undergraduate and (completed) graduate courses of study (original transcript plus four copies), and certification of completion of coursework and language requirements, as well as general and preliminary examinations. This material, together with a letter of nomination by the chairperson and support letters from at least two other faculty members who have worked with the applicant, should be forwarded to the dean of the center.

Deadline(s) Applications should be forwarded by November 15.

112. Center for Advanced Study in the Visual Arts
National Gallery of Art
Washington, DC 20565
(202) 842-6480

Predoctoral Program: The David E. Finley Fellowship

Program Description The National Gallery of Art, Center for Advanced Study in the Visual Arts, announces its annual program of predoctoral fellowships for productive scholarly work in the history of art, architecture, and urban form in the western world. The David E. Finley Fellowship is a three-year fellowship, intended usually as a two-year period for travel and research in Europe on a dissertation topic already well advanced, and an additional year in residence at the National Gallery of Art, Center for Advanced Study in the Visual Arts. Half-time of the year in residence will be devoted to gallery research projects designed to complement the subject of the dissertation. A primary requirement for the award of this fellowship is that the candidate have a significant interest in museum work, which could be furthered during travel to visit European and other collections, as well as during the period of residency at the center in Washington; there is, however, no requirement as to the candidate's subsequent choice of a career.

Eligibility/Limitations Applicants must have completed their residence requirements and coursework for the Ph.D. and general or preliminary examinations before the date of application, and have devoted at least one-half year's full-time research to their proposed dissertation topic before the commencement of the fellowship. Candidates may begin fellowships in the fourth year of their graduate studies. Applicants must be either U.S. citizens or enrolled in a university in the U.S.

Fiscal Information The fellowship extends for three years and carries a stipend of $10,000 annually.

Application Information Applications may be made only through the chairpersons of graduate departments of art history who should act as sponsors for applicants from their respective schools. The candidate must assemble the following material (in quintuplicate) for transmittal by the chairperson: a title for the dissertation, a description of the dissertation project, and a report on the preparatory research; a tentative schedule of work to be accomplished during the grant; a short personal biography with current and permanent addresses and telephone numbers; a curriculum vitae and four offprints of each published work, or typescripts of work accepted for publication (with indication of place of publication); a list of other applications for fellowships for the same period; official transcripts of both undergraduate and (completed) graduate courses of study (original transcript plus four copies), and certification of completion of coursework and language requirements, as well as general and preliminary examinations. This material, together with a letter of nomination by the chairperson and support letters from at least two other faculty members who have worked with the applicant, should be forwarded to the dean of the center.

Deadline(s) Applications should be forwarded by November 15.

113. Center for Advanced Study in the Visual Arts
National Gallery of Art
Washington, DC 20565
(202) 842-6480

Predoctoral Program: The Mary Davis Fellowship

Program Description The National Gallery of Art, Center for Advanced Study in the Visual Arts, announces its annual program of predoctoral fellowships for productive scholarly work in the history of art, architecture, and urban form in the western world. The Mary Davis Fellowship is to be held partly in residence at the National Gallery of Art, Center for Advanced Study in the Visual Arts, and partly elsewhere in the U.S. or abroad. The Davis Fellow is expected to spend one year of the two-year fellowship period on dissertation research, and one year at the center, devoting half-time to gallery research projects designed to complement the subject of the dissertation, and to provide curatorial experience.

Eligibility/Limitations Applicants must have completed their residence requirements and coursework for the Ph.D. and general or preliminary examinations before the date of application, and have devoted at least one-half year's full-time research to their proposed dissertation topic before the commencement of the fellowship. Candidates may begin fellowships in the fourth year of their graduate studies. Applicants must be either U.S. citizens or enrolled in a university in the U.S.

Fiscal Information The Davis Fellowship extends for two years and carries a stipend of $10,000 annually.

Application Information Applications may be made only through the chairpersons of graduate departments of art history who should act as sponsors for applicants from their respective schools. The candidate must assemble the following material (in quintuplicate) for transmittal by the chairperson: a title for the dissertation, a description of the dissertation project, and a report on the preparatory research; a tentative schedule of work to be accomplished during the grant; a short personal biography with current and permanent addresses and telephone numbers; a curriculum vitae and four offprints of each published work, or typescripts of work accepted for publication (with indication of place of publication); a list of other applications for fellowships for the same period; official transcripts of both undergraduate and (completed) graduate courses of study (original transcript plus four copies), and certification of completion of coursework and language requirements, as well as general and preliminary examinations. This material, together with a letter of nomination by the chairperson and support letters from at least two other faculty members who have worked with the applicant, should be forwarded to the dean of the center.

Deadline(s) Applications should be forwarded by November 15.

114. Center for Advanced Study in the Visual Arts
National Gallery of Art
Washington, DC 20565
(202) 842-6480

Predoctoral Program: The Paul Mellon Fellowship

Program Description The National Gallery of Art, Center for Advanced Study in the Visual Arts, announces its annual program of predoctoral fellowships for productive scholarly work in the history of art, architecture, and urban form in the western world. The Paul Mellon Fellowship is a three-year fellowship, usually including a two-year period of research in Europe or elsewhere on a dissertation topic already well advanced, and an additional year in residence at the National Gallery of Art, Center for Advanced Study in the Visual Arts. The fellowship is intended to allow a candidate of exceptional promise to develop expertise in a specific region or locality abroad.

Eligibility/Limitations Applicants must have completed their residence requirements and coursework for the Ph.D. and general or preliminary examinations before the date of application, and have devoted at least one-half year's full-time research to their proposed dissertation topic before the commencement of the fellowship. Candidates may begin fellowships in the fourth year of their graduate studies. Applicants must be either U.S. citizens or enrolled in a university in the U.S.

Fiscal Information The fellowship extends for three years and carries a stipend of $10,000 annually.

Application Information Applications may be made only through the chairpersons of graduate departments of art history who should act as sponsors for applicants from their respective schools. The candidate must assemble the following material (in quintuplicate) for transmittal by the chairperson: a title for the dissertation, a description of the dissertation project, and a report on the preparatory research; a tentative schedule of work to be accomplished during the grant; a short personal biography with current and permanent addresses and telephone numbers; a curriculum vitae and four offprints of each published work, or typescripts of work accepted for publication (with indication of place of publication); a list of other applications for fellowships for the same period; official transcripts of both undergraduate and (completed) graduate courses of study (original transcript plus four copies), and certification of completion of coursework and language requirements, as well as general and preliminary examinations. This material, together with a letter of nomination by the chairperson and support letters from at least two other faculty members who have worked with the applicant, should be forwarded to the dean of the center.

Deadline(s) Applications should be forwarded by November 15.

115. Center for Advanced Study in the Visual Arts
National Gallery of Art
Washington, DC 20565
(202) 842-6480

Predoctoral Program: The Robert H. and Clarice Smith Fellowship

Program Description The National Gallery of Art, Center for Advanced Study in the Visual Arts, announces its annual program of predoctoral fellowships for productive scholarly work in the history of art, architecture, and urban form in the western world. The Robert H. and Clarice Smith Fellowship supports work in Dutch or Flemish art history, intended for the advancement or completion either of a doctoral dissertation, or of a resulting publication. The Smith Fellow may use the grant to study either in the U.S. or abroad; there are no residence requirements at the National Gallery of Art, Center for Advanced Study in the Visual Arts, although the fellow may be based at the center if so desired.

Eligibility/Limitations Applicants must have completed their residence requirements and coursework for the Ph.D. and general or preliminary examinations before the date of application, and have devoted at least one-half year's full-time research to their proposed dissertation topic before the commencement of the fellowship. Candidates may begin fellowships in the fourth year of their graduate studies. Applicants must be either U.S. citizens or enrolled in a university in the U.S.

Fiscal Information The one-year fellowship carries a stipend of $10,000.

Application Information Applications may be made only through the chairpersons of graduate departments of art history who should act as sponsors for applicants from their respective schools. The candidate must assemble the following material (in quintuplicate) for transmittal by the chairperson: a title for the dissertation, a description of the dissertation project and a report on the preparatory research; a tentative schedule of work to be accomplished during the grant; a short personal biography with current and permanent addresses and telephone numbers; a curriculum vitae and four offprints of each published work, or typescripts of work accepted for publication (with indication of place of publication); a list of other applications for fellowships for the same period; official transcripts of both undergraduate and (completed) graduate courses of study (original transcript plus four copies), and certification of completion of coursework and language requirements, as well as general and preliminary examinations. This material, together with a letter of nomination by the chairperson and support letters from at least two other faculty members who have worked with the applicant, should be forwarded to the dean of the center.

Deadline(s) Applications should be forwarded by November 15.

116. Center for Advanced Study in the Visual Arts
National Gallery of Art
Washington, DC 20565
(202) 842-6480

Predoctoral Program: The Samuel H. Kress Fellowship

Program Description The National Gallery of Art, Center for Advanced Study in the Visual Arts, announces its annual program of predoctoral fellowships for productive scholarly work in the history of art, architecture, and urban form in the western world. The Samuel H. Kress Fellowship is a two-year fellowship, to be held partly in residence at the National Gallery of Art, Center for Advanced Study in the Visual

Arts, and partly elsewhere in the U.S. or abroad. The Kress Fellow is expected to spend one year of the fellowship period on dissertation research, and one year at the center, devoting half-time to gallery research projects designed to complement the subject of the dissertation, and to provide curatorial experience.

Eligibility/Limitations Applicants must have completed their residence requirements and coursework for the Ph.D. and general or preliminary examinations before the date of application, and have devoted at least one-half year's full-time research to their proposed dissertation topic before the commencement of the fellowship. Candidates may begin fellowships in the fourth year of their graduate studies. Applicants must be either U.S. citizens or enrolled in a university in the U.S.

Fiscal Information The fellowship extends for two years and carries a stipend of $10,000 annually.

Application Information Applications may be made only through the chairpersons of graduate departments of art history who should act as sponsors for applicants from their respective schools. The candidate must assemble the following material (in quintuplicate) for transmittal by the chairperson: a title for the dissertation, a description of the dissertation project, and a report on the preparatory research; a tentative schedule of work to be accomplished during the grant; a short personal biography with current and permanent addresses and telephone numbers; a curriculum vitae and four offprints of each published work, or typescripts of work accepted for publication (with indication of place of publication); a list of other applications for fellowships for the same period; official transcripts of both undergraduate and (completed) graduate courses of study (original transcript plus four copies), and certification of completion of coursework and language requirements, as well as general and preliminary examinations. This material, together with a letter of nomination by the chairperson and support letters from at least two other faculty members who have worked with the applicant, should be forwarded to the dean of the center.

Deadline(s) Applications should be forwarded by November 15.

117. Center for Advanced Study in the Visual Arts
National Gallery of Art
Washington, DC 20565
(202) 842-6480

Predoctoral Program: The Wyeth Fellowship

Program Description The National Gallery of Art, Center for Advanced Study in the Visual Arts, announces its annual program of predoctoral fellowships for productive scholarly work in the history of art, architecture, and urban form in the western world. The Wyeth Fellowship supports research in American art, to be held partly in residence at the National Gallery of Art, Center for Advanced Study in the Visual Arts, and partly elsewhere in the U.S. or abroad. The Wyeth Fellow is expected to spend the second year of the fellowship at the center to complete the dissertation.

Eligibility/Limitations Applicants must have completed their residence requirements and coursework for the Ph.D. and general or preliminary examinations before the date of application, and have devoted at least one-half year's full-time research to their proposed dissertation topic before the commencement of the fellowship. Candidates may begin fellowships in the fourth year of their graduate studies. Applicants must be either U.S. citizens or enrolled in a university in the U.S.

Fiscal Information The two-year fellowship carries an annual stipend of $10,000.

Application Information Applications may be made only through the chairpersons of graduate departments of art history who should act as sponsors for applicants from their respective schools. The candidate must assemble the following material (in quintuplicate) for transmittal by the chairperson: a title for the dissertation, a description of the dissertation project, and a report on the preparatory research; a tentative schedule of work to be accomplished during the grant; a short personal biography with current and permanent addresses and telephone numbers; a curriculum vitae and four offprints of each published work, or typescripts of work accepted for publication (with indication of place of publication); a list of other applications for fellowships for the same period; official transcripts of both undergraduate and (completed) graduate courses of study (original transcript plus four copies), and certification of completion of coursework and language requirements, as well as general and preliminary examinations. This material, together with a letter of nomination by the chairperson and support letters from at least two other faculty members who have worked with the applicant, should be forwarded to the dean of the center.

Deadline(s) Applications should be forwarded by November 15.

118. Center for Advanced Study in the Visual Arts
National Gallery of Art
Washington, DC 20565
(202) 842-6480

Senior Fellowships and Visiting Senior Fellowships

Program Description The Center for Advanced Study in the Visual Arts, a part of the National Gallery of Art, was founded in 1979 to facilitate study of the history, theory, and criticism of art, architecture, and urbanism. Scholars in the history, theory, and criticism of the visual arts (painting, sculpture, architecture, landscape architecture, urbanism, graphics, film, photography, decorative arts, industrial design, etc.) of any geographical area and of any period are supported. Applications are also solicited from scholars in other disciplines whose work examines physical objects or has the implication for the analysis and criticism of physical form. The notable resources represented by the collections of the gallery, the library, and the photographic archives will be available to fellows as will the Library of Congress and other specialized libraries and collections in Washington. Lectures, colloquia, and informal discussions will complement the fellowship program.

Eligibility/Limitations Senior fellowships are limited to those who have held the Ph.D. for five years or more or who possess a record of professional accomplishment at the time of application. Fellowships are awarded without regard to the age or nationality of the applicant. Senior fellowships will normally be awarded for an academic year, early fall to late spring. Applications for a single academic term or quarter are also possible. In exceptional cases, application may be made for a period of two years. There are, in addition, a number of short-term (maximum sixty days) visiting senior fellowships. Qualifications for visiting senior fellows are the same as for senior fellows. Senior and visiting fellowships may not be postponed or renewed. Scholars are expected to reside in Washington throughout their fellowship period and participate in the activities of the center.

Fiscal Information All grants are based on individual need. A senior fellowship award will normally be limited to one-half of the applicant's annual salary; in no case can it exceed the applicant's annual salary. Senior fellows receive a monthly stipend and additional allowances for research materials, round-trip travel, and housing. Visiting senior fellows receive a stipend that includes travel, research, and local expenses. Senior and visiting senior fellows are provided with a study and subsidized luncheon privileges.

Application Information Separate application forms are required for senior fellowships and visiting senior fellowships. For a descriptive brochure and application forms, write to the center.

Deadline(s) Applications for senior fellowships must be received by October 15; for visiting senior fellowships by March 21 for the award period September-February and September 21 for the award period March-August.

119. The Center for Field Research
680 Mount Auburn Street, Box 403
Watertown, MA 02172
(617) 926-8200

Private Grants for Field Research

Program Description The Center for Field Research exists to strengthen and refine public understanding of the world's natural and human resources, and of their interdependence, through participant funding of significant scholarship in the sciences and humanities. To these ends EARTHWATCH, a private volunteer research corps, was created in 1971 to enable "participant funding"—whereby qualified members of the public both join research expeditions as co-workers and help underwrite expedition costs. The center defines "field research" broadly, to include any research in the sciences and humanities that directly addresses primary sources—whether natural, artifactual, or archival—and especially favors projects of clear scholarly and public value. The center neither awards nor distributes grants. All funds are distributed by EARTHWATCH, on recommendations by the center, and derive from the contributions of the working volunteers.

Sample Grants Support for a study of immigration and aggregation: the dynamics of the settlement of Homolovi IV and the Little Colorado River Valley, Arizona, to Arizona State Museum. Support for a survey of a 19th century shipwreck, the *Edwin Fox*, New Zealand, to Western Australian Maritime Museum. Support for a study of volcanology and birth of a tropical forest: Arenal Volcano, Costa Rica, to the Smithsonian Institution. Support for a study of biology, ecology, and taxonomy of neotropical katydids, Peru, to the National Museum of Natural History, Smithsonian Institution.

Eligibility/Limitations Awards principally support advanced postdoctoral scholars of any nationality. Women and minority applicants are encouraged to apply. Research teams supported must include qualified volunteers from EARTHWATCH.

Fiscal Information Grants range from $5,000 to $85,000 and average $18,000. Grants cover all expenses for maintaining research teams (including both scholarly staffs and volunteers) in the field, the travel of the principal investigator to and from the field, plus expendable and leased or rented field equipment. Faculty salaries, university overhead, or major (capital) equipment purchases are not allowed.

Application Information The application procedure is designed to be informal and straightforward. There are three stages involved. In a preliminary proposal, outline the project in two or three pages. After submission of the preliminary proposal, candidates will hear from the center staff in thirty days. Eligible projects will be invited to submit a full proposal which will be scheduled for peer review. Approved projects are recommended to EARTHWATCH for publication and funding. Questions regarding the application procedure, eligibility requirements, or submission deadlines should be directed to a program officer at the center.

Deadline(s) Preliminary proposals should be submitted nine to twelve months before project date. Full proposals should be submitted nine months before project date.

120. Center for Italian Renaissance Studies
Harvard University, Department of Comparative Literature
401 Boylston Hall
Cambridge, MA 02138
(617) 495-2543

Villa I Tatti Fellowships

Program Description The Harvard Center for Italian Renaissance Studies at Villa I Tatti will award stipendiary fellowships for independent study on any aspect of the Italian Renaissance.

Eligibility/Limitations Villa I Tatti offers fellowships for scholars of any nationality, normally postdoctoral and in the earlier stages of their careers. Fellows must be free to devote full time to study. It is in keeping with the purposes of I Tatti that fellows not be absent for very protracted periods during the academic year, although they certainly are expected to come and go in the course of carrying out necessary work and making visits elsewhere.

Fiscal Information Stipends will be given in accord with the individual needs of the approved applicants and the availability of funds. The maximum grant will be no higher than $22,000; most are considerably less. Each fellow is offered a place to study, use of the Biblioteca Berenson and Fototeca, lunches during weekdays, participation in the activities of the center, and an opportunity to meet scholars from the United States and other countries working in related fields.

Application Information Applicants should send their curriculum vitae and a description of their project to the director at Via di Vincigliata, 50135 Florence, Italy, and duplicates to Professor Walter Kaiser at the above address.

Deadline(s) Applications must be received by November 1.

Additional Information I Tatti offers a limited number of non-stipendiary fellowships for scholars working in Florence on Renaissance subjects with support from other sources. Non-stipendiary fellows should have the same qualifications and will have the same privileges as those whose stipends are derived from I Tatti funds. Scholars interested in these fellowships should apply by November 1.

121. Champion International Corporation
Contributions Department
One Champion Plaza
Stamford, CT 06921
(203) 358-7000

Contributions

Program Description Champion International Corporation is a leading producer of paper and forest products. The company employs more than 24,000 people in locations across the U.S. As a company whose roots reach back to the 1890s, Champion has a long heritage of community involvement and good corporate citizenship. Over the years the focus of contributions has largely been oriented towards broad-based, nationally recognized causes. In response to the 1984 Champion-St. Regis merger and subsequent divestitures of major operations, Champion recognized the importance of redirecting the focus of contributions activities and chose to concentrate more on the needs of local communities in the following areas: community support, aid to education, natural resources and environment, human services support, national organizations, and visual and graphic arts. In the last category, Champion's commitment to producing high quality papers provides an inherent interest in programs that promote the visual and graphic arts, including support of selected art exhibitions at galleries and museums in Champion communities.

Eligibility/Limitations Champion prefers not to contribute to: individuals; organizations which do not have a 501(c)(3) tax-exempt status from the IRS; political candidates or organizations; religious, veterans, or fraternal organizations, unless they furnish services to benefit the general public; dinners, benefits, exhibits, conferences, sports events, and other one-time, short-term activities; journal advertisements and the purchase of tickets; supplementary operating funds for agencies in a United Way supported by Champion; and community organizations not located in a Champion community.

Fiscal Information While there is no limitation on grant requests, it may be helpful for prospective grantees to know that most grants range between $2,500 and $5,000.

Application Information Programs that meet Champion guidelines are encouraged to apply, addressing the following specific points: name, address and telephone number of organization requesting support; contact person and title; the names of the executive director, directors, and their affiliations; copy of IRS exemption letter ensuring the organization's status as a tax-exempt organization; description of how the proposed project relates to Champion's interests; description of how success of the project will be determined; and description of the experience and qualifications the organization has for implementing the project. The following should also be included in the grant request: a copy of the most recent audited financial statement; sources of income; and budget for the organization and for the proposed project. This information should be sent either to the nearest Champion facility, or the the corporate contributions office in Stamford.

Deadline(s) Contributions are planned a year in advance and based on a calendar-year budget. Grant applications are accepted at any time. Within three weeks of receipt of a request, Champion will respond with written notification as to whether the grant request fits within guidelines and will be considered at an upcoming contributions committee meeting. Following that meeting, applicants will be notified of the committee's decision within ten days.

122. The Champlin Foundations
P.O. Box 637
Providence, RI 02901
(401) 421-3719

Program Description The foundations were established for the purpose of making grants to qualified charitable organizations. Grants have been made to youth and health agencies, libraries, hospitals, secondary and public schools, colleges and universities, social welfare agencies, humane societies, the arts, sciences, and historic preservation. Funds are awarded in the following areas: environment, education, information/cultural, hospitals/health, youth/fitness, social services, and historic preservation.

Eligibility/Limitations The foundations make direct grants for capital needs to tax-exempt organizations, substantially all in Rhode Island. Typical capital needs are the purchase of equipment, construction, renovations, purchases of real property, and reduction of mortgage indebtedness. Grants are not awarded for program or operating expenses, or to individuals. Grants are not awarded on a continuing basis, but applicants may qualify annually.

Fiscal Information In 1986, grants ranged from a low of $1,500 to a high of $2 million; the general range of grants was from $15,000 to $50,000.

Application Information An initial contact should be made by mail, addressed to The Champlin Foundations, Attention: Executive Director. This should consist of a very brief (one page) letter describing concisely the project and its intended purpose, its cost, and the amount requested; the status of any fund-raising effort, and other sources of funds available. Submit one copy only. Copies of IRS Section 501 exemption and 509(a) letters must be furnished. Financial statements may be required on request. In order to consider a request, Champlin needs specifics on fund-raising efforts—the applicant must perform fund-raising activities, and must have some results to show for it; the applicant must tell what is wanted from Champlin, what will be done if fund-raising is not totally successful, what parts of the project will be carried out, and their cost.

Deadline(s) For consideration at a November meeting, requests should be submitted between April 1 and August 31. (Funds are seldom available for applications filed at the last minute.)

123. Chevron Corporation
P.O. Box 7753
San Francisco, CA 94120
(415) 894-5464

Grants

Program Description Chevron contributes to a broad variety of civic, cultural, social, health, and educational activities. The company gives priority to programs that encourage local initiative and demonstrate creative long-term solutions to human and community needs.

Eligibility/Limitations Eligible applicants are usually private, tax-exempt organizations with certified 501(c)(3) status under the Internal Revenue Code. Generally excluded from consideration are grants to: individuals; religious, veterans, labor, fraternal, athletic, or political organizations—except for specific projects that benefit the broad community; capital funds for buildings and equipment (exceptions may be made to renovate existing facilities for selected institutions that have broad community support in areas where Chevron has significant business operations); endowment funds; conferences and seminars; operating expenses for organizations receiving support through the United Way; school-related bands and sports organizations and events; sports activities; national health, medical, and human service organizations specializing in research; travel funds; films, videotapes, or audio productions; fund-raising events or benefits; tickets for benefits; courtesy advertising; or product requests.

Fiscal Information Total contributions in 1986 exceeded $22 million.

Application Information Requests should be in concise letter form, preferably not more than two pages, plus attachments, and should include: organization name, address, phone number and contact person; brief statement of the organization's history, goals, and accomplishments; geographic area and number of people served by the organization; purpose for which the grant is requested; amount requested and funding period; number of volunteers participating in the organization's activities; a copy of the organization's most recent IRS tax-exemption 501(c)(3) determination letter; the names and affiliations of the organization's governing board and brief background of the executive director and key staff members; a copy of the organization's most recent audited financial statement or current operating budget containing amounts and percentages of income utilized for program administration, fund-raising and general expense and a list of current sources of unrestricted and restricted funds; and a copy of the organization's most recent Form 990, including state supplement, if applicable. Specific project requests, if applicable, should include: brief description of activity or project; description of need, and how the project meets identified needs not being met by other community groups; timetable for project implementation; expected results (who will benefit and how); plans for continued funding, if activity or project will be ongoing; method of evaluating project effectiveness and communicating results to donors and similar organizations; and project budget, including sources of financial support and amounts received, committed, or pending.

Deadline(s) Proposals are accepted and reviewed on a continuing basis.

124. The Chicago Community Trust

222 North LaSalle Street, Suite 1400
Chicago, IL 60601
(312) 372-3356

Grants

Program Description The Chicago Community Trust awards grants in the following areas: hospitals, health, and medical programs; social services; education; civic affairs; and the arts and humanities.

Sample Grants Toward support of the second year of its Chicago Collecting Project, $5,000 to Archives of American Art, Chicago, IL (1986). To provide technical assistance, $2,500 to American Curling History Museum, Chicago, IL (1986). For support of its membership and public relations activities, $75,000 to the Du Sable Museum, Chicago, IL (1986). A one-year grant toward the support and related costs of hiring an executive director, $75,000 to Museum of Broadcast Communications, Chicago, IL (1986). A five-year outright grant for support of its capital campaign, $100,000 and a five-year matching grant, $300,000 to Chicago Zoological Society (1986). A five-year outright grant in support of "The Landmark Campaign," $200,000 and a five-year matching grant, $600,000 to Field Museum of Natural History, Chicago, IL (1986).

Eligibility/Limitations Organizations which receive funds from the trust are nonprofit groups whose services improve the quality of life in the greater Chicago community. The trust, as a matter of policy, will not make grants: for scholarships, to individuals, for religious purposes, for endowments, or for operating support of government agencies.

Fiscal Information In 1986, support to organizations in the arts and humanities totaled over $1.2 million in discretionary funds and $3.4 million in capital campaign grants.

Application Information The trust does not use a printed application form nor has it established a particular format for applications or proposals. However, all applications must include: a cover letter and brief summary of the background and purposes of the request for funds; approval in writing for the submission of the request from the chief executive officer or other authorized individual; a copy of the requesting agency's 501(c)(3) tax-exemption letter from the IRS; a list of the members of the governing board of the requesting agency; and a copy of the requesting agency's most recent audited financial statement, if available, and its current financial statement and current operating budget. Requests which do not contain this information will not be considered. The applicant should submit two copies of the proposal. Proposals should be sent to the attention of the assistant director.

Deadline(s) Grants are awarded by the executive committee at its grant meetings in January, March, June and September.

Additional Information In 1978 the trust established the Cultural Arts Fund to provide ongoing support for the area's cultural arts agencies and institutions. The fund income is regularly devoted to the maintenance, support, and promulgation of the cultural arts in the Chicago metropolitan area, including, but not limited to art, music, dance, poetry, drama, and literature. The CityArts II Program was established in 1982 as a joint project involving the trust, NEA, and the City of Chicago/Council on Fine Arts. The program was developed to support smaller community arts organizations with budgets of under $250,000, utilizing the trust's Cultural Arts Matching Grant Program. Contact the trust for more information about these programs.

125. Chrysler Corporation Fund
P.O. Box 1919
Detroit, MI 48288
(313) 956-2564

Grants

Program Description In an effort to use its limited resources prudently, the Chrysler Corporation Fund has established guidelines for review of grant requests. The fund contributes to organizations grouped under the following general categories: education, health and human services, civic and community, and culture and the arts. Fund support for cultural institutions is generally directed toward local art and cultural organizations serving the communities in which Chrysler has a major presence as well as selected cultural organizations of national scope, with an emphasis on the performing arts. Within these categories, grants are made for the public welfare, or for charitable, scientific, educational, environmental, safety and affirmative action purposes.

Eligibility/Limitations It is the policy of the fund to make contributions in support of the well-being of the communities in which it operates. This support is also extended to selected national organizations, in light of Chrysler Corporation's nationwide involvement in the manufacture and distribution of motor vehicles. The fund does not make contributions to: individuals; organizations without IRS 501(c)(3) tax-exempt, public charity status; organizations that discriminate by race, religion, color, creed, sex, age, or national origin; endowment funds; primary or secondary schools; purchase of courtesy advertising; support for conferences, seminars or similar events; or organizations or projects outside the U.S.

Fiscal Information Total grants paid in 1986 exceeded $5.7 million, including $514,900 in support of culture and the arts.

Application Information All grant requests must be in writing and must contain: the goals/objectives/historical description of the organization; the sum being requested together with a total budget or project cost amount; a list of current contributors, particularly companies and foundations; an explanation of the relationship, if any, to a United Way organization or governmental agency; a list of officers and board of directors; a copy of IRS 501(c)(3) tax-exemption letter; and a copy of the most recent audited financial statement.

Deadline(s) Applications are accepted throughout the year.

126. Citicorp
200 South Wacker Drive
Chicago, IL 60606
(312) 993-3064

Corporate Contributions Program

Program Description Citicorp awards corporate grants under six major headings: cultural, education/research, health, community revitalization and civic organizations, International and United Way. In the cultural category, Citicorp supports both major cultural institutions and the less visible, medium- and small-sized groups which encourage new talent and stimulate neighborhood development. Citicorp places particular emphasis on performing arts programs, museums of art, history and science, libraries, zoological societies, botanical gardens, and public broadcasting stations. Citicorp looks for strong community outreach programs that make the arts accessible to broad audiences, including programs with free admission and projects that bring the arts to the handicapped or young people.

Eligibility/Limitations Citicorp makes grants to nonprofit organizations. Citicorp does not make grants from corporate funds for: individuals, for educational or any other purposes; political causes or candidates; religious, veterans, or fraternal organizations unless they are engaged in a significant project benefiting the entire community; fundraising dinners, benefits, or events; or courtesy advertising.

Fiscal Information Grants in 1986 totaled over $10.3 million, including over $2.5 million in the cultural category.

Application Information Any qualified organization should send a request containing the following information: amount requested; brief statement of history, goals and accomplishments to date; statement of objectives of proposal; current annual report; IRS tax-exemption letter 501(c)(3); current year's budget showing anticipated expense and income; current Form 990; list of current corporate and foundation funding sources, public and/or private, with amounts contributed within the most recent twelve months or last fiscal year; most recent independently audited financial statement; list of members of applicant organization's governing board; and list of accrediting agencies, where appropriate. Cultural organizations should submit their most recent twelve months' audience statistics.

Deadline(s) Applications are accepted throughout the year.

Additional Information Since 1969, Citicorp has matched its employees contributions to certain nonprofit organizations located in the U.S. or its territories that have been granted tax-exempt status by the IRS under Section 501(c)(3). Cultural organizations supported include: libraries; museums of art, history, or science; performing arts companies; botanical gardens; zoological societies; and public broadcasting. Contact Citicorp for additional information about this program.

127. Robert Sterling Clark Foundation, Inc.
112 East 64th Street
New York, NY 10021
(212) 308-0411

Grants

Program Description The Robert Sterling Clark Foundation was incorporated in 1952, and since then has provided financial assistance to a wide variety of charitable organizations. Over the years, program guidelines have evolved and changed. At present, the foundation is concentrating its resources in the following three fields: improving the performance of public institutions; ensuring access to family planning services; and strengthening the management of cultural institutions. For many years, the foundation has been particularly interested in cultural institutions in New York City and the greater metropolitan area. This interest has led the foundation to develop a program designed to promote the long-term financial viability of these important institutions. While a substantial part of foundation support is aimed at helping institutions effectively manage their resources, additional funds are available to enhance financial stability through unrestricted support. Types of assistance through this program include: (1) Management Support Grants made to cultural institutions and arts service organizations for one-time projects designed to: increase earned income as a percentage of total operating budget, improve internal management, reduce operating costs through resource sharing, and increase contributions from individuals; and (2) Foundation-Initiated Grants which provide general support to a limited number of small cultural institutions.

Sample Grants To develop and implement a plan to strengthen its management and fund-raising capabilities, $15,000 to Alternative Museum, New York, NY (1985). To retain a fund-raising and management consultant firm to review the museum's fund-raising efforts to date, analyze future needs, and prepare an economic forecast and feasibility study to be used as the basic tools for fund-raising activities, $33,000 to Parrish Art Museum, Southampton, NY (1985).

Eligibility/Limitations Nonprofit organizations are eligible to apply.

Fiscal Information Grants paid in 1985 totaled more than $1.7 million.

Application Information The foundation is interested in learning as much as possible about applicants. Consequently, the foundation requires that the following information accompany all proposals: one page proposal summary; organization budget for the past year, current year, and projected; most recent audited financial statement; IRS letter explaining tax status; names and occupations of board of directors; major sources of current financial support; resumes of key staff; and examples of past accomplishments. The main body of the application should not exceed ten pages. If the applicant is requesting support for a particular project, the proposal should include the following information: description of project; project budget; expected results; detailed workplan; plans for evaluation; plans for future support; other contributors; and names of other organizations where the proposal has been submitted.

Deadline(s) The board of directors considers proposals throughout the year.

128. William Andrews Clark Memorial Library
The Fellowship Secretary
2520 Cimarron Street
Los Angeles, CA 90018
(213) 731-8529

American Society for Eighteenth-Century Studies/Clark Library Fellowships

Program Description The principal collection of the library is broadly representative of seventeenth- and eighteenth-century English culture, with particular concentration on the period 1640 to 1740. Other major collections include Oscar Wilde and his circle, Montana history, and modern fine printing. The Clark Library and ASECS are jointly funding one-month fellowships each for research in the library's extensive collection of Restoration and eighteenth-century works.

Eligibility/Limitations Members of ASECS in good standing who are not more than ten years beyond the Ph.D. or equivalent are eligible.

Fiscal Information The one-month fellowships carry a stipend of $1,250.

Application Information Application forms are available from the fellowship secretary.

Deadline(s) Applications are due October 15 and March 1.

129. William Andrews Clark Memorial Library
The Fellowship Secretary
2520 Cimarron Street
Los Angeles, CA 90018
(213) 731-8529

Short-Term Fellowships for Individual Research

Program Description The principal collection of the library is broadly representative of seventeenth- and eighteenth-century English culture, with particular concentration on the period 1640 to 1740. Other major collections include Oscar Wilde and his circle,

Montana history, and modern fine printing. Short-term fellowships are available for up to three months' research on any subject appropriate to the Clark's collections.

Eligibility/Limitations Applicants must hold the Ph.D. or equivalent; preference is given to younger scholars from outside the southern California area.

Fiscal Information Awards are made for periods of up to three months during the academic year or summer, with a stipend of $1,250 per month.

Application Information Application forms are available from the fellowship secretary.

Deadline(s) Applications are due October 15 and March 1.

130. William Andrews Clark Memorial Library

The Fellowship Secretary
2520 Cimarron Street
Los Angeles, CA 90018
(213) 731-8529

Summer Postdoctoral Fellowships

Program Description The principal collection of the library is broadly representative of seventeenth- and eighteenth-century English culture, with particular concentration on the period 1640 to 1740. Other major collections include Oscar Wilde and his circle, Montana history, and modern fine printing. Summer postdoctoral fellowships are available for an intensive six-week summer study program each year on a specific topic. A highly renowned and qualified scholar is appointed each year to direct this program. Dates, topic, and director are usually announced in the previous September.

Eligibility/Limitations The fellows, who are chosen from applicants not more than five years beyond their doctorate, will meet as a group in weekly seminars, with informal discussions at other times.

Fiscal Information The fellowships are for $2,500 each, plus travel allowance within the continental U.S.

Application Information Application forms are available from the fellowship secretary.

Deadline(s) Applications are due January 15.

131. Columbia Foundation

1090 Sansome Street
San Francisco, CA 94111
(415) 986-5179

Program Description The Columbia Foundation is currently focusing its grant program on projects that address critical issues and offer promise of significant positive impact in the following areas: preservation of the natural environment; enhancement of urban community life and culture; international and cross-cultural understanding; reversal of the arms race worldwide; and protection of basic human rights.

Sample Grants To support the national museum to be constructed on the Mall in Washington, DC, $50,000 to United States Holocaust Memorial Museum, Washington, DC (1987). To support production costs for "Sound Sculptures Through the Golden Gate," a live acoustical portrait of the area between the Golden Gate Bridge and the Farallon Islands, $1,000 to San Francisco Museum of Modern Art (1987). To support the Freud Museum campaign to establish a museum and public education program in the home occupied by Freud and his family in London, $5,000 to Sigmund Freud Archives, Inc., New York (1987).

Eligibility/Limitations The foundation focuses its program primarily on projects that seek common ground between the San Francisco community and the shared global concerns facing an interdependent world. The foundation will consider grants only to organizations certified by the IRS as "public charities."

Fiscal Information Total grants awarded in the year ending May 31, 1987 exceeded $1.4 million. Grants ranged in size from $1,000 to $250,000. The foundation generally does not provide support for operating budgets of established agencies, recurring expenses for direct services or ongoing administrative costs, individual fellowships or scholarships, nor to agencies that are wholly supported by federated campaigns or heavily subsidized by government funds.

Application Information Preliminary inquiry by letter to the executive director at the address listed above is preferred. This preliminary letter of inquiry should include a brief summary of the proposed project or activity, the financial support needed, and a brief profile of the organization, its purpose, activities, and personnel. A full proposal will be requested if the application is to be considered further by the foundation. Foundation profile and grants list are available on request.

Deadline(s) Grant applications are accepted on an ongoing basis. Application review can take two to three months.

132. The Columbus Foundation
1265 Neil Avenue
Columbus, OH 43201
(614) 294-7300

Grants

Program Description The Columbus Foundation welcomes grant requests from organizations in central Ohio. Grants are made in the fields of the arts and humanities, civic affairs, conservation, education, health, and social services. In the field of arts and humanities, the foundation awards grants in music, theater, arts, dance, preservation, and history to further cultural development in central Ohio.

Sample Grants To support acquisition of a private collection of nineteenth- and twentieth-century European art (payable through 1989), $700,000 to the Columbus Museum of Art (1985). To support the capital development campaign, $70,000 to the Columbus Museum of Art (1985). To support construction of a historical museum at Port Columbus Airport, $25,000 to Ohio History of Flight, Inc. (1985).

Eligibility/Limitations Grants are made to organizations in central Ohio having recognition under Section 501(c)(3) of the Internal Revenue Code. Grant applications must have direct relevance to the central Ohio region. The foundation makes no grants to individuals.

Fiscal Information During 1985, grants were made to 330 charitable organizations. In all, grants paid totaled more than $5.5 million, including over $1.2 million in the arts and humanities category. Grant requests for religious purposes, budget deficits, endowments, conferences, scholarly research, or projects that are normally the responsibility of a public agency are generally not funded.

Application Information The foundation awards grants for definite purposes and for projects covering a specified period of time. Applicants are encouraged to discuss their project with the foundation's program staff prior to submitting a formal proposal. Grant applications should include four copies each of the formal proposal and the request for information form, available from the foundation.

Deadline(s) The foundation considers grants four times a year. Grant requests must be submitted by the first Friday in December, March, May, and August in order to be considered at meetings held in February, May, July, and October. Proposals are due at the foundation's office by 5 p.m. on deadline dates.

133. Committee on Scholarly Communication with the People's Republic of China
National Academy of Sciences
2101 Constitution Avenue, NW
Washington, DC 20418
(202) 334-2718

National Program for Advanced Study and Research in China: Graduate Program

Program Description The Committee on Scholarly Communication with the People's Republic of China (CSCPRC) was founded in 1966 under the joint sponsorship of the

American Council of Learned Societies (ACLS), the National Academy of Sciences (NAS), and the Social Science Research Council (SSRC). The CSCPRC supports the exchange of scholars between the PRC and the United States. The Graduate Program provides support for American graduate students in the social sciences and humanities to carry out long-term (ten to twelve months) study or research in affiliation with Chinese universities and research institutes.

Eligibility/Limitations The program offers support for individuals between the bachelor's and Ph.D. levels of coursework. It requires a high degree of Chinese language skill. Application is open to U.S. citizens and permanent residents regardless of national origin, race, sex, or religious affiliation.

Fiscal Information Grants for the National Program include transportation to and from China, a stipend, living and travel allowances while in China, and a limited research and educational materials allowance. They do not cover travel or support for dependents.

Application Information Address requests for information to CSCPRC, National Academy of Sciences.

Deadline(s) Applications must be postmarked by October 12.

134. Committee on Scholarly Communication with the People's Republic of China
National Academy of Sciences
2101 Constitution Avenue, NW
Washington, DC 20418
(202) 334-2718

National Program for Advanced Study and Research in China: Research Program

Program Description The Committee on Scholarly Communication with the People's Republic of China (CSCPRC) was founded in 1966 under the joint sponsorship of the American Council of Learned Societies (ACLS), the National Academy of Sciences (NAS), and the Social Science Research Council (SSRC). The CSCPRC supports the exchange of scholars between the PRC and the United States. The Research Program awards grants for support of research to scholars in the social sciences and humanities. It involves a tenure of three to twelve months.

Sample Grants A 1987-1988 research program grant was awarded to a museum professional from the Freer Gallery of Art, Smithsonian Institution, to research "Shang Daquian (1899-1983): The Great Synthesis of Traditional Chinese Painting in the 20th Century" at the State Cultural Relics Bureau, People's Republic of China.

Eligibility/Limitations Applicants must have the Ph.D. or its equivalent. There is no minimum language requirement, but the necessity of Chinese language skills for a particular research plan is considered in reviewing the feasibility of proposals. Application is open to U.S. citizens and permanent residents regardless of national origin, race, sex, or religious affiliation.

Fiscal Information Grants for the program include transportation to and from China, a stipend, living and travel allowances while in China, and a limited research and educational materials allowance. They do not cover travel or support for dependents.

Application Information Address requests for information to CSCPRC, National Academy of Sciences.

Deadline(s) Applications must be postmarked by October 12.

135. Committee on Scholarly Communication with the People's Republic of China
National Academy of Sciences
2101 Constitution Avenue, NW
Washington, DC 20418
(202) 334-2718

Visiting Scholar Exchange Program (VSEP)

Program Description The Visiting Scholar Exchange Program provides short-term (one to three months) research and lecturing opportunities for American and Chinese scholars of all disciplines. Through a program of lecturing, exploratory research, and meeting professional colleagues, participants are expected to further academic understanding and collaborative research in their respective disciplines.

Sample Grants A VSEP grant was awarded to the Head, Department of Insect Taxonomy and Faunistics, Institute of Zoology, Chinese Academy of Sciences, to study "Entomology: The Bees of China" at the National Museum of Natural History (1986-1987).

Eligibility/Limitations American scholars at the associate professor level and above or its equivalent for social sciences and humanities, and at the postdoctoral level and above or its equivalent for scientists are eligible to apply. Chinese scholars at the assistant professor level and above in all fields are eligible.

Fiscal Information The CSCPRC will customarily provide travel funds for American scholars to China, with Chinese hosting organizations covering living costs. The CSCPRC will also provide financial support for Chinese scholars while they are in the United States.

Application Information Address requests for information to CSCPRC, National Academy of Sciences.

Deadline(s) Applications must be postmarked by October 12.

Additional Information Under this program half of the participants—both American and Chinese—are nominated by the CSCPRC; half are nominated by the sponsoring Chinese institutions.

136. Compton Foundation
10 Hanover Square
New York, NY 10005
(212) 510-5040

Program Description The foundation's directors determine funding priorities. The areas of interest given precedence may change from time to time when, in the opinion of the directors, adjustments are appropriate in response to social change, unanticipated needs of the community, or emerging opportunities. At present, the foundation's priorities include: global human survival, education, social welfare and social justice, religion, and culture and the arts. The objectives of the culture and the arts program are to improve the quality of life in the United States; to promote community participation in cultural affairs; to encourage the development of creative talent in the arts; and to improve the quality of cultural institutions.

Sample Grants For general support, $1,000 to Art Museum Association of America (1985). For a cultural institutions management program, $5,000 to Museums Collaborative (1985). For general support, $6,500 to Oakland Museum Association (1985). For general support, $5,500 to San Francisco Museum of Modern Art (1985). For a capital fund, $5,000 to Triton Museum of Art (1985).

Eligibility/Limitations The Compton Foundation makes grants only to organizations and institutions that qualify under requirements of the federal Tax Reform Act of 1969. No grants are awarded to individuals.

Fiscal Information Grants authorized and paid in 1985 totaled more than $1.5 million, including $166,350 in the culture and the arts category.

Application Information The Compton Foundation has no application forms. Inquiries may be made by writing a concise letter clearly stating the objectives of the proposal, the means by which they are to be accomplished, the qualifications of the personnel involved, and a budget. Evidence of the organization's status under provisions of the Internal Revenue Code should be included. Prospective applicants are encouraged to determine before making an application that the proposal is relevant to the foundation's interests. An annual report, delineating the foundation's interests and grant-making policies, and significant grants made, is available on request from the foundation.

Deadline(s) Not announced.

137. Cooper Industries Foundation

P.O. Box 4446
Houston, TX 77210
(713) 739-5632

Grants

Program Description It is the policy of Cooper Industries, in carrying out the respon-sibilities of corporate citizenship, to support nonprofit organizations in areas where employees are located, and which best serve the educational, health, welfare, civic, cultural, and social needs of our communities. All gifts should be consistent with the company's objectives to enhance the quality of life and to honor the principles and freedoms that have enabled our company to grow and prosper.

Eligibility/Limitations To be eligible to receive gifts from the foundation, charitable organizations must be exempt from taxation under Section 501(c)(3) of the Internal Revenue Code. No grants are made to religious, political, labor, lobbying, fraternal, veterans, or national or state health and welfare organizations, except through United Way and through the company's program of matching the gifts of its employees. No grants are made to public or private elementary and secondary schools; endowment funds; individuals; trips or tours; tickets, tables, or advertising for benefit purposes; intermediary funding agencies; or any organization whose policies are inconsistent with national equal opportunity policies.

Fiscal Information The average grant ranges from $1,000 to $5,000.

Application Information Nonprofit organizations in communities where Cooper has a plant facility should direct their requests to local Cooper management for consider-ation. Other requests should be directed to Patricia B. Mottram, Secretary, Cooper Industries Foundation, P.O. Box 4446, Houston, TX 77210.

Deadline(s) Budgets are compiled annually each fall for the following year (January-December).

138. Adolph Coors Company

Community Affairs Department, NH410
Golden, CO 80401
(800) 277-3397

Corporate Contributions Program

Program Description The Corporate Contributions Program is a resource which helps the company to identify community concerns, participate in solutions, and develop close working relationships with community organizations and special interest groups. Coors activities and donations are concentrated in the metro Denver area and with organizations of national scope and membership. Coors donations include: cash grants, products, advertising items, obsolete equipment, and in-kind services. Coors does not donate to specific charitable categories, preferring to consider each request for support on its own merit.

Eligibility/Limitations Coors awards the majority of its donations inside Colorado, but requests from company operating areas are considered. Coors is generally unable to: fund individuals in personal projects; sponsor teams, groups, races, or "-athons" of any kind; provide funding for travel expenses; accept telephone solicitations; loan company vehicles; commit resources to politically oriented endeavors; or provide support to any group or organization which discriminates on the basis of race, creed, gender, or sexual orientation.

Fiscal Information Total contributions in 1985 reached $3 million, including cash, products, equipment, and in-kind services.

Application Information All requests for donation of any corporate resource must: be submitted in writing; include the complete name of the organization with address, telephone number, and name of contact; contain a complete description of the organization, including goals and purpose; and provide for sufficient lead time, depending on request, for processing of application.

Deadline(s) A minimum of 30 days advance time is required to process a request; 60 days is preferred.

139. Corning Glass Works Foundation
MP-HF-02-1
Corning, NY 14831
(607) 974-8719

Grants

Program Description The Corning Glass Works Foundation was established in 1952 to administer the company's philanthropic activities and to initiate creative programs of corporate giving. The foundation supports four general areas: educational institutions and programs; human services; civic organizations and programs; and cultural institutions and programs. Within the area of cultural institutions and programs, libraries, museums, and performing arts organizations receive a major portion of the funds awarded. The foundation's principal emphasis in giving is on activities which enhance the living environment of communities where the company has manufacturing facilities.

Sample Grants For audiovisual equipment, $1,000 to Danville Chapter of the Virginia Museum of Fine Arts, Danville, VA (1986). For a new facility, $2,000 to Five Civilized Tribes Museum, Muskogee, OK (1986). For education programs, $1,000 to Museum of the American Indian-Heye Foundation, New York, NY (1986). For Rembrandt Gallery, $25,000 to Metropolitan Museum of Art, New York, NY (1986).

Eligibility/Limitations Grants are made only to organizations which are tax-exempt under Section 501(c)(3) of the Internal Revenue Code. Grants usually are restricted further to public charities as defined by the IRS under Section 509(a) of the code. Donations are not made to individuals. By policy, the foundation does not support political causes, labor or veterans organizations, religious groups or fraternal orders.

Fiscal Information Grants paid in 1986 totaled over $1.9 million, including $238,487 to cultural institutions and programs.

Application Information All proposals for financial assistance should be made in writing. No application forms are used. The write-up should provide a description of the project, including its objectives and the techniques for evaluating results; a detailed budget; a list of known and potential sources of revenue; and information on the sponsoring group, including officers and board members. A copy of the IRS letter certifying tax-exemption should accompany the proposal. During the review process, a copy of the organization's Form 990 may be requested. Inquiries and proposals should be mailed to the executive director of the foundation at the address listed above.

Deadline(s) Applications are accepted throughout the year.

Additional Information In addition to its direct grants, the foundation sponsors a matching gifts program under which certain donations made by employees and retirees are matched one-for-one. To qualify, a contribution must be at least $25. An individual can give up to $4,000 in a two-year period. Participating institutions may receive up to $20,000 a year in matching payments. During 1986 the foundation distributed $497,552 in matching gifts to colleges, universities, performing and visual arts organizations, historical societies, nature centers, libraries, museums, and other organizations.

140. The Dr. M. Aylwin Cotton Foundation
c/o Albany Trustee Company Limited
P.O. Box 232, Pollet House
The Pollet, St. Peter Port, Guernsey, Channel Islands

Fellowship Awards

Program Description The Dr. M Aylwin Cotton Foundation invites applications for fellowship awards for studies in the archaeology, architecture, history, language, and art of the Mediterranean. In this contest the word "Mediterranean" is used without geographical limitations.

Sample Grants Towards research on "Le tombe da Poggio Gallinaro nel Museo Archeologico di Firenze. Aspetti della cultura tarquiniese nel corso dell'Orientalizzante e del primo arcaismo," 2,500 pounds to a graduate of the University of Florence (1987-1988).

Eligibility/Limitations Fellowships are open to men and women of all nationalities. These fellowships will be awarded to persons engaged in personal academic research, normally of postdoctoral standard (although no formal academic qualifications will be necessary). Fellowships will not be granted for the furtherance of doctoral research, other than in exceptional circumstances.

Fiscal Information Fellowships will normally be of one year's duration and may exceptionally be renewable. The sums awarded will each have a maximum value of 5,000 pounds and will be expected to cover the costs of accommodation, travel, photography, photocopying, and all other expenses relating to the work for which the fellowship was awarded. Fellows will be expected to arrange for the publication of their research.

Application Information Applicants should supply a curriculum vitae and an outline of the research they intend to undertake. The trustees of the foundation will require an indication of the likely cost of the project, a statement of alternative sources of funding (including other current applications), and an assurance that applicants can obtain access to relevant material. Eight completed copies or photocopies of the application form, together with eight copies of the additional information required, and including the names and addresses of two referees who should be asked by the applicant to forward their references directly to the foundation, should be sent to the foundation.

Deadline(s) The closing date for receipt of applications and letters from referees will be February 29.

141. The Dr. M. Aylwin Cotton Foundation
c/o Albany Trustee Company Limited
P.O. Box 232, Pollet House
The Pollet, St. Peter Port, Guernsey, Channel Islands

Publication Grants

Program Description The Dr. M. Aylwin Cotton Foundation invites application for fellowship awards for studies in the archaeology, architecture, history, language, and art of the Mediterranean. In this contest the word "Mediterranean" is used without geographic limitations. Publication grants are available toward the costs of publication of academic research already completed or imminently available for publication.

Sample Grants Towards the publication of "Il Pittore di Micali ed i suoi seguaci," the catalogue to an exhibition at the Museo Nazionale di Villa Guilia, Rome, 250 pounds to a Research Fellow, Emmanuel College, Cambridge (1987-1988). Towards the publication of "Etruscan and Iron Age Tomb-Groups in the Field Museum," 500 pounds to an associate professor, School of Art and Art History, University of Iowa (1985-1986).

Eligibility/Limitations Applicants should be either the author or the editor of the work. Awards are open to men and women of all nationalities.

Application Information Applicants should supply a brief account of the proposed publication, the name of the publisher, and an estimate of the likely cost of publication. Eight completed copies or photocopies of the application form, together with eight copies of the additional information required, and including the names and addresses of two referees who should be asked by the applicant to forward their references directly to the foundation, should be sent to the foundation.

Deadline(s) The closing date for receipt of applications and letters from referees will be February 29.

142. Council for International Exchange of Scholars
Eleven Dupont Circle, NW, Suite 300
Washington, DC 20036-1257
(202) 939-5401

Fulbright Scholar Program—Faculty Grants for Lecturing

Program Description The Fulbright Scholar Program serves two primary purposes. It enables Americans to learn firsthand about other countries and cultures; and it promotes academic and professional development. Some 700 awards are offered in support of university lectureships; many of these also offer some opportunity for research.

Eligibility/Limitations Prospective applicants should have United States citizenship at the time of application. For lecturing, usually a doctoral degree at the time of application and postdoctoral college or university teaching experience at the level and in the field of the lectureship is required. In some programs, language proficiency may be required. Persons who have lived abroad for the full ten-year period immediately preceding the time of application are ineligible. In general, preference is given to persons who have not already had lecturing or research grants. A previous grantee may, however, apply for a second award if three years have elapsed between the end of the first grant period and the beginning of the second. In accordance with a new ruling by the Board of Foreign Scholarships, scholars who have already held two (or more) Fulbright scholar awards are no longer prohibited from making application. Such applicants should bear in mind, however, that preference will be given to those who have not participated in the program and who do not have substantial recent experience abroad.

Fiscal Information Grant benefits include: round-trip travel for the grantee and for a principal dependent of a grantee whose appointment is for a full academic year; a maintenance allowance, paid either in local currency, in dollars, or in local currency with a dollar supplement (allowance amounts vary by grant category, the country and duration of the grant, and family status); incidental allowances for baggage, books and services essential to the assignment, and travel within the host country; housing (or housing allowance) in certain countries; and tuition allowance in certain countries (where available, tuition reimbursement is provided for tuition costs of accompanying dependents enrolled in elementary or secondary schools of the host country).

Application Information Only one application may be filed in an annual competition, but applicants may name up to three alternate countries. To obtain an application form and more detailed information, write or call CIES.

Deadline(s) Application deadline for faculty lectureship awards vary from country to country. Contact CIES for specific deadlines. A brochure is produced in November announcing awards for which there are insufficient numbers of candidates. For those unfilled awards, applications will continue to be accepted. Applications will also be accepted for some lecturing awards after the announced deadline. Interested persons may inquire at any time during the year.

143. Council for International Exchange of Scholars
Eleven Dupont Circle, NW, Suite 300
Washington, DC 20036-1257
(202) 939-5401

Fulbright Scholar Program—Faculty Grants for Lecturing/Research

Program Description The Fulbright Scholar Program serves two primary purposes. It enables Americans to learn firsthand about other countries and cultures; and it promotes academic and professional development. Some awards are designed to combine both lecturing and research.

Eligibility/Limitations Prospective applicants should have United States citizenship at the time of application. For lecturing, usually a doctoral degree at the time of application and postdoctoral college or university teaching experience at the level and in the field of the lectureship is required. In some programs, language proficiency may be required. Persons who have lived abroad for the full ten-year period immediately preceding the time of application are ineligible. In general, preference is given to persons who have not already had lecturing or research grants. A previous grantee may, however, apply for a second award if three years have elapsed between the end of the first grant period and the beginning of the second. In accordance with a new ruling by the Board of Foreign Scholarships, scholars who have already held two (or more) Fulbright scholar awards are no longer prohibited from making application. Such applicants should bear in mind, however, that preference will be given to those who have not participated in the program and who do not have substantial recent experience abroad.

Fiscal Information Grant benefits include: round-trip travel for the grantee and for a principal dependent of a grantee whose appointment is for a full academic year; a maintenance allowance, paid either in local currency, in dollars, or in local currency with a dollar supplement (allowance amounts vary by grant category, the country and duration of the grant, and family status); incidental allowances for baggage, books and services essential to the assignment, and travel within the host country; housing (or housing allowance) in certain countries; and tuition allowance in certain countries (where available, tuition reimbursement is provided for tuition costs of accompanying dependents enrolled in elementary or secondary schools of the host country).

Application Information Only one application may be filed in an annual competition, but applicants may name up to three alternate countries. To obtain an application form and more detailed information, write or call CIES.

Deadline(s) A brochure is produced in November announcing awards for which there are insufficient numbers of candidates. For those unfilled awards, applications will continue to be accepted. Applications will also be accepted for some lecturing awards after the announced deadline. Interested persons may inquire at any time during the year.

144. Council for International Exchange of Scholars
Eleven Dupont Circle, NW, Suite 300
Washington, DC 20036-1257
(202) 939-5401

Fulbright Scholar Program—Faculty Grants for Research

Program Description The Fulbright Scholar Program serves two primary purposes. It enables Americans to learn firsthand about other countries and cultures; and it promotes academic and professional development. Some 300 grants are offered in support of research in most disciplines.

Eligibility/Limitations Prospective applicants should have United States citizenship at the time of application. A doctorate at the time of application, or comparable professional qualifications is required. In some programs, language proficiency may be required. Persons who have lived abroad for the full ten-year period immediately preceding the time of application are ineligible. In general, preference is given to persons who have not already had lecturing or research grants. A previous grantee may, however, apply for a second award if three years have elapsed between the end of the first grant period and the beginning of the second. In accordance with a new ruling by the Board of Foreign Scholarships, scholars who have already held two (or more) Fulbright scholar awards are no longer prohibited from making application. Such applicants should bear in mind, however, that preference will be given to those who have not participated in the program and who do not have substantial recent experience abroad.

Fiscal Information Grant benefits include: round-trip travel for the grantee and for a principal dependent of a grantee whose appointment is for a full academic year; a maintenance allowance, paid either in local currency, in dollars, or in local currency with a dollar supplement (allowance amounts vary by grant category, the country and duration of the grant, and family status); incidental allowances for baggage, books and services essential to the assignment, and travel within the host country; housing (or housing allowance) in certain countries; and tuition allowance in certain countries (where available, tuition reimbursement is provided for tuition costs of accompanying dependents enrolled in elementary or secondary schools of the host country).

Application Information Only one application may be filed in an annual competition, but applicants may name up to three alternate countries. To obtain an application form and more detailed information, write or call CIES.

Deadline(s) Application deadlines for faculty research awards vary with country. Contact CIES for specific deadlines. Applications for research normally are not accepted after the deadline. Interested persons may inquire at any time during the year.

145. Council for International Exchange of Scholars
Eleven Dupont Circle, NW, Suite 300
Washington, DC 20036-1257
(202) 939-5401

Fulbright Scholar Program—Junior Lecturing and Junior Research

Program Description The Fulbright Scholar Program serves two primary purposes. It enables Americans to learn firsthand about other countries and cultures; and it promotes academic and professional development. These awards are designed primarily for younger scholars who are recent Ph.D. recipients or advanced Ph.D. candidates.

Eligibility/Limitations Prospective applicants should have United States citizenship at the time of application. In some programs, language proficiency may be required. Persons who have lived abroad for the full ten-year period immediately preceding the time of application are ineligible. In general, preference is given to persons who have not already had lecturing or research grants. A previous grantee may, however, apply for a second award if three years have elapsed between the end of the first grant period and the beginning of the second. In accordance with a new ruling by the Board of Foreign Scholarships, scholars who have already held two (or more) Fulbright scholar awards are no longer prohibited from making application. Such applicants should bear in mind, however, that preference will be given to those who have not participated in the program and who do not have substantial recent experience abroad.

Fiscal Information Grant benefits include: round-trip travel for the grantee and for a principal dependent of a grantee whose appointment is for a full academic year; a maintenance allowance, paid either in local currency, in dollars, or in local currency with a dollar supplement (allowance amounts vary by grant category, the country and duration of the grant, and family status); incidental allowances for baggage, books and services essential to the assignment, and travel within the host country; housing (or housing allowance) in certain countries; and tuition allowance in certain countries (where available, tuition reimbursement is provided for tuition costs of accompanying dependents enrolled in elementary or secondary schools of the host country).

Application Information Only one application may be filed in an annual competition, but applicants may name up to three alternate countries. To obtain an application form and more detailed information, write or call CIES.

Deadline(s) Application deadline for junior research and lecturing awards vary with country. A brochure is produced in November announcing awards for which there are insufficient numbers of candidates. For those unfilled awards, applications will continue to be accepted. Applications will also be accepted for some lecturing awards after the announced deadline. Interested persons may inquire at any time during the year.

146. Council for International Exchange of Scholars
Eleven Dupont Circle NW, Suite 300
Washington, DC 20036-1257
(202) 939-5404

Fulbright Scholar-in-Residence Program

Program Description This program supports American colleges and universities hosting a visiting scholar in the humanities or social sciences, or in scientific or professional specializations with a strong international focus. Of particular interest for the current program are proposals to bring foreign specialists in the fields of communications, education, US constitutional law and related subjects, as well as foreign scholars in US studies (history, literature, and politics).

Eligibility/Limitations American colleges and universities are eligible to apply.

Fiscal Information Grants support visiting scholars for all or part of the academic year. The program provides round-trip travel for the grantee, and for awards for the full academic year, one accompanying dependent; a maintenance allowance; and incidental allowances. The host institution is expected to share in the support of the visiting scholar.

Application Information Detailed program guidelines, proposal forms and further information is available on request.

Deadline(s) The deadline for receipt of proposals is November 1.

147. Council for International Exchange of Scholars
Eleven Dupont Circle, NW
Washington, DC 20036-1257
(202) 939-5426

Regional Awards: African Regional Research Program

Program Description About ten awards in all academic fields are made for research in one to four sub-Saharan African countries over periods of three to nine months. African specialists are encouraged to apply, but applications are also welcome from scholars who may have had no previous experience in Africa.

Eligibility/Limitations Both Africanists and non-Africanists are expected to include evidence in their proposals of host-country support for their research. This can be done by enclosing a letter of invitation or one expressing interest in the research from an African colleague or university. Applicants for non-English-speaking countries should have sufficient language ability to conduct the proposed research.

Fiscal Information The grant carries an award of approximately $1,860 to $3,400 per month (in U.S. dollars), plus initial allowance of $2,710 to $4,970 to cover such items as international travel and excess baggage, depending on country and number of dependents (figures quoted are for AY 1987-1988). Separate allowance will be provided for purchase of educational materials to be left in host country. Tuition reimbursement of $12,000 is available for accompanying K-12 children for grants of nine months and over, or $8,000 for grants of four to eight months. Deductions may be made if the host institution provides a local salary, international travel, or housing.

Application Information Because grantees are responsible for obtaining their own research clearances and visas, scholars should request information on procedures from colleagues in Africa and/or the U.S. Information Agency at an early date. Applicants are also encouraged to discuss their proposals with CIES Africa area staff well in advance of the application deadline.

Deadline(s) The application deadline is September 15.

148. Council for International Exchange of Scholars
Eleven Dupont Circle, NW, Suite 300
Washington, DC 20036-1257
(202) 939-5458

Regional Awards: American Republics Research Program

Program Description This program offers up to twenty research awards, each for six months, in any discipline for one or more countries of the Caribbean, Mexico, or South America. Applications are encouraged from scholars whose projects involve collaboration with colleagues in the host country and who are willing to give occasional lectures.

Eligibility/Limitations Applicants for non-English-speaking countries should have sufficient language ability to conduct the proposed research.

Fiscal Information The grant carries an award of approximately $1,800 to $3,000 per month (in U.S. dollars or local currency), depending on country and number of dependents. In addition, international travel for grantee, and in some countries, tuition reimbursement for accompanying K-12 children (up to $8,000) is awarded.

Application Information Additional information and application guidelines are available from CIES.

Deadline(s) The application deadline is June 15.

149. Council for International Exchange of Scholars
Eleven Dupont Circle, NW, Suite 300
Washington, DC 20036-1257
(202) 939-5464

Regional Awards: Central American Republics Research and Lecturing Program

Program Description CIES offers an expanded program of Fulbright awards for research and lecturing with Belize, Costa Rica, El Salvador, Guatemala, Honduras, Nicaragua, and Panama. Up to fifteen awards are offered for from three to nine months of research in any field in one or several countries of the area (fields may be restricted in some countries). Awards for lecturing in a variety of fields are offered for periods of from six to twelve months.

Eligibility/Limitations With few exceptions, lecturing awards require good to fluent Spanish.

Fiscal Information Awards carry stipends of from $1,800 to $2,600 per month (in U.S. dollars), plus an initial allowance of $1,635 to $1,820 to cover such items as international travel, excess baggage, settling in, books, and services. Tuition reimbursement for accompanying K-12 children is offered (up to $12,000) for grants over nine months, or $8,000 for shorter grants. Deductions may be made if the host institution provides local salary, international travel, or housing.

Application Information Additional information and application guidelines are available from CIES.

Deadline(s) The application deadline is June 15.

150. Council for International Exchange of Scholars
Eleven Dupont Circle, NW
Washington, DC 20036-1257
(202) 939-5467 or (202) 939-5470

Regional Awards: Islamic Civilization Research Program

Program Description Six to ten awards for three to nine months are offered in any field of research on some aspect of civilization, society, or science in one or more Muslim countries or among communities of Africa, Asia, and the Middle East with substantial Muslim populations. Research may be on contemporary or historical topics; collaborative research with foreign scholars is encouraged. Applications are welcome in established fields of Islamic studies, as well as in fields in which there is a growing interest in comparative and Islamic studies, such as architecture, law, planning, education, environmental studies, and science and technology in society. If a proposal is designed to analyze social, political, and economic conditions of a Muslim country or Muslim community, it should explicitly outline those variables of Islamic beliefs and practices that will be factors examined in the research to be undertaken.

Eligibility/Limitations Appropriate language facility required. For research in francophone countries, a French summary of the proposed research is requested with the application.

Fiscal Information Awards carry a stipend of approximately $2,040 to $4,200 per month (in U.S. dollars), plus initial allowance of $4,000 to $8,200 to cover such items as international travel, excess baggage, settling-in expenses, books, and services, depending on country and number of dependents (figures quoted are for AY 1986-1987).

Application Information Applications and additional information are available from CIES.

Deadline(s) Application deadline is September 15.

151. Council for International Exchange of Scholars
Eleven Dupont Circle, NW
Washington, DC 20036-1257
(202) 939-5467 or (202) 939-5470

Regional Awards: Middle East, North African, and South Asian Regional Research Program

Program Description A limited number of nine-month awards are offered within the social sciences and the humanities for research on how the U.S. is perceived in the Middle East, North Africa, and South Asia, and how present images have been formed. The research is expected to be comparative, preferably undertaken in more than one of the following countries: Algeria, Bahrain, Bangladesh, Egypt, India, Iraq, Israel, Jordan, Kuwait, Mauritania, Morocco, Nepal, Oman, Pakistan, Qatar, Saudi Arabia, Sri Lanka, Sudan, Syria, Tunisia, United Arab Emirates, West Bank, or Yemen. Collaborative research with a foreign scholar/professional abroad is encouraged. Academic fields of interest include: anthropology, area studies, communications, economics, education, history, language and literature, political science, psychology, and sociology and social work.

Eligibility/Limitations Candidates must have the Ph.D. or equivalent professional status. Appropriate language facility is required.

Fiscal Information Awards carry a stipend of approximately $2,040 to $4,200 per month (in U.S. dollars), plus initial allowances of $4,000 to $8,200 to cover such items as international travel, excess baggage, settling in, books, and services, depending on country and number of dependents.

Application Information Applications and additional information are available from CIES.

Deadline(s) Application deadline is September 15.

152. Council for International Exchange of Scholars
Eleven Dupont Circle, NW
Washington, DC 20036-1257
(202) 939-5475

Regional Awards: Southeast Asian Regional Research Program

Program Description Up to ten awards for three to ten months to conduct research on Southeast Asian society and culture are available. Fields include humanities, social sciences, communications, education, law, and business. Countries of study include Indonesia, Malaysia, Philippines, Singapore, and Thailand.

Eligibility/Limitations Proposals with intercountry travel and collaborative research will be considered. Degree of language facility will be considered.

Fiscal Information Benefits vary, depending on country. Contact CIES for specific information.

Application Information Applications and additional information are available from CIES.

Deadline(s) Application deadline is September 15.

Additional Information Under this program, proposals will be considered that request support for translation of a significant work or anthology of Southeast Asian literature. It is expected that the translation will be carried out in the country of the source language and will be completed during the period of the grant. Contact CIES for additional information on translation support.

153. Council for International Exchange of Scholars
Eleven Dupont Circle, NW
Washington, DC 20036-1257
(202) 939-5416 or (202) 939-5411

Regional Awards: Western European Regional Research Program

Program Description Approximately fifteen awards for research on European politics, society, and culture, past and present, are available. Applications are accepted in any discipline within the social sciences and humanities *only*. Preference is given to scholars with professional interest in European area studies. Projects should be regional or comparative in scope, historical or contemporary in focus, and must involve significant time in each of two or more of the following countries: Austria, Belgium, Cyprus, Denmark, Finland, France, the Federal Republic of Germany, Greece, Iceland, Ireland, Italy, Luxembourg, Malta, the Netherlands, Norway, Portugal, Spain, Sweden, Switzerland, Turkey, and the United Kingdom. Research in Eastern Europe is not funded under this program.

Eligibility/Limitations Where appropriate, applicants should submit documentation demonstrating access to archives, individuals to be interviewed, or European colleagues. Language competency or arrangements for translation must be demonstrated if required for completion of the project.

Fiscal Information Grants are for a minimum of three months and a maximum of nine months, with a preference for projects of six months or less. Benefits include $2,000 per month stipend, prorated for periods involving parts of a month, plus a travel/incidental allowance of $3,000 to cover such items as international travel, excess baggage, settling in, books and services, etc.

Application Information Applications and additional information are available from CIES.

Deadline(s) Application deadline is September 15.

154. Council for International Exchange of Scholars
Eleven Dupont Circle, NW, Suite 300
Washington, DC 20036-1257
(202) 939-5414

Spain Research Fellowships

Program Description Approximately twenty postdoctoral fellowships of three to ten months' duration will be awarded for research under the Agreement of Friendship, Defense, and Cooperation between the U.S. and Spain. Fields of preference are: anthropology, archaeology, arts, communications, economics, education, geography, history, law, linguistics, literature, logic, philosophy, political science, psychology, and sociology.

Eligibility/Limitations Competence in oral and written Spanish is required, according to the needs of the proposed research project. The doctorate is required at the time of application.

Fiscal Information Fellowships carry an award of approximately $1,200 to $1,800 per month, the total to be based on the number of accompanying dependents; $1,000 for books and settling-in expenses; round-trip travel for grantee, and, if the grant period is seven or more months, for one accompanying dependent.

Application Information Special application forms are available from CIES.

Deadline(s) Application deadline is January 1.

155. The Cowles Charitable Trust
630 Fifth Avenue, Suite 1612
New York, NY 10111-0144
(212) 765-6262

Grants

Program Description Grants are made to art museums, museums, institutions of higher education, and some medical facilities.

Sample Grants To the American Craft Museum, $2,500 (1986). To the Brooklyn Museum $3,750 (1986). To the Museum of Modern Art, $75,000 (1986). To Parrish Art Museum, $25,000 (1986). To New York Zoological Society, $1,625 (1986).

Eligibility/Limitations No grants are awarded to individuals.

Fiscal Information Total contributions in 1986 were over $1 million.

Application Information The trust requires seven complete sets of each proposal submitted for financial assistance.

Deadline(s) In order for a proposal to be considered at the next quarterly trustees meeting, all materials must be received thirty days prior to meeting date. Quarterly trustees meetings are usually held on the third Thursday in January, April, July, and October.

156. Cummins Engine Foundation
Mail Code 60814, Box 3005
Columbus, IN 47202-3005
(812) 377-3114

Program Description The foundation gives special consideration for funding to programs in three major categories: youth and education; equity and justice; and quality of life. In the area of youth and education, the foundation seeks ways to help young people grow up to be full participants in a complex world. In equity and justice, the foundation's focus is on those who face discrimination, are dispossessed, or are poorly served by society. The foundation also encourages opportunities for leadership development among women and minorities. A limited number of grants is made annually to promote economic development and human rights abroad. In quality of life, the foundation looks for programs that refresh the spirit and enhance the general environment in communities where Cummins and its subsidiaries have manufacturing plants. The foundation also seeks new and unusual ways to support the arts and artists.

Eligibility/Limitations Cummins does not support political causes or candidates, or sectarian religious activities. No grants are made to individuals. The foundation makes virtually all its local grants in communities where Cummins and its subsidiaries have manufacturing plants.

Fiscal Information Grant awards range from $500 to $30,000.

Application Information A preliminary proposal should include a brief description of the problem being addressed, specifically what the program hopes to achieve, operating plan and cost, description of key leadership and how one will be able to tell whether or not the program worked. Upon receipt of the proposal, the foundation staff will respond regarding the possibility of funding.

Deadline(s) Inquiries and proposals may be submitted in writing at any time during the year, though to be on the agenda for a specific meeting, proposals should be received no later than the first of the previous month. The foundation directors meet in February, July, September, and December to consider new programs and approve grants. The staff has authority to make small grants from its discretionary budget between meetings.

157. Charles and Margaret Hall Cushwa Center
University of Notre Dame
Room 614, Memorial Library
Notre Dame, IN 46556
(219) 239-5441

Hibernian Research Award

Program Description This award is designed to promote scholarly study of the Irish in the United States.

Eligibility/Limitations Applicants must be postdoctoral scholars from any academic discipline who are engaged in a research project related to the study of the Irish people in the United States.

Fiscal Information The award carries a stipend of $2,000.

Application Information Application forms are available from the center on request.

Deadline(s) Applications must be postmarked no later than December 31.

158. Charles and Margaret Hall Cushwa Center
University of Notre Dame
Room 614, Memorial Library
Notre Dame, IN 46556
(219) 239-5441

Research Grant Program

Program Description This program is designed to foster research in the archives and library of the University of Notre Dame. The library collection is particularly rich in the following areas: Catholic newspapers, history of midwestern Catholicism, Catholic literature, and history of Catholicism in the United States. The archives have manuscripts of historical personages, records of twentieth century Catholic organizations, reports of European missionary societies, and much more material related to the American Catholic community.

Eligibility/Limitations Applicants must be postdoctoral scholars of any academic discipline who are engaged in projects which require substantial use of the collection of the library and/or archives. The research project must be related to the study of the American Catholic community and must indicate as specifically as possible how the use of the Notre Dame library and archives is pertinent to the study.

Fiscal Information Grants range from $1,000 to $2,000.

Application Information Application forms and procedures are available from the center on request.

Deadline(s) Applications must be postmarked no later than November 30.

159. Dart & Kraft Foundation
2211 Sanders Road
Northbrook, IL 60062

Corporate Giving

Program Description Dart & Kraft is committed to the long-term objective of contributing two percent of domestic pretax income to benefit nonprofit organizations whose work improves the well-being of society and, therefore, the environment in which the company operates. A sprectrum of activities is supported through four major program categories: arts and culture, civic affairs, education, and health and welfare. In the arts and culture category, proposals will be considered from arts funds and councils, performing arts groups, cultural centers, libraries, museums, and for the general operating needs of public broadcasting stations. Priority is given to those proposals which are most responsive to the focus areas of company concern: nutrition and physical fitness; strengthening educational institutions; economic development; and community development. Additionally, programs addressing the needs of minorities, women, and persons with a disability are of particular interest and constitute a special focus.

Eligibility/Limitations Generally, the foundation will not consider requests for funding: individuals; organizations with a limited constituency; organizations which restrict their services to members of one religious group; political organizations or those whose primary purpose is to influence legislation or political viewpoint, or the promotion of a particular candidate; travel, tuition, and registration fees; membership dues; or good-will advertisements of any kind.

Application Information Initial contact should be made by mail. An application form is not required, however, a concise statement of the following information is required: general program information including a brief statement of the history, purpose, and achievements of the organization; a proposal including an indication of how the applicant and/or its project meet one or more of the objectives of the focus areas, innovatively responds to an important need, is supported by the targeted constituency it intends to serve and is cost effective; total organization and/or project budgets for both the current and previous fiscal year, if applicable; an audited financial statement for the previous year, or a Letter of Auditability; an IRS letter certifying the applicant as 501(c)(3) or equivalent organization; list of officers and board members; list of other donors; list of accrediting agencies; and statement of fund-raising expenses as a percentage of overall organization, administrative, and program costs.

Deadline(s) Proposals are reviewed on a continuous basis.

160. Data General
4400 Computer Drive
Westboro, MA 01580
(617) 366-8911

Contributions and Donations Program

Program Description Data General considers proposals requesting cash contributions and equipment donations from nonprofit organizations which provide benefits to company employees and/or the communities in which they live.

Eligibility/Limitations Applicant organizations must be certified as nonprofit by the IRS.

Application Information Applications should be made in writing to the attention of the donations administrator at the above address and should include the following: proof of tax-exempt status; an itemized budget; summary of proposed program; specifics of support requested; statement of organizational history and objectives; summary of benefits to DG employees and/or communities; and specifics of DG employee involvement in the organization.

Deadline(s) No deadlines are announced.

161. Dayton Hudson Foundation
777 Nicollet Mall
Minneapolis, MN 55402
(612) 370-6553

Grants

Program Description Dayton Hudson's policies emphasize a strong commitment to serve communities where the corporation has operating facilities. The corporation's giving, therefore, is principally local (in forty-seven states). Dayton Hudson has established the following priority funding categories and has assigned guidelines to each: social action (40 percent); arts (40 percent); and miscellaneous (20 percent) support for the efforts of community-based institutions, organizations, and programs that are dedicated to meeting other critical community needs. In the arts category, support is available for the efforts of community-based arts organizations and programs of quality that exhibit and interpret our artistic heritage or encourage contemporary artistic expression. Priority is given to full-time arts organizations that pay their artistic personnel. In smaller communities, consideration may be given to part-time or volunteer organizations of quality.

Sample Grants For general support for national organization of art museums, $5,000 to Art Museum Association of America (1986). For capital support, $5,000 to New Mexico Museum of Natural History, Albuquerque, NM (1983). For general support, $15,000 to Phoenix Art Museum, Phoenix, AZ (1983). For a concert and an exhibition, $30,000 to California International Arts Foundation, Los Angeles, CA (1983). For materials development, $120,000, and exhibition support, $12,625, to Children's Museum, Denver, CO (1983). For artworks purchase, $25,000 to the Museum of Fine Arts of Houston, Houston, TX (1983).

Eligibility/Limitations Dayton Hudson strives to be a contributions leader in its Twin Cities headquarters area (Minneapolis-St. Paul) and in the communities where the corporation has operating company headquarters: Hayward, CA; Detroit, MI; Oklahoma City, OK; Phoenix, AZ; and Woburn, MA. On a more limited basis, grants are made in other communities where there is a major Dayton Hudson presence. Dayton Hudson, its operating companies, and the foundation consider requests from organizations which have been given 501(c)(3) tax-exempt status by the IRS. Dayton Hudson rarely funds organizations during their first year of operation. Grants are not made to individuals. Grants are rarely made to educational institutions or research groups.

Fiscal Information Grant funds distributed in 1986 totaled more than $8.4 million. Grants are made for general operations, special projects, and occasionally capital purposes. Grants are not normally made for endowments.

Application Information Requests from organizations in Minnesota should be sent directly to the foundation. Requests from organizations located outside Minnesota should be sent to the grants officer of the Dayton Hudson facility in the local community; a list of companies and locations is available from the foundation at the address listed above. Informal inquiries in advance of a formal application are encouraged. Dayton Hudson does not use an application form. It is acceptable to use another funder's application form or to send a letter of not more than two typewritten pages (four handwritten pages). In either case, the following items should be included: a request for a specific amount of money with an explanation of how the funds will be used; a description of the organization, including a statement of the organization's purposes and objectives; if the request is to support a capital drive or specific project, the applicant should include a statement of the need the project intends to address, the geographic area and population to be served, and a timetable; and, the name(s) and qualifications of the person(s) who will administer the grant. The formal application letter should have the following attachments: a copy of the organization's most recent tax-exempt ruling statement from the IRS; a list of the organization's officers and directors; a financial statement for the most recently completed year of operation; an organizational budget for the current operating year showing anticipated expenses and income by sources (if the request is for a capital drive or specific project, a budget showing both expenses and income for the drive or project should be included); and a donors list, either complete or representative, showing private, corporate, and foundation contributions to the organization during the past twelve months.

Deadline(s) No deadlines are announced.

162. The Gladys Krieble Delmas Foundation
40 West 57th Street, 27th Floor
New York, NY 10019

Grants for Venetian Research

Program Description The foundation announces its program of predoctoral and post-doctoral grants for research in Venice, Italy. The following areas of study will be considered: the history of Venice and the former Venetian empire in its various aspects—art, architecture, archaeology, theater, music, literature, natural science, political science, economics, and the law; also studies related to the contemporary Venetian environment such as ecology, oceanography, and urban planning and rehabilitation.

Eligibility/Limitations Applicants must be citizens of the United States, have some experience in advanced research, and, if graduate students, have fulfilled all doctoral requirements except for completion of the dissertation.

Fiscal Information Applications will be entertained for grants from $500 up to a maximum of $10,000. Funds will also be available eventually for aid in the publication of such studies resulting from research made possible by those grants as are deemed worthy by the trustees and advisory board.

Application Information There are no formal application forms. For application guidelines contact the foundation.

Deadline(s) Applications for grants should be received by December 15.

163. Geraldine R. Dodge Foundation, Incorporated
95 Madison Avenue, P.O. Box 1239R
Morristown, NJ 07960
(201) 540-8442

Grants

Program Description For the effective focus of the foundation's energies, the trustees have found it necessary to exclude major fields from consideration. Among these are higher education, health, and religion. The foundation's focus is on four areas: animal welfare and local projects; secondary education; the arts; and public issues. The foundation's focus in the area of animal welfare is directed toward projects with national implications. Humane activities at local levels fall outside the foundation's programs. Projects within the state of New Jersey in the public interest and in the arts are considered. The foundation's focus on secondary education includes projects in New Jersey and at NALIS schools in the Northeast and Middle Atlantic states and programs with a national audience.

Sample Grants In support of three five-day seminars to train high school teachers and zoo educators, including representatives from Belize, in the use of zoological collections for science collections, $48,000 to New York Zoological Society, New York, NY (1986). For the production of a handbook, *Wild Mammals in Captivity, Guide to Management*, which will provide zoo managers and scientists with the latest knowledge about the care of animals, especially the rare and endangered species facing extinction in the wild, $25,000 to Smithsonian Institution, Washington, DC (1986). For publication of a catalog documenting a printmaking and photography exhibit and for a three-month sequence of educational programs relevant to the museum's participation in the New Jersey Arts Annual program, $10,000 to The Jersey City Museum, Jersey City, NJ (1986). For an art exhibition, a concert, a symposium, and other events celebrating Black History Month, $25,000 to The Montclair Art Museum, Montclair, NJ (1986). To develop a valid methodology for assessing the effect of the zoo and individual exhibits upon the casual visitor, thus finding ways to make the zoo more valuable educationally, $35,000 to Zoological Society of Philadelphia (1987). For mounting a two-year exhibit for children, entitled "Westward Ho!," a simulation of the westward migration of the mid-1800s, $20,000 to Monmouth Museum, Lincroft, NJ (1987). For a program of conserving endangered plant species of New Jersey and for research on their survival, $76,000 to Center for Plant Conservation, The Arnold Arboretum, Harvard University, Jamaica Plain, MA (1987).

Eligibility/Limitations The foundation does not support scholarship funds or make direct awards to individuals, nor does it administer programs which it supports. Also, it does not typically consider requests for grants to conduit organizations. The foundation does not ordinarily consider proposals for capital purposes, endowment funds, or deficit operations.

Fiscal Information Grants in 1987 totaled over $7.3 million.

Application Information A grant request should be initiated by a letter describing the proposed project, its expected impact, the qualifications of staff, a detailed expense budget and certified audit of the financial statements, the time frames, and other funding sources, as well as copies of the applicant organization's tax-exempt rulings stating that it is described in Section 501(c)(3) of the Internal Revenue Code and is not a private foundation. A preliminary inquiry prior to the submission of a detailed proposal is advisable.

Deadline(s) Proposals should be postmarked no later than the following deadlines, to allow adequate time for review: January 1 for animal welfare and local projects; April 1 for secondary education; July 1 for the arts; and October 1 for public issues.

164. Dow Chemical Company Foundation
2030 Willard H. Dow Center
Midland, MI 48674
(517) 636-1162

Contributions

Program Description The Dow Chemical Company financial contributions are devoted to four general categories: health and community programs; arts and culture; aid to education; and other interests. The company is especially interested in programs or projects that focus on: environment and safety; community service; education; and women and minorities.

Eligibility/Limitations No grants are awarded to individuals.

Fiscal Information The foundation awarded grants totaling over $13.2 million in 1984.

Application Information Additional information about foundation giving is available from the Public Interest Committee at the address listed above.

Deadline(s) No deadlines are announced.

165. Dresser Foundation, Inc.
P.O. Box 718
Dallas, TX 75221
(214) 740-6741

Grants

Program Description The principal interests of the foundation are health, education, welfare, and cultural activities which broadly benefit the communities of which Dresser is a part, or to a more limited extent, society in general. Primary and secondary schools are not included in the aid to education program.

Eligibility/Limitations Foundation policy prohibits contributions directly to individuals.

Fiscal Information Total contributions in 1986 were over $2.4 million.

Application Information The foundation does not publish an annual report nor does it have unique guidelines with respect to the development of a grant proposal. Applicants should send the foundation an outline of their proposed project or program, the funding needed, the overall outreach of the activity, the 501(c)(3) exemption letter, and any other materials which might be helpful to the deliberations of the foundation. The foundation will be happy to consider the request.

Deadline(s) The foundation has no deadlines for submission; proposals are reviewed as they are received.

166. Dumbarton Oaks Center for Byzantine Studies
1703 32nd Street, NW
Washington, DC 20007
(202) 342-3232

Fellowships

Program Description Dumbarton Oaks offers fellowships in the areas of Byzantine studies (including related aspects of late Roman, early Christian, western medieval, Slavic, and Near Eastern studies), Pre-Columbian studies, and the history of landscape architecture.

Eligibility/Limitations Fellowships are available for scholars who at the time of application hold a doctorate (or appropriate final degree) or who have established themselves in their field and wish to pursue their own research. Applications will also be accepted from graduate students who expect to have the Ph.D. in hand prior to taking up residence at Dumbarton Oaks. (Successful applicants will revert to the status and stipend of junior fellows if the degree has not been conferred.)

Fiscal Information Fellowships are normally awarded for the academic year from September 15 until June 1, during which recipients are expected to be in residence at Dumbarton Oaks and to devote full time to their fellowship projects, without undertaking other major activities. Applications are also accepted for either the first (September 15-January 20) or the second (February 1-June 1) term or for shorter periods. The maximum annual stipend (which is prorated for shorter periods) is $9,000, to which is added $1,250 for each dependent who accompanies the recipient and is without other means of support. Fellows also receive: (a) furnished housing or housing allowance adjusted to need; (b) an expense account of $500 for the academic year for approved research expenses (such as typing, since secretarial and other support services are not provided); and (c) lunch in the Fellows Building on weekdays. Fellowships are not renewable, but initial application may be made for two successive years (two annual fellowships and an intervening summer fellowship, part of which may be spent away from Dumbarton Oaks). Applications from former fellows are accepted but reappointments are not normally made (except for fellows previously appointed for less than three months) before five years have elapsed since the tenure of the previous fellowship.

Application Information There is no application form. Application guidelines are available from the assistant director.

Deadline(s) Applications for all awards are due on or before November 15.

Additional Information Inquiries concerning long-term appointments, which are occasionally made for senior scholars, on both a full- and part-time basis, should be addressed to the director of Dumbarton Oaks. Dumbarton Oaks also makes grants to assist with scholarly projects in the three fields with which it is concerned. These can cover expenses such as travel, photography, supplies, and occasionally modest stipends to replace salary otherwise lost. Preference is given to projects for limited periods of time conducted in cooperation with other institutions.

167. Dumbarton Oaks Center for Byzantine Studies
1703 32nd Street, NW
Washington, DC 20007
(202) 342-3232

Junior Fellowships

Program Description Dumbarton Oaks offers fellowships in the areas of Byzantine studies (including related aspects of late Roman, early Christian, western medieval, Slavic, and Near Eastern studies), Pre-Columbian studies, and the history of landscape architecture.

Eligibility/Limitations Junior fellowships are available to students who at the time of application have fulfilled all preliminary requirements for a higher degree and are working on a dissertation or final project under the direction of a faculty member at their own university. In exceptional cases applications will be accepted from students before fulfilling preliminary requirements.

Fiscal Information Junior fellowships are normally awarded for the academic year from September 15 until June 1, during which recipients are expected to be in residence at Dumbarton Oaks and to devote full time to their fellowship projects, without undertaking other major activities. Applications are also accepted for either the first (September 15-January 20) or the second (February 1-June 1) term or for shorter periods. The maximum annual stipend (which is prorated for shorter periods) is $6,750, to which is added $1,250 for each dependent who accompanies the recipient and is without other means of support. Junior fellows also receive: (a) furnished housing or housing allowance adjusted to need; (b) an expense account of $500 for the academic year for approved research expenses (such as typing, since secretarial and other support services are not provided); and (c) lunch in the Fellows Building on weekdays. Fellowships are not renewable, but initial application may be made for two successive years (two annual fellowships and an intervening summer fellowship, part of which may be spent away from Dumbarton Oaks). Applications from former fellows are accepted but reappointments are not normally made (except for fellows previously appointed for less than three months) before five years have elapsed since the tenure of the previous fellowship.

Application Information There is no application form. Application guidelines are available from the assistant director.

Deadline(s) Applications for all awards are due on or before November 15.

168. Dumbarton Oaks Center for Byzantine Studies
1703 32nd Street, NW
Washington, DC 20007
(202) 342-3232

Summer Fellowships

Program Description Dumbarton Oaks offers fellowships in the areas of Byzantine studies (including related aspects of late Roman, early Christian, western medieval, Slavic, and Near Eastern studies), Pre-Columbian studies, and the history of landscape architecture.

Eligibility/Limitations Scholars (on any level of advancement) who are not incumbent fellows or residents of the Washington area are eligible to apply.

Fiscal Information Summer Fellowships are awarded for periods of four to ten weeks between June 15 and September 1. They include housing, lunch in the Fellows Building on weekdays, travel expenses between the fellow's home and Washington (if other support is unavailable) and an allowance of $100 a week. Accommodations for families are not available.

Application Information There is no application form. Application guidelines are available from the assistant director.

Deadline(s) The deadline for submission of applications for all awards is November 15.

169. Early American Industries Association
The Winterthur Museum
Winterthur, DE 19735
(302) 656-8591

Grants-in-Aid

Program Description Awards are made to support individuals conducting graduate- or postgraduate-level research or publication projects relating to the purposes of the EAIA. The association encourages the study and better understanding of early American industries in homes, shops, farms, and on the sea. The discovery, identification, classification, preservation, and exhibition of obsolete tools, implements, and mechanical devices used in early America has also been a primary goal.

Eligibility/Limitations Individual applicants may be sponsored by an institution or be engaged in self-directed projects. While grants-in-aid are available to all qualified applicants, in general, those who have completed the undergraduate level of their education will be given preference. This is in keeping with the goal of the program to assist serious students and scholars in work paralleling the purposes of the association.

Fiscal Information Non-renewable grants of up to $1,000 are made each year. Grants-in-aid may be used to supplement existing scholarships, fellowships, or other forms of aid. They are not to be used as a substitute for such assistance.

Application Information Application information is available on request.

Deadline(s) Applications must be received by the Grants-in-Aid Committee no later than March 15 of each year.

170. Eastern National Park & Monument Association
P.O. Box 671
Cooperstown, NY 13326
(607) 547-8511

Herbert E. Kahler Research Fellowship

Program Description This fellowship is granted to support scholarly study other than a doctoral thesis focusing on cultural, historical, and natural resources of the National Park System.

Eligibility/Limitations The applicant must propose a project focusing on the historical, cultural, or natural resources of the National Park System.

Fiscal Information The fellowship carries a stipend of $5,000, granted annually.

Application Information There is no application form, but applicants must present a comprehensive statement on the research proposal, together with a research and writing schedule.

Deadline(s) Applications should be sent no later than August 1.

171. Eastern National Park & Monument Association
P.O. Box 671
Cooperstown, NY 13326
(607) 547-8511

Ronald F. Lee Fellowships

Program Description Fellowships are granted to graduate students whose doctoral thesis deals with the conservation, geological, archaeological, architectural, ecological, historical, biological, environmental, scientific, and preservation interests of the national parks.

Eligibility/Limitations The applicant must be a candidate for the doctorate.

Fiscal Information The fellowships carry a stipend of $5,000. The award money may be used for travel and support during the period of research and writing leading to the presentation of the doctoral thesis.

Application Information There is no application form, but applicants must present a comprehensive statement on their thesis proposal, as approved by their thesis adviser(s), together with a research and writing schedule and curriculum vitae.

Deadline(s) Applications should be sent no later than August 1.

172. Eastman Kodak Company
Corporate Contributions Committee
343 State Street
Rochester, NY 14650
(716) 724-3127

Corporate Contributions Program

Program Description Kodak's financial contributions program has four chief areas of concentration: education, health and human services, culture and the arts, and civic and community. Within the category of culture and the arts, Kodak believes that cultural and arts organizations enrich and enhance the communities in which major facilities are located. Support is available for museums, libraries, zoos, theaters, music schools, arts centers, symphonies and orchestras, public television, arts councils and service organizations, and a variety of special projects. Through these many outlets, the company hopes to make the arts and humanities available to as many people as possible.

Eligibility/Limitations Kodak's investments focus on projects and organizations that enhance the quality of life in communities where principal facilities are located. Kodak contributes usually to preselected, nonprofit institutions and programs.

Fiscal Information Contributions in 1986 totaled over $14.1 million, including over $1.57 million in the culture and the arts category.

Application Information Kodak attempts to respond to all requests for support; not all are supported, but all do receive consideration. Contact the company for additional information on the Kodak contributions program.

Deadline(s) No deadlines are announced.

173. Eaton Corporation

Eaton Center
Cleveland, OH 44114

Grants

Program Description Eaton supports educational institutions, health and human services groups, cultural and arts organizations, and civic endeavors. Eaton believes that its first obligation is to the communities in which it operates. High priority is given to local organizations which serve the needs of company employees and which offer them the opportunity to provide leadership, voluntary service, and personal financial support.

Eligibility/Limitations Organizations requesting charitable contributions should forward a copy of their IRS 501(c)(3) classification letter, and where applicable, their 509(a) letter, or their Canadian public charity registration number. Grants are not made to religious, fraternal, or labor organizations, or to individuals.

Fiscal Information During 1986 Eaton's contributions totaled over $5.9 million.

Application Information All requests must be in writing. Each should include a description of the organization's history and purpose, copies of the most recent audited financial statements and the current budget, a listing of corporate donors and their amounts, and a roster of officers and directors.

Deadline(s) No deadlines are announced.

174. El Pomar Foundation

P.O. Box 158
Colorado Springs, CO 80901
(303) 633-7733

Grants

Program Description The El Pomar Foundation was established in 1937 as a nonprofit charitable foundation which makes grants in the areas of: arts and humanities, education, health and welfare, religion, and specific projects. The foundation is limited to making grants for activities that take place within the state of Colorado.

Sample Grants For operations, $250,000 to Cheyenne Mountain Museum and Zoological Society (1986). For perimeter fence, directional signage, and walkway modifications, $193,800 to Cheyenne Mountain Museum and Zoological Society (1986). For program funds, $5,000 to Children's Museum (1986). For museum renovations, $10,000 to Children's Museum (1986).

Eligibility/Limitations The foundation does not make grants to individuals. Foundation policy generally precludes grants under the following circumstances: grants to another foundation or organization which distributes money to entities of its own selection; grants to cover deficits or for endowment; grants for the making of films or other media projects; grants to tax-supported institutions, however, municipalities may apply for a grant for a specific project; grants to organizations which discriminate by reason of race, religion, sex, national origin, or physical handicap; grants for travel, conferences, conventions, group meetings; and grants for camps or seasonal facilities.

Fiscal Information The foundation awarded grants totaling over $7.3 million in 1986.

Application Information There are no forms for making application to the trustees for grants. Applicants should submit one copy of a detailed and complete application which contains the following: name and address of tax-exempt organization; relationship, capacity, or title of person signing the application; a list of officers and directors of the organization; statement of the amount requested and a complete explanation of the necessity therefor; and a statement of whether aid has been sought during the preceding three years from other foundations and, if so, the names of the foundations and the amount received, if any. Applicants should furnish: a photocopy of the current U.S. Treasury tax-exempt letter; a photocopy of the organization's classification under Section 509(a) of the code; its latest audited balance sheet; and its latest audited income statement. Include also: a brief history of the organization and its principal program accomplishments, particularly if this is the organization's first application to the foundation; a concise and clear description of the project or program, supplemented by other material showing the need or problem and the proposed solution, its social or other significance, its expected benefit to the citizens of Colorado, and other related information; a detailed budget of the project or program for the full term and for the period for which assistance is requested; and the endorsement of the principal officer of the organization.

Deadline(s) All applications are acted upon, usually within ninety days of receipt.

175. Eleutherian Mills Historical Library
Eleutherian Mills-Hagley Foundation, Inc.
P.O. Box 3630, Greenville
Wilmington, DE 19807
(302) 658-2400 ext. 242

Grants-in-Aid

Program Description The purpose of these grants is to provide opportunities for a limited number of scholars each year to use the Eleutherian Mills Historical Library's rich manuscript, pictorial, and imprint collections relating to French history, 1760-1820, and to American history, 1800-1950, with special emphasis on business, industrial, and technological developments in the lower Delaware River Valley area. There is no restriction on the applicant's field of study.

Eligibility/Limitations This program is designed for scholars holding the degree of Doctor of Philosophy or having equivalent status and for a limited number of doctoral candidates.

Fiscal Information The Grants-in-Aid will not exceed $750 per month. The actual amount will depend upon the individual needs of the recipient. Grants-in-Aid will not be made for periods shorter than one month.

Application Information Application forms and additional information may be obtained by writing the director.

Deadline(s) Applications for Grants-in-Aid may be submitted throughout the year and will be processed as received.

176. Enron Foundation—Houston
P.O. Box 1188
Houston, TX 77001
(713) 654-6318

Grants

Program Description The Enron Foundation—Houston supports a broad range of charitable organizations which fall into these general categories: education, health and human services, arts and culture, and civic and community development. In the arts and culture category, the foundation provides financial support to the arts and humanities as important aspects of community life. Typical recipients are symphony/orchestral associations, museums of art and science, performing arts including dance and drama, historic preservation societies, public radio and television, zoological societies, and libraries.

Eligibility/Limitations The foundation's main focus is nonprofit organization requests from the southern tier of states of Alabama, Arizona, California, Florida, Louisiana, Mississippi, New Mexico, and Texas. The Enron Foundation does not fund the following: organizations without proper IRS nonprofit status; support for individuals; political causes, lobbying efforts, or candidates; programs for organizations outside the U.S. and its territories; and veterans groups not qualifying for 501(c)(3). In general, the foundation does not support these activities: endowment funds; projects of religious denominations or sects other than institutions of higher education with religious affiliations; tickets or tables for benefit purposes; advertising for benefit purposes; travel for individuals or groups; elementary and secondary schools and colleges with less than a four-year curriculum.

Fiscal Information In 1986, foundation grants totaled over $2.3 million. A matching program also exists for Enron employees' gifts (2 to 1) to cultural organizations, funded by the foundation.

Application Information The foundation does not provide a grant application, preferring that the requesting nonprofit organization submit a letter of request. Such letters should be typewritten and normally not more than three pages in length. The letter of proposal should cover: a brief description of the requesting organization and its purposes; a description of the particular cause or program for which funds are being sought; a statement of rationale for the proposal including an indication of its goals, the need for such a program, any unique elements, and the population benefited; total amount of monies sought in this campaign; what portion of the total goal is targeted for corporate support and where will remaining funds come from; a specific indication of how much is requested from the foundation and desired timing; indication of broad-based community and corporate support; and project evaluation plans and methods of reporting such evaluation to donors. In addition to the letter of proposal, a number of attachments should be enclosed, including: a copy of the nonprofit organization's 501(c)(3) tax-exempt ruling from the IRS; an itemized budget for the program or project involved; a detailed organizational budget for the current operating year covering both income and expenses; a financial statement for the organization's most recent fiscal year, preferably audited; a listing of officers and directors, as well as their principal affiliations.

Deadline(s) Routine requests will normally be answered within 30-45 days. Requests for major grants (over $10,000) may require 90-120 days, since such applications are considered at board meetings, held quarterly.

Additional Information Enron Corp. now maintains two philanthropic foundations—one based in its corporate headquarters city, Houston, TX, and another in Omaha, NE, former headquarters of its predecessor corporation, HNG/InterNorth. National nonprofit organizations may continue to deal with either of the foundations if a previous association existed with that foundation. Otherwise, national organizations applying for the first time should contact the foundation office at corporate headquarters in Houston.

177. Enron Foundation—Omaha
2600 Dodge Street
Omaha, NE 68131
(402) 633-5812

Grants

Program Description The Enron Foundation—Omaha supports a broad range of charitable organizations which fall into these general categories: education, health and human services, arts and culture, and civic and community development. In the arts and culture category, the foundation provides financial support to the arts and humanities as important aspects of community life. Typical recipients are symphony/ orchestral associations, museums of art and science, performing arts including dance and drama, historic preservation societies, public radio and television, zoological societies, and libraries.

Eligibility/Limitations The foundation concentrates principally on requests from the corporation's area of operations in the Midwest. The Enron Foundation does not fund the following: organizations without proper IRS nonprofit status; support for individuals; political causes, lobbying efforts, or candidates; programs for organizations outside the U.S. and its territories; and veterans groups not qualifying for 501(c)(3). In general, the foundation does not support these activities: endowment funds; projects of religious denominations or sects other than institutions of higher education with religious affiliations; tickets or tables for benefit purposes; advertising for benefit purposes; travel for individuals or groups; elementary and secondary schools and colleges with less than a four-year curriculum.

Fiscal Information A matching program also exists for Enron employees' gifts (2 to 1) to cultural organizations, funded by the foundation.

Application Information The foundation does not provide a grant application, preferring that the requesting nonprofit organization submit a letter of request. Such letters should be typewritten and normally not more than three pages in length. The letter of proposal should cover: a brief description of the requesting organization and its purposes; a description of the particular cause or program for which funds are being sought; a statement of rationale for the proposal including an indication of its goals, the need for such a program, any unique elements, and the population benefited; total amount of monies sought in this campaign; what portion of the total goal is targeted for corporate support and where will remaining funds come from; a specific indication of how much is requested from the foundation and desired timing; indication of broad-based community and corporate support; and project evaluation plans and methods of reporting such evaluation to donors. In addition to the letter of proposal, a number of attachments should be enclosed, including: a copy of the nonprofit organization's 501(c)(3) tax-exempt ruling from the IRS; an itemized budget for the program or project involved; a detailed organizational budget for the current operating year covering both income and expenses; a financial statement for the organization's most recent fiscal year, preferably audited; a listing of officers and directors, as well as their prinicpal affiliations.

Deadline(s) Routine requests will normally be answered within 30-45 days. Requests for major grants (over $10,000) may require 90-120 days, since such applications are considered at board meetings, held quarterly.

Additional Information Enron Corp. now maintains two philanthropic foundations— one based in its corporate headquarters city, Houston, TX, and another in Omaha, NE, former headquarters of its predecessor corporation, HNG/InterNorth. National nonprofit organizations may continue to deal with either of the foundations if a previous association existed with that foundation. Otherwise, national organizations applying for the first time should contact the foundation office at corporate headquarters in Houston.

178. Exxon Education Foundation

111 West 49th Street
New York, NY 10020-1198
(212) 333-6327

Grants

Program Description The mission of the Exxon Education Foundation is to support improvements in the quality of education. Proposals for funding may be submitted under the foundation's Curriculum & Teaching program (higher education portion) and their Management in Higher Education program. Curriculum & Teaching grants support efforts that will lead to improvement in instructional methodology and content as well as the evaluation and dissemination of such efforts. The foundation is especially interested in projects that cross traditional lines between disciplines, professions, and institutions, and in projects that promote interaction between humanists and social scientists and representatives of scientific, technical, and professional fields. Priority is given to projects involving re-examination of basic educational purposes, programs, and requirements and to efforts to introduce consideration of values issues into professional and graduate training. Preference is given also to projects that reflect a concern for the international dimension of education and the need for heightened awareness of global issues. Under the Management of Higher Education program, the foundation is interested in projects that will foster improved allocation and use of resources among and within educational institutions and systems, improved understanding of the economic forces affecting educational services and institutions, and improved institutional response to economic change.

Sample Grants For an international exhibit, $150,000 to Guggenheim Museum, New York, NY (1986). For an exhibit of ancient ivories, $10,000 to Anchorage Fine Arts Museum, Anchorage, AK (1986). For a program to help teachers find ways to incorporate the arts in their curricula, $20,000 to Museum of Fine Arts of Houston, TX (1986). To assist in the renovation and expansion of the museum, $12,500 ($25,000, two years) to Newark Museum Association, NJ (1986).

Eligibility/Limitations Educational institutions or organizations that are located in the United States, its territories or possessions, and that are qualified as eligible charitable donees by the Internal Revenue Service are eligible for grants. The foundation makes no grants to individuals. Grants are not ordinarily made to: (1) support the adoption of established educational or administrative methods or materials; (2) provide funds for capital purposes (equipment, buildings, or endowment); (3) support institutional scholarship funds; or (4) fund those standard course or curriculum development activities normally covered by institutional budgets. (This does not include special course or curriculum development efforts that would involve unusual expenditures for the institution.) The foundation is less likely to respond to requests for operating funds for an existing college or university program.

Fiscal Information In 1986, Exxon organizations made contributions of $46.1 million in the U.S. and $11.1 million in countries outside the U.S.

Application Information An institution or organization wishing to submit a project for consideration should send the foundation a proposal outline. Guidelines for the proposal outline are available from the foundation.

Deadline(s) There are no specific closing dates for submission of the proposal outline; each will be reviewed as it is received.

179. Federal Council on the Arts and the Humanities

Museum Program, National Endowment for the Arts
1100 Pennsylvania Avenue, NW
Washington, DC 20506
(202) 682-5442

Arts and Artifacts Indemnity

CFDA Program Number 45.201

Program Description The objective of this program is to provide for indemnification against loss or damage for eligible art works, artifacts, and objects: (1) when borrowed from abroad on exhibition in the U.S.; and (2) from the U.S. for exhibition abroad, preferably when there is an exchange exhibition from a foreign country. Certificates of Indemnity will be issued for the following items insuring them against loss or damage: (1) works of art including tapestries, paintings, sculpture, folk art, graphics, and craft arts; (2) manuscripts, rare documents, books, and other printed or published materials; (3) other artifacts or objects; and (4) photographs, motion pictures, or audio and video tapes; which are of educational, cultural, historical or scientific value; and the exhibition of which is certified by the United States Information Agency to be in the national interest.

Sample Grants Thirty-three Certificates of Indemnity were issued in fiscal year 1986 for thirty-three exhibitions insuring $540 million out of a $650 million ceiling. Certificates of Indemnity will be issued in fiscal year 1988 for thirty exhibitions insuring a $650 million ceiling.

Eligibility/Limitations Federal, state, and local government entities, nonprofit agencies, institutions, and individuals may apply.

Fiscal Information No indemnity agreement for a single exhibition shall exceed $75 million. There is a $15,000 deductible for exhibitions of up to $2 million in value; a $25,000 deductible for exhibitions of $2 million to $10 million; and a $50,000 deductible for exhibitions above $10 million. The applicant must assume the deductible for the exhibition. The total amount of indemnities which can be outstanding at any one time is $650 million. The program has a very low loss record; it does not anticipate having to pay any claims.

Application Information Applicants should request guidelines and application forms from: The Museum Program, National Endowment for the Arts.

Deadline(s) The deadlines for receipt of applications are April 1 and October 1 of each year.

180. Federal Express Corporation

Grants and Community Services
P.O. Box 727
Memphis, TN 38194-1850
(901) 369-3600

Grants

Program Description The company directs its philanthropic efforts to health and welfare, education, culture/arts, and civic assistance. Believing in the power of concentrated giving, Federal Express channels the majority of its resources into community service activities and programs servicing the greater Memphis area, where half of its employees are located.

Eligibility/Limitations Nonprofit organizations may be considered for either financial or people support. The organization must show evidence, however, of competent management, low administrative/fund-raising expense ratios, and a non-discriminatory program benefiting broad segments of the community. Corporate funds generally are not available to exclusively tax-supported educational institutions, labor or political organizations, sectarian or religious denominations, or special occasion advertising.

Fiscal Information Corporate financial contributions totaled $2 million in 1986.

Application Information Applicant organizations should first present the project's goals, objectives, and financial needs in writing accompanied by a concisely written proposal that includes: brief description of the organization, including its membership, goals, and objectives, mailing address, zip code, and telephone number; purpose of the project or activity, expected benefits, plan for implementation, area served, and individuals reached; complete financial data, total operating budget by line item, funds already committed, and other funding sources; name and qualifications of person(s) responsible for project implementation; specification of how the Federal Express funds will be used and their impact on the project's success; and a timetable for reporting the project's progress and method for evaluating its effectiveness.

Deadline(s) No deadlines are announced.

181. Leland Fikes Foundation
3206 Republic Bank Tower
Dallas, TX 75201
(214) 754-0144

Grants

Program Description The foundation gives generally to health and welfare, education, cultural programs and organizations, and for medical research, but any project or program may be considered within giving guidelines. The foundation "has such broad interests" that it hesitates to publish guidelines.

Eligibility/Limitations Nonprofit organizations are eligible to apply.

Application Information The foundation encourages applicants to submit concise and complete written proposals in whatever format seems best to the applicant. The foundation does not have application forms, but does expect ordinarily to find the following in a written proposal: a cover letter, written on the organization's letterhead and signed by the chief executive officer of the governing body, which briefly describes the program or project for which funds are needed, the amount of funds requested, and the date by which funds are needed; a copy of all currently applicable letters from the IRS pertaining to tax-exempt status under sections 501(c)(3) and 509(a) of the Internal Revenue Code; the names and affiliations of the organization's board of directors or trustees; a brief history of the organization's work and purpose; a specific description of the program or project for which support is requested; a copy of the organization's total budget for the current year and the year immediately past; appropriate budget information pertaining to the program or project for which funding is requested; information about the principal staff or volunteers who will implement the program or project; the name and phone number of someone who could be contacted for additional information; other funding sources that have responded favorably or currently are considering the program or project for funding; plans for future funding of the program, project, or organization; and plans for evaluating the effectiveness of the project or program.

Deadline(s) Applications for grants are accepted at any time throughout the year.

182. First Bank System Foundation
Community Affairs Department
517 Marquette Avenue
Minneapolis, MN 55402
(612) 370-5080

Grants

Program Description Corporate giving is concentrated primarily in five areas: United Way, human services, arts and culture, civic and community, and education. Grants are pledged generally to programs and causes located in and serving the needs of First Bank System communities. FBS Foundation represents the pooled contribution dollars of all affiliate and branch banks and other affiliates such as trust companies, insurance agencies, leasing companies, etc.

Eligibility/Limitations First Bank System Foundation provides grants to tax-exempt nonprofit organizations in communities where FBS affiliates are located in order to fulfill its commitment of preserving and improving the quality of life. The following requests will not be considered: organizations and causes that do not serve the FBS affiliate geographical area; organizations and programs primarily designed to influence legislation; grants to individuals or organizations that are not designated by the IRS to be 501(c)(3) nonprofits; endowment funds; tickets or tables for benefit purposes; or advertising in programs and annuals for fund-raising and benefit purposes.

Fiscal Information In 1986, First Bank System and its foundations and affiliates made charitable donations totaling over $7.3 million, including over $1.1 million in the arts and culture category.

Application Information Organizations serving the Minneapolis/St. Paul metropolitan area should send a completed FBS application form to: First Bank System Foundation, P.O. Box 522, Minneapolis, MN 55480. Organizations serving Minnesota (non-metro), Montana, North Dakota, South Dakota, Washington, and Wisconsin should send a complete FBS application form to the local FBS affiliate managing officer. Application forms and procedures for applying for a grant are available from the foundation.

Deadline(s) The grants committee meets monthly to consider requests up to $25,000. Requests can be made at any time and are usually decided within ninety days. Capital request grants are considered once per year during the third quarter. Additional capital grant requests will generally not be considered until at least two years have elapsed since the final payment of a previous grant.

183. First Interstate Bank of California Foundation
707 Wilshire Boulevard, W15-3
Los Angeles, CA 90017
(213) 614-3302

Grants

Program Description The foundation is the bank's vehicle for receiving and administering funds to promote, develop, and support exclusively charitable, scientific, literary, and educational activities. Priority is given to four categories of program activities: educational, health and welfare, arts and culture, and urban and civic causes. Arts and culture donations are contributed to the continued development of the visual and performing arts through funding of cultural arts facilities, outstanding performances, exhibits and acquisitions. Aid to urban and civic causes include grants to organizations which help the individual cope with the complexities of urban life. Funds are also distributed to groups whose purpose is to maintain and protect the natural environment.

Eligibility/Limitations Foundation grants are limited to public, nonprofit organizations which possess tax-exempt status as prescribed in Section 501(c)(3) of the Internal Revenue Code and who serve without any form of discrimination with regards to race, sex, age, religion, physical handicap, or national origin. Organizations must rely on private support for the bulk of their operating revenue. In general, the foundation limits its philanthropic efforts to support programs in those communities in which First Interstate is located. The foundation will not support organizations which represent strictly sectarian, fraternal, veterans, religious, social, or athletic purposes, or organizations which are supported in part or in whole by the United Fund or other federated subsidiary. In addition, the foundation will not make grants to individuals.

Fiscal Information In 1986, the foundation made over $2.2 million in contributions.

Application Information A written request for an application should be directed to: Secretary-Treasurer, First Interstate Bank of California Foundation, 707 Wilshire Boulevard-15th Floor, Los Angeles, CA 90017.

Deadline(s) No deadlines are announced.

184. The Fluor Foundation
Community Affairs Coordinator
3333 Michelson Drive
Irvine, CA 92730
(714) 975-2000

Grants

Program Description The Fluor Foundation has been established in order to handle philanthropic matters for the Fluor Corporation. Contributions are given in the areas of education, health and welfare, cultural activities, and civic programs.

Eligibility/Limitations The foundation does not support the endeavors of individuals, medical research, guilds, auxiliaries, support groups. It is the policy of the foundation to consider contribution requests from nonprofit, 501(c)(3) organizations as determined by the IRS. These organizations must be located in the communities where Fluor has permanent offices. Contribution requests from national organizations will only be considered when local organizations do not exist.

Fiscal Information Contributions in 1986 totaled over $1.2 million.

Application Information The proper procedure for financial consideration is to submit a letter of introduction explaining your purpose and goals, the amount you are requesting, and how the grant will be used. If the request falls within foundation guidelines, a contribution request application will be forwarded.

Deadline(s) No deadlines are announced.

185. FMC Foundation
200 East Randolph Drive
Chicago, IL 60601
(312) 861-6135

Grants

Program Description The FMC Foundation was incorporated in 1953 for the purpose of receiving, administering, and expending funds "for charitable, scientific, educational, and cultural purposes in the furtherance of the public welfare and the well-being of mankind." The foundation makes grants in the following general categories: health and welfare, education, community improvement, urban affairs, public issues/economic education, and other. Grants for community improvement include support for youth groups, cultural organizations, and civic groups in plant communities.

Eligibility/Limitations Contributions provide assistance to charitable and educational organizations that strive to improve communities in which FMC employees live and work, and improve the environment in which FMC does business. Contributions are made to organizations and institutions that have proven their effectiveness in producing results, that have a broad base of community support, and that qualify under Section 501(c)(3) of the Internal Revenue Code. Priority is given to organizations and institutions that promote the values of the free enterprise system The link between employees and community organizations and educational institutions is an important criterion for giving. Grants are made in communities where FMC has a significant number of employees.

Fiscal Information In 1986, contributions totaled over $2 million, with 15-20 percent going to the community improvement category.

Application Information Applications must be submitted in a typewritten letter not more than two pages containing: a brief description of the organization and a statement of the organization's activities and programs; request for a specific amount of money with an explanation of how funds will be used; and, if the request is to support a specific program or project, the purpose of the project, the location, and the timetable. The foundation discourages the submission of unsolicited and voluminous supporting materials. If, on the basis of the brief description outlined above, funding from the FMC appears possible, the foundation will request additional information.

Deadline(s) No deadlines are announced. The board of directors meets regularly to consider requests.

186. Folger Shakespeare Library
Fellowship Committee
201 East Capitol Street, SE
Washington, DC 20003
(202) 544-4600

NEH Senior Fellowships and Folger Senior Fellowships

Program Description A limited number of NEH Senior Resident Fellowships and Folger Senior Fellowships are available to senior scholars who are pursuing research projects appropriate to the collections of the Folger. The Folger Library houses one of the world's finest collections of Renaissance books and manuscripts. Its principal collections are in the following areas: Shakespeareana; English, American, and European literature and drama (1500-1800); English, American, and continental history (1500-1715); political, economic, and legal history (1500-1715); history of philosophy, art, music, religion, science and medicine, and exploration (1500-1715). Applications are welcome in all areas covered by the Folger collection for work on projects which draw significantly on Folger holdings.

Eligibility/Limitations Senior scholars who have made substantial contributions in their fields of research and who are pursuing research projects appropriate to the collections of the Folger are eligible to apply.

Fiscal Information Fellowships are for a period of six to nine months and carry stipends of $13,750 to $20,625.

Application Information Applicants should submit five copies of both a 500-word description of the research project and curriculum vitae including a list of publications. Applicants should also have three letters of reference sent directly to the fellowship committee.

Deadline(s) The deadline for application is November 1.

Additional Information Short-term postdoctoral fellowships with stipends of up to $1,500 per month for a term of one to three months are available. A completed application will consist of three copies of the applicant's curriculum vitae and three copies of a 500-word description of the research project plus three letters of recommendation submitted directly to the fellowship committee. The deadline for application is March 1.

187. The Ford Foundation
320 East 43rd Street
New York, NY 10017
(212) 573-5000

Grants

Program Description The Ford Foundation's domestic and international work is coordinated within six areas of general concern: urban poverty; rural poverty and resources; human rights and social justice; governance and public policy; education and culture; and international affairs. In the U.S., the foundation's work in education has three principal objectives: broadening access to learning and improving the effectiveness of programs that serve disadvantaged groups; deepening the engagement of faculty in their teaching; and strengthening curricula and curricular resources in selected fields. Support for the arts in the U.S. has two major goals: to assist the development of new work and innovative forms of expression in the performing arts and to enhance pluralism and diversity in the arts. Overseas, the foundation assists programs to preserve and interpret traditional cultures and to enhance their contributions to contemporary society. The foundation is also deeply involved in work on a range of domestic and international issues, including the efficacy of government, the quality of education, the vitality of cultural pursuits, world peace and interdependency, and the rights of individuals in free and closed societies.

Sample Grants For outreach activities aimed at increasing membership and support of this Hispanic arts institution, $50,000 to Friends of the Barrio Museum, New York, NY (1987). For equipment and supplies for the academy's conservation laboratory and for training of archivists, $60,000 to National Academy of History, Peru (1987). For the Museum of Contemporary Hispanic Art, $50,000 to Friends of Puerto Rico, New York, NY (1987). To microfilm and repair rare manuscripts that record the early history of Christianity in Ethiopia, $175,000 (two-year supplement) to the Government of Ethiopia (Ministry of Culture and Sports) and $30,000 to St. John's University, MN (1987). For a survey of Black and Hispanic art museums, $84,040 to Studio Museum of Harlem, New York, NY (1986). To establish an archive of the records of El Teatro

Campesino, and of the papers of its founder, playwright-director Luis Valdez, $135,673 over three years to University of California, Santa Barbara (1986).

Eligibility/Limitations Activities supported by foundation grants must be charitable, educational, or scientific as defined under the appropriate provisions of the U.S. Internal Revenue Code and treasury regulations. Most of the foundation's grant funds are given to organizations. Although the foundation also makes grants to individuals, such grants are few in number relative to demand; limited to research, training, and other activities related to the foundation's program interests; and subject to certain limitations and procedural requirements of the U.S. Internal Revenue Code. In the main, foundation grants to individuals are awarded either through publicly announced competitions or on the basis of nominations from universities and other nonprofit institutions.

Fiscal Information The program budget for 1988-1989, $505 million, represents an increase of 17 percent over the budget for the previous biennium. The program budget includes a general reserve, which serves as a flexible instrument for meeting unanticipated needs and responding to unusual program opportunities.

Application Information Before any detailed formal application is made, a brief letter of inquiry is advisable in order to determine whether the foundation's present interests and funds permit consideration of the proposal. There is no application form. Proposals should set forth: objectives; the proposed program for pursuing objectives; qualifications of persons engaged in the work; a detailed budget; present means of support and status of applications to other funding sources; and legal and tax status.

Deadline(s) Applications are considered throughout the year.

188. Ford Motor Company Fund
The American Road, P.O. Box 1899
Dearborn, MI 48121-1899
(313) 845-8711

Grants

Program Description The fund contributes to the betterment and improvement of mankind through grants to organizations operating exclusively for charitable, scientific, literary, or educational purposes, primarily in geographic areas of interest to the fund. A major segment of the fund's activities in these communities concern grants in support of cultural organizations, United Way, urban affairs projects, social welfare, educational institutions, and selected national charities and associations.

Eligibility/Limitations Grants are made only to organizations and institutions and never directly to individuals.

Fiscal Information Contributions in 1986 totaled over $12.3 million.

Application Information Proposals are generally submitted in brief narrative form, and, if the project appears to be in the fund's area of interest, further data and detailed exhibits will be requested. For applicants interested in more detailed information, an annual report on the fund's activities is available for a $3.00 charge.

Deadline(s) No deadlines are announced.

189. Gannett Foundation, Inc.
Lincoln Tower
Rochester, NY 14604
(716) 262-3315

Community Priority Program

Program Description The Community Priorities Program (CPP), established in 1981, is the foundation's single largest competitive grant program. It is designed to identify a community's most pressing problems and propose projects to address them. These priorities vary from community to community, and from year to year, and are determined by a community-based ascertainment process or needs assessment. On occasion, the foundation will limit proposals to a special topic.

Eligibility/Limitations The foundation makes grants only in communities served by Gannett Co., Inc. subsidiaries. As a general rule, grants are not made to: individuals, or organizations not determined by the U.S. Internal Revenue Service to be nonprofit and tax-exempt; local organizations not located in Gannett Co., Inc.-served communities; endowment funds; national or religious organizations not related to journalism; or multiple-year campaigns.

Fiscal Information CPP awards range in amount from about $20,000 to a maximum of $150,000; in recent years these grants totaled more than $2 million annually.

Application Information Each individual ascertainment process, conducted under guidelines developed by the foundation, draws upon the expertise and input of community representatives from all walks of life who know the community and its needs. Contact the foundation for additional information.

Deadline(s) The foundation accepts proposals at any time throughout the year. Its executive committee approves grants monthly and the full board of trustees meets quarterly. Applicants should plan on 90 to 120 days for processing and a decision.

Additional Information Decisions to compete in CPP, the types of projects submitted, and the organization(s) chosen to carry them out are the individual responsibilities of Gannett Co., Inc. local CEOs. Individual organizations, therefore, may not apply directly to the foundation for CPP awards.

190. Gannett Foundation, Inc.
Lincoln Tower
Rochester, NY 14604
(716) 262-3315

Local Grants

Program Description In its local grant program, the Gannett Foundation funds a wide range of community-based projects designed to address many needs. The local grants support a broad array of efforts to help all kinds of people live healthier, safer, and more productive and fulfilling lives. While there is a great diversity of purpose among local grants, the foundation requires that at least one-third of each area's local grants address key community problems identified as part of each area's Community Priorities Program ascertainment process.

Sample Grants For a reception, interim report, and publication of a book in connection with the institution's international symposium on the bicentennial of the U.S. Constitution in May 1987, $39,500 to Smithsonian Institution, Washington, DC (1987).

Eligibility/Limitations The foundation makes local grants only in communities served by Gannett Co., Inc. subsidiaries. As a general rule, grants are not made to: individuals, or organizations not determined by the U.S. Internal Revenue Service to be nonprofit and tax-exempt; local organizations not located in Gannett Co., Inc.-served communities; endowment funds; national or religious organizations not related to journalism; or multiple-year campaigns.

Fiscal Information Traditionally, most local grants are relatively small, averaging less than $4,000 each.

Application Information If a local nonprofit organization wishes to apply for a grant, it should contact the Gannett Co., Inc. chief executive officer in the community for additional information. Grant applications must be in writing. They can be in either letter or proposal form, and elaborate presentations or personal interviews are not required. However, the following information is needed: the project's purpose and cost; amount requested from the foundation; completion date or timetable; other sources of revenue, actual or anticipated, and budgeted expenditures; background on the organization's general operations and personnel responsible for the project; and documentation of the organization's IRS tax-exempt status.

Deadline(s) The foundation accepts proposals at any time throughout the year. Its executive committee approves grants monthly and the full board of trustees meets quarterly. Applicants should plan on 90 to 120 days for processing and a decision.

Additional Information The Gannett Foundation periodically supports a number of special projects. These grants differ from the foundation's local grant programs in several ways. Often they reflect programmatic interests that are more national in scope, or at least extend to programs operating in a number of Gannett Co., Inc.-served communities. These grants are usually larger in amount and normally represent unusual, one-time funding opportunities related to the foundation's historic or current interests. Occasionally the foundation starts a program and seeks a grantee or grantees to operate it; less frequently the proposal comes unsolicited to the foundation. The nature of these special projects varies from year to year. Information about them can be found in the foundation's annual reports.

191. General Electric Foundations
3135 Easton Turnpike
Fairfield, CT 06431
(202) 373-3216

Program Description The foundations seek to improve the way we educate our young, care for our health, protect our natural environment, nurture our arts, assist people and communities whose jobs have been lost to competition, and provide for those least able to provide for themselves. The role of the foundations is to stimulate change in all these areas. The foundations see their grants as "risk capital" seeding the ideas of those whose imagination and drive are already at work.

Eligibility/Limitations The foundations do not award scholarships or fellowships directly to individuals, nor do they support requests from individuals for research or study grants. Assistance is not customarily provided for capital, endowment, or other special purpose campaigns.

Fiscal Information Foundation grants totaled over $17.4 million in 1985.

Application Information The foundations do not have formal grant application forms. Requests for funding should be made by letter and should include the following information: brief description of the organization, including its legal name, its primary purpose and history; amount of grant request and how it will be used; clear statement of the purpose of the organization's program(s), including the benefits it is expected to provide, and the official contact person; budget information; any additional factual information related to the organization or the request that may be useful for evaluation (e.g., list of support from other donors); and documents affirming that the organization is exempt from federal income tax under section 501(c)(3) of the Internal Revenue Code.

Deadline(s) No deadlines are announced.

192. General Foods
Corporate Contributions & The General Foods Fund, Inc.
250 North Street
White Plains, NY 10625
(914) 335-7961

Corporate Contributions

Program Description General Foods' Contributions Program consists of cash contributions made directly by General Foods Corporation and its U.S. and foreign subsidiaries and grants made by The General Foods Fund, Inc. Gifts are made at the local and national levels. GF supports programs or projects in the following categories: education in nutrition and the food sciences, general education, socio-economic development, cultural affairs, and public policy and food industry issues. In the cultural affairs category, GF assists local civic and cultural organizations and programs, including performing arts, museums, libraries, parks, and zoos. On a highly selective basis, GF contributes to nationally prominent performing arts companies, and cultural organizations and programs.

Sample Grants For general support, $10,000 to Whitney Museum of Art, New York, NY (1986). For capital campaigns, $50,000 to New York Zoological Society, New

York, NY (1986). For general support, $45,000 to American Museum of Natural History, New York, NY (1986). For a capital program, $37,500 to Binder Park Zoological Society, Battle Creek, MI (1986).

Eligibility/Limitations General Foods and subsidiaries intend to support nonprofit, tax-exempt organizations and programs which: address needs, issues, and concerns of society consistent with GF's contributions policy and program objectives; benefit a broad segment of the community served; through responsible sponsorship and competent management have demonstrated their effectiveness and/or promise for producing desired results in the future; hold themselves accountable to donors and beneficiaries, regularly reporting on their financial condition, including sources of funding, fund-raising practices, costs, and administrative expenses; and, if in the U.S., qualify as tax-exempt under Section 501(c)(3) of the Internal Revenue Code. GF will not contribute to: organizations which discriminate by race, color, or national origin; religious organizations or activities for the propagation of a particular faith or creed; individuals; or goodwill advertising. GF prefers not to make donations for capital or endowment funds, memorial purposes, testimonial dinners, conferences, or related travel expenses.

Fiscal Information Annual contributions and grants combined totaled $9.9 million in 1986.

Application Information All requests and proposals should be in brief and concise written form, stating the purpose for which funds are sought and containing a brief description of the sponsoring organization, its history, leadership, services offered, constituencies served, accomplishments, current financial statements, support sources, and evidence of tax-exempt status. Where applicable—primarily in local communities—the extent of actual or potential use of facilities and services by employees of GF and/or subsidiary companies and their families should be furnished. Requests for support in local GF communities should be addressed to the senior official at the GF subsidiary unit. Requests for support of organizations and programs of national scope, and specifically for education in nutrition and food sciences, general education, and public policy and food industry issues should be addressed to the secretary of the Corporate Contributions Committee, General Foods Corporation, White Plains, NY 10625.

Deadline(s) No deadlines are announced.

193. General Mills Foundation
P.O. Box 1113
Minneapolis, MN 55440
(612) 540-3337

Grants

Program Description The General Mills Foundation originally focused its primary attention on education, but in 1969 widened its range of interest to include the areas of social service, health, cultural affairs, and civic affairs. Its current giving favors those communities where substantial numbers of General Mills employees live and work, and favors grants that address the current needs of families, children, and the disadvantaged.

Sample Grants For a young Minnesota artists touring exhibition, $7,500 to University of Minnesota Foundation, University Art Museum, Minneapolis, MN (1987). For general support, $35,000 to Science Museum of Minnesota, St. Paul, MN (1987). For support of the United States Holocaust Memorial Museum $5,000 to the United States Holocaust Memorial Council, Washington, DC (1987).

Eligibility/Limitations It is the practice of the foundation to make grants to organizations that have secured their own 501(c)(3) and 509(a) Internal Revenue Service rulings and not to make "pass-through" grants to fiscal agents for expenditure by another agency. The foundation does not make grants to: individuals; support travel, either by groups or individuals; basic or applied research; for-profit organizations; or advertising. Generally, the foundation will not make grants to: subsidize publications; support conferences, seminars, workshops, or symposia, endowment campaigns, or capital funds; or testimonial dinners or fund-raisers. In distributing its grants, the foundation gives most of its attention to those communities in which its parent company has a major facility and a substantial number of employees.

Fiscal Information Total grants by General Mills Foundation in 1987 were over $6.6 million.

Application Information Proposals to the foundation do not require a prescribed application form. A brief letter, with adequate documentation, is an acceptable application. Such a letter should include: a description of the purpose for which the grant is sought; specific details on how this purpose will be achieved by the grant; description of the constituency which will benefit from the project; evidence that there is a need for the activity or project; evidence that the persons proposing a project are able to carry it to completion; a planned method for evaluating the proposed program after its completion; a specific budget for the project, as well as the operating budget for the organization's current fiscal year showing anticipated sources of revenue and expenses; a brief description of the organizations requesting support, with a list of its officers and board members; an audited financial statement and the most recent Form 990 (including Schedule A); a major donor list for the most recent and the current fiscal years listing the amount of support from each donor and sources of assured or anticipated support for the project proposed; and evidence that the organization requesting support has been granted tax-exemption under Section 501(c)(3) of the Internal Revenue Code and is not a private foundation within the meaning of Section 509(a). The foundation earnestly requests that all initial inquiries from prospective applicants be made by mail, not by telephone or by personal visits to the foundation office.

Deadline(s) The General Mills Foundation trustees meet periodically throughout the year. There is, therefore, no "best" time to submit applications to the foundation.

194. General Motors Foundation, Inc.
General Motors Building, Room 13-145
3044 West Grand Boulevard
Detroit, MI 48202-3091
(313) 556-4260

Grants

Program Description The General Motors Foundation makes contributions to local and national organizations. With regard to local contributions, the foundation places primary emphasis on communities in which a significant number of GM employees work and live. Similarly, contributions are made to national organizations that have a broad appeal and are recognized for their excellence. The categories of primary interest to the foundation are education and community relations. Included in the latter category are support for health and welfare, cultural, and various other activities.

Eligibility/Limitations The foundation contributes only to publicly supported organizations exempt from federal income tax under section 501(c)(3) of the Internal Revenue Code. The foundation does not generally support endowments or special interest groups or projects.

Fiscal Information In 1986, combined charitable and educational contributions from General Motors and the General Motors Foundation totaled $61.2 million.

Application Information Contribution requests should include: a statement summarizing the expected use of the proposed grant; a copy of the organization's 501(c)(3) IRS determination letter; historical organizational information; detailed budget information for the previous three years; a detailed budget proposal; a list of major annual contributors for the previous three years; and a brief description of the organization's activities and operations for the current year.

Deadline(s) No deadlines are announced.

195. General Services Administration
Property Management Division
Federal Supply Service
Washington, DC 20406
(703) 557-1234

Donation of Federal Surplus Personal Property

CFDA Program Number 39.003

Program Description The objective of this program is to transfer surplus property to the states for donation to state and local public agencies for public purposes or to certain nonprofit, tax-exempt education and public health activities and programs for older individuals; to public airports; and to educational activities of special interest to the armed forces.

Eligibility/Limitations State participation is contingent upon the acceptance by the General Services Administration (GSA) of a state plan of operation in conformance with Public Law 94-519. This state plan must establish a state agency which is responsible for the distribution of federal surplus personal property to eligible recipients within the state on a fair and equitable basis. Eligible donee categories for the distribution of property through the state agencies are defined as: (1) public agencies and (2) nonprofit, tax-exempt activities such as schools, colleges, universities, public libraries, and museums.

Fiscal Information The following items are representative of those donated: office machines and supplies, furniture, hardware, textiles, special purpose motor vehicles, boats, airplanes, and construction equipment. In fiscal 1986, surplus personal property with an original government acquisition cost of $375 million was donated; fiscal year 1987 is estimated at $350 million; and fiscal year 1988 is estimated at $376.1 million.

Application Information Initial contacts should be at the regional or local level. Contact the GSA Federal Supply Service Bureau in your area.

Deadline(s) There are no deadlines.

196. The Wallace Alexander Gerbode Foundation
470 Columbus Avenue, Suite 209
San Francisco, CA 94133
(415) 391-0911

Grants

Program Description The foundation's interests generally fall under the following categories: arts, education, environment, health, and urban affairs.

Eligibility/Limitations The foundation is primarily interested in programs and projects impacting the residents of Alameda, Contra Costa, Marin, San Francisco, and San Mateo counties in California and the state of Hawaii. However, the foundation will, on occasion, and as a second priority, award grants to efforts that it finds to be exceptionally compelling in other northern California communities. The foundation generally does not support: direct services, deficit budgets, general operating funds, building and equipment funds, general fund-raising campaigns, religious purposes, publications, scholarships and grants to individuals.

Fiscal Information Grants in 1986 totaled over $1.6 million.

Application Information The preferred form of contact is a letter of inquiry with a short description of the project and a proposed budget.

Deadline(s) Applications are accepted on an ongoing basis.

197. The Getty Center for the History of Art and the Humanities
401 Wilshire Boulevard, Suite 400
Santa Monica, CA 90401-1455
(213) 458-9811

Dissertation Residencies

Program Description The Getty Center for the History of Art and the Humanities is an institution dedicated to the research in the history of art broadly conceived as an integral part of human history and society. It brings together art historians and scholars in the social sciences and the humanities to foster the critical reexamination of the meaning of art in cultures past and present. Students are chosen according to qualifications and current departmental and scholarly projects. Students spend the residency at the Getty Center, pursuing their own research on topics in which the center's resources are particularly strong.

Eligibility/Limitations Eligible applicants are Ph.D. candidates in the humanities or social sciences working on dissertations in the arts or cultural history of Western Europe, or recent recipients rewriting their dissertations for publication.

Fiscal Information The residency amounts to $15,000 for a full-year period that may begin between July 1 and September 1. Residencies are not renewable.

Application Information Applications must include: a description of the topic of research, including a timetable for thesis completion, a synopsis, and a sample chapter; an official statement from your institution that course work is completed and the qualifying exams have been passed; a copy of a current transcript; a resume, including description of related studies, projects, languages, work experience, and travel; and the names of three references (one of whom is to be outside the area of academic specialization).

Deadline(s) Applications must be postmarked no later than February 15.

198. The Getty Center for the History of Art and the Humanities
401 Wilshire Boulevard, Suite 400
Santa Monica, CA 90401-1455
(213) 458-9811

Internships: MA Students

Program Description The Getty Center for the History of Art and the Humanities is an institution dedicated to the research in the history of art broadly conceived as an integral part of human history and society. It brings together art historians and scholars in the social sciences and the humanities to foster the critical reexamination of the meaning of art in cultures past and present. Students are chosen according to qualifications and current departmental and scholarly projects. The purpose of the internship program is to provide training and educational experiences for persons planning a career of scholarship or administration in the arts or humanities. Interns will be assigned to one of the center's departments: the Library Photo Archive, the Archives, the History of Art and Administration, or Visiting Scholars.

Eligibility/Limitations Applicants must be MA candidates currently enrolled in a university program.

Fiscal Information Internships are for nine months, starting in September, and carry a stipend of $23,000. They are not renewable.

Application Information Applications should include a letter stating reasons for interest in the program; a copy of a current transcript; a resume including a description of applicable course work, languages, work experience, and travel; and the names of three references (one of whom is to be outside the area of academic specialization).

Deadline(s) Applications must be postmarked no later than February 15.

199. The J. Paul Getty Trust
1875 Century Park East, Suite 2300
Los Angeles, CA 90067
(213) 277-9188

Conservation: Conservation of Major Works of Art

Program Description The J. Paul Getty Trust is a private operating foundation with programs in the visual arts and related areas of the humanities. The purpose of the grant program is to make possible work of vital importance to the visual arts and related areas of the humanities for which resources are limited. It supports projects throughout the world involving research in the history of art and the humanities, advancement of the understanding of art, and conservation. In order to increase the level and quality of art conservation around the world, the trust supports the treatment of major works of art. Proposals will be evaluated on the basis of the aesthetic significance of the works of art, the appropriateness of the conservation plan, the qualifications of the conservator, and the institution's long-range plans for the conservation of its collection.

Eligibility/Limitations Any institution with an ongoing exhibition program, open to the public on a regular basis, may apply for a matching grant for conservation of works of art in the permanent collection. Proposals are accepted from institutions but not from individuals.

Fiscal Information While grants may vary based on the requirements of the particular project, they do not usually exceed $50,000. These grants, which require a one-to-one match, are available for up to three years in order to bring outside conservation experts in-house or to fund work by regional laboratories or by qualified conservators.

Application Information Before any proposal is developed, a preliminary letter (not more than two pages) describing the project and an outline of its general financial requirements should be submitted. The trust will respond with an initial determination as to whether or not a full proposal should be submitted.

Deadline(s) There are no specific deadlines.

Additional Information Treatment reports and photographic documentation submitted with the final report on the project will become part of the Getty Conservation Institute's Documentation Program archive.

200. The J. Paul Getty Trust
1875 Century Park East, Suite 2300
Los Angeles, CA 90067
(213) 277-9188

Conservation: Libraries

Program Description The J. Paul Getty Trust is a private operating foundation with programs in the visual arts and related areas of the humanities. The purpose of the grant program is to make possible work of vital importance to the visual arts and related areas of the humanities for which resources are limited. It supports projects throughout the world involving research in the history of art and the humanities, advancement of the understanding of art, and conservation. In order to increase the level and quality of art conservation around the world, the trust supports specialized conservation libraries. Grants may support library acquisitions and related staff and services and projects to organize and make accessible existing conservation archives.

Eligibility/Limitations Only an institution engaged in training activity, which has an existing conservation library systematically collected and organized to provide a research service to conservators, is eligible for support.

Fiscal Information While grants may vary based on the requirements of the particular project, they do not usually exceed $50,000.

Application Information Before any proposal is developed, a preliminary letter (not more than two pages) describing the project and an outline of its general financial requirements should be submitted. The trust will respond with an initial determination as to whether or not a full proposal should be submitted.

Deadline(s) There are no specific deadlines.

201. The J. Paul Getty Trust
1875 Century Park East, Suite 2300
Los Angeles, CA 90067
(213) 277-9188

Conservation: Publications

Program Description The J. Paul Getty Trust is a private operating foundation with programs in the visual arts and related areas of the humanities. The purpose of the grant program is to make possible work of vital importance to the visual arts and related areas of the humanities for which resources are limited. It supports projects throughout the world involving research in the history of art and the humanities, advancement of the understanding of art, and conservation. In order to increase the level and quality of art conservation activities around the world, the trust supports the publication of manuscripts valuable to the conservation profession.

Eligibility/Limitations Support is available for publications that further knowledge of conservation science and practice. Eligible projects include: book-length manuscripts; collected papers from symposia; special issues of journals; and enhancements of journal articles. Only completed manuscripts already accepted for publication will be considered. Exceptions to this policy are special issues of journals, which need not be completed prior to submission.

Application Information Further details about the publication grants are explained in special guidelines available from the trust. For an application form and specific guidelines, contact the Publication Grants program of the trust.

Deadline(s) There are no specific guidelines.

202. The J. Paul Getty Trust
1875 Century Park East, Suite 2300
Los Angeles, CA 90067
(213) 277-9188

Conservation: Surveys of the Conservation Needs of Art Museums

Program Description The J. Paul Getty Trust is a private operating foundation with programs in the visual arts and related areas of the humanities. The purpose of the grant program is to make possible work of vital importance to the visual arts and related areas of the humanities for which resources are limited. It supports projects throughout the world involving research in the history of art and the humanities, advancement of the understanding of art, and conservation. In order to increase the level and quality of art conservation activities around the world, the trust supports surveys to determine the conservation needs of art museum collections. Support is available for surveys to analyze the conservation requirements of art collections in a single institution or group of institutions.

Eligibility/Limitations Single institutions or groups of institutions are eligible to apply.

Fiscal Information While grants vary based on the requirements, they do not usually exceed $50,000. They may extend over multi-year periods.

Application Information Applications must include the qualifications of the conservator who will undertake the survey, a description of the collection, and a plan for future implementation of the survey results. Before any proposal is developed, a preliminary letter (not more than two pages) describing the project and an outline of its general financial requirements should be submitted. The trust will respond with an initial determination as to whether or not a full proposal should be submitted.

Deadline(s) There are no specific deadlines.

203. The J. Paul Getty Trust
1875 Century Park East, Suite 2300
Los Angeles, CA 90067
(213) 277-9188

Conservation: Training

Program Description The J. Paul Getty Trust is a private operating foundation with programs in the visual arts and related areas of the humanities. The purpose of the grant program is to make possible work of vital importance to the visual arts and related areas of the humanities for which resources are limited. It supports projects throughout the world involving research in the history of art and the humanities, advancement of the understanding of art, and conservation. In order to increase the level and quality of art conservation activities around the world, the trust supports the training of young conservators.

Eligibility/Limitations Training programs that integrate art history, science, and conservation practice are eligible for consideration. Museums and regional conservation centers are also eligible to apply for support of internships. Applications for support of a specific individual may be submitted only by a sponsoring institution.

Fiscal Information While grants vary based on the requirements of the particular project, they do not usually exceed $50,000 a year. Proposals may include support for visiting faculty, acquisition of resource materials, and first- and second-year internships.

Application Information Before any proposal is developed, a preliminary letter (not more than two pages) describing the project and an outline of its general financial requirements should be submitted. The trust will respond with an initial determination as to whether or not a full proposal should be submitted.

Deadline(s) There are no specific deadlines.

204. The J. Paul Getty Trust
1875 Century Park East, Suite 2300
Los Angeles, CA 90067
(213) 277-9188

Documentation and Interpretation of Art Museum Collections: Cataloguing Projects

Program Description The J. Paul Getty Trust is a private operating foundation with programs in the visual arts and related areas of the humanities. The purpose of the grant program is to make possible work of vital importance to the visual arts and related areas of the humanities for which resources are limited. It supports projects throughout the world involving research in the history of art and the humanities, advancement of the understanding of art, and conservation. In order to assist museums to develop their collections as both scholarly and educational resources, the trust supports research projects to catalogue works of art in permanent collections. Proposals will be evaluated on the basis of the significance of the collection, the qualifications of the scholars/curators involved, a realistic plan for the implementation of the project, and the way in which the results of the research will be made available to the broader scholarly community. The institution's demonstrated commitment to the cataloguing of its collection will also be a consideration.

Eligibility/Limitations Cataloguing projects that result in full documentation of an art collection are eligible for consideration. Inventories, checklists, or summary catalogues are not eligible.

Fiscal Information While grants vary based on the requirements of the particular project, they do not usually exceed $50,000 a year. Awards may be made for up to two years for the following: support for a visiting scholar/curator to work on a particular aspect of a museum's collection and funds for a substitute position so that staff members may undertake catalogue research. Related costs may be included in the grant request. Cataloguing grants are not intended to include publication of the results. However, a finished manuscript may be eligible for support under the publication grant category of the trust's grant programs.

Application Information Before any proposal is developed, a preliminary letter (not more than two pages) describing the project and an outline of its general financial requirements should be submitted. The trust will respond with an initial determination as to whether or not a full proposal should be submitted.

Deadline(s) There are no specific deadlines.

205. The J. Paul Getty Trust

1875 Century Park East, Suite 2300
Los Angeles, CA 90067
(213) 277-9188

Documentation and Interpretation of Art Museum Collections: Education Programs

Program Description The J. Paul Getty Trust is a private operating foundation with programs in the visual arts and related areas of the humanities. The purpose of the grant program is to make possible work of vital importance to the visual arts and related areas of the humanities for which resources are limited. It supports projects throughout the world involving research in the history of art and the humanities, advancement of the understanding of art, and conservation. In order to assist museums to develop their collections as both scholarly and educational resources, the trust supports education projects that make art works more understandable to the general public. Examples of eligible projects are explanatory labels, self-guides, handbooks, on-site audiovisual programs, and other projects that create a permanent resource for the institution. Proposals will be evaluated on the basis of the content of the program, the plan for its implementation, its potential as a model for other institutions, and the institution's long-term financial commitment to sustain a serious level of educational activity.

Eligibility/Limitations The trust will consider support for programs that enhance the general public's appreciation and understanding of permanent collections. Projects should involve curators as well as educators. Outside experts may be brought in for extended periods of time.

Fiscal Information While grants vary based on the requirements of the particular project, they do not usually exceed $50,000 a year. Awards may be made for up to three years. Lectures, symposia, and workshops are not eligible for support.

Application Information Before any proposal is developed, a preliminary letter (not more than two pages) describing the project and an outline of its general financial requirements should be submitted. The trust will respond with an initial determination as to whether or not a full proposal should be submitted.

Deadline(s) There are no specific deadlines.

206. The J. Paul Getty Trust

1875 Century Park East, Suite 2300
Los Angeles, CA 90067
(213) 277-9188

Scholarship in the History of Art and the Humanities: Archival Projects

Program Description The J. Paul Getty Trust is a private operating foundation with programs in the visual arts and related areas of the humanities. The purpose of the grant program is to make possible work of vital importance to the visual arts and related areas of the humanities for which resources are limited. It supports projects throughout the world involving research in the history of art and the humanities, advancement of the understanding of art, and conservation. In order to develop the relationship between art history and other disciplines of the humanities and to further the vitality of advanced research in these areas, the trust supports projects to organize selected archival holdings of major importance to the field of art history. Proposals will be evaluated on the basis of the importance of the materials, the arrangement and catalogue procedures proposed, the qualifications of the project staff, and the commitment of the institution to maintain the collection and make it readily accessible to the scholarly community.

Eligibility/Limitations Only a nonprofit repository that owns the materials may apply. Also eligible for consideration are cooperative proposals from institutions or associations for projects designed to prepare and make accessible registers or archival holdings in a number of repositories.

Fiscal Information While grants vary based on the requirements of the particular project, they do not usually exceed $50,000 a year. Grants may be made for a maximum of three years and are nonrenewable. Requests may include support for a project archivist or archivists, for specialized scholarly consultants to analyze and describe the materials, and for other related project expenses. The institution seeking the grant will be expected to provide facilities and support services as required.

Application Information Before any proposal is developed, a preliminary letter (not more than two pages) describing the project and an outline of its general financial requirements should be submitted. The trust will respond with an initial determination as to whether or not a full proposal should be submitted.

Deadline(s) There are no specific deadlines.

207. The J. Paul Getty Trust
1875 Century Park East, Suite 2300
Los Angeles, CA 90067
(213) 277-9188

Scholarship in the History of Art and the Humanities: Corpora and Other Art Historical Reference Tools

Program Description The J. Paul Getty Trust is a private operating foundation with programs in the visual arts and related areas of the humanities. The purpose of the grant program is to make possible work of vital importance to the visual arts and related areas of the humanities for which resources are limited. It supports projects throughout the world involving research in the history of art and the humanities, advancement of the understanding of art, and conservation. In order to develop the relationship between art history and other disciplines of the humanities, and to further the vitality of advanced research in these areas, the trust supports international projects for the creation of research tools in the field of art history. Projects must be international multi-institutional research efforts that will result in the creation of a corpus of information or a major reference tool useful to a large segment of the art historical community. Proposals will be evaluated on the basis of the scope, feasibility, and organization of the project; its importance to the field in general; and the method proposed for dissemination of information.

Eligibility/Limitations Applications may be made by a sponsoring institution or an international committee if it has registered nonprofit status. Research projects concerned with a single artist, or projects undertaken by a single individual or institution, are not eligible.

Fiscal Information While grants vary based on the requirements of the particular project, they do not usually exceed $50,000 a year. They may extend over multi-year periods.

Application Information Before any proposal is developed, a preliminary letter (not more than two pages) describing the project and an outline of its general financial requirements should be submitted. The trust will respond with an initial determination as to whether or not a full proposal should be submitted.

Deadline(s) There are no specific deadlines.

208. The J. Paul Getty Trust
1875 Century Park East, Suite 2300
Los Angeles, CA 90067
(213) 277-9188

Scholarship in the History of Art and the Humanities: Library and Photo Archive Projects at Centers for Advanced Research in the History of Art

Program Description The J. Paul Getty Trust is a private operating foundation with programs in the visual arts and related areas of the humanities. The purpose of the grant program is to make possible work of vital importance to the visual arts and related areas of the humanities for which resources are limited. It supports projects throughout the world involving research in the history of art and the humanities, advancement of the understanding of art, and conservation. In order to develop the relationship between art history and other disciplines of the humanities, and to further the vitality of advanced research in these areas, the trust supports library and photo archive projects at centers for advanced research in the history of art and the humanities. Grants may be made for library acquisitions and related staff services and for projects to organize and make accessible existing significant photographic archives.

Eligibility/Limitations Only an independent research center, which has its own extensive library holdings in the history of art and architecture and which provides services for scholars internationally, is eligible for support. University and museum libraries do not qualify.

Fiscal Information While grants vary based on the requirements of the particular project, they do not usually exceed $50,000 a year. They may extend for up to four years.

Application Information Before any proposal is developed, a preliminary letter (not more than two pages) describing the project and an outline of its general financial requirements should be submitted. The trust will respond with an initial determination as to whether or not a full proposal should be submitted.

Deadline(s) There are no specific deadlines.

209. The J. Paul Getty Trust
1875 Century Park East, Suite 2300
Los Angeles, CA 90067
(213) 277-9188

Scholarship in the History of Art and the Humanities: Postdoctoral Fellowships

Program Description The Getty Postdoctoral Fellowships are designed to strengthen the history of the visual arts of all periods and areas by supporting the work of outstanding young scholars in the field considered broadly to include other humanistic studies that draw substantially on the materials, methods, and/or findings of art history.

Eligibility/Limitations Scholars who have received their doctorates within the six years prior to applying for a grant and who demonstrate an unusual potential to contribute to knowledge in the history of art and the humanities are eligible to apply.

Fiscal Information All awards normally will provide a $21,000 stipend for the fellow for twelve months and a subvention of up to $4,000 to be allocated to the institution or institutions at which the fellow is based during the year of the award. The program of Getty Fellowships in the History of Art and the Humanities is made possible by a grant from the trust to the Woodrow Wilson National Fellowships Foundation, which administers the fellowship program.

Application Information Inquiries should be addressed to Getty Postdoctoral Fellowships in the History of Art and the Humanities at the address listed above.

Deadline(s) The last date completed applications will be accepted is January 10.

210. The J. Paul Getty Trust

1875 Century Park East, Suite 2300
Los Angeles, CA 90067
(213) 277-9188

Scholarship in the History of Art and the Humanities: Publications

Program Description The J. Paul Getty Trust is a private operating foundation with programs in the visual arts and related areas of the humanities. The purpose of the grant program is to make possible work of vital importance to the visual arts and related areas of the humanities for which resources are limited. It supports projects throughout the world involving research in the history of art and the humanities and advancement of the understanding of art, and conservation. In order to develop the relationship between art history and other disciplines of the humanities, and to further the vitality of advanced research in these areas, the trust supports scholarly publications that disseminate the results of art historical research. Support is available for the publication of a broad range of manuscripts that make an important contribution to research and scholarship in the history of art.

Eligibility/Limitations Eligible projects include the following: manuscripts already accepted for publication that could be substantially improved in quality or reduced in price for wider distribution; scholarly catalogues of major museum collections (support must be requested on a matching basis); special exhibition catalogues that contain new scholarly contributions; completed excavation reports; collected papers from symposia; special issues of journals; and enhancements of journal articles. In addition, support is available on a highly selective basis (and for no more than three years) for start-up costs for new scholarly journals where there is a demonstrated need that is not met by existing publications. Only completed manuscripts already accepted for publication will be considered. Exceptions to this policy are special exhibition catalogues and special issues of journals, which need not be completed prior to submission. Manuscripts from a foreign publisher and/or manuscripts written in a foreign language are eligible for consideration.

Fiscal Information While grants vary based on the requirements of the particular project, they do not usually exceed $50,000 a year. They may extend over multi-year periods.

Application Information Applications should normally be submitted by the publisher. Further details about publication grants are explained in special guidelines available from the trust.

Deadline(s) There are no specific deadlines.

211. Florence J. Gould Foundation

Chahill Gordon & Reindel
Eighty Pine Street
New York, NY 10005
(212) 701-3292

Grants

Program Description The primary focus of the Florence J. Gould Foundation is in the area of French-American cultural affairs.

Sample Grants For a Lucien Clergue exhibition, $5,000 to International Center of Photography, New York, NY (1986). For a Franco-American exhibition to celebrate the Statue of Liberty, $50,000 to The New York Public Library, New York, NY (1986). To the Fine Art Museums of San Francisco Foundation, San Francisco, CA, $750,000 (1986).

Fiscal Information Grants awarded in 1986 totaled over $2.9 million.

Application Information No formal guidelines are available at this time. Inquiries with respect to specific projects should be directed to John R. Young, president of the foundation at the address listed above.

212. Graham Foundation
4 West Burton Place
Chicago, IL 60610
(312) 787-4071

Program Description It is the general policy of the Graham Foundation to limit its activities to matters relating to contemporary architecture, planning, and the study of urban problems.

Eligibility/Limitations Individuals and institutions are eligible to apply. In the case of individuals, consideration is given to those demonstrating mature creative talents and who have specific project objectives.

Application Information The foundation does not require special application forms. Procedures for applying are available upon request from the foundation.

Deadline(s) The foundation does not have a specific funding schedule.

213. Philip L. Graham Fund
1150 Fifteenth Street, NW
Washington, DC 20071
(202) 334-6640

Grants

Program Description The Philip L. Graham Fund was established in 1963 in the District of Columbia as a trust in the memory of the late Philip L. Graham, who was for many years the president of The Washington Post company. The fund has as its purpose the awarding of grants for charitable, scientific, literary, and educational concerns of the kind that were of particular interest to Mr. Graham during his lifetime. Grants are awarded in the following categories: arts and humanities, civic and community, education, health and human services, journalism and communications.

Sample Grants For an $8.5 million capital campaign to finance the building and equipping of a new Science Center and Space Theater/Planetarium, $10,000 to Jacksonville Museum of Arts and Science, Jacksonville, FL (1986). To purchase a computerized information system designed specifically for museums, $24,000 (fulfills pledge of $48,000) to Phillips Collection, Washington, DC (1986). Toward $100 million campaign to build and equip museum and provide for research and education programs, $20,000 (second payment toward pledge of $100,000) to United States Holocaust Memorial Museum, Washington, DC (1986). For Discover Graphics, a museum seminar and studio training program in printmaking for area art students and teachers, $20,000 to Smithsonian Resident Associates, Washington, DC (1986).

Eligibility/Limitations Applications are accepted only from organizations that have been ruled to be tax-exempt under Section 501(c)(3) of the Internal Revenue Code and that are not private foundations as defined in the code. No grants are made to individuals. At the present time, the fund is not accepting proposals for the following types of projects: research; conferences, workshops, seminars, or travel expense; production of films or publications; tickets for benefits or support for fund-raisers; courtesy advertising; national or international purposes or concerns; or annual campaigns. The fund also operates under strict geographical restrictions, making grants primary in the Washington, DC, metropolitan area. To a limited degree and on the initiative of the fund only, grants are also made in communities where The Washington Post Company has significant business interests.

Fiscal Information Grants in 1986 totaled more than $1.7 million.

Application Information Proposals should be brief (a letter format is encouraged) and should contain the following information: a general statement describing the organization, its purpose and its goals; a description of the project for which funding is sought and its anticipated benefits; a budget for the project; the specific amount requested from the fund and a list of other funding sources from which the organization is seeking assistance (if any); a copy of the organization's most recent financial statement; a copy of the IRS determination of the organization's tax status; and if the program is expected to be a continuing one, information on how it will be funded in the future.

Deadline(s) The fund's trustees meet three times each year to decide on grants. Deadlines for these meetings are April 1, August 1, and November 1.

214. Mary Livingston Griggs and Mary Griggs Burke Foundation
1400 Norwest Center, 55 East Fifth Street
Saint Paul, MN 55101
(612) 227-7683

Grants

Program Description The foundation supports projects and programs in the following categories: arts and culture, conservation, education, and social services.

Eligibility/Limitations Applicant organizations must be tax-exempt. Most grants are awarded in St. Paul, MN and New York, NY.

Application Information Grant requests need not take any particular form. The request should, however, make clear the organization's tax-exempt status by inclusion of a copy of the letter issued by the IRS. The request should set out, clearly and concisely, the purposes of the grant, the amount requested, the budget for the project, and whether or not assistance is sought from any other foundation. Include a copy of the latest audited financial statement. If a request for a grant is submitted, six copies of the covering letter should also be included.

Deadline(s) No deadlines are announced.

215. GTE Foundation
One Stamford Forum
Stamford, CT 06904
(203) 965-3620

Grants

Program Description The foundation awards support in the following areas: education, health and welfare, social services, United Way, public affairs, arts and humanities, and international policy. Awards in the arts and humanities category includes support of libraries, museums, and for historic preservation.

Eligibility/Limitations Organizations that are tax-exempt under Section 501(c)(3) of the Internal Revenue Code are eligible for support.

Fiscal Information Contributions in 1985 totaled over $16 million.

Application Information The GTE Foundation is in the process of preparing new guidelines and will make them available after June 1988. Contact the foundation for these guidelines and additional information.

Deadline(s) No deadlines are announced.

216. The Daniel and Florence Guggenheim Foundation
950 Third Avenue
New York, NY 10022
(212) 755-3199

Grants

Program Description The foundation's resources are devoted to the promotion, through charitable and benevolent activities, of the well-being of mankind throughout the world. Of the many grants made since 1924 by the foundation, a large number have been in support of civic, educational, religious, charitable, cultural, and other causes.

Eligibility/Limitations No grants are awarded to individuals.

Application Information Application information is available upon request from the foundation.

Deadline(s) Contact the foundation for deadlines.

217. The Harry Frank Guggenheim Foundation
527 Madison Avenue
New York, NY 10022-4301
(212) 644-4907

Contributions

Program Description From time to time the foundation makes contributions to selected worthy causes, in addition to the awards made in support of its regular programs. Although the purposes of these contributions are generally not central to the foundation's present program of research and study, they fall within the stated general purpose of the foundation: to provide grants for "furthering or improving the physical, mental, or moral condition of humanity."

Sample Grants For their public program of museum exhibits and festivals on the estate itself and outdoor education programs on the nature preserve formed by the surrounding property, $112,500 to the Friends for Long Island's Heritage (1982-1985).

Application Information Unsolicited applications for contributions are not accepted.

218. The Harry Frank Guggenheim Foundation
527 Madison Avenue
New York, NY 10022-4301
(212) 644-4907

Grants to Individuals for Research and Study

Program Description The principal object of this program is to provide seed money to get new projects started rather than to lend continuing support to already well-established endeavors. The foundation gives the individual investigator as much leeway in the choice of problem and method of approach as is consistent with its overall aims and objectives. Whatever the discipline and whatever the method, the principal criteria for support of a project proposed to the foundation are the same: excellence and relevance.

Sample Grants A research grant was awarded in support of cataloguing the papers of Robert Ardrey (1983-1984).

Eligibility/Limitations The foundation makes awards to individuals (or to institutions on behalf of individuals).

Fiscal Information The foundation expects to make most awards in the range of $15,000 to $25,000 a year for periods of one or two years.

Application Information Guidelines and application forms for grants are available from the foundation.

Deadline(s) The biannual deadlines are August 1 and February 1.

219. John Simon Guggenheim Memorial Foundation
90 Park Avenue
New York, NY 10016
(212) 687-4470

Fellowships to Assist Research and Artistic Creation

Program Description In order to improve the quality of education and the practice of the arts and professions, to foster research, and to provide for the cause of better international understanding, the John Simon Guggenheim Memorial Foundation offers fellowships to further the development of scholars and artists by assisting them to engage in research in any field of knowledge and creation in any of the arts, under the freest possible conditions and irrespective of race, color, or creed.

Eligibility/Limitations Fellowships are awarded through two annual competitions: one open to citizens and permanent residents of the United States and Canada, and the other open to citizens and permanent residents of all the other American states, of the Caribbean, the Philippines, and the French, Dutch, and British possessions in the

Western Hemisphere. Fellows are usually between thirty and forty-five years of age, but there are no age limits. The fellowships are awarded to men and women of high intellectual and personal qualifications who have already demonstrated unusual capacity for productive scholarship or unusual creative ability in the arts.

Fiscal Information Appointments are ordinarily made for one year, but in no instance for less than six consecutive months. The amount of each grant will be adjusted to the needs of the fellows, considering their other resources and the purpose and scope of their studies. Members of the teaching profession receiving sabbatical leave on full or part salary are eligible for appointment, as are holders of appointments under the Fulbright program, but Guggenheim Fellowships may not be held concurrently with other fellowships. In 1987, the foundation awarded 273 United States and Canadian fellowships for a total of $6,336,000. There were 3,421 applicants.

Application Information Application forms will be mailed on request.

Deadline(s) Applications for fellowships must be made in writing on or before October 1 by the applicants themselves in the form prescribed. Fellows of the foundation who seek further assistance must apply before October 15 of each year. It should be noted that the foundation does not grant immediate renewals of its fellowships.

220. Hagley Museum and Library
P.O. Box 3630
Wilmington, DE 19807
(302) 658-2400

Grants-in-Aid

Program Description The Hagley Museum and Library announces the availability of grants-in-aid designed to support short-term (two to eight weeks) research in Hagley's imprint, manuscript, pictorial, and artifact collections relating to French history, 1760-1820, and to American history, 1800-1950, with special emphasis on business, industrial, and technological developments in the lower Delaware River Valley area. There is no restriction on the applicant's field of study.

Eligibility/Limitations Grants are available to degree candidates as well as to advanced scholars working in Hagley's areas of collecting and research interest.

Fiscal Information The Grants-in-Aid will not exceed $750 per month.

Application Information To apply, send the following information to the Executive Administrator, Center for the History of Business, Technology, and Society, Hagley Museum and Library: current curriculum vitae or resume; a brief (one to three pages) description of the research project to be pursued at Hagley (be certain to include a discussion of specific collections, artifacts, buildings, gardens or archaeological digs to be studied, and a statement of purpose for the study, whether for publication, exhibition, restoration, etc.); a statement of the period in which you expect to use the grant; and the amount of stipend requested.

Deadline(s) Applications for Grants-in-Aid may be submitted throughout the year and will be processed as received. Awards will be made in February, June, and October.

221. Hagley Museum and Library
P.O. Box 3630
Wilmington, DE 19807
(302) 658-2400

Research Fellowships

Program Description The fellowship program is designed to promote integrative and comparative research into the social context and consequences of industrialization of the U.S. in the century following 1850. The Hagley contains over 160,000 volumes, 20,000 linear feet of manuscript and archival materials, and 350,000 photographs. There are records of hundreds of different Middle-Atlantic businesses, with particular strengths in railroads, electric utilities, iron and steel, shipbuilding, chemicals, coal mining, petroleum refining, and computers. Holdings also include the records of such business organizations as the National Association of Manufacturers and the Conference Board. Approximately 20,000 catalogs document the changing nature of technology and material culture during industrialization.

Eligibility/Limitations Scholars from any humanistic discipline or from related social sciences are encouraged to apply. Under endowment guidelines, NEH fellowships may not be awarded to degree candidates or for study leading to advanced degrees.

Fiscal Information Funded by the National Endowment for the Humanities and the Andrew W. Mellon Foundation, the fellowship carries a maximum stipend of $27,500 for an academic year, and the minimum residency is six months.

Application Information Application forms and additional information are available from the Hagley.

Deadline(s) Completed applications must be received by February 15.

222. The Hall Family Foundations
P.O. Box 419580
Kansas City, MO 64141-6580

Grants

Program Description The Hall Family Foundations concentrate their philanthropic efforts on four specific areas of concern: the needs of young people, particularly in regard to education; the needs of older persons; the economic development of central Kansas City; and the support of major visual and performing arts institutions. Within this final category, the foundations currently focus on the special needs and opportunities of the community's major performing and visual arts institutions. The foundations value programs which provide long-term benefits, encourage strong management, broaden existing funding bases and increase community impact and audience support. Programs that foster cooperation among Kansas City's major arts groups and promote the arts locally are also of interest.

Sample Grants For Oriental art acquisition, $1 million to Nelson-Atkins Museum of Art (1983-1986). Final payment on three-year grant for administrative support, $40,000 (total commitment $121,000) to Nelson-Atkins Museum of Art (1986).

Eligibility/Limitations Grants are made to charitable organizations which qualify as tax-exempt under section 501(c)(3) of the Internal Revenue Code. The foundations do not normally make grants to or for the following: individuals; international or religious organizations; general endowment funds; scholarly or medical research; event promotion; past operating deficits, travel, or conference expenses.

Fiscal Information Grants payable in 1986 totaled over $10.9 million. During fiscal year 1987, the foundations' board of directors made grants in excess of $10 million, with the majority of the recipients located within the greater Kansas City area.

Application Information Initial contact should be by letter, briefly outlining the proposed project or program and the amount requested from the foundations. If the proposal meets the foundations' guidelines and funding priorities, further correspondence containing more specific information will be requested.

Deadline(s) No deadlines are announced. The average period of initial review is six to eight weeks.

223. Hallmark Cards, Inc.
Charitable & Crown Investment 323
2501 McGee, Box 580
Kansas City, MO 64108
(816) 274-8515

Corporate Contribution Program

Program Description Hallmark Cards, Inc., is dedicated to taking an active role in improving the communities in which it operates through its support of causes which contribute to the community's economic and social development. To this end, the company annually commits a portion of its resources to each of its operating facilities to be distributed in ways that will best serve to improve the quality of life in these locations. The company supports a broad range of programs in areas such as education, social welfare, health care, civic affairs, and arts and the humanities. In the area of arts and humanities, interest is expressed through support of local professional arts organizations which have an impact on a broad segment of the community.

Eligibility/Limitations Applicants must be either a charitable or civic organization. An organization qualifies as charitable if it has received a 501(c)(3) designation from the IRS. The company contributes funds mainly in Kansas City and other communities in which Hallmark facilities are located. Generally, the company does not make grants to the following: individuals; religious, fraternal, or international organizations; endowment funds; labor groups; social clubs; or veterans organizations. In addition, funds will generally not be awarded when the purpose is to cover past operating deficits, travel, conferences, scholarly research, charitable advertisements, or mass media campaigns.

Fiscal Information Total contributions in 1986 were over $7 million.

Application Information The preferred method of initial contact is for the grant applicant to submit a letter describing the need, purpose, and general activities of the requesting organization. If the request appears to fall within an area of company interests, and meets the guidelines, additional information may be requested.

Deadline(s) Proposals are accepted and reviewed throughout the year.

224. The Armand Hammer Foundation
10889 Wilshire Boulevard
Los Angeles, CA 90024
(213) 879-1700

Program Description The foundation was established in 1968 by Dr. Hammer to advance the cause of international peace and understanding. The foundation is a private operating foundation with a form of incorporation which limits program funding to those projects in which the foundation is directly involved. The board of trustees has identified programs to support including: a national and international traveling exhibition program drawn from the objects of the Armand Hammer Collections; a program of international exchange exhibitions developed and supervised by foundation staff; the Armand Hammer Cancer Research Prize (administered by others); and the United World College of the American West, located in Las Vegas, New Mexico (administered by others).

Application Information Applicants who believe that their program qualifies for consideration under one of the foundation programs should send a letter to the attention of the director of exhibitions of the foundation outlining as briefly as possible the nature of the program/activity and how the foundation could become involved. Do not send a full proposal. Proposals sent without a preliminary letter will not be given proper consideration.

225. James G. Hanes Memorial Fund/Foundation
c/o Wachovia Bank and Trust Co., N.A., Trustee and Foundation
   Administrator
P.O. Box 3099
Winston-Salem, NC 27150
(919) 770-5269

Grants

Program Description The purposes of the fund/foundation are very broad. Support is granted for a wide range of charitable requests including conservation, local and regional health and education projects, arts and cultural institutions and projects, social service organizations, and community-based programs.

Eligibility/Limitations Grants are disbursed to IRS designated tax-exempt section 501(c)(3) organizations only. Organizations must also have been determined by the

IRS to be public foundations. Although the main thrust of the fund/foundation's efforts is directed toward North Carolina and the Southeast, applications from organizations outside this geographic area will be accepted. In general, grants are awarded for seed money, matching funds, and general purposes.

Fiscal Information In the last few years, annual disbursements have ranged from $1 million to $1.5 million in grants to a wide range of recipients.

Application Information Any qualified organization may apply for a grant by completing the designated application form. Application forms may be obtained from the Charitable Funds Management Section, Wachovia Bank and Trust Company, N.A. at the address above.

Deadline(s) The distribution committee meets quarterly at the end of January, April, July, and October of each year. To be considered, requests with completed application forms must be submitted no later than the first day of the month in which the meeting is held. Requests received after the deadline will be carried over to the next scheduled meeting for consideration.

226. Hawaiian Electric Industries Charitable Foundation
P.O. Box 730
Honolulu, HI 86808-0730

Grants

Program Description In accordance with the Hawaiian Electric Industries mission to be a responsible corporate and individual citizen, the foundation continually assesses the needs of local communities in the areas of education, health and rehabilitation, culture and the arts, social welfare, and youth services.

Eligibility/Limitations The purpose of the foundation is to make grants to appropriate nonprofit organizations primarily within the state of Hawaii. Generally excluded from consideration are requests from political, religious, veterans, or fraternal organizations and requests in support of operational and maintenance activities.

Fiscal Information Contributions granted by the foundation totaled over $492,000 in 1987.

Application Information Written requests for funds should be submitted to the foundation.

Deadline(s) Requests should be submitted prior to December 1 and June 1 for consideration, respectively, at the February and August board of directors meetings.

227. Charles Hayden Foundation
One Bankers Trust Plaza, 130 Liberty Street
New York, NY 10006
(212) 938-0790

Grants

Program Description The foundation makes contributions only to institutions and organizations that serve school-age children from the metropolitan areas of New York City and Boston. Grants are restricted to institutions and organizations that are primarily concerned with the mental, moral, and physical development of youth.

Sample Grants For construction of the Discovery Cove project in the New York Aquarium, $300,000 to New York Zoological Society, Bronx, NY (1986). For relocating the educational department and the Junior Museum in new facilities, $35,000 to Newark Museum Association, Newark, NJ (1986). For an addition to the administration building, $15,000 to Queens Botanical Garden Society, Flushing, Queens, NY (1986). For a new facility at Snug Harbor Cultural Center, $75,000 to Staten Island Children's Museum, Staten Island, NY (1986). For modernization and expansion of exhibits, $150,000 to Museum of Science, Boston, MA (1986). For renovation of school reception center, $250,000 to American Museum of Natural History, New York, NY (1987). For construction of an Educational Building, $75,000 to Brooklyn Botanic Garden Corporation, Brooklyn, NY (1987).

Eligibility/Limitations Grants are awarded only to organizations and institutions that have a current charitable exemption from federal income tax under section 501(c)(3) of the Internal Revenue Code. Grants are not ordinarily made to: organizations that have been awarded a grant from the foundation in the prior two and one half years for the facility for which the grant is dedicated; purchase transportation equipment; individuals; projects intended to raise revenue to offset operating costs; or endowments. If the foundation has declined a grant request, reapplication can be made after a period of six months from the date of the denial letter. The request can be for the same project or for another project.

Fiscal Information Total grants authorized in the fiscal year ended September 30, 1986 were over $5.6 million. This amount was shared by 163 organizations.

Application Information Written applications for grants may be submitted. There is no application form, but applications should include: a concise description of the proposed project, its goals, and the make-up of the youth group to be served; total costs, based on professional estimates; if the request is for less than the total amount, the plans for raising the balance of those costs; if the request is for the full amount, whether or not a lesser amount would be of assistance and how in that event the balance of the funds can be raised from other sources; the sources, if needed, for additional operating funds once the capital project is completed; an audited copy of the most recent financial report; and IRS letter stating that the applicant has a 501(c)(3) tax-exempt status as an organization and is not a private foundation. For first applications, or when the activities of the grant applicant have materially changed, the application should also contain a narrative statement, a brief history of the organization and, if available, a catalog or other printed material concerning the activities of the institution.

Deadline(s) No deadlines are announced.

228. The Hearst Foundations
90 New Montgomery Street, Suite 1212
San Francisco, CA 94105
(415) 543-0400

Grants

Program Description The Hearst Foundation, Inc., was founded in 1945 by publisher/philanthropist William Randolph Hearst. In 1948, the California Charities was established. Soon after Mr. Hearst's death in 1951, the name was changed to the William Randolph Hearst Foundation. Both foundations reflect the philanthropic interests of William Randolph Hearst: social welfare, education, health care, and culture. The foundations have established the following priority areas of interest: programs to aid poverty level and minority groups; education programs with emphasis on private secondary and higher education; health delivery systems and medical research; cultural programs with records of public support; and programs affiliated with religious institutions. Organizations serving larger geographical areas are generally favored over those of a neighborhood or narrow community nature. Charitable goals of the two foundations are essentially the same. For economy they are administered as one. Grant proposals should be addressed to 'ι he Hearst Foundations.

Eligibility/Limitations Grants from the foundations must be used exclusively for charitable purposes within the U.S. and its possessions. Grants are not made to individuals. Grants may not be used for political purposes. The foundations do not purchase tickets, tables, or advertising for fund-raising events. Grants will be made only to tax-exempt organizations that are not private foundations.

Application Information The foundations do not have formal application forms. Proposals need not be elaborate and should include the following: amount requested; brief description of basic needs and objectives of project or program; budget showing project costs and how funds will be used; brief history of organization making request; names and primary affiliations of officers and board members; most recent audited financial report; other actual and potential sources of funding; IRS documentation certifying applicant is tax-exempt under section 501(c)(3) and not a private foundation under section 509(a).

Deadline(s) Board meetings on grant decisions are held in March, June, September, and December. Proposals may be submitted throughout the year.

Additional Information Applicants headquartered east of the Mississippi River should mail appeals to: The Hearst Foundations, 888 Seventh Avenue, 27th Floor, New York, NY 10106, telephone (212) 586-5404. Applicants headquartered west of the Mississippi River should mail appeals to The Hearst Foundations at the address listed above.

229. H. J. Heinz Company Foundation
P.O. Box 57
Pittsburgh, PA 15230
(412) 456-5772

Grants

Program Description Foundation grants frequently reflect concerns of the H.J. Heinz Company, and are made to address problems that confront communities and the nation...to organizations and projects encompassing educational, medical/health related activities, charitable, civic, and cultural endeavors in geographic areas served by the company and/or its affiliates.

Eligibility/Limitations Each applicant must present evidence of a charitable, tax-exempt status, under section 501(c)(3) of the Internal Revenue Code. The foundation does not make grants to individuals, nor does it make travel grants, grants for political campaigns, sectarian religious purposes, or general scholarships/fellowships.

Fiscal Information During 1984 contributions totaled over $3.7 million.

Application Information The foundation does not have a standard application form. Requests should be submitted in a written format describing the program, its objectives and impact, and specifying the amount of funds needed. A budget should be appended, including information about other possible sources of support, and any recent financial statements for the organization.

Deadline(s) The foundation's trustees meet quarterly in July, October, January, and April. Those submitting an application should permit adequate time for consideration prior to the project date/period.

230. Howard Heinz Endowment
301 Fifth Avenue, Suite 1417
Pittsburgh, PA 15222-2494
(412) 391-5122

Grants

Program Description The endowment supports projects in the following areas: the arts, human services, education, health, urban affairs, and international affairs. In the arts category, the endowment supports and encourages the cultural climate in western Pennsylvania. It also continues the policy of funding professional arts organizations on three levels: annual support is provided to seven large arts institutions; periodic support is awarded to middle-size organizations with a proven record of artistic quality; and three-year start-up grants are given to new professional arts groups, some of whom specialize in experimental or nontraditional art.

Sample Grants For a traveling exhibition program, $95,000 to Carnegie Institute Museum of Art (1984). To document, record, and conserve the Margo Lovelace puppet and mask collection, $17,500 to Pittsburgh Children's Museum (1984).

Eligibility/Limitations The endowment generally awards grants to organizations in Pittsburgh and Allegheny County.

Fiscal Information Grants approved in 1984 totaled over $2.9 million.

Application Information To be considered for a grant, an organization should submit a proposal describing the purpose of the grant, the amount requested, the procedures to be employed, the personnel involved, and a complete financial statement. If the proposal is within the endowment's areas of interest, the applicant will be requested to fill out a brief application form relevant to the proposal.

Deadline(s) The trustees of the endowment generally meet two times a year, in the spring and the fall.

231. The William R. and Flora L. Hewlett Foundation
525 Middlefield Road
Menlo Park, CA 94025
(415) 329-1070

Grants

Program Description The foundation's broad purpose, as stated in its articles of incorporation, is to promote the well-being of mankind by supporting selected activities of a charitable, religious, scientific, literary, or educational nature, as well as organizations or institutions engaged in such activities. More particularly, to date the foundation has concentrated its resources on activities in the performing arts, education, particularly at the university and college level, population issues, environmental issues, and more recently, conflict resolution.

Sample Grants For general support, $100,000 to Folger Shakespeare Library, Washington, DC (1986). To implement a cooperative program to convert card catalog records to computer form, $350,000 to Research Libraries Group, Inc., Stanford, CA (1986).

Eligibility/Limitations Normally, the foundation will not consider for support: grants or loans to individuals, grants for basic research, capital construction funds, grants in the medical or health-related fields, or general fund-raising drives. It will not make grants intended directly or indirectly to support candidates for political office or to influence legislation. Although the Hewlett Foundation is a national foundation, with no geographic limit stipulated in its charter, a modest proportion of disbursable funds has been earmarked for projects in the San Francisco Bay Area.

Fiscal Information Grants authorized in 1986 totaled over $32.7 million.

Application Information The most efficient means of initial contact with the Hewlett Foundation is a letter of inquiry, addressed to the president. The letter should contain a brief statement of the applicant's need for funds and enough factual information to enable the staff to determine whether or not the application falls within the foundation's areas of preferred interests or warrants consideration as a special project. Applicants who receive a favorable response to their initial inquiry will be invited to submit a formal proposal.

Deadline(s) Grants must be approved by the board of directors, which meets quarterly. Meeting dates are available upon request, but applicants should realize that even proposals which are recommended for board approval cannot in every case be reviewed at the first meeting following their receipt. All inquiries and proposals are reported to the board, including both those that lie clearly outside the foundation's declared interests and those declined at the staff level.

232. Hewlett-Packard Company Foundation
3000 Hanover Street
Palo Alto, CA 94304
(415) 857-3053

Philanthropic Grants

Program Description Hewlett-Packard, since its founding in 1939, has sought to be an economic, intellectual, cultural, and social asset for each area—technical and geographical—within which it functions. One important means to this end is a wide array of carefully developed equipment and cash grants programs. These philanthropic programs can be grouped generally into four main categories: (1) community grants; (2) national grants in causes related to science, engineering, technology, and medicine; (3) employee-driven grants; and (4) international grants in those countries where direct contributions of cash and equipment are permitted and encouraged.

Eligibility/Limitations Hewlett-Packard does not make philanthropic grants to: organizations which are not tax-exempt; individuals; sectarian or denominational groups; agencies which practice or promote discriminatory or partisan policies; political activities; causes which offer specific direct benefits to grantors; university-industry associates programs; individual's research projects; or conferences, seminars, or meetings.

Application Information Local arts agencies should send their cash and equipment proposals to the Community Contributions Committee at the major company facility in their vicinity. National equipment requests may be addressed to the Director of Corporate Grants, Hewlett-Packard Company, 3000 Hanover Street, Palo Alto, CA, 94304. National cash requests falling within company guidelines and emphases may be submitted to the Executive Director, Hewlett-Packard Company Foundation, P.O. Box 10301, Palo Alto, CA 94303-0890.

Deadline(s) Deadlines vary depending upon the backlog of prior cases and upon the monthly, quarterly, or annual cycle of the program category involved. Contact Hewlett-Packard for specific information.

Additional Information Hewlett-Packard Company designs and manufactures computers and computer peripherals, test and measurement instruments, handheld calculators, electronic components, medical electronic equipment, and instrumentation for chemical analysis.

233. The Hillman Foundation, Inc.
2000 Grant Building
Pittsburgh, PA 15219
(412) 566-1480

Grants

Program Description Since its founding in 1951 the Hillman Foundation has concentrated its resources primarily on locally-oriented programs designed to improve and enrich the quality of life within the city of Pittsburgh and the southwestern Pennsylvania region. The foundation provides support for organizations in a wide range of program areas. There areas include community/civic affairs, human/social services, cultural advancement/the arts, all levels of education, youth and youth services, health and medicine, and religion.

Sample Grants Towards The Henry L. Hillman Fund to purchase painting by Elizabeth Murray entitled "Don't Be Cruel," $58,500 to The Carnegie Museum of Art, Pittsburgh, PA (1986). Support of Hillman Hall of Minerals and Gems, $92,475 to The Carnegie Museum of Natural History, Pittsburgh, PA (1986). Toward exhibit programing and general support, $15,000 to Pittsburgh Children's Museum (1986-1987). Toward construction of The Quadrangle, A Center for African, Near Eastern, and Asian Cultures as part of $75 million capital campaign, $25,000 (final payment of an authorized four-year pledge of $100,000) to Smithsonian Institution, Washington, DC (1986).

Eligibility/Limitations Preference is given to proposals submitted by tax-exempt organizations located in the Pittsburgh/southwestern Pennsylvania area. No contributions are made to individuals or to organizations outside the U.S.

Fiscal Information During 1986 a total of over $1.7 million was distributed to sixty-one organizations.

Application Information The foundation does not have a standard application form. Requests should be presented in a cover letter which describes the program and its objectives, and specifies the amount of funds needed. The letter should convey justification for the request and be signed by a fully authorized official of the organization. Included as part of the application should be an annual budget of the organization, a listing of the organization's directors/trustees, detailed information concerning costs of the project or program to be funded, and a time schedule (if appropriate). Additional information deemed necessary by the applicant will be welcomed. Each applicant must present evidence of a charitable, tax-exempt status. For additional information write to the foundation.

Deadline(s) The board of directors of the foundation meets quarterly for the purpose of considering applications.

234. Historic Deerfield
Summer Fellowship Program
Deerfield, MA 01342
(413) 774-5581

Summer Fellowships

Program Description Historic Deerfield will offer between six and ten summer fellowships to men and women who have completed two or more years of college and are of undergraduate status as of January 1. The fellowships are intended to encourage young people to consider careers in museums, historic preservation, and the study of American culture. Fellows will participate in a program of independent study and field experience in museum interpretation to be held at Deerfield, MA. Historic Deerfield operates twelve historic house museums with substantial collections of American decorative arts. The Memorial Libraries at Deerfield contain an outstanding collection of reference works, monographs, rare books, manuscripts, microfilm, newspapers, and periodicals that provide an opportunity for the study of local history, the culture of the Connecticut Valley, and early American arts. These libraries enable Summer Fellows to study the community of Deerfield from the 17th century to the 20th.

Eligibility/Limitations Applicants must have completed two or more years of college and be of undergraduate status as of January 1.

Fiscal Information Students may apply for full, partial, or tuition fellowships.

Application Information For applications and further information contact the Summer Fellowship Program.

Deadline(s) The application deadline is March 1.

235. The Hitachi Foundation
1725 K Street, NW, Suite 1403
Washington, DC 20006
(202) 457-0588

Grants

Program Description The Hitachi Foundation has been established to help develop the human resources, skills, and understanding necessary to enrich the lives of individuals in the increasingly complex and technological world of today and tomorrow. The foundation is committed to supporting programs which enable individuals to lead more productive lives and help them to participate with more awareness as citizens in an increasingly international environment. Grants are made to programs that have practical purpose and far-reaching impact. Finally, the foundation encourages proposals that will bring together diverse institutions and organizations to help resolve human and social concerns, to stimulate learning, and to address the humanistic dimension of technological development. The foundation supports the following program areas: community and economic development, education, technology and human resource development, and the arts. Within the arts category, the foundation supports projects in the visual and performing arts, particularly those which enhance the understanding of both American and/or Japanese cultures. Additionally, the foundation is interested in those projects which use the arts to improve education and learning.

Eligibility/Limitations Applicant organizations must be tax-exempt. The foundation will not consider requests related to: organizations whose activities or policies include specific political purposes; capital improvement projects/building funds; projects in which the primary purpose is publications, conferences, seminars or research; sectarian or denominational religious activities; endowments, fund-raising campaigns, recruitment or advertising; or funds for individuals.

Application Information A request for funding is considered in two stages. The preliminary stage should take the form of a letter no more than three pages in length.

The preliminary request should include the following: a statement of need for the project, and a description of those whom it will serve; a summary of the proposed project activities, its specific purpose, and how the project is an improvement upon present practice; the amount of the grant being requested, and other sources of funds to be committed to the project; a brief description of the applicant organization, its objectives, activities, and scope (this may be may be appended); and verification of tax-exempt status. If the proposed project is of interest to the foundation, a more detailed proposal will be invited for formal consideration.

Deadline(s) The foundation will review preliminary requests three times a year. These review periods begin in February, June, and October. Preliminary requests received by the first of February, June, and October will be reviewed and given a response regarding foundation interest within four weeks. Any preliminary requests received after the beginning of each of the review periods will be considered automatically in the following review period.

236. Hoblitzelle Foundation
1410 Tower 1, First Republic Bank Center
Dallas, TX 75201
(214) 979-0321

Grants

Program Description The foundation makes grants for educational, scientific, literary, and charitable purposes in the state of Texas.

Sample Grants Contributions of paintings, $906,800 (appraised value) to Dallas Museum of Art (1987). Contribution of antique English silver collection, $1,761,669 (appraised value) to Dallas Museum of Art (1987). Contribution of various historic photographs of The Louisiana Purchase Exhibition in St. Louis, $960 (appraised value) to Winterthur Museum, Winterthur, DE (1987).

Eligibility/Limitations No grants are made to individuals. Under present policy, contributions are not made to operating budgets, debt retirement, research, media productions or publications, scholarships, or endowment. No grants are made for religious purposes. Before an application can be considered, proof is required that the applicant has an exempt classification as described in section 501(c)(3) of the Internal Revenue Code, and that it is considered "not a private foundation" within the meaning of section 509(a) of the code. An applicant may qualify under section 170(c)(1) if its requested grant is shown to be for public purposes only as described in the code.

Fiscal Information Grants paid in the fiscal year ending April 30, 1987 totaled over $6.1 million.

Application Information It is preferred that the initial approach be through a brief narrative letter describing the project for which funds are requested, its justification, the cost based upon reliable estimates, the amount already realized or anticipated, from what other sources funding is expected, and the amount to be requested. If the project falls within the areas of the foundation's interest, purpose, and current funding policies, more detailed information will be requested.

Deadline(s) The board meets to consider applications for grants in the latter part of January, May, and September. The proper processing of applications precludes the consideration of any proposal not received in the foundation office on or before the 15th of the month prior to the month in which the meeting is scheduled.

237. Honeywell Foundation
MN12-5259, Honeywell Plaza
Minneapolis, MN 55408
(612) 870-2231

Grants

Program Description Honeywell earmarks each year approximately two percent of its U.S. pretax profits for contributions in communities where it has major operations.

Those contributions are made through the Honeywell Foundation in three priority categories: education, human services, and arts and civic organizations.

Eligibility/Limitations The foundation makes grants only to nonprofit organizations with a 501(c)(3) IRS tax-exempt code. The foundation tends to support organizations where Honeywell facilities are located. Minnesota organizations receive approximately fifty percent of funding.

Fiscal Information Contributions in 1986 totaled over $7.9 million.

Application Information The foundation requires no specific application form. It favors proposals that address a well-defined need with a sound strategy, from organizations who have the skills and commitment to achieve the proposal's objectives. Proposals should be submitted in writing and include the following information: a brief description of the organization submitting the proposal, including its legal name, primary purpose and history; the amount requested and how funds will be used; a clear statement of purpose, including specific outcomes or expected results; financial information, including budget for the proposed project; an audited financial statement, if available for previous fiscal year; a current operational budget; a copy of the most recent IRS 990 report; any additional factual information related to the organization or the request that may be useful for evaluation of the request; copy of the organization's IRS 501(c)(3) tax-exemption letter; and a list of members of the governing board and their affiliations.

Deadline(s) The foundation board meets quarterly to act on funding requests.

238. Hoover Presidential Library Association, Inc.
P.O. Box 696
West Branch, IA 52358
(319) 643-5327

Herbert Hoover Presidential Fellowship and Grant Program

Program Description The purpose of this program is to encourage original scholarship into the personal and public careers of Herbert Hoover, and secondarily, into national public policy during the Hoover Period, 1921-1933. Priority is given to projects which utilize the primarily historical resources of the Herbert Hoover Presidential Library and Museum, and which have the highest probability for publication and subsequent discussion and use by educators and policymakers.

Eligibility/Limitations Graduate and postdoctoral researchers are eligible to apply.

Fiscal Information Fellowships generally will be awarded as stipends for extended postdoctoral research and will range to an annual maximum of $10,000 per fellow. Grants generally will be awarded to defray travel and per diem expenses for pre- and postdoctoral research of a more limited duration and will range to an annual maximum of $1,000 per grantee.

Application Information Application forms are available from the association.

Deadline(s) Deadline for receipt of applications is March 1.

239. The George A. and Eliza Gardner Howard Foundation
Brown University
42 Charlesfield Street, Box 1867
Providence, RI 02912
(401) 863-2640

Fellowships

Program Description The Howard Foundation seeks to aid the personal development of promising individuals at the crucial middle stages of their careers. Fellowships offered in 1988-1989 will support persons engaged in independent projects in the following fields: history, anthropology, political science, and sociology.

Eligibility/Limitations Candidates should be in the "middle stages of their careers," and free of all professional responsibilities during the fellowship years. While no age limit is prescribed, ordinarily grantees are not younger than twenty-five or older than forty-five years. No grants are made to or through organizations, nor for institutional or programmatic support, but only to individuals. No fellowships are awarded for work leading to any academic degree or for coursework or training of any sort. Awards are made for projects requiring essentially full-time work over an extended period of time. Fellows must therefore be eligible for sabbatical or other leave, or make arrangements with the institution involved for time released from normal duties.

Fiscal Information Stipends of $18,000 will be given for a period of one year beginning July 1 and ending June 30. No grants are made for summer research or other short-term projects. Awards are made for projects requiring essentially full-time work over an extended period of time.

Application Information The Howard Foundation does not accept any direct application. Application forms are forwarded to candidates only upon the foundation's acceptance of a suitable nomination, submitted according to the following guidelines: (1) for all individuals associated with a college or university, a nomination should be submitted by the president of the institution, or a designated representative; and (2) independent scholars and others without academic institutional connections may be nominated by an editor of a professional journal, a museum director, or a person of equivalent professional standing in the relevant field.

Deadline(s) Nominations will be accepted between September 1 and November 15 for the fellowship year beginning on July 1 and ending on June 30. The deadline for accepted nominee completed applications is December 15.

240. The Huntington Library
Committee on Awards
1151 Oxford Road
San Marino, CA 91108
(213) 792-6141

Research Awards

Program Description The Huntington Library is a research institution devoted primarily to the study of British and American history, literature, science, and art. The library welcomes applications from scholars for awards to help them carry on significant research in the collections of the institution. In selecting persons to receive awards, attention is paid to the value of the project, the ability of the scholar, and the degree to which special strengths of the library will be utilized.

Eligibility/Limitations In general, the competition is such that awards can be made only to persons who have demonstrated, to a degree commensurate with their age and experience, unusual abilities or promise through publications of great merit. A few awards of three months or less are available for persons writing doctoral dissertations.

Fiscal Information Awards for a period of less than six months carry normal stipends of $1,500 per month. One month is the minimum period for which awards are made. Holders of awards are expected to be in residence at the library throughout their tenure.

Application Information An application should be in the form of a letter and include: an outline of the project, the period of proposed residence at the library, personal data, previous scholarly work, references, and financial need. More detailed guidelines are available from the library.

Deadline(s) Applications are received from October 1 to December 1 of each year for awards within the twelve-month period beginning on the following June 1.

Additional Information Through funds made available by grants from the National Endowment for the Humanities, three or four awards for periods of six to twelve months are currently being offered each year. These awards, called Huntington Library-NEH Fellowships, carry stipends adjusted to need. Ordinarily they are set at half the current cash salary of the applicant, but they may not exceed $2,250 per month; the minimum period is six consecutive months. NEH Fellowships may not be awarded to foreign nationals unless they have been residents in the U.S. for at least three years.

241. IBM Corporation
Director, Corporate Support Programs
2000 Purchase Street
Purchase, NY 10577
(914) 697-7519

Corporate Support Program

Program Description IBM's philanthropic activities are founded in the corporation's self-interest. Support categories include: education, health and welfare, civic, and cultural. In the cultural category, support is awarded to museums, performing arts groups, public broadcasting, and other cultural organizations.

Eligibility/Limitations Political or religious organizations will not be considered for support. Proof of tax-exemption is required.

Fiscal Information IBM offers the following types of support: fellowships, scholarships, capital campaigns, general operating support, special projects, employee loans, matching grants, and loaned/donated equipment.

Application Information Local community organizations should contact a local plant/branch office; all others should contact headquarters at the address listed above.

Deadline(s) Applicant evaluation decision time varies, averaging two to three months.

242. IC Industries, Inc.
One Illinois Center, 111 East Wacker Drive
Chicago, IL 60601
(312) 565-3000

Grants

Program Description IC Industries makes donations in the following general areas: United Way, education, health and welfare, youth, and culture and the arts. Many grants are focused in the greater Chicago area.

Eligibility/Limitations No grants are made to individuals. Organizations must be tax-exempt.

Fiscal Information Contributions in 1986 totaled $2 million.

Application Information Initial contact with the company should be by letter or phone. Additional information is available from the director of advertising and public affairs at the address listed above.

Deadline(s) Deadline for application is August 1.

243. Indian Arts and Crafts Board
Department of the Interior
Washington, DC 20240
(202) 343-2773

Indian Arts and Crafts Development

CFDA Program Number 15.850

Program Description The objective of this program is to encourage and promote the development of American Indian arts and crafts. The program supports program planning assistance, such as the development of innovative educational, production, promotion, and economic concepts related to native cultures.

Eligibility/Limitations Eligible applicants include Native Americans; Indian, Eskimo, Aleut individuals and organizations; federally recognized Indian tribal governments; state and local governments; and nonprofit organizations.

Fiscal Information Types of assistance offered include: use of property, facilities, and equipment; advisory services and counseling; and investigation of complaints. No grants or direct financial assistance are offered.

Application Information Applications should be submitted to the headquarters office.

Deadline(s) There are no deadlines for application.

244. Institute of Early American History and Culture

Box 220
Williamsburg, VA 23187
(804) 253-5117

Postdoctoral Fellowships

Program Description The staff of the Institute of Early American History and Culture includes two postdoctoral fellows. The fellowship is a two-year appointment awarded to a promising junior scholar in any area of early American studies. Institute fellows are at an early stage of their careers when, under prevailing circumstances, they are likely to be diverted from research by a burdensome teaching load in their first academic position. At the institute, however, the fellows devote most of their time to research and writing and reap the benefit of critical judgment of their work at close range. Fellows may achieve publication in the *William and Mary Quarterly* and have the good prospect of acceptance of their book manuscript by the institute, which holds first claim on it.

Eligibility/Limitations The fellowship is open to all eligible persons equally. The following restrictions apply: Candidates (1) must not have published a book previously, (2) must have satisfied all requirements for the doctorate before commencing their term, and (3) must be able to provide a copy of at least a significant portion of their dissertation with the initial application. Foreign nationals are not eligible unless they have lived in the U.S. for the three years immediately preceding the date of the fellowship award.

Fiscal Information The fellowship will be supported for the twelve-month period of the calendar year by a grant from NEH. Among the perquisites of the fellowship are travel funds for research and the opportunity to participate in conferences and seminars sponsored by the institute. Funds are also available for purchase of photographic copies of manuscript and printed sources.

Application Information Further instructions for applying for the fellowship and the necessary forms may be obtained by writing to the director of the institute.

Deadline(s) The deadline for application is November 15.

245. Institute of International Education

809 United Nations Plaza
New York, NY 10017

Fulbright Fixed Sum Grants

Program Description The Institute of International Education is under contract to the U.S. Information Agency to organize publicity, receive and process applications, and, through its National Screening Committee, make recommendations to the Board of Foreign Scholarships for graduate study grants under the Fulbright Program. Under agreements with foreign governments, universities, and private donors, the institute performs the same functions with regard to grants sponsored by them. Fulbright Fixed Sum Grants provide a fixed sum payment in U.S. dollars for predoctoral study or research abroad.

Eligibility/Limitations Applicants must be United States citizens and have received the majority of their high school and undergraduate college education at educational institutions in the United States. Applicants must hold a B.A. degree or the equivalent before the beginning date of the grant. Applicants may not hold a doctoral degree at the time of application. Applicants must have sufficient proficiency in the written and spoken language of the host country to communicate with the people and to carry out the proposed study. Such proficiency is especially important to students wishing to undertake projects in the social sciences and humanities. Although the majority of these grants are reserved for graduate students who, in most cases, will be engaged in research for the doctoral dissertation, it is the policy of the Board of Foreign Scholarships that awards also be available to other graduate students, graduating seniors, and candidates who wish to further their careers in the creative and performing arts.

Fiscal Information Most grants will be awarded for programs of study or research that will require an academic year. Grant amounts vary from country to country. In certain countries, grantees who, upon arrival, can submit proof that they have been admitted to doctoral candidacy and have completed all requirements except the writing of their dissertations may receive higher stipends.

Application Information Application forms and additional information are available from IIE. Before filling out an application, a prospective candidate should confirm that there will be awards in the country in which he or she is interested. Applicants who are enrolled in U.S. colleges and universities should contact their Fulbright Program Advisers for the latest information. Others should write to IIE.

Deadline(s) Deadlines vary from year to year and from country to country. Contact IIE for up-to-date information.

246. Institute of International Education
809 United Nations Plaza
New York, NY 10017

Fulbright Full Grants

Program Description The Institute of International Education is under contract to the U.S. Information Agency to organize publicity, receive and process applications, and, through its National Screening Committee, make recommendations to the Board of Foreign Scholarships for graduate study grants under the Fulbright Program. Under agreements with foreign governments, universities, and private donors, the institute performs the same functions with regard to grants sponsored by them.

Eligibility/Limitations Applicants must be United States citizens and have received the majority of their high school and undergraduate college education at educational institutions in the United States. Applicants must hold a B.A. degree or the equivalent before the beginning date of the grant. Applicants may not hold a doctoral degree at the time of application. Applicants must have sufficient proficiency in the written and spoken language of the host country to communicate with the people and to carry out the proposed study. Such proficiency is especially important to students wishing to undertake projects in the social sciences and humanities. Although the majority of these grants are reserved for graduate students who, in most cases, will be engaged in research for the doctoral dissertation, it is the policy of the Board of Foreign Scholarships that awards also be available to other graduate students, graduating seniors, and candidates who wish to further their careers in the creative and performing arts.

Fiscal Information Most grants will be awarded for programs of study or research that will require an academic year. Full Grants provide round-trip transportation, language or orientation courses (where appropriate), tuition, books, maintenance for one academic year in only one country, and health and accident insurance. Most of these benefits are payable in local currency. The maintenance allowance is based on living costs in the host country and is sufficient to meet the normal expenses of a single person.

Application Information Application forms and additional information are available from IIE. Before filling out an application, a prospective candidate should confirm that there will be awards in the country in which he or she is interested. Applicants who are enrolled in U.S. colleges and universities should contact their Fulbright Program Advisers for the latest information. Others should write to IIE.

Deadline(s) Deadlines vary from year to year and from country to country. Contact IIE for up-to-date information.

247. Institute of International Education

809 United Nations Plaza
New York, NY 10017

Fulbright Travel Grants

Program Description The Institute of International Education is under contract to the U.S. Information Agency to organize publicity, receive and process applications, and, through its National Screening Committee, make recommendations to the Board of Foreign Scholarships for graduate study grants under the Fulbright Program. Under agreements with foreign governments, universities, and private donors, the institute performs the same functions with regard to grants sponsored by them. In general, Fulbright Travel Grants are tied to specific maintenance and tuition scholarships and may not used to supplement awards other than these.

Eligibility/Limitations In general, applicants must be candidates for Fulbright maintenance and tuition scholarships.

Fiscal Information Travel Grants provide round-trip transportation to the country where the student will pursue studies for an academic year, health and accident insurance, and the cost of an orientation course abroad, if applicable.

Application Information Application forms and additional information are available from IIE. Before filling out an application, a prospective candidate should confirm that there will be awards in the country in which he or she is interested. Applicants who are enrolled in U.S. colleges and universities should contact their Fulbright Program Advisers for the latest information. Others should write to IIE.

Deadline(s) Deadlines vary from year to year and from country to country. Contact IIE for up-to-date information.

248. Institute of International Education

U.S. Students Programs Division
809 United Nations Plaza
New York, NY 10017
(212) 984-5326

Fulbright Collaborative Research Grants

Program Description The Institute of International Education is under contract to the U.S. Information Agency to organize publicity, receive and process applications, and, through its National Screening Committee, make recommendations to the Board of Foreign Scholarships for graduate study grants under the Fulbright Program. Under agreements with foreign governments, universities, and private donors, the institute performs the same functions with regard to grants sponsored by them. The Board of Foreign Scholarships has approved the introduction of a new project under the Fulbright program which will fund proposals for joint research abroad by teams of two or three U.S. graduate students or recent post-graduate researchers. The program is available for research in all countries of the world where conditions permit, except for most countries in Eastern Europe, the USSR, and Indochina. It is expected that all members of a team involved in a joint grant will carry out their research in one country abroad in the same academic year, although research does not need to be carried out simultaneously and the duration of the grant need not be the same in all cases. However, individual team members are required to carry out research within the host country for a minimum of six months. Application must include evidence of affiliation with a host country institution or ongoing project that will oversee the collaborative research. The program does not impose restrictions as to fields of research.

Eligibility/Limitations Applicants must be United States citizens at the time of application. They must hold a B.A. degree or its equivalent before the beginning date of the grant. Those with a Ph.D. at the time of application may have obtained the degree no earlier than June 1984. Researchers in the creative arts need not hold a degree, but must have at least four years of relevant training and/or experience. Applicants in medicine must have an M.D. degree or the equivalent (e.g., O.D., D.D.S.) at the time of application. Applicants must have received the majority of their high school and undergraduate college educations at educational institutions in the United States. Applicants must have sufficient proficiency in the written and spoken language of the host country to communicate with the people and to carry out the proposed study. Such proficiency is especially important to those wishing to undertake projects in the social sciences and the humanities. Applicants must be in good health. There are no restrictions as to age, sex, race, or religion. Full-time permanent employees of the U.S. Information Agency are ineligible for grants for a period of one year following the termination of their employment. This limitation applies to members of their immediate families. Employees of any agency involved in administering the educational and cultural exchange programs of the U.S. Information Agency, and members of their immediate families, should check with IIE on their eligibility.

Fiscal Information The Fulbright Collaborative Research Grants will provide equal monthly fixed sum payments to each member of the research team, based on the cost of living in the host country. These payments are intended to cover the normal travel and living expenses of a grantee for the tenure of the award, normally 6-10 months. No extra funds for research expenses, translators, or other resource persons will be included. There is no allowance for dependent support, nor is it recommended that dependents accompany grantees abroad. Grantees will also receive basic health and accident insurance coverage as part of the award. Renewals or extensions of the grants will not be made.

Application Information Application forms and additional information are available from IIE. Before filling out an application, a prospective candidate should confirm that there will be awards in the country in which he or she is interested. Applicants who are enrolled in U.S. colleges and universities should contact their Fulbright Program Advisers for the latest information. Others should write to IIE.

Deadline(s) Completed applications for each team must reach IIE by January 16.

249. Institute of Museum Services
1100 Pennsylvania Avenue, NW, Room 609
Washington, DC 20202
(202) 786-0539

Grants

CFDA Program Number 45.301

Program Description The Institute of Museum Services (IMS) awards grants to support the efforts of museums to conserve the nation's historic, scientific, and cultural heritage; to maintain and expand their educational role; and to ease the financial burden borne by museums as a result of their increasing use by the public. The IMS currently makes grants in four categories: (1) General Operating Support (GOS); (2) Conservation Project Support (CP); (3) the Museum Assessment Program (MAP); and (4) the Museum Assessment Program II (MAP II). GOS grants are one-year competitive awards to maintain or improve the operation of museums. CP grants fund a variety of functions as applied to living and nonliving collections including: surveys of collections and environmental conditions, treatment of collections, and research and training. MAP grants are one-time awards made on a first-come, first-served basis, which provide funds for an independent professional assessment of the institution's operations. Institutions that have received a MAP grant are eligible to apply for a MAP II grant which provides for an independent professional assessment of the institution's collection care and maintenance. To participate in MAP and MAP II the institution must complete a self-study questionnaire provided by the American Association of Museums.

Eligibility/Limitations A museum located in the fifty States of the Union, the Commonwealth of Puerto Rico, American Samoa, the Virgin Islands, the Northern Mariana Islands, the Trust Territories of the Pacific Islands, Guam, or the District of Columbia may apply for a grant. No museum is eligible to apply unless it has provided museum services including exhibiting objects to the general public on a regular basis for at least two years prior to application. A public or private nonprofit agency, such as a municipality, college, or university which is responsible for the operation of a museum may, if necessary, apply on behalf of the museum. A museum operated by a department or agency of the Federal government is not eligible to apply. Under the IMS definition, a museum is a public or private nonprofit institution which is organized on a permanent basis for essentially educational or aesthetic purposes and which, using a professional staff: (1) owns or uses tangible objects, whether animate or inanimate; (2) cares for these objects; and (3) exhibits them to the general public on a regular basis. A museum must have at least one staff member, paid or unpaid, who devotes his or her time primarily to the acquisition, care, or exhibition of objects. The definition makes clear that the term "museum" includes aquariums and zoological parks; botanical gardens and arboreta; nature centers; museums relating to art, history (including historic buildings), natural history, children's general and specialized museums, science and technology centers, and planetariums.

Fiscal Information The maximum grant is currently $75,000 or up to ten percent of the applicant museum's nonfederal income, whichever is less, through the GOS program. CP awards will not exceed $25,000 and require a fifty percent match by the applicant museum from nonfederal sources, but may include in-kind contributions. MAP and MAP II awards will be $1,000 each.

Application Information The standard application forms as furnished by the Federal agency and required by OMB Circular No. A-102 must be used for this program. For GOS and CP grants, applications, on the required forms, are submitted directly to the Institute of Museum Services. Application procedures and guidelines are available from the Institute. To participate in MAP and MAP II, application is made to the American Association of Museums (AAM), 1055 Thomas Jefferson Street, NW, Washington, DC, 20007. A self study questionnaire provided by AAM must be completed to participate in MAP and MAP II.

Deadline(s) The deadline for GOS applications is in the fall. The deadline for CP grants is in the winter. The deadline for MAP awards is May 1; MAP II deadlines are throughout the year. Contact the appropriate office for specific dates.

250. International Paper Company Foundation
Two Manhattanville Road
Purchase, NY 10577
(914) 397-1500

Contributions

Program Description Since its incorporation in 1953, International Paper Company Foundation has sought out and funded programs which address existing and emerging educational, social, and civic needs. As the demand for support has grown, experience has convinced the foundation that limited resources are most effectively utilized in support of specific projects in the following categories: community and civic, arts and culture, economic education, health and welfare, higher education, minority education, and pre-college education. Within the arts and culture category, the foundation will consider support for cultural organizations, including libraries, and projects in the visual and performing arts in communities with substantial numbers of company employees.

Eligibility/Limitations Special attention is given to the needs in communities where International Paper Company operates mills and plants and to programs in which company employees demonstrate their interest by serving as volunteers. To this end, the foundation does not generally support national programs unless they have specific impact on a community in which the company operates. The foundation does not provide funds for: individuals; organizations which are not tax-exempt; organizations which discriminate on the basis of sex, race, or creed; general operating expenses; endowments and capital expenses of cultural, civic, or educational institutions; organizations in foreign countries or organizations whose contributed funds go outside the U.S. or its territories; or tables at charitable functions or courtesy advertising.

Fiscal Information Contributions in 1985 totaled over $1.6 million.

Application Information A nonprofit organization with a program meeting foundation guidelines may wish to submit a preliminary proposal. If the organization is located in a community where the company maintains a facility, initial contact should be made with the mill, plant, or communications manager. If there is sufficient interest, company personnel will refer the request in the form of a preliminary proposal to the foundation with a recommendation. A preliminary proposal should include: brief background of the organization; most recent audited financial statement; program budget, including amount requested; concise description of the program and its specific objectives; IRS tax determination letter, indicating 501(c)(3) status; list of current funding sources with specific amounts; and current annual report.

Deadline(s) Normally a decision will be made within six to eight weeks.

251. International Research & Exchanges Board
126 Alexander Street
Princeton, NJ 08540-7102
(609) 683-9500

Developmental Fellowships: Disciplinary Fellowships

Program Description IREX offers fellowships to faculty, postdoctoral researchers, and Ph.D. candidates for Soviet or East European language and area studies. This program prepares fellows to undertake field research in the USSR and Eastern Europe and to establish working relationships with Soviet and East European colleagues and institutions. By enabling scholars in a variety of disciplines to use Soviet and East European sources and materials, IREX seeks to stimulate research on these countries. Disciplinary Fellowships are open to applicants outside of Soviet and East European studies in fields such as archaeology, anthropology, business, economics, geography and demography, law, musicology, political science, psychology, and sociology, to gain the language and area background necessary to conduct research in the USSR and Eastern Europe.

Eligibility/Limitations Applicants must be U.S. citizens planning doctoral dissertations or postdoctoral research requiring field access to the USSR or Eastern Europe. Fellows are required to apply to an appropriate IREX program following their tenure.

Fiscal Information Applicants may apply for academic tuition; language training allowance for summer work; academic year work or tutoring; and stipend support.

Application Information Contact IREX by mail or phone giving: program for which an application is contemplated, academic affiliation or job title, highest degree and date received, age, citizenship, proposed time abroad, field of specialization, and the proposed project.

Deadline(s) The deadline for application is February 15.

252. International Research & Exchanges Board
126 Alexander Street
Princeton, NJ 08540-7102
(609) 683-9500

Developmental Fellowships: Fellowships for the Study of Soviet Nationalities

Program Description IREX offers fellowships to faculty, postdoctoral researchers, and Ph.D. candidates for Soviet or East European language and area studies. This program prepares fellows to undertake field research in the USSR and Eastern Europe and to establish working relationships with Soviet and East European colleagues and institutions. By enabling scholars in a variety of disciplines to use Soviet and East European sources and materials, IREX seeks to stimulate research on these countries. IREX offers a limited number of fellowships to strengthen American scholarship on the USSR and Eastern Europe. Fellowships for the Study of Soviet Nationalities are open to applicants who already have strong preparation in Soviet area studies but need additional training in a minority language at an appropriate center.

Eligibility/Limitations Applicants must be U.S. citizens planning doctoral dissertations or postdoctoral research requiring materials available through exchange participation.

Fiscal Information Applicants may apply for academic tuition; language training allowance for summer work, academic year work, or tutoring; and stipend support.

Application Information Contact IREX by mail or phone giving: program for which an application is contemplated, academic affiliation or job title, highest degree and date received, age, citizenship, proposed time abroad, field of specialization, and the proposed project.

Deadline(s) The application deadline is February 15.

253. International Research & Exchanges Board
126 Alexander Street
Princeton, NJ 08540-7102
(609) 683-9500

Developmental Fellowships: Fellowships to Develop Dual Area Competence

Program Description IREX offers fellowships to faculty, postdoctoral researchers, and Ph.D. candidates for Soviet or East European language and area studies. This program prepares fellows to undertake field research in the USSR and Eastern Europe and to establish working relationships with Soviet and East European colleagues and institutions. By enabling scholars in a variety of disciplines to use Soviet and East European sources and materials, IREX seeks to stimulate research on these countries. Fellowships to Develop Dual Area Competence are open to applicants with expertise in a specific world area, including the USSR and Eastern Europe, who propose to develop competence in a second world region for the purpose of comparative research. While either the present expertise or that to be acquired can be the USSR and/or Eastern Europe, the applicant must be planning to conduct future research in Eastern Europe or the Soviet Union.

Eligibility/Limitations Applicants must be U.S. citizens planning doctoral dissertations or postdoctoral research requiring materials available through exchange participation.

Fiscal Information Applicants may apply for academic tuition; language training allowance for summer work, academic year work or tutoring; and stipend support.

Application Information Contact IREX by mail or phone giving: program for which an application is contemplated, academic affiliation or job title, highest degree and date received, age, citizenship, proposed time abroad, field of specialization, and the proposed project.

Deadline(s) The application deadline is February 15.

254. International Research & Exchanges Board
126 Alexander Street
Princeton, NJ 08540-7102
(609) 683-9500

Grants for Collaborative Activities and New Exchanges

Program Description To encourage the development of individual and institutional collaboration and exchange involving humanists and social scientists from the United States and from Eastern Europe and the USSR, as well as Albania and Mongolia, IREX makes a very limited number of grants in support of specific collaborative projects and new exchanges. Such undertakings as bilateral and multinational symposia, collaborative and parallel research, joint publications (but not publication costs), exchanges of data, comparative surveys, and the like, as well as brief visits necessary in the planning of such projects, will be considered for support.

Eligibility/Limitations Applicants must present evidence that they will be received by the appropriate institutions in one of these countries and that appropriate scholars are prepared to consider the proposed project or exchange. Only those proposals will be considered which give evidence of exceptional merit, feasibility, and substantial prior planning and consultation. Grants are not available to support individual study, research, or attendance at international scholarly conferences. In the case of university-sponsored exchanges between students and faculty, IREX will support the initial planning of such programs, but will not finance the resulting exchanges.

Fiscal Information Applicants should bear in mind that the funds for these grants are severely limited; accordingly, grants average under $2,000 and will seldom cover the full cost of any project. Applicants presenting projects which involve sums in excess of $5,000 or which will require support beyond a one-year period should seek aid from other sources. Grant recipients are responsible for their visa and travel arrangements.

Application Information Contact IREX by mail or phone, giving: program for which an application is contemplated, academic affiliation or job title, highest degree and date received, age, citizenship, proposed time abroad, field of specialization, and the proposed project.

Deadline(s) The application deadlines are October 15 and April 15.

255. International Research & Exchanges Board
126 Alexander Street
Princeton, NJ 08540-7102
(609) 683-9500

Grants for Independent Short-Term Travel to the USSR and Eastern Europe

Program Description These grants are designed for senior scholars (Ph.D. or equivalent professional degree) who need to make brief visits to Eastern Europe or the Soviet Union in connection with ongoing research and who do not require academic or administrative assistance in carrying out their proposed projects.

Eligibility/Limitations Grantees are expected to make all their own housing, visa, and academic arrangements.

Fiscal Information Awards will provide recipients with an APEX round-trip air fare and a lump sum support allowance. Support is offered for up to two weeks, although participants may stay longer at their own expense.

Application Information Contact IREX by mail or phone, giving: program for which an application is contemplated, academic affiliation or job title, highest degree and date received, age, citizenship, proposed time abroad, field of specialization, and the proposed project.

Deadline(s) Application deadlines are October 1 and April 1 for fellowship tenure after January 1 and June 1, respectively.

256. International Research & Exchanges Board
126 Alexander Street
Princeton, NJ 08540-7102
(609) 683-9500

Research Exchanges: Eastern Europe

Program Description IREX conducts research exchange programs open to applicants in all disciplines with all of the socialist countries of East Central and Southeastern Europe except Albania, including Bulgaria, Czechoslovakia, the German Democratic Republic, Hungary, Poland, Romania, and Yugoslavia.

Eligibility/Limitations Applicants should be U.S. citizens, have command of the language of the host country sufficient for research, and, normally, have full-time affiliation with a North American college or university and be faculty members or advanced doctoral candidates who will have completed all requirements for the Ph.D. (or equivalent professional degree) except the thesis by the time of participation. However, many scholars not academically employed and candidates for the M.A. degree may also be qualified if they are proposing professional-level independent research projects. Inquiries about eligibility are welcome.

Fiscal Information IREX provides domestic and international transportation; an internal travel allowance for graduate students; for married graduate student participants, a family allowance determined by the number of dependents; for salaried participants, partial stipend-in-lieu-of-salary less the value of benefits received from the host country, including housing. Stipends are adjusted to take into account such other resources as fellowships, sabbatical salaries, etc. Host countries provide a stipend in local currency and book and microfilm allowances. Preliminary language training is provided under certain conditions except in the German Democratic Republic. With the exception of Yugoslavia, where only a nominal housing allowance is provided and IREX also pays a housing allowance, host countries pay for housing for the participant and accompanying dependents. Medical and dental care is provided for participants and accompanying dependents except in the German Democratic Republic and Yugoslavia, where medical and dental care is provided for participants only. Details of host support vary from country to country and may vary from year to year. Current information is included in application materials.

Application Information Contact IREX by mail or phone, giving: program for which an application is contemplated, academic affiliation or job title, highest degree and date received, age, citizenship, proposed time abroad, field of specialization, and the proposed project.

Deadline(s) The application deadline for all East European programs is November 1 for periods of participation beginning September 1 or later of the following year.

257. International Research & Exchanges Board
126 Alexander Street
Princeton, NJ 08540-7102
(609) 683-9500

Travel Grants for Senior Scholars

Program Description IREX makes available a very limited number of travel grants in order to facilitate communication between prominent American humanists and social scientists and their colleagues in Eastern Europe and the USSR, as well as Albania and Mongolia. In order to encourage wider participation in East-West scholarly contacts, preference will be given to scholars outside the field of Soviet and East European studies.

Eligibility/Limitations Applicants should be U.S. citizens and must have received a formal invitation from an appropriate institution in one of these countries, such as an academy of science or one of its institutes.

Fiscal Information The grants are intended for support of short visits (normally less than two months) for the purposes of consultation and/or lecturing. They are not intended to support attendance at international scholarly conferences or individual study and research. Grants to American applicants consist of round-trip economy transportation only. Grant recipients are responsible for all their visa and travel arrangements.

Application Information Contact IREX by mail or phone, giving: program for which an application is contemplated; academic affiliation or job title; highest degree and date received; age; citizenship; proposed time abroad; field of specialization; and the proposed project.

Deadline(s) The application deadlines are October 15 and April 15.

258. International Research & Exchanges Board
126 Alexander Street
Princeton, NJ 08540-7102
(609) 683-9500

Union of Soviet Socialist Republics: ACLS-Academy Exchange for Senior Scholars

Program Description The agreement between the American Council of Learned Societies and the Academy of Sciences of the USSR provides for visits of senior American scholars totaling one hundred months annually. Sixty of these months are reserved for individual research visits; the remaining forty are allocated for joint research projects under the Commission on the Humanities and Social Sciences.

Eligibility/Limitations Applicants should be U.S. citizens and, normally, have full-time affiliation with a North American college or university. Senior scholar status and distinction in a discipline of the humanities or social sciences are also required. In exceptional cases, applications will be accepted from assistant professors.

Fiscal Information The program supports periods of stay abroad between one and ten months. The academy prefers that scholars not plan exchange participation during the summer months. The Academy of Sciences provides housing, medical coverage, a per diem ruble allowance, some expenses for research materials, and internal travel directly related to research. The academy has agreed to assist in providing suitable accommodations for accompanying family members. IREX provides domestic and international transportation for participants and for salaried participants, a partial stipend-in-lieu-of-salary less the value of housing and other benefits received from the host country. Stipends are adjusted to take into account such other resources as fellowships, sabbatical salaries, etc.

Application Information Contact IREX by mail or phone, giving: program for which an application is contemplated, academic affiliation or job title, highest degree and date received, age, citizenship, proposed time abroad, field of specialization, and the proposed project.

Deadline(s) Contact IREX for deadline information.

259. International Research & Exchanges Board
126 Alexander Street
Princeton, NJ 08540-7102
(609) 683-9500

Union of Soviet Socialist Republics: Ministry Exchange—Long-Term Advanced Research

Program Description Allowance is made in an intergovernmental agreement for at least forty U.S. participants annually to stay in the USSR for periods of from one semester to an academic year. Affiliation is normally limited to institutions under the jurisdiction of the Ministry of Higher and Specialized Secondary Education (i.e., universities).

Eligibility/Limitations Applicants should be U.S. citizens, have command of the language of the host country sufficient for research, and, normally, have full-time affiliation with a North American college or university and be faculty members or advanced doctoral candidates who will have completed all requirements for the Ph.D. (or equivalent professional degree) except the thesis by the time of participation. However, many scholars not academically employed and candidates for the M.A. degree may also be qualified if they are proposing professional-level independent research projects. Inquiries about eligibility are welcome.

Fiscal Information The program supports periods of stay abroad between one semester to an academic year. The ministry prefers that scholars not plan exchange participation during the summer months. One-semester applications from graduate students are strongly discouraged and will not be approved for the spring semester except in unusual cases. The ministry provides housing, medical coverage, and a monthly ruble allowance. IREX provides domestic and international transportation for participants; for graduate students, a small monthly maintenance allowance; for married graduate students, a family allowance determined by the number of participants; and for salaried participants, a partial stipend-in-lieu-of-salary less the value of housing and other benefits received from the host country. Stipends are adjusted to take into account such other resources as fellowships, sabbatical salaries, etc.

Application Information Contact IREX by mail or phone, giving: program for which an application is contemplated, academic affiliation or job title, highest degree and date received, age, citizenship, proposed time abroad, field of specialization, and the proposed project.

Deadline(s) The application deadline is November 1.

260. International Research & Exchanges Board
126 Alexander Street
Princeton, NJ 08540-7102
(609) 683-9500

Union of Soviet Socialist Republics: Ministry Exchange—Short-Term Advanced Research

Program Description Allowance is made in an intergovernmental agreement for the participation of at least ten U.S. scholars annually for stays not to exceed a total of fifty months. Affiliation is normally limited to institutions under the jurisdiction of the Ministry of Higher and Specialized Secondary Education (i.e., universities).

Eligibility/Limitations Applicants should be U.S. citizens, have command of the language of the host country sufficient for research, and, normally, have full-time affiliation with a North American college or university. Preference is given to those who are associate or full professors, but assistant professors may apply. Inquiries about eligibility are welcome.

Fiscal Information The program supports periods of stay abroad between two to five months. The ministry prefers that scholars not plan exchange participation during the summer months. The ministry provides housing, medical coverage, as well as a monthly ruble allowance for the participant. The ministry has agreed to assist in providing suitable accommodations for accompanying family members, but it is not responsible for the additional cost involved. IREX provides domestic and international transportation for participants, and for salaried participants, a partial stipend-in-lieu-of-salary less the value of housing and other benefits received from the host country. Stipends are adjusted to take into account such other resources as fellowships, sabbatical salaries, etc.

Application Information Contact IREX by mail or phone, giving: program for which an application is contemplated, academic affiliation or job title, highest degree and date received, age, citizenship, proposed time abroad, field of specialization, and the proposed project.

Deadline(s) Contact IREX for deadline information.

261. The James Irvine Foundation
One Market Plaza, Steuart Street Tower, Suite 2305
San Francisco, CA 94105
(415) 777-2244

Grants

Program Description The James Irvine Foundation was established in 1937 to promote the general welfare of the people of California. Though its historic roots are in Orange County, the foundation is dedicated to enhancing the social, economic, and physical quality of life throughout California, and enriching the state's intellectual and cultural climate. Within these broad purposes, the foundation supports higher education, the cultural arts, medicine and health care, community services, and youth programs.

Sample Grants For construction of a wildlife center, $75,000 to Coyote Point Museum for Environmental Education, San Mateo (1986). Toward additional renovation of the museum, $50,000 to Fresno Museum of Art, History and Science (1986). To hire a full-time fund-raising director and for further development of the desert gardens, $60,000 to Living Desert Reserve aka The Living Desert, Palm Desert (1986). To fund a two-year membership campaign, $80,000 to Los Angeles Children's Museum (1986). For furnishings and equipment for museum expansion, $300,000 to Museum Associates/Los Angeles County Museum of Art (1986). Challenge grant to be matched from new and increased contributions, $250,000 to San Francisco Museum of Modern Art (1986).

Eligibility/Limitations Grants are limited to charitable uses in the State of California and for the benefit of charities which do not receive a substantial part of their support from taxation nor exist primarily to benefit tax-supported entities. The foundation is willing to consider requests for institutional and program development, policy studies, and capital projects. Grants generally are not made for basic research, films or publishing activities, or for festivals or conferences. Exceptions to these policies may occur from time to time solely upon the initiative of the foundation.

Fiscal Information Grant authorizations in 1986 totaled more than $18.6 million, including over $5.6 million to cultural programs.

Application Information Grant seekers should submit one copy of the proposal with a cover letter signed by an appropriate officer of the organization. The cover letter should briefly summarize the proposed project; identify the applicant, the problem or need to be addressed, the proposed objectives, and strategy to accomplish the objectives; and the amount of support requested from the foundation and total estimated project costs. The proposal narrative should include the following components: applicant background, problem statement, and proposed project. In addition, the proposal should include: complete financial statements for the last two fiscal years; current year's budget to include year-to-date financial information; copies of original federal and state tax-exemption letters and IRS notification of foundation status under Section 509(a) of the Tax Reform Act of 1969; list of officers and directors/trustees, including names, addresses, occupations/affiliations, board responsibilities, and length of term; a current annual report and/or program brochure, if available; and board endorsement, signed by an officer of the board of directors/trustees, indicating that the proposal is made with board approval.

Deadline(s) The distribution committees meet semi-annually, generally in May and November, to consider applications. These meetings are followed by a meeting of the board of directors at which final action is taken.

Additional Information For the purpose of processing inquiries and applications only, the foundation has divided California into northern and southern sections. Applicants from the northern section, which is the area north of San Luis Obispo, Kern and San Bernardino counties, should address their applications to the San Francisco office at the address listed above. Applications from the southern section, which is the area south of and including San Luis Obispo, Kern, and San Bernardino counties, should be directed to: The James Irvine Foundation, 450 Newport Center Drive, Suite 545, Newport Beach, CA 92660, telephone (714) 644-1362.

262. Jerome Foundation, Inc.
West 2090 First National Bank Building
Saint Paul, MN 55101
(612) 224-9431

Project Grants

Program Description The foundation supports projects in the arts, including programs in creative writing, dance, film and video, music, theater, visual arts, and in the humanities, including programs directed to increasing the understanding of the cultural heritage of our nation and the cultures of other regions of the world and programs which search for enduring values and increase appreciation of the importance of ethics and value judgments in American society. The functions of the Jerome Foundation are geographically limited to organizations and artists located and working in New York City, the state of Minnesota, and adjoining Midwest states.

Eligibility/Limitations The foundation confines its program to contributing to the support of projects and programs sponsored by appropriate, established, and tax-exempt organizations which have demonstrated that they have the essential skills and expertise in the arts and humanities encompassed in the foundation's program. Institutions applying for grants must provide evidence that they are tax-exempt and have been declared to be "nonprivate foundations" by the Federal Internal Revenue Service. Grants are not generally made to individuals or private foundations.

Fiscal Information Grants paid during the most recent fiscal year totaled approximately $1.18 million. The foundation ordinarily does not operate any projects, institutions, or organizations; conduct research, experiments, or studies; contribute to the operating budgets of established institutions; contribute to the support of general educational programs in the arts and humanities; fund capital campaigns; or support projects over extended periods of time. Specific program policies are available upon request.

Application Information All requests to the foundation must be in writing. A program brochure describing application procedures and content is available on request.

Deadline(s) Applications are reviewed and acted upon by the board of directors, generally in bimonthly meetings. Applicants should allow 90 to 120 days for the evaluation of proposals.

263. George Frederick Jewett Foundation
One Maritime Plaza, Suite 1340
San Francisco, CA 94111
(415) 421-1351

Program Description The Jewett Foundation is a family foundation whose grant-making activities respond in substantial part to the philanthropic interests of the members of the founding family. It is concerned primarily with people and values. The program focuses on the future and on stimulating and supporting activities and projects of established, voluntary, nonprofit organizations which are of importance to human welfare. The foundation makes grants in the following fields: arts and humanities, conservation and preservation, education, health care and medical services, population, religion, and social welfare. The foundation may support research on and studies of important problems of public concern, but when it does, it is solely for the purpose of aiding in the gathering and presenting of facts which may assist the public to better understand such problems and to arrive at realistic and effect solutions to them. The foundation confines its grants largely to the Pacific Northwest region of the United States, with priority given to requests from eastern Washington and northern Idaho.

Eligibility/Limitations No grants are made to individuals. From time to time, support may be given to the scholarship, fellowship, and research programs of established institutions when sufficient evidence is available to establish clearly that the applicant organization is awarding such grants in accordance with the regulations established by the Internal Revenue Code. Grants usually are not made to other private foundations and, as a rule, are not made to operating foundations. Preference is given to those voluntary organizations that are classified under the Tax Reform Act of 1969 as "public charities" or "nonprivate foundations."

Application Information Inquiries for clarification of the foundation's policy and program emphasis are welcomed and may save the inquirer time and effort in submitting a formal proposal.

Deadline(s) Deadlines for receipt of completed applications are February 15, May 15, August 15, November 1.

264. Johnson Controls Foundation
5757 North Green Bay Avenue, P.O. Box 591
Milwaukee, WI 53201
(414) 228-2219

Contributions

Program Description The Johnson Controls Foundation is organized and directed to be operated for charitable purposes which include the distribution and application of financial support to soundly managed and operated organizations or causes which are fundamentally philanthropic, give service with broad scope and impact, and contribute to the general welfare. In evaluating requests for funds, the foundation has developed policies and guidelines for giving in the following categories: health and social service; education; culture and the arts; civic activities; and miscellaneous. In the culture and the arts category, the foundation recognizes that the vitality of the arts and cultural activities significantly enriches the quality of life in any community. To assist such programs, it will consider contributions to visual, performing, and literary arts, public radio and television, libraries, museums, and other related cultural activities.

Eligibility/Limitations Contributions are limited to organizations which are exempt from taxation under the IRS code. Grants are not usually given to public or private preschools, elementary, or secondary institutions, but are limited to colleges and universities. No distribution will be made to a private individual for support of personal needs. No gifts are made to sectarian groups or programs. In general, no gifts are made for testimonial dinners, fund-raising events, tickets to benefits, shows or advertising. Grants are not made to provide monies for travel or tours, seminars and conferences, or for publication of books and magazines. Grants are not usually made for individual academic research. No gifts are made to foreign-based institutions. The foundation does not donate equipment, products, or labor.

Fiscal Information Contributions in 1985 totaled over $1.8 million.

Application Information There is no formal application procedure. Proposals, preferably in concise letter form, should include the following information: statement regarding tax-exempt status under Section 501(c)(3) of the IRS code; description of the structure, purpose, history, and programs of the organization, with a list of its officers and governing board members, including their outside affiliations; summary of the need for support and how it will be used; geographic areas served by the organization; current income and expense budget information of the organization and a copy of most recent audited financial statement; and statement regarding other sources of income from corporations and foundations, community support, and involvement.

Deadline(s) Proposals are accepted and reviewed throughout the year. In order to permit evaluation of proposals, notification of final action may take up to 120 days. Contributions are generally made bi-annually.

265. Edward C. Johnson Fund

82 Devonshire Street
Boston, MA 02109
(617) 570-6806

Grants

Program Description The fund offers support to youth programs, community development programs, higher education and secondary schools, museums, historic preservation, and protection and improvement of the environment.

Eligibility/Limitations The fund awards grants to qualified charitable institutions and nonprofit organizations, usually within Massachusetts. No grants or loans are made to individuals.

Fiscal Information The fund provides operating support, endowment, building funds, and funds for special projects.

Application Information Application is made in a brief letter of request along with supporting materials including history and objectives; current audited financial statements; IRS nonprofit status determination letter; list of officers and directors; and specific project request and project budget.

Deadline(s) Deadlines are March 30 for consideration by the trustees in June; October 30 for consideration by the trustees in December.

266. The Johnson's Wax Fund, Inc.

1525 Howe Street
Racine, WI 53403
(414) 631-2000

Grants

Program Description The fund has defined several broad-based areas of interest: education; scholarships and fellowships; and social welfare, civic, cultural, and environmental protection. Grants within the social welfare, civic, cultural, and environmental protection category are concentrated on programs which are a resource to the employees of Johnson's Wax and which benefit the community as a whole. The fund contributes to a small number of national, regional, and state organizations whose activities are far-ranging in effect and which reflect its current interests and concerns.

Sample Grants To help underwrite the Wooden Ship Era exhibit, $10,000 (second payment on a $25,000, three-year commitment) to the Manitowoc Maritime Museum (1986-1987). For the Great Circus Parade, $2,500 to Circus World Museum (1986-1987).

Eligibility/Limitations A grant seeking organization must have received a ruling from the IRS determining that it is an organization described in Section 501(c)(3) and Section 509(a)(1), (2), (3), or (4) of the Internal Revenue Code. Preference is given to agencies and programs in the geographic area of the headquarters of Johnson's Wax in Racine, Wisconsin, and to organizations and projects which are not primarily or normally financed by public tax funds. The fund does not contribute to the direct benefit of individual, nor does it make contributions for conferences, workshops, or seminars.

Fiscal Information Grants awarded in 1986 totaled more than $2 million, including $826,306 to social, cultural, and community concerns.

Application Information Applications for grants must be in written form. Initial contact should be by letter and proposals should include: a statement of purpose and brief history of the organization, a description of the overall program, an explanation regarding the specific request for support, an itemized annual and project budget, and a list of other corporate and foundation donors.

Deadline(s) There are no deadlines for submitting requests, which are reviewed on an ongoing basis.

Additional Information The corporation approved more than $6.5 million to organizations or institutions during the year ended June 30, 1987. Support by the corporation, however, is directed to requests from worthy recipients who do not fall within the established guidelines of the fund.

267. The Fletcher Jones Foundation
One Wilshire Building, Suite 1210, 624 South Grand Avenue
Los Angeles, CA 90017
(213) 689-9292

Grants

Program Description The trustees of the foundation give consideration to charitable, scientific, literary, and education areas, plus a minor portion to general purpose grants. However, from time to time, the trustees may give special emphasis to any of the above-listed areas. At present, special emphasis is being given to private colleges and universities, particularly those in California.

Sample Grants To assist "Need Scholarship" Program for summer science workshops, $5,000 to California Museum Foundation (1986). For general operating support, $7,500 to Craft and Folk Art Museum (1986). To assist in construction cost of Children's Zoo, $5,000 to Greater Los Angeles Zoo Association (1986). Final payment on grant to endow Fletcher Jones Chair in British & American Studies, $200,000 to Henry E. Huntington Library and Art Gallery (1986).

Eligibility/Limitations Grants are made to qualified, nonprofit organizations. Grants are not made to individuals, to carry on propaganda, to influence legislation, or to organizations engaged in such activities. The foundation generally does not favor requests for projects which should be financed by governmental agencies, nor does it normally make grants to operating funds, secondary schools, deficit financing, or contingencies. As a general rule, it does not make grants for conferences, seminars, workshops, travel exhibits, or surveys.

Fiscal Information Grants paid in 1986 totaled over $2.6 million.

Application Information An organization which believes it meets the foundation's criteria for a grant may wish to test the foundation's interest before preparing a formal grant application by submitting a short "Test Letter," highlighting the proposal and stating the amount of the grant to be requested. Each such letter will be acknowledged. Two replies are possible: (1) without commitment, the foundation will be pleased to receive and give consideration to an application for the grant as outlined or (2) the proposal does not appear feasible for foundation support. For applications deemed appropriate, no special application format is required. To facilitate trustee consideration, however, it is suggested that all applications be submitted on one typewritten page. A short cover letter should summarize the essential information. There is no limitation on the number of supporting documents. The following information assists the trustees in making a proper judgment: a fact sheet summarizing significant statistics and background about the applicant organization, its objectives, its current programs and services, and its chief sources of support; a description of the project, why it is needed, goals to be accomplished and how; applicant's qualifications to carry out the project; detailed financial information relative to the project; the amount requested from the foundation; how and when the project will be evaluated. Support documents forwarded should include: the most recent financial report, including balance sheet and profit-and-loss statement; IRS Classification Letter showing that the organization is a Section 501(c)(3) nonprofit public charity and not a private foundation; most recent Form 990 filed with the IRS; state Franchise and Income Tax Exemption Letter; list of organization's officers and directors, including their business or professional affiliations; applicant's most recent annual program report and name, address and telephone number of the organization's attorney.

Deadline(s) The foundation accepts and processes applications for grants throughout the year.

268. W. Alton Jones Foundation
433 Park Street
Charlottesville, VA 22901
(804) 295-2134

Arts Program

Program Description In 1986, a two-year arts pilot program was launched. This program seeks to nurture creative and venturesome initiatives in the visual arts, music, theater, and architecture. Throughout the period of the pilot program the foundation is operating proactively, researching and seeking out suitable grantees. The foundation does not solicit or accept applications. The theme of the program is the "best of tomorrow," and there are two parts: (1) up-and-coming organizations—general operating and special project support to young, emerging organizations with a distinct and convincing artistic mission, the potential to fulfill that mission, and to gain recognition as leaders in their genre, and (2) established organizations—new ventures involving traditional art, and special project support to encourage new art.

Sample Grants For support for the "Objects of Adornment" exhibit, $50,000 to Walters Art Gallery, Baltimore, MD (1986). For restoration and cataloguing of the 250-piece collection of works by Palmer Hayden, the doyen of the Harlem Renaissance movement of the 1930s, $20,000 to Museum of African American Art, Los Angeles, CA (1986).

Eligibility/Limitations Grants are restricted to seven geographic areas: New York City, Baltimore, Los Angeles, Palm Beach, New Jersey, Colorado, and Virginia.

Application Information Contact the foundation for additional information about this program.

269. W. Alton Jones Foundation
433 Park Street
Charlottesville, VA 22901
(804) 295-2134

Sustainable Society Program

Program Description The Sustainable Society Program seeks to keep the earth suitable for long-term habitation by preserving the natural resource base. The program supports proposals for projects which address the conservation of biological diversity worldwide. The goal of this program is to preserve the diversity of the earth's plants, animals, natural communities, and ecosystems, and to preserve the ecosystem services required to maintain a livable biosphere.

Sample Grants For support of their "Alternatives to Destruction Project," $138,930 (fifth year of a five-year $1,029,200 grant) to Smithsonian Tropical Research Institute (1986). For support of botanical gardens, $60,000 to International Union for Conservation of Nature and Natural Resources, Gland, Switzerland (1986).

Eligibility/Limitations The foundation does not support scholarship funds or make direct awards to individuals. The foundation has in the past supported projects which educate the public and the government; monitor the government; foster conservation through land purchases, easements, parks and preserves; include basic and applied research; initiate policy development, litigation, and mediation; and train resource specialists or develop indigenous organizations, especially in the tropics and other species-rich areas.

Fiscal Information Grant awards range from $4,000 to over $300,000. The foundation ordinarily will not consider proposals for capital purposes, endowment funds, or deficit operations.

Application Information A preliminary inquiry prior to the submission of a detailed proposal is advisable. A grant request should be initiated by a letter describing the proposed project, its expected impact, the qualifications of the staff, a detailed expense budget, the time frames, and other funding sources, as well as copies of the applicant organization's tax-exempt rulings stating that it is described in Section 501(c)(3) of the Internal Revenue Code and is not a private foundation.

Deadline(s) The commitment of grant funds is the responsibility of the board of trustees. The board meets in March, June, September, and December. Proposals should be submitted to the foundation's executive director prior to January 15, April 15, July 15, and October 15 to allow adequate time for review before the quarterly meetings.

270. The J. M. Kaplan Fund, Inc.
330 Madison Avenue
New York, NY 10017
(212) 661-8485

Grants

Program Description The fund's program is mainly concerned with the public interest of New York, including some issues that go beyond local borders such as the natural environment and human rights. The fund contributes to organizations based in New York; most grants stay near home. Grants fall into three principal categories: the city and state; the arts; and civil liberties and human needs. Within the city and state category, the fund support programs in New York City and New York state to improve the physical environment. This means architecture and landscape design, city planning, and historic preservation; help for parks, open space, trees and city gardens; neighborhood stability and amenity; monitoring public responsibility for basic services; and natural resource protection. Within the arts category, the fund supports the arts and cultural life in New York City and New York in limited and specific ways: with assistance for libraries and writers' organizations; grants to distinguished, small-scale music groups; and varied forms of help to museums and to certain cultural centers.

Sample Grants For general support for this association of sixty historic house museums, $5,000 to Metropolitan Historic Structures Association (1986). For an exhibition on "Louis H. Sullivan: The Function of Ornament," the most extensive display of materials ever assembled on the work of America's great 19th century architect, $62,500 to Cooper-Hewitt National Museum of Design (Smithsonian Institution) (1986). To produce a catalogue to accompany their exhibition on "Building the Borough: Architecture and Planning in the Bronx," $35,000 to Bronx Museum of the Arts (1986). For an exhibition on Russia and the Jews, 1880-1980, presented in conjunction with Yivo Institute, $50,000 to The Jewish Museum (1986).

Eligibility/Limitations The fund generally does not contribute to: operating budgets of educational, medical, and cultural institutions; building programs; charitable organizations that solicit contributions from the general public; organizations whose main activities take place outside the New York area; films or video; scholarships, fellow-ships, research, conferences, prizes, study or travel; or the personal sponsorship of books, dances, plays, musical compositions, or other works of art. The fund contributes only to tax-exempt, publicly supported organizations, and is prohibited from making grants to individuals.

Fiscal Information At the end of fiscal year 1986 the fund awarded grants totaling $4,967,500 to 162 programs.

Application Information A clear, concise letter describing the organization and the program for which it seeks support serves as application—and should be accompanied by budgets, sources of income, lists of board and staff members, IRS determination letter, and Form 990. Further material may be requested if there is trustee interest in the proposal. Initial inquiries by brief letter or telephone are preferred, after which the fund will send its application checklist for the complete materials if the project is appropriate.

Deadline(s) Requests are considered between March 1 and October 15, and grant decisions are made on a rolling schedule.

271. W. M. Keck Foundation
555 South Flower Street, Suite 3230
Los Angeles, CA 90071
(213) 680-3833

Grants

Program Description The W. M. Keck Foundation makes grants to eligible institutions for the following purposes: to strengthen studies and programs in the areas of earth sciences, involving development of natural resources; engineering; medical education and research; and, to some extent, other sciences and liberal arts. The foundation gives some consideration, focused in southern California, to support organizations and institutions in arts and culture, civic and community services, health care, and primary and secondary education. In addition to supporting the above purposes, the foundation may from time to time initiate special, major grants for potentially significant endeav-ors that require levels of funding not commonly available, for the advancement of knowledge which the foundation believes will ultimately benefit mankind.

Eligibility/Limitations Funding will not be considered for the following types of requests: organizations that have not received permanent, tax-exempt ruling determina-tion from the federal government and the state of California (if state exemption is applicable); routine institutional expenses, general endowments, or deficit reduction; general and federated campaigns, including fund-raising events, dinners, or mass mailings; direct aid to individuals; conduit organizations; sponsorship of conferences and seminars; publication of books or production of films; public policy research; and requests which do not fall within the foundation's specific areas of interest, set forth above.

Fiscal Information Grants awarded in 1986 totaled over $36.5 million, including over $1.5 million in the arts and culture category.

Application Information Initial contact must be made by letters of inquiry which must contain: a narrative, not to exceed three pages, describing the project and including a brief statement of the institution's background and a cost summary of the project or program for which support is being sought; a copy of the institution's current audited financial statements; a copy of the institution's determination letter from the IRS, stating that the institution is exempt from taxation as defined by Section 501(c)(3) of the Internal Revenue Code and is not a private foundation as defined in Section 509(a) of the code; if the institution is located in the state of California, or is conducting operations within the state, a copy of the current documentary evidence from the State of California Franchise Tax Board showing that the institution is exempt from California State Franchise or Income Tax under Section 23701(d), Revenue and Taxation Code. Upon review of these initial inquiries, the foundation will invite full proposals from selected organizations. Full proposals are accepted upon invitation of the foundation only.

Deadline(s) Initial contacts by letter of inquiry are accepted year-round.

272. Peter Kiewit Foundation
Woodmen Tower, Suite 1145, Farnam at Seventeenth
Omaha, NE 68102
(402) 344-7890

Grants

Program Description The objective of the foundation is to provide charitable grants to worthy tax-exempt organizations carrying on religious, charitable, scientific, literary, or educational activities exclusively. Grants may also be made to a state or any political subdivision thereof but only if the grant is made exclusively for public purposes.

Sample Grants For program expansion and acquisition of research/resource materials, $5,000 to Great Plains Black Museum, Omaha, NE (1982). For improvements to museum and supporting facilities, $500,000, and for operating support, $70,000 to Joslyn Liberal Arts Society, Omaha, NE (1982). For program support, $23,500 to Omaha Children's Museum (1982).

Eligibility/Limitations Preference will be given to those organizations which will use and apply substantially all of the distribution in the state of Nebraska; that part of Iowa which is within a 100-mile radius of Omaha, Nebraska; the city of Sheridan, Wyoming and the immediate vicinity thereof. Also receiving preference is the area of Rancho Mirage, California. Grants will be made only to such organizations that are tax-exempt as defined in Section 501(c)(3) of the Internal Revenue Code and which are not private foundations as defined in Section 509 of the code. The foundation is prohibited from making grants to individuals.

Fiscal Information Contributions awarded in 1982 totaled over $6 million.

Application Information Additional information and guidelines are available from the foundation.

Deadline(s) The board meets at least quarterly (on a selected date in March, June, September, December) and all commitments of grant funds are made by the board. Grant applications are to be submitted seventy-five days prior to the board meeting at which consideration of the application is desired.

273. Robert J. Kleberg, Jr. and Helen C. Kleberg Foundation
700 North St. Mary's Street, Suite 1200
San Antonio, TX 78205
(512) 271-3691

Grants

Program Description The foundation supports medical research, veterinary and animal sciences, wildlife research and preservation, health services, higher education, community organizations, and the arts and humanities. Over the last twelve years a large portion of the foundation's funds has been directed into medical research.

Sample Grants For historic site and museum support, $1,000 to Henry Francis duPont Winterthur Museum, Winterthur, DE (1986). For management of Texas bird sanctuaries, $15,000 to National Audubon Society, New York (1986). For construction project, $20,000 to National Museum of Racing, Saratoga Springs, NY (1986). For archives of American art project, $5,000 to Smithsonian Institution, Washington, DC (1986).

Eligibility/Limitations As a general policy, the foundation refrains from making grants to: individuals; endowments, deficit financing, or ongoing operating expenses; community organizations outside the state of Texas; organizations limited by race or religion; and organizations which are not tax-exempt.

Fiscal Information Grant awards range from $1,000 to $400,000.

Application Information Proposals should include: a brief background of the organization; a description of the proposed project and a concise statement of the necessity for such a project; an explanation of the proposed use of funds, a detailed project budget, other potential sources of funding, and a specific amount requested from the foundation; evidence of tax-exempt status; and a statement of approval of the request for funds signed by the chief administrator of the organization.

Deadline(s) The foundation directors convene twice annually to consider grant applications.

274. Knight Foundation
1 Cascade Plaza, 8th Floor
Akron, OH 44308
(216) 253-9301

Cities Program

Program Description The Knight Foundation supports worthy causes and organizations in communities in which the Knight-Ridder company has newspaper and other business enterprises. In making grants, the foundation seeks to enhance the quality of life in these communities and encourage educational, cultural, economic, social, and civic betterments as promising opportunities present themselves. The foundation also makes selected national grants in these various fields of interest.

Sample Grants To encourage minority exposure to the arts by exhibiting the works of five contemporary ethnic artists and providing outreach programs and workshops, $5,000 to Long Beach Museum of Art Foundation, Long Beach, CA (1986). To build a new chimpanzee exhibit, $500,000 to Detroit Zoological Society, Royal Oak, MI (1986). For general operating support, $30,000 to Akron Art Museum, Akron, OH (1986). To participate in creating The Technology Center, an educational institution that will promote an understanding and awareness of technology, $1 million to High Technology Museum, San Jose, CA (1986). To support the Patrons' Permanent Fund, $400,000 to National Gallery of Art, Washington, DC (1986).

Eligibility/Limitations Applicant organizations must have received a letter of determination from the IRS granting them 501(c)(3) tax-exempt status and be considered not a private foundation according to the definition in Section 509(a) of the Internal Revenue Code. Applicant organizations must be located in cities in which Knight-Ridder newspapers or other enterprises are based. The foundation does not make grants to individuals. The trustees prefer not to fund participation in annual fund-raising campaigns, ongoing requests for general operating support, although some repeat grants are made, or operating deficits.

Fiscal Information Grants awarded during 1986 totaled over $19 million.

Application Information The foundation does not use application forms. Qualified organizations seeking grant support should submit a brief letter on the letterhead of the organization to the president of the foundation. In general, the form of the letter is less important than the contents. However, the following information must be included: a brief description of the organization; the need for the project, what it will accomplish, and a timetable for its duration; the total cost of the project and the specific amount requested from Knight Foundation and, if other foundations are being approached, they should be listed and any commitments noted. Other materials to be attached to the proposal letter include: a list of the applicant's governing body and its officers, showing their business, professional, and community affiliations; a copy of the most recent letter from the IRS determining the organization's tax-exempt status; a copy of the organization's most recent audited financial statements; a written endorsement by the organization's CEO, when the request comes from someone other than the CEO. If additional information is needed, it will be requested. Only written applications will be considered.

Deadline(s) The foundation meets four times a year to consider grant requests. Any eligible request that arrives too late for one meeting will be placed upon the agenda of the following meeting. Proposals must be received at foundation offices by 5:00 p.m. on the following dates to be included in the agendas noted: January 15 for the March agenda; April 15 for the June agenda; July 15 for the September agenda; October 15 for the December agenda. The trustees prefer not to consider applications from any institution or organization more frequently than once every twelve months, whether the result of the previous application was positive or negative.

275. The Kresge Foundation
3215 West Big Beaver Road, P.O. Box 3151
Troy, MI 48007-3151
(313) 643-9630

Grants

Program Description Grants are awarded *only* toward projects involving (a) construction of facilities, (b) renovation of facilities, (c) the purchase of major capital equipment or an integrated system at a cost of at least $75,000, and (d) the purchase of real estate.

Sample Grants For renovation of facilities, $80,000 to The Ann Arbor Hands-On Museum, Ann Arbor, MI (1986). For Phase I and Phase II renovation and expansion of facility, $350,000 to Cedar Rapids Museum of Art, Cedar Rapids, IA (1986). For renovation and expansion of museum facilities, $150,000 to Ella Sharp Museum, Jackson, MI (1986). For construction of wing to house Shin'enKan Collection, $325,000 to Los Angeles County Museum of Art, Los Angeles, CA (1986). For renovation and construction of facilities, $500,000 to The Saint Louis Art Museum, St. Louis, MO (1986). For construction of children's zoo at Phoenix Zoo, $150,000 to Arizona Zoological Society, Phoenix, AZ (1986). For renovation of Lehmann Building, $350,000 to Missouri Botanical Garden, St. Louis, MO (1986). For Phase I construction of Asian elephant forest exhibit, $250,000 to Seattle Zoological Society, Seattle, WA (1986).

Eligibility/Limitations Eligible applicants include tax-exempt charitable organizations operating in the fields of four-year college and university education, health care, social services, science and conservation, arts and humanities, and public affairs.

Fiscal Information In 1986, the foundation awarded over $45.1 million to 151 charitable organizations after reviewing 915 eligible applications. Grants are awarded on a challenge basis. No matching formula is involved. The challenge is to raise whatever balance is needed to assure full project funding. The purpose is to encourage additional gift support. The foundation does not grant initial funds or total project support. Grants are for a portion of the costs remaining at the time of grant approval.

Application Information An application must include the following: a covering letter, signed by the senior administrative official, which briefly describes the grant request; a fact sheet form (from the foundation); organizational, project, and fund-raising information; and attachments including most recent audited financial statement; IRS ruling letters indicating that the organization is tax-exempt and not classified as a private foundation under IRS code Section 509(a), and a complete copy of the most recent accreditation and/or licensure report.

Deadline(s) Applications may be submitted at any time throughout the year, but only one in any twelve month period.

276. Samuel H. Kress Foundation
221 West 57th Street
New York, NY 10019
(212) 586-4450

Fellowships in Art Conservation

Program Description Advanced students in the conservation of works of art may compete for funds to support their studies.

Eligibility/Limitations Applicants must be citizens of the United States, and must be already accepted into a training program.

Application Information Further information is available on written request to the foundation.

Deadline(s) Application deadline is January 31.

277. Samuel H. Kress Foundation
221 West 57th Street
New York, NY 10019
(212) 586-4450

Grants

Program Description Continuing its traditional concerns, the Kress Foundation concentrates its funding in the history and preservation of art. Present program areas of interest include: (1) fellowships for predoctoral research in art history; (2) training and research in conservation of works of art; (3) development of scholarly resources in the fields of art history and conservation; (4) conservation and restoration of monuments and works of art; (5) archaeological fieldwork emphasizing art history; and (6) occasional related projects.

Eligibility/Limitations The foundation does not consider grants for living artists, films, art history programs below the predoctoral level, or the purchase of works of art.

Fiscal Information Grants awarded in 1984 ranged in amount from $1,500 to $261,500.

Application Information The foundation does not have formal application forms. A simple letter describing the project and the funds to be requested will ensure consideration.

Deadline(s) Proposals for projects within the program areas listed above may be submitted to the foundation at any time.

278. Samuel H. Kress Foundation
221 West 57th Street
New York, NY 10019
(212) 586-4450

Research Fellowships in Art History

Program Description Travel grants to enable predoctoral candidates in the history of art to pursue essential research are available annually through a program administered by the foundation.

Eligibility/Limitations Applicants must be citizens of the United States, and must anticipate the completion of all requirements for the Ph.D. degree except the dissertation at the time the grant will be received.

Application Information Further information is available on written request to the foundation.

Deadline(s) Application deadline is November 30.

279. Lannan Foundation
12555 West Jefferson Boulevard, Suite 218
Los Angeles, CA 90066
(213) 301-7683

Grants for the Visual Arts

Program Description The Lannan Foundation is dedicated to fostering the creation and appreciation of contemporary art. Toward this end the foundation has developed and instituted four programs: grants for varied programs and activities in the field of contemporary art; exhibition and interpretation of the Lannan Foundation collection; acquisition of contemporary art for its permanent collection; and the fostering of serious scholarship and criticism in contemporary art. The foundation supports quality projects and activities in the field of contemporary visual arts at its facilities and other qualifying institutions in the United States. The visual arts grant program was developed to achieve the following: bring the work of emerging and contemporary artists to a wider audience; further the careers of emerging and under-recognized artists; give museums incentives to focus attention and scholarship on their own collections of contemporary art; and encourage spontaneity in institutional programming so as to respond with greater flexibility to new art. The foundation, therefore, is especially interested in proposals from institutions that: feature the work of emerging or under-recognized living artists; give established contemporary artists exposure where their work is not represented; feature and interpret the applying institution's own collection of contemporary art; feature work that is unlikely to be sponsored by other sources because it is too controversial or experimental.

Eligibility/Limitations Funding for this program is available to institutions for exhibitions, exhibition series, temporary installations, and interdisciplinary activities. The foundation may consider other types of projects as well. Funds are not available for individuals, general operating expenses or endowment funds, juried exhibitions, annuals, biennials, internationals, or maintenance and conservation of sponsored projects and commissions.

Application Information Interested institutions must obtain grant application forms from the foundation. Requests for funding are to be sent to the director of art programs. Application forms must be completed and delivered to the foundation with proof of tax-exempt status, resumes of individuals involved in the activity, a list of the board of trustees or other governing body, up to twenty slides (each labeled with artist's name, media, dates, and applicant's name), and/or up to thirty minutes of video, and a self-addressed post card. Proposals for exhibition series must: include slides showing installations of similar exhibitions organized by the institution; catalogues or brochures and reviews of similar exhibitions; explanation of the institution's procedure for selecting artists for the series; description of the assigned gallery space (including location and size); and include slides and resumes of artists included in the series if they are determined by the application date.

Deadline(s) Grant requests are reviewed three times a year, with application deadlines on the first day of October, February, and May. The application must be delivered to the foundation by the due date.

280. Eli Lilly and Company Foundation
Contributions Committee
Lilly Corporate Center
Indianapolis, IN 46285
(317) 276-2000

Grants

Program Description The foundation was established in 1968 to complement the charitable activities and interests of Eli Lilly and Company. The contributions of the foundation are directed toward programs in the areas of health and welfare, education, local civic and cultural activities, and public affairs.

Eligibility/Limitations While a number of national programs are supported, emphasis is placed upon those endeavors serving communities where Lilly employees reside. The foundation also reviews other programs that address the needs of society and are consistent with corporate objectives. Typically, the company and its foundation are unable to provide assistance for: grants to individuals; scholarships, loans, or fellowships; operating support for organizations already receiving United Way funds; memorial programs; or debt financing.

Fiscal Information Contributions in 1986 totaled over $3.3 million.

Application Information Requests for financial assistance should include information explaining the purpose of the organization, the amount of money requested, the reason for the grant, the latest IRS classification, and any other general information that might help the foundation in its decision making process.

Deadline(s) No deadlines are announced.

281. The Lincoln Electric Foundation
22801 St. Clair Avenue
Cleveland, OH 44117
(216) 481-8100

Grants

Program Description The foundation contributes to the Cleveland United Way Drive, certain cultural institutions, and to a number of local independent colleges and hospitals.

Eligibility/Limitations Grants are awarded in the Cleveland, Ohio geographic area, in which the foundation is located. No grants are awarded to individuals.

Fiscal Information Contributions in 1985 totaled over $500,000.

Application Information Applicants should send an initial letter of inquiry outlining their proposed project or program.

Deadline(s) Contact the foundation for deadlines.

282. The Charles A. Lindbergh Fund, Inc.
Grants Office
Box O
Summit, NJ 07901
(201) 522-1392

The Lindbergh Grants Program

Program Description This program offers grants to individuals working for a balance between technological progress and the preservation of our natural and human environment to achieve a better quality of life for all. The board of directors of the fund is interested in increasing representation in the following areas: aeronautics/astronautics/aviation, agriculture, biomedical research, conservation of natural resources, health and population sciences, intercultural communication, oceanography and water resources, waste disposal management, and wildlife preservation.

Eligibility/Limitations The Lindbergh Grants Program is international in scope. Citizens of all countries are eligible. The fund welcomes candidates who are affiliated with an academic or nonprofit institution. Grants are awarded to individuals, not to affiliated institutions for institutional programs.

Fiscal Information Grants of up to $10,580 will be awarded annually. In 1986, the average grant size was $8,625.

Application Information Copies of the Lindbergh Grants Announcement and application guidelines can be obtained by writing the fund.

Deadline(s) Complete applications should be received by the fund before October 15.

283. The Henry Luce Foundation, Inc.
111 West 50th Street
New York, NY 10020
(212) 489-7700

The Luce Fund for Chinese Scholars

Program Description This program brings senior Chinese humanists and social scientists to spend periods of six months to one year at leading American China studies centers.

Eligibility/Limitations Participation in the program is limited to seventeen American universities with outstanding programs in the field of Chinese studies. The program is not competitive: a request that meets the requirements of the program will receive funding.

Fiscal Information In 1985, foundation grant awards in all categories exceeded $8.4 million.

Application Information The foundation publishes no formal guidelines, nor does it use special application forms. The staff of the foundation is always happy to answer telephone requests for additional information about specific application procedures.

Deadline(s) Requests for the Luce Fund for Chinese Scholars will be considered at any time, but no more than twelve months before the anticipated arrival of a scholar.

284. The Henry Luce Foundation, Inc.
111 West 50th Street
New York, NY 10020
(212) 489-7700

Luce Fund for Scholarship in American Art Grants

Program Description The Luce Fund for Scholarship in American Art was designed to encourage the growth of serious scholarship on every aspect of American fine and decorative arts, a field that has frequently—and surprisingly—been undervalued by art historians. A secondary purpose is to encourage American museums to place greater emphasis on research and scholarship than has been possible in recent years.

Sample Grants For a catalogue of the Herbert Bayer Archive, $100,000 to The Denver Art Museum (1985-1986). For a catalogue of the American paintings and sculpture in the institute, $95,000 to Sterling and Francine Clark Art Institute (1985-1986). For research, preparation, and publication of "American Silver at Winterthur," $120,000 to Henry Francis duPont Winterthur Museum (1985-1986).

Eligibility/Limitations Application is open to American museums identified by the foundation. In the future, special project requests from a sharply curtailed group of designated museums will continue to be considered. Awards of this nature are likely to be few in number.

Fiscal Information Through 1986, a total of seventy-nine separate research grants totaling $7 million were made to forty different museums.

Application Information Contact the foundation for additional information about this program.

Deadline(s) June 15 is the deadline for submission of proposals.

285. The Henry Luce Foundation, Inc.
111 West 50th Street
New York, NY 10020
(212) 489-7700

Luce Scholars Program

Program Description The Luce Scholars Program is one aspect of the foundation's continuing efforts to improve American understanding of Asia. Each year, fifteen young Americans of outstanding promise are selected by the foundation and sent to East and Southeast Asia to undertake internships in their chosen fields under the guidance of leading Asian professionals. A distinguishing feature of the program is that it is directed toward those who are not—and do not plan to become—specialists in Asian affairs. Its object is to develop among a broad cross section of future American leaders an understanding of the nature of Asian societies and cultures. The program is experimental rather than academic in nature. At its core are the individual internships and job placements arranged for the scholars on the basis of their individual career interests, experience, and training. Though it is hoped that the work of the scholars will be useful to their Asian hosts, a scholar's most significant contribution may simply be an honest attempt to assimilate the wealth of Asian experience and, in the process, to develop a much broader world perspective.

Eligibility/Limitations To be eligible for the program, nominees must be American citizens under thirty years of age with a bachelor's degree as a minimum.

Fiscal Information In 1985, foundation grant awards in all categories exceeded $8.4 million.

Application Information The program relies for its nominations on a network of sixty colleges and universities. Individual applications submitted directly to the foundation cannot be considered. A brochure describing the program in detail is available on request.

Deadline(s) Applications for the Luce Scholars Program must reach the foundation from the nominating institutions by the first Monday of December.

286. The Henry Luce Foundation, Inc.
111 West 50th Street
New York, NY 10020
(212) 489-7700

Program Grants

Program Description General program grants are made each year to a wide range of qualified nonprofit organizations active in fields of particular interest to the foundation. Through such responsive grants, the foundation preserves its flexibility and its freedom to respond quickly to new ideas and situations. More often, general program grants are made in support of specific projects in the areas of the foundation's overall program interests: public affairs, Asian affairs, theology, and higher education and the arts. Specific program emphasis may change from time to time to reflect shifts in the national and international scene.

Sample Grants To complete construction of the museum's new facilities, and to retire obligations incurred by the museum in moving, $500,000 to The New Museum of Contemporary Art (1985-1986). To support the cataloguing of a collection of original drawings of Central Park and other New York City parks and public institutions, $28,000 to New York Archival Society (1985-1986). To support the preservation and cataloguing of the academy's archives, $30,000 to the Academy of American Poets (1985-1986).

Eligibility/Limitations Qualified nonprofit organizations are eligible to apply.

Fiscal Information In 1985, foundation grant awards in all categories exceeded $8.4 million.

Application Information The foundation publishes no formal guidelines, nor does it use special application forms. The staff of the foundation is always happy to answer telephone requests for additional information about specific application procedures.

Deadline(s) Requests for general program grants can be submitted at any time, although the foundation's awards in this category are normally made late in the year.

287. The J. E. and L. E. Mabee Foundation, Inc.
Mid-Continent Tower
401 South Boston, 30th Floor
Tulsa, OK 74103-4017
(918) 584-4286

Grants

Program Description The general objectives and purposes of the Mabee Foundation are to assist religious, charitable, and educational organizations.

Sample Grants For a print gallery and study area, $168,000 to the Museum of the Southwest, Midland, TX (1985).

Eligibility/Limitations The foundation has a geographical area of giving which includes only the states of Arkansas, Kansas, Missouri, New Mexico, Oklahoma, and Texas. Although it is a broad-based foundation, the Mabee Foundation does not generally favor: grants for deficit financing; grants for operating funds or annual fund-raising campaigns; grants for reserve purposes or for projects likely to be long delayed; grants for endowments; and grants for government-owned or -operated institutions and/or facilities.

Fiscal Information Most of the foundation grants are made toward building and facility construction, renovation projects, and to the purchase of major capital equipment. Ordinarily, grants in these areas are made on a challenge or conditional basis so as to provide incentive for enlisting the support of other donors. No matching formula is involved.

Application Information The Mabee Foundation does not use a standard application form and there is no formal procedure for making application. Elaborate presentations are not required and only one application need be furnished. Proposals must contain all of the items listed below that are pertinent to the request and that will assist the foundation in judging the proposal: the legal name and address of the organization making application; name, title, address, and telephone number of the person designated as the primary proposal contact; brief description of the organization, including a summary of its background and its qualifications in the area for which funds are sought; description of the project for which funds are sought, what it is expected to achieve, and why it is important to undertake; description of the people, organizations, or groups expected to benefit from the project and the ways they would benefit; substantiation of the extent of need for those benefits and comments on past or present attempts by the applicant or others to address this need; detailed expenditure budget for the project, indicating how the major elements of expense were estimated, how the requested funds are to be spent and during what time periods; description of other possible sources of support which have been or will be solicited for the project, including a statement of funds which have been received or pledged as of the date of the application; the amount of the grant sought from the foundation; if a challenge grant is requested, the time within which the challenge will be met; a time schedule for start of construction or the anticipated commencement of the project; explanation of how the project will be sustained, if appropriate, after the period for which support has been requested. In addition to the actual proposal, the following support information must be included as an appendix: photocopies of the most recent ruling from the IRS that the organization is tax-exempt under Section 501(c)(3) and is not a "private foundation" under Section 509(a); a statement on the organization's letterhead, signed by the organization's chief executive officer, that there has been no change in the purpose, character, or method of operation subsequent to the issuance of the IRS determination letter; a copy of the organization's audited financial statement for the most recently completed fiscal year; interim financial statement for the current fiscal period; a list of names and primary professional affiliations of members of the organization's governing body and names and titles of the officers.

Deadline(s) An application may be submitted at any time throughout the year. The trustees of the foundation meet four times a year, in January, April, July, and October, to decide on grants. An application filed on or before the first day of the month preceding a meeting date is normally considered at such meeting date.

288. The John D. and Catherine MacArthur Foundation
140 South Dearborn Street
Chicago, IL 60603
(312) 726-8000

Chicago Cultural Grants Program

Program Description The Chicago Cultural Grants Program reflects the foundation's commitment to Chicago, the urban community which was the founders' home and place of business for many years. The principal goal of this program is to enhance the quality of life for people living in this community by supporting cultural activities and helping organizations that are addressing important community needs. The foundation's criteria for cultural grants include artistic merit, organizational soundness, financial accountability, and community outreach activities.

Sample Grants In renewed support of general operations (over two years) $100,000 to Adler Planetarium, Chicago, IL (1986). In renewed support of general operations (over two years), $120,000 to Chicago Zoological Society, Brookfield, IL (1986). In renewed support of general operations (over four years), $200,000 Museum of Broadcast Communications, Chicago, IL (1986).

Eligibility/Limitations As a matter of policy, the foundation does not consider requests to support special cultural events or projects. Chicago cultural grants provide unrestricted annual support to both established institutions and emerging artistic efforts within the city.

Fiscal Information Grant authorizations in 1986 totaled over $5.2 million.

Application Information Letters of inquiry from cultural organizations not previously supported by the foundation should describe the organization's artistic program, management and board capabilities, sources of financial support, and unique contribution to Chicago's cultural environment. Foundation staff will request more detailed information and arrange a site visit if appropriate. Cultural organizations that have previously received foundation grants are automatically reviewed each year for consideration of continued support.

Deadline(s) Letters of inquiry are reviewed throughout the year.

289. The John D. and Catherine MacArthur Foundation
140 South Dearborn Street
Chicago, IL 60603
(312) 726-8000

General Grants Programs

Program Description The foundation's General Grants Program reflects its interests in a variety of important public issues. While the scope of the program is broad, the foundation has specified four areas of emphasis: education, governance, justice, and mass communications. Within the mass communications category, interests include the role of the press and the performance of the journalism community in our democratic society; the impact of media on public opinion and public policy formation; the educational use of broadcast television and newer communications technologies; and the role of nonprofit media enterprises in American communications.

Sample Grants To purchase a complete interformat editing system, a broadcast camera, and a field recorder, $30,000 to Capital Children's Museum, Washington, DC (1986). To upgrade existing editing decks, purchase a new recorder, implement a broadcast post-production system, and build another studio, $30,000 to Long Beach Museum of Art Foundation, Long Beach, CA (1986). To create a retrospective exhibition of the video art of Bill Viola, $30,000 to Museum of Modern Art, New York, NY (1986). To underwrite costs of publications, program notes, advertising, and promotion, $15,000 to Whitney Museum of American Art, New York, NY (1986).

Eligibility/Limitations The program reflects the foundation's interest in creative approaches to general problems rather than the ongoing financial needs of organizations. In general, support will not be considered for local scope or local impact projects, service delivery, operating programs, professional education or training, or single-investigator, single-issue research projects. The foundation does not make awards to individuals, except by way of the MacArthur Fellows Program. Increasingly, grants are made in support of foundation-generated initiatives rather than in response to grant requests.

Fiscal Information Grant awards in this category totaled over $18 million in 1986.

Application Information The program accepts brief letters of inquiry and intent from nonprofit organizations which are pursuing or are interested in pursing these goals and objectives. Unsolicited proposals are not considered, and may be returned without review. The letter of inquiry, usually not more than four pages in length, should succinctly state a problem or issue to be addressed, the significance of that problem, the way that problem relates to the interests of the program, and the solution or resolution being proposed. It should also discuss summarily the financial aspects of the undertaking proposed, and include a brief description of the applicant organization to explain its appropriateness for the tasks being suggested.

Deadline(s) The board of directors meets regularly to conduct foundation business and to make decisions on funding authorizations recommended by program committees.

290. William Hammond Mathers Museum
601 East Eighth Street
Bloomington, IN 47405
(812) 335-6873

Graduate Assistantships

Program Description Graduate Assistantships at the William Hammond Mathers Museum offer an opportunity for sponsored training in museum work.

Eligibility/Limitations While assistantships are not limited to students in anthropology, history, and folklore, a graduate assistant must be enrolled in the graduate school of Indiana University during his or her term of appointment. Any award will be contingent upon acceptance by and enrollment in the graduate school. Previous museum training and experience are not absolute prerequisites for appointment as a graduate assistant, but preference is normally given to applicants with such qualifications. Graduate assistants may be appointed for a single semester or a full academic year. Upon reapplication, appointments may be renewed at the discretion of the museum.

Fiscal Information Assistantships provide financial support for graduate students who are carrying out projects under the supervision of one or more members of the museum's staff.

Application Information There is no standard application form. Instead, the museum requests that applicants write a letter (one to two pages) discussing museum training and experience, if any, and the aspects of museum work that interest the applicant. Applicants not currently enrolled in Indiana University should include an official transcript from their most recently attended college or university. The museum also requests letters of reference from someone qualified to evaluate the applicant's work; this person should send the letter directly to the museum. All applications should be sent to the director of the museum.

Deadline(s) Applications received by April 1 will be assured of consideration for the upcoming academic year.

291. The May Stores Foundation, Inc.
611 Olive Street
Saint Louis, MO 63101
(314) 342-6300

Grants

Program Description The foundation focuses its activities on the areas of health and welfare, education, culture and the arts, and civic causes.

Eligibility/Limitations The foundation directs particular attention to the needs of the communities in which the May Company operates. The foundation only awards financial assistance to nonprofit organizations.

Fiscal Information Contributions in 1986 totaled approximately $6 million.

Application Information The foundation does not have a formal set of guidelines. To apply to the foundation for financial assistance, an organization must address its request in writing. The letter should state the purpose of the request and if applicable, briefly discuss the organization's history, goals, and the breadth of support it receives from its constituents.

Deadline(s) No deadlines are announced.

292. McGraw-Hill Foundation, Inc.
1221 Avenue of the Americas
New York, NY 10020
(212) 512-6480

Grants

Program Description The McGraw-Hill Foundation was established in 1979 to formalize the corporation's philanthropic activities begun twenty-one years earlier and to meet emerging issues in a planned, constructive manner. Wholly funded by contributions from McGraw-Hill, Inc., the foundation is the corporation's principal vehicle for providing charitable support. While responsive to a broad range of issues, the foundation, with limited resources, cannot be a partner to all causes. Its strongest emphasis is placed on education, culture and the arts, health and human services, and civic affairs.

Eligibility/Limitations The foundation prefers to support projects and programs that address problems that affect communities in which McGraw-Hill has a substantial presence and qualify as public charities under the U.S. Internal Revenue Code. The foundation does not sponsor advertising, nor subscribe to tables or tickets for charitable events. In addition, it does not contribute to: institutions and agencies clearly outside company geographic concerns and interests; individuals; publication of books, magazines, or films; endowment funds; conferences, trips or tours; nor make loans of any kind.

Fiscal Information Foundation contributions in 1986 totaled over $1.9 million.

Application Information The foundation welcomes requests for support. Organizations falling within the guidelines listed here who wish to seek support are invited to do so by submitting a preliminary proposal letter that should include the following information: a brief background of the organization including its goals and objectives, staff, and outside directors; a concise description of the program and objectives for which support is being sought; a copy of the most recent audited financial statement and annual report; a current year's budget and the sources from which funding is derived; the budget for the program for which support is requested and the sum requested; evidence of public charity status under U.S. Internal Revenue Code.

Deadline(s) The board of directors of the foundation meets quarterly and decisions on pending grants are made at those times.

293. McKesson Foundation, Inc.
One Post Street
San Francisco, CA 94104
(415) 983-8673

Grants

Program Description The McKesson Foundation emphasizes support to organizations located in the San Francisco Bay area and other areas where McKesson has a sizable employee representation. Although the foundation funds a variety of social, civic, and cultural projects, priority is given to youth programs and emergency services for families in crises. The foundation recognizes the value of new programs created to respond to changing needs and will consider grants to projects of an original or pioneering nature. Contributions to cultural organizations are generally for the purpose of funding programs which reach youth, senior citizens, and the disabled.

Sample Grants For support for the museum's community outreach program, $2,500 to Oakland Museum Association (1987). General operating support for the M. H. de Young Memorial Museum and the California Palace of the Legion of Honor, $5,000 to Fine Arts Museums of San Francisco (1987). To complete pledge for construction of the Primate Discovery Center, $20,000 to San Francisco Zoological Society (1987). For general support, $1,000 to the Heard Museum, Phoenix, AZ (1987).

Eligibility/Limitations Grants are not made to endowment campaigns, individuals, religious organizations for religious purposes, advertising, charitable publications, or political organizations, and rarely to capital campaigns, film, or research projects.

Fiscal Information Grants range from $1,500 to $50,000. Most are in the $5,000 to $15,000 range. Grants in 1987 totaled over $1.3 million, including $141,750 for culture and the arts.

Application Information Applications for a grant must include: a letter of not more than two pages which includes but is not limited to a description of the organization, a statement of purpose and objectives, a request for a specific amount of money, and an explanation of how the funds will be used; a list of the board of directors; an organizational budget for the current operating year, showing both expenses and income sources; a list of corporate, foundation, and other contributors and amounts for the current or past year; a copy of the IRS letter designating the organization as a nonprofit, tax-exempt entity; a current financial statement, audited if available.

Deadline(s) There is no deadline for receipt of applications.

294. The Mead Corporation Foundation
Courthouse Plaza Northeast
Dayton, OH 45463
(513) 222-6323

Grants

Program Description Most of the foundation's grants fall into one of two areas: support for charitable and civic groups, and aid to higher education. Programs in the charitable and civic area include health and welfare agencies, hospitals, support of the arts and humanities, minority or civil rights organizations, environmental protection or community improvement efforts, and similar social development agencies. The aid to education program includes two types of support: direct donations to colleges, universities and education-related organizations and a matching gifts program. The program places emphasis on: community needs rather than national programs; development and support of community priorities; coordination of social services; and support of agencies which encourage citizen involvement and which maximize their effectiveness through the use of volunteers.

Eligibility/Limitations The foundation's primary concern is for those communities in which Mead people live and work. Since it is impossible for the foundation's distribution committee to be familiar with all eligible organizations in the more than ninety Mead communities, local Mead management plays an important role in assessing local needs. Priorities may vary from community to community. National organizations are not normally recipients of the foundation's support, nor are organizations which operate outside Mead communities. Only organizations classified as public charities under Section 501(c)(3) of the Internal Revenue Code can be considered for support.

Fiscal Information Contributions in 1985 totaled over $1.8 million.

Application Information Potential applicants for grants should contact or apply to the local Mead unit manager. If the manager determines that the grant request meets established local criteria, the manager will forward it with a recommendation to the foundation for final approval. All requests must be submitted to the local manager in writing, and should contain the following: basic description of the organization, its area of service and the number of people served; audited financial statement; budget for current year; statement on how the foundation's funds would be expended and the benefits those funds would provide; and documentation of charitable tax-exempt status. Requests for education grants outside Mead communities, support for Dayton area organizations, or inquiries of a general nature should be directed to the foundation. The foundation has developed application forms to be used for requests. Interested organizations should write or call, giving a brief description of the proposal, to obtain a copy of the required form.

Deadline(s) Grant requests are accepted at any time. The distribution committee normally meets on a monthly basis, except for January and August.

295. The Meadows Foundation
Wilson Historic Block
2922 Swiss Avenue
Dallas, TX 75204-5928
(214) 826-9431

Grants

Program Description Grants are made in five areas of interest: arts, social services, health, education, and civic and cultural affairs.

Sample Grants For partial underwriting for new exhibit on sports and support for development personnel, $44,490 to Austin Children's Museum (1986). To complete restoration of the DeGolyer Gardens, $199,000 to Dallas Arboretum & Botanical Society (1986). To conserve pieces of the art collection in the library of the Alamo, $14,000 to Daughters of the Republic of Texas, San Antonio (1986). Additional support for research/fabrication of exhibit on Spanish colonial culture in Texas, $10,000 to Dallas County Heritage Society (1986). Toward improvements to the compound of Mission Concepcion and to establish a docent program for the four National Historical Park mission sites, $400,000 to Los Compadres De San Antonio Missions (1986). For restoration of the 1914 Santa Fe parlor club car at the Age of Steam Museum at Fair Park, $25,000 to Southwest Railroad Historical Society, Dallas (1986).

Eligibility/Limitations The foundation can distribute grants only to qualified public entities or 501(c)(3) charities serving the state of Texas. The foundation does not make grants or loans to individuals, nor does it favor contributions for annual fund-raising drives, or media projects in initial planning stages.

Fiscal Information Grants awarded during 1986 totaled more than $13.9 million.

Application Information Persons who represent an organization which they believe qualifies for support are welcome to submit a formal application, which must be in writing. An application should contain, in order, a brief narrative history of the organization's work and purpose; a specific description of the program or project for which support is asked; a project budget; statement of the amount of funds requested and the preferred payment date; a copy of all documents from the IRS pertaining to tax-exempt status under Section 170 of the Internal Revenue Code; and a listing of trustees or directors and principal staff. Additionally, fiscal year-to-date and last complete fiscal year's financial statements should be included. A concise and brief proposal will speed the foundation's processing of a grant application. Only one unbound proposal copy should be submitted.

Deadline(s) Formal applications may be submitted at any time of the year; however, requests from the same organization can be considered only once every twelve months. Please do not call the foundation offices to inquire about a proposal until at least three weeks after mailing.

296. The Andrew W. Mellon Foundation
140 East 62nd Street
New York, NY 10021
(212) 838-8400

Grants

Program Description The purpose of the foundation is to "aid and promote such religious, charitable, scientific, literary, and educational purposes as may be in the furtherance of the public welfare or which tend to promote the well-doing or well-being of mankind." Within this broad charter the foundation currently makes grants on a selective basis to institutions of higher education; in cultural affairs and the performing arts; in medical, public health, and population education and research; and in certain areas of conservation, natural resources, the environment, and public affairs.

Sample Grants Toward costs of cataloguing the library of the Center for Hellenic Studies, $245,000 to Harvard University (1986). Matching endowment to strengthen the society's capacity to catalogue its collections, $400,000 to American Antiquarian

Society, Worcester, MA (1986). Matching endowment for the conservator training program at the university and the Winterthur Museum, $500,000 to University of Delaware, Newark, DE (1986). Matching endowment for research and publication at its Art Museum, $175,000 to Princeton University (1986). For its advanced programs in conservation, $285,000 to Intermuseum Conservation Association, Oberlin, OH (1986). Endowment for its Center for Advanced Study in the Visual Arts to be designated the Paul Mellon Fund, $2.5 million to National Gallery of Art, Washington, DC (1986). To develop a conservation program for its anthropology collections, $725,000 to American Museum of Natural History, New York, NY (1986). For its computer software project, $25,000 to Art Museum Association of America, San Francisco, CA (1986).

Eligibility/Limitations The foundation does not award fellowships or other grants to individuals or make grants to primarily local nonprofit organizations.

Fiscal Information Grants awarded in fiscal 1986 totaled approximately $66.8 million.

Application Information No special application forms are required. Ordinarily a simple letter setting forth the need, the nature, the amount of the request and the justification for it, together with evidence of suitable classification by the Internal Revenue Service and any supplementary exhibits an applicant may wish to submit, will suffice to assure consideration.

Deadline(s) Applications are considered throughout the year.

297. Mellon Bank Corporation
Community Affairs Division
One Mellon Bank Center, Room 368
Pittsburgh, PA 15258
(412) 234-2732

Grants

Program Description Mellon assists nonprofit organizations by making available money, people, goods, and services in the general areas of health and welfare, education, neighborhood and economic development, and arts and culture.

Eligibility/Limitations Organizations requesting support must have 501(c)(3) tax-exempt charitable status and must be public charities as defined under section 509(a)(1) of the Internal Revenue Code. No support is available for loans or assistance to individuals, or organizations engaged in subversive activities or propaganda. As a general rule, support is not available for: scholarships, fellowships, and travel grants; conference or seminar attendance; goodwill advertising in benefit publications; highly specialized projects with little or no apparent impact in the immediate community.

Fiscal Information Grants awarded in 1986 totaled over $3.8 million, including $397,154 in the arts and culture category.

Application Information There is no standard form of application for requests. Requests must be made in writing and should be directed to the Mellon affiliate located in the organization's area of operation. Organizations are asked to include the following when making a request: general purpose and objectives; copy of letter of determination from the IRS indicating the section of the code under which contributions are judged to be tax deductible and status as a public charity; audited financial statement; current operating budget; representative list of recent sources and amounts of public and private support, both cash and in-kind; and current officers and directors. The request should include: specific purpose and amount of request; brief statement of the need or problem to be addressed; other sources of cash and in-kind support; a description of service area and beneficiaries; itemized budget and explanation of future plans; procedure and criteria for evaluating results.

Deadline(s) There is no deadline for requests; they are considered upon receipt.

298. Metropolitan Life Foundation
One Madison Avenue
New York, NY 10010
(212) 578-3515

Grants

Program Description The Metropolitan Life Foundation was created for the purpose of supporting various scientific, educational, health and welfare, and civic and cultural organizations. In the area of culture, the foundation's goal is to enrich society's cultural resources on the national and local level and to contribute to the vitality and quality of life. Contributions are made to both established and pioneering organizations in order to provide opportunities for the development of artists and to bring cultural experiences to wider audiences.

Eligibility/Limitations The foundation limits its support to tax-exempt organizations in the areas of health, education, civic affairs, and culture. Grants are not made to private foundations; religious, fraternal, political, athletic, social, or veterans organizations; hospital fund campaigns; individuals; organizations receiving support from United Way; local chapters of national organizations; disease-specific organizations; labor groups; organizations whose activities are mainly international; organizations primarily engaged in patient care or direct treatment, drug treatment centers and community clinics; elementary and secondary schools; endowments; or courtesy advertising or festival participation.

Fiscal Information Foundation giving in 1986 totaled more than $7 million.

Application Information Metropolitan Life Foundation welcomes requests for support within the guidelines and program areas set forth. Requests must be made in writing and should include the following information: a brief description of the organization, including its legal name, history, activities, purpose, and governing board; the purpose for which the grant is requested; the amount requested and a list of other sources of financial support; a copy of the organization's most recent audited financial statement; a copy of the IRS determination letter indicating 501(c)(3) tax-exempt status as an organization that is not a private foundation; and a copy of the organization's most recent Form 990.

Deadline(s) Requests are accepted and reviewed throughout the year.

299. The Metropolitan Museum of Art
Asian Art Conservation
Fifth Avenue and 82nd Street
New York, NY 10028
(212) 879-5500

Starr Fellowship in Asian Paintings Conservation

Program Description The Starr Foundation has made it possible for the Metropolitan Museum of Art to award a fellowship for training in the conservation and mounting of Asian paintings. The department is concerned with the complete mounting, remounting, and restoration of hanging scrolls, handscrolls, folding screens, prints, albums, books, etc. This apprenticeship program includes learning the properties of various materials such as silk and paper, the use of specialized tools, carpentry, and the development of technical, practical, and manual skills.

Eligibility/Limitations Since work in this field does not require the use of specialized materials and tools, no prior experience is anticipated or required. Eligibility of the applicant will be judged by those responsible for the formulation and supervision of the program.

Fiscal Information The amount of the stipend will depend on funds and may vary with particular circumstances. Duration of the grant is determined by annual review.

Application Information Before a formal application can be made, a brief letter stating one's particular interest in this program must be sent to the department. Following a reply, a typed application should include: name, address, and telephone number; resume of education, and professional experience; three recommendations, at least one professional and one academic. As a rule, a personal interview is required before acceptance.

Deadline(s) Applications may be made at any time of the year.

300. The Metropolitan Museum of Art
Fellowship Program, Office of Academic Programs
Fifth Avenue and 82nd Street
New York, NY 10028
(212) 879-5500

Andrew W. Mellon Fellowships

Program Description These fellowships are provided by the Andrew W. Mellon Fund for promising young scholars with commendable research projects related to the museum's collections, as well as for distinguished visiting scholars from this country and abroad who can serve as teachers and advisers and make their expertise available to catalogue and refine the collections.

Sample Grants Fellowships were awarded in 1987: to do a comparative study of Phyrgian and coeval Near Eastern findings; to study Dutch mannerist printmaking, 1585-1610; to study the symbolism of divine kingship in Akan art and its implications for the history of African art; to study the Romanesque sculpture of Canterbury Cathedral.

Eligibility/Limitations Applicants should have received the doctorate or have completed substantial work toward it.

Fiscal Information The stipend amount varies with particular circumstances. Usually a fellowship will be given for a maximum of one year, most of which should be spent at the Metropolitan Museum.

Application Information There are no application forms. Applicants must submit a typed application including the following (in triplicate); name, home and present address, and telephone number; full resume of education and employment; official undergraduate and graduate transcripts (original transcript plus two copies); a two-part statement, not to exceed two thousand words, specifying what the applicant wishes to accomplish during the fellowship period, and detailing how the Metropolitan Museum's resources can be utilized to accomplish the applicant's goals; and tentative schedule of work to be accomplished and travel required during the fellowship period. Three recommendations (at least one academic and one professional) should be sent directly to the above address (in triplicate).

Deadline(s) Applications for fellowships must be made by letter and must be submitted by November 20 to the Fellowship Program.

Additional Information For all fellowships offered by the museum, it is the responsibility of the applicant, in connection with any project that may reasonably be expected to require assistance from a particular museum department, to discuss the project with the department concerned and to obtain that department's approval before submitting the application. Such departmental approval should not, however, be construed as assurance that a fellowship will be awarded by the grants committee. Fellowships generally cannot be given for projects proposing that an exhibition be organized and presented within the fellowship period.

301. The Metropolitan Museum of Art
Fellowship Program, Office of Academic Programs
Fifth Avenue and 82nd Street
New York, NY 10028
(212) 879-5500

The Chester Dale Fellowship

Program Description Individuals whose fields of study are related to the fine arts of the western world are eligible for Chester Dale Fellowships for research at the Metropolitan Museum.

Sample Grants Fellowships were awarded in 1987 for study of the arts of Brescia after the League of Cambria; for studies of the Arca of San Millan de la Cogolla; for study of the early illuminted Bibles of the Bolognese school of miniature painting.

Eligibility/Limitations Applicants are preferably American citizens under the age of forty.

Fiscal Information The grants typically cover periods from three months to one year. Stipend amount may vary with particular circumstances.

Application Information There are no application forms. Applicants must submit a typed application including the following (in triplicate): name, home and present address, and telephone number; full resume of education and employment; official undergraduate and graduate transcripts (original transcript plus two copies); a two-part statement, not to exceed two thousand words, specifying what the applicant wishes to accomplish during the fellowship period, and detailing how the Metropolitan Museum's resources can be utilized to accomplish the applicant's goals; and tentative schedule of work to be accomplished and travel required during the fellowship period. Three recommendations (at least one academic and one professional) should be sent directly to the above address (in triplicate).

Deadline(s) Applications for fellowships must be made by letter and must be submitted by November 20 to the Fellowship Program.

Additional Information For all fellowships offered by the museum, it is the responsibility of the applicant, in connection with any project that may reasonably be expected to require assistance from a particular museum department, to discuss the project with the department concerned and to obtain that department's approval before submitting the application. Such departmental approval should not, however, be construed as assurance that a fellowship will be awarded by the grants committee. Fellowships generally cannot be given for projects proposing that an exhibition be organized and presented within the fellowship period.

302. The Metropolitan Museum of Art
Fellowship Program, Office of Academic Programs
Fifth Avenue and 82nd Street
New York, NY 10028
(212) 879-5500

The Classical Fellowship

Program Description An annual fellowship is awarded to an outstanding graduate student who has been admitted to the doctoral program of a university in the United States, and who has submitted an outline of thesis dealing with Greek and Roman art. Preference will be given to the applicant who will profit most from utilizing the resources of the Department of Greek and Roman Art: its collections, library, photographic, and other archives, and the guidance of its curatorial staff.

Eligibility/Limitations Applicants must have been admitted to the doctoral program of a university in the United States and have submitted an outline of a thesis dealing with Greek and Roman art. The thesis outline must already have been accepted by the applicant's thesis adviser at the time of application for the fellowship. Recipients will generally be expected both to conduct research on the particularly scholarly project with respect to which their fellowships were awarded and to participate in ongoing activities of the curatorial department to which they will be attached.

Fiscal Information The stipend amount varies with particular circumstances.

Application Information There are no application forms. Applicants must submit a typed application including the following (in triplicate): name, home and present address, and telephone number; full resume of education and employment; official undergraduate and graduate transcripts (original transcript plus two copies); a two-part statement, not to exceed two thousand words, specifying what the applicant wishes to accomplish during the fellowship period, and detailing how the Metropolitan Museum's resources can be utilized to accomplish the applicant's goals; and tentative schedule of work to be accomplished and travel required during the fellowship period.

Three recommendations (at least one academic and one professional) should be sent directly to the above address (in triplicate).

Deadline(s) Applications for fellowships must be made by letter and must be submitted by November 20 to the Fellowship Program.

Additional Information For all fellowships offered by the museum, it is the responsibility of the applicant, in connection with any project that may reasonably be expected to require assistance from a particular museum department, to discuss the project with the department concerned and to obtain that department's approval before submitting the application. Such departmental approval should not, however, be construed as assurance that a fellowship will be awarded by the grants committee. Fellowships generally cannot be given for projects proposing that an exhibition be organized and presented within the fellowship period.

303. The Metropolitan Museum of Art
Fellowship Program, Office of Academic Programs
Fifth Avenue and 82nd Street
New York, NY 10028
(212) 879-5500

The Norbert Schimmel Fellowship for Mediterranean Art and Archaeology

Program Description This is an annual fellowship awarded to an outstanding graduate student. Preference will be given to a candidate who, in the opinion of the grants committee, would profit most from utilization the resources of the Ancient Near Eastern Art or Greek and Roman Art Departments: their collections, libraries, photographic, and other archives, and the guidance of their curatorial staffs.

Sample Grants Fellowship was awarded in 1987 to study the glazed-wares of pre-Archaemenid Iran.

Eligibility/Limitations Applicants must have been admitted to a graduate program of a university in the United States and have submitted an outline of a thesis dealing with ancient Near Eastern art and archaeology or with Greek and Roman art.

Fiscal Information The amount of the stipend varies with particular circumstances.

Application Information There are no application forms. Applicants must submit a typed application including the following (in triplicate): name, home and present address, and telephone number; full resume of education and employment; official undergraduate and graduate transcripts (original transcript plus two copies); a two-part statement, not to exceed two thousand words, specifying what the applicant wishes to accomplish during the fellowship period, and detailing how the Metropolitan Museum's resources can be utilized to accomplish the applicant's goals; and tentative schedule of work to be accomplished and travel required during the fellowship period. Three recommendations (at least one academic and one professional) should be sent directly to the above address (in triplicate).

Deadline(s) Applications for fellowships must be made by letter and must be submitted by November 20 to the Fellowship Program.

Additional Information For all fellowships offered by the museum, it is the responsibility of the applicant, in connection with any project that may reasonably be expected to require assistance from a particular museum department, to discuss the project with the department concerned and to obtain that department's approval before submitting the application. Such departmental approval should not, however, be construed as assurance that a fellowship will be awarded by the grants committee. Fellowships generally cannot be given for projects proposing that an exhibition be organized and presented within the fellowship period.

304. The Metropolitan Museum of Art
Fellowship Programs, Office of Academic Programs
Fifth Avenue and 82nd Street
New York, NY 10028
(212) 879-5500

J. Clawson Mills Scholarships

Program Description Scholars interested in pursuing research projects in any branch of the fine arts related to the Metropolitan Museum's collections are eligible for J. Clawson Mills Scholarships.

Sample Grants Fellowships were awarded in 1987: to write on tomb structures and burials of the Middle Kingdom; to study the early paintings of Shih-t'ao; to do research for a catalogue raisonne on the photographs of Roger Fenton.

Eligibility/Limitations The scholarships are generally reserved for mature scholars of demonstrated ability.

Fiscal Information The scholarships provide for study or research at the museum for one year with the possibility of renewal for a second year.

Application Information There are no application forms. Applicants must submit a typed application including the following (in triplicate): name, home and present address, and telephone number; full resume of education and employment; official undergraduate and graduate transcripts (original transcript plus two copies); a two-part statement, not to exceed two thousand words, specifying what the applicant wishes to accomplish during the fellowship period, and detailing how the Metropolitan Museum's resources can be utilized to accomplish the applicant's goals; and tentative schedule of work to be accomplished and travel required during the fellowship period. Three recommendations (at least one academic and one professional) should be sent directly to the above address (in triplicate).

Deadline(s) Applications for fellowships must be made by letter and must be submitted by November 20 to the Fellowship Program.

Additional Information For all fellowships offered by the museum, it is the responsibility of the applicant, in connection with any project that may reasonably be expected to require assistance from a particular museum department, to discuss the project with the department concerned and to obtain that department's approval before submitting the application. Such departmental approval should not, however, be construed as assurance that a fellowship will be awarded by the grants committee. Fellowships generally cannot be given for projects proposing that an exhibition be organized and presented within the fellowship period.

305. The Metropolitan Museum of Art
Fellowships in Conservation, Office of Academic Programs
Fifth Avenue and 82nd Street
New York, NY 10028
(212) 879-5500

Andrew W. Mellon Fellowships in Conservation

Program Description The Andrew W. Mellon Foundation has made it possible for The Metropolitan Museum of Art to award annual conservation fellowships for training in one or more of the following departments of the museum: Paintings Conservation, Objects Conservation (including such materials and objects as metal, arms and armor, stone, wood, musical instruments, glass and ceramics), Paper Conservation, Textile Conservation, the Costume Institute, and Asian Art Conservation.

Eligibility/Limitations Whenever possible, fellowship applicants should already have reached an advanced level of experience or training.

Fiscal Information Fellowship recipients will receive stipends appropriate to their level of training or experience. Additional funds may be available for travel, books, photographs, and other reasonable or necessary expenses incident to the fellowship. Fellowships will typically be one year in duration with the possibility of renewal for up to two additional years. Fellowship recipients are expected to spend the fellowship in residence in the department with which they are affiliated.

Application Information There are no application forms. Applicants must submit a typed application including the following (in duplicate): name, home and present address, and telephone number; full resume of education and professional experience; a statement, not to exceed one thousand words, describing what the applicant expects to accomplish during the fellowship period, and detailing how the Metropolitan Museum's resources can be utilized to accomplish the applicant's goals; tentative schedule of work to be accomplished and travel required during the fellowship period; and three recommendations (at least one academic and one professional).

Deadline(s) Applications for fellowships must be submitted by January 15.

Additional Information For all fellowships offered by the museum, it is the responsibility of the applicant, in connection with any project that may reasonably be expected to require assistance from a particular museum department, to discuss the project with the department concerned and to obtain that department's approval before submitting the application. Such departmental approval should not, however, be construed as assurance that a fellowship will be awarded by the grants committee.

306. The Metropolitan Museum of Art
Fellowships in Conservation, Office of Academic Programs
Fifth Avenue and 82nd Street
New York, NY 10028
(212) 879-5500

Fellowships in Conservation: Objects Conservation

Program Description The L.W. Frohlich Charitable Trust enables the museum to award a fellowship in the Department of Objects Conservation.

Eligibility/Limitations Fellowship applicants should be conservators, art historians, or scientists who are at an advanced level in their training and who have demonstrated commitment to the physical examination and treatment of art objects.

Fiscal Information Fellowship recipients will receive stipends appropriate to their level of training or experience. Additional funds may be available for travel, books, photographs, and other reasonable or necessary expenses incident to the fellowship. Fellowships are for two years.

Application Information There are no application forms. Applicants must submit a typed application including the following (in duplicate): name, home and present address, and telephone number; full resume of education and professional experience; a statement, not to exceed one thousand words, describing what the applicant expects to accomplish during the fellowship period, and detailing how the Metropolitan Museum's resources can be utilized to accomplish the applicant's goals; tentative schedule of work to be accomplished and travel required during the fellowship period; and three recommendations (at least one academic and one professional).

Deadline(s) Applications for fellowships must be submitted by January 15.

Additional Information For all fellowships offered by the museum, it is the responsibility of the applicant, in connection with any project that may reasonably be expected to require assistance from a particular museum department, to discuss the project with the department concerned and to obtain that department's approval before submitting the application. Such departmental approval should not, however, be construed as assurance that a fellowship will be awarded by the grants committee.

307. The Metropolitan Museum of Art
McCloy Fellowships, Office of Academic Programs
Fifth Avenue and 82nd Street
New York, NY 10028
(212) 879-5500

John J. McCloy Fellowships in Art for Museum Professionals

Program Description The Metropolitan Museum of Art, in cooperation with the American Council on Germany, Inc., is seeking applications for three John J. McCloy Fellowships in Art. The fellowships are for the purposes of study, research, travel, and cultural exchange with colleagues in German museums.

Sample Grants Fellowships were awarded in 1987: to study head reliquaries from Limoges housed in German collections; to study the African collections in German museums; to study German expressionist art for a catalogue for the Lawrence University Art Collection.

Eligibility/Limitations The fellowships are open to anyone currently employed by a museum in the U.S., including, but not limited to, curators, educators, conservators, and librarians. Preference will be given to applicants who have had no prior opportunity to work in Germany.

Fiscal Information Although the McCloy Fellowship will pay travel and living expenses for the recipient, each recipient's institution is also expected to continue the employee at full salary during the fellowship leave of absence.

Application Information A typed application in triplicate should include the following: resume of education and professional experience; brief statement outlining the applicant's study proposal; two professional letters of reference.

Deadline(s) Applications for these fellowships must be made by letter and submitted by November 20.

308. The Metropolitan Museum of Art
Theodore Rousseau Fellowship
Fifth Avenue and 82nd Street
New York, NY 10028
(212) 879-5500

Theodore Rousseau Fellowships

Program Description Annual fellowships made possible by a bequest from the late curator-in-chief of the museum, are awarded for the training of students whose goal is to enter museums as curators of painting, by enabling them to undertake related study in Europe. The purpose of these fellowships is to develop the skills of connoisseurship by supporting first-hand examination of paintings in major European collections, rather than to support library research for the completion of degree requirements.

Sample Grants Fellowships were awarded in 1987: to study Bloomsbury art, re-imagining the domestic; to study Caspar Netscher and late seventeenth century Dutch painting.

Eligibility/Limitations Applicants should be enrolled in an advanced degree program in the field of art history.

Fiscal Information The stipend amount may vary with particular circumstances.

Application Information There are no application forms. Applicants must submit a typed application including the following (in triplicate): name, home and present address, and telephone number; full resume of education and employment; official undergraduate and graduate transcripts (original transcript plus two copies); a two-part statement, not to exceed two thousand words, specifying what the applicant wishes to accomplish during the fellowship period, and detailing how the Metropolitan Museum's resources can be utilized to accomplish the applicant's goals; and tentative schedule of work to be accomplished and travel required during the fellowship period. Three recommendations (at least one academic and one professional) should be sent directly to the above address (in triplicate).

Deadline(s) Applications for fellowships must be made by letter and must be submitted by November 20 to the Fellowship Program.

Additional Information For all fellowships offered by the museum, it is the responsibility of the applicant, in connection with any project that may reasonably be expected to require assistance from a particular museum department, to discuss the project with the department concerned and to obtain that department's approval before submitting the application. Such departmental approval should not, however, be construed as assurance that a fellowship will be awarded by the grants committee. Fellowships generally cannot be given for projects proposing that an exhibition be organized and presented within the fellowship period.

309. The Milwaukee Foundation
1020 North Broadway
Milwaukee, WI 53202
(414) 272-5805

Grants

Program Description The Milwaukee Foundation has identified the following broad charitable fields as those particularly deserving support by the foundation: health, social services, arts and culture, education, conservation and historic preservation, and community development/other. Of particular interest are innovative programs which cross the fields of social services, health, and education and which prevent problems rather than address symptoms. Grants within the arts and culture category are made to encourage the development of programs in the performing and visual arts, to strengthen the performing groups, museums, libraries, zoos, and other institutions which substantially enhance the quality of life in the greater Milwaukee community. The foundation designated conservation and historic preservation as a separate grant category for the first time in 1986, to reflect a long standing interest of the foundation in efforts to promote more efficient use of natural resources, enhance the quality of the environment, and preserve the community's heritage. It is also committed to the preservation of buildings and areas of historical significance to the community as well as preserving its cultural heritage and values.

Sample Grants For development of biosphere exhibit: Life on the Third Planet, $30,000 to Friends of the Museum (1986). For facility development and expansion, $75,000 to Zoological Society of Milwaukee County (1986).

Eligibility/Limitations The foundation is a community trust with a commitment mainly to the people of the Greater Milwaukee area, and it gives priority to programs whose principal thrust benefits that geographic region. Geographically, the target area includes the following counties: Milwaukee, Waukesha, Ozaukee, and Washington. Grants may also be made to agencies outside the geographic area for purposes specifically relevant to the people of the Greater Milwaukee community, or as directed in the creation of certain funds. Grants are made only to nonprofit organizations exempt from federal taxation under Section 501(c)(3) of the Internal Revenue Code and, on occasion, to governmental agencies. Except for prize awards, grants are not made to individuals. The foundation ordinarily does not support: endowments; debt reductions; churches or sectarian religious purposes; specific medical or scientific research projects; annual fund drives for sustaining support; agencies and organizations which are discriminatory with respect to age, race, religion, sex, or national origin.

Fiscal Information Grants approved in 1986 totaled over $3.3 million, including $684,603 in the arts and culture category and $99,546 in the conservation and historic preservation category.

Application Information To assist potential applicants, the foundation offers regular information sessions to discuss the foundation's current priorities and guidelines. To register for these sessions, contact the foundation office.

Deadline(s) The foundation board meets every three months to act on grant applications. To allow time for review and analysis, applications must be submitted at least eight weeks prior to a meeting. Applications submitted in advance of these dates are appreciated. Application deadlines are January 4 for March meeting (special projects); April 1 for June meeting (capital and special projects); July 1 for September meeting (special projects); and October 1 for December meeting (capital and special projects).

Additional Information In May 1986, the foundation announced the establishment of the Fund for the Arts, a new and permanent source of support for small and medium-sized arts organizations in the Milwaukee metropolitan area. Contact the foundation for more information about this fund.

310. Mobil Foundation, Inc.
150 East 42nd Street
New York, NY 10017
(212) 883-2174

Grants

Program Description Mobil Foundation, Inc., offers grants to civic, health, art and cultural organizations, hospitals, and educational institutions. The foundation supports art and cultural activities which are national in scope or which are located in communities where Mobil has a significant business presence.

Eligibility/Limitations Charitable, federally tax-exempt organizations who meet funding criteria are eligible to apply. Grants are not made to individuals.

Fiscal Information Contributions in 1986 totaled over $10.4 million, including over $1 million in the culture category.

Application Information Inquiries in the art and culture category should be made to the nearest local office to establish whether or not a particular area is included in the local giving program. All grant applications to the foundation must be in writing and include the following: a brief description of the organization and its goals; amount requested and the specific purpose for it; other sources of funding; a budget and audited financial statement; other pertinent supporting data, such as an annual report, if available; a copy of the organization's most recent tax-exemption letter under Section 501(c)(3) of the Internal Revenue Code.

Deadline(s) The foundation has no application deadlines. Local offices may have deadlines for submitting proposals in the art and culture category. Contact the local office for deadline information.

311. The Moody Foundation
704 Moody National Bank Building
Galveston, TX 77550
(409) 763-5333

Grants

Program Description The foundation supports projects and programs in the state of Texas in the areas of education, arts and humanities, health and science, and community and social services.

Sample Grants Assistance with underwriting the costs of an exhibition of Oriental and Eastern sculpture and woven artworks from a private collection, $12,500 to Amarillo Art Center (1986). Support of operation needs of "The Colonel," a paddlewheeler-style riverboat which provides daily narrated historical cruises of Galveston Harbor, $300,000 to The Colonial Museum, Inc. (1986). Assistance with the construction of a lagoon sculpture garden as part of the Texas State Fair Park renovation, $5,000 to For the People, Inc./The Fair Park Lagoon Sculpture Garden, Dallas (1986).

Eligibility/Limitations Eligible applicants are qualified nonprofit Texas organizations.

Fiscal Information Grant awards in 1986 totaled over $25.9 million.

Application Information Grant guidelines are available to qualified nonprofit Texas organizations.

Deadline(s) No deadlines are announced.

312. Morgan Guaranty Trust Company of New York
Community Relations and Public Affairs
23 Wall Street
New York, NY 10015
(212) 483-2058

Contributions to the Community

Program Description Corporate policy states that the company has a responsibility to those cities where business is carried out, and where staff members live and work. To carry out this policy, the company awards grants in education, urban affairs, health care, international affairs, and the arts. Morgan has consistently sought to enrich the quality of education through support of many different kinds of schools. For more than twenty-five years Morgan has contributed both human resources and funds to major universities and small colleges, independent and public elementary and secondary schools, as well as community education programs. As Morgan's business has become more international, the trust has committed substantial resources to help organizations working around the world break down the barriers between people by fostering study and exchange, to promote economic and social development in less-developed countries, and to present the best of American values, traditions, and technologies abroad. Morgan's goal in the arts is to encourage the growth of the arts through support for both major cultural institutions and smaller, less-established organizations. The trust is especially interested in organizations that produce, perform, or exhibit the work of outstanding contemporary American artists.

Sample Grants For capital purposes, $25,000 to the Metropolitan Museum of Art (1986). For visual arts, $20,000 to the Brooklyn Museum (1986). For environmental organization, $35,000 to New York Botanical Garden (1986). For contributions to organizations based abroad having a U.S. presence, $12,000 to the American Museum in Britain (1986).

Eligibility/Limitations Grants are made to charitable organizations to which contributions are deductible for federal income tax purposes under section 501(c)(3) of the Internal Revenue Code and that are not classified as private foundations. No grants are made to individuals. The trust rarely contributes to projects outside of New York City except in the fields of higher education and international affairs. Those few grants made outside New York are likely to be to those organizations whose work is undertaken nation wide.

Fiscal Information In 1986, contributions totaled over $6 million.

Application Information Proposals for funding should be made by submitting two copies of an application form which may be obtained from Roberta A. Ruocco, Community Relations and Public Affairs, at the address listed above. Proposals will not be considered until the trust has received all requested information, after which a decision will be reached within three months. Proposals that remain incomplete two months after receipt will not be considered.

Deadline(s) Morgan's contributions committees meet frequently, and therefore applications may be submitted at any time.

313. Philip Morris Companies Inc.
Corporate Contributions
120 Park Avenue
New York, NY 10017
(212) 880-5000

Corporate Contributions

Program Description Program guidelines channel support to those arts, health and welfare, educational, and cultural organizations that provide direct service to plant communities across the country.

Eligibility/Limitations Applicant organizations must provide proof of status as a nonprofit 501(c)(3) corporation.

Fiscal Information Contributions in 1986 totaled over $15 million.

Application Information To apply for a grant, please send: a short letter including a description of applicant organization, the amount of the request, and to what specific purpose the contribution would be put; proof of tax-exempt status; a current annual report; the list of the board of directors; a list of sponsors; and current and projected budget.

Deadline(s) Proposal review process takes up to three months.

314. Mountain Bell Foundation

1801 California Street, Room 5050
Denver, CO 80202
(303) 896-3572

Grants

Program Description The foundation supports nonprofit endeavors in the areas of human services, education, health, arts and culture, and civic and community development. In the arts and culture category, the foundation is committed to helping ensure the financial viability of performing arts groups, libraries, museums, natural history museums, and public radio and television stations. The foundation gives special consideration to local and regional art and cultural programs that emphasize the unique western heritage of this part of the country. The foundation also administers corporate grants to nonprofit and for-profit organizations involved with economic development initiatives.

Eligibility/Limitations The foundation makes charitable contributions to nonprofit, tax-exempt organizations that have a 501(c)(3) Internal Revenue Service designation. Organizations from the following states are supported: Arizona, Colorado, Idaho, Montana, New Mexico, Utah, and Wyoming. The foundation does not make contributions to: organizations which discriminate by race, creed, color, sex, age, or national origin; scholarships or athletic funds; endowment funds; national health organizations; individuals; political or religious organizations; debt financing funds; international organizations; organizations not based in the foundation's seven-state territory, with the exceptions of institutions of higher learning which may benefit from the foundation's educational matching gifts program.

Fiscal Information Contributions in 1986 totaled over $5.2 million, including $638,864 in the arts and culture category.

Application Information Requests for grants must be submitted in writing to the local Mountain Bell public relations office. Each grant request must include: the name, address, and telephone number of the organization and a representative who may be contacted for further information; a profile of the organization including its history, purpose, objectives, and accomplishments; a description of the number and types of people and groups who benefit from the organization's work; the grant amount requested from the foundation and a description of how these funds will be used; the names and amounts of requests and contributions made or received from other corporate and foundation sources; the program/organization budget; the organization's financial statement for the immediate past year; the most recent copy of the organization's IRS tax-exempt status letter; the names, addresses, and areas of expertise of the organization's board of directors; and the names and qualifications of agency staff members and project administrators.

Deadline(s) Requests for contributions are considered annually; deadline for submission of applications is October 1.

315. M. J. Murdock Charitable Trust

P.O. Box 1618
Vancouver, WA 98668
(206) 694-8415

Grants

Program Description The trust, in order to produce impact, focuses its attention on a few fields of activity and on certain priorities within those fields. Projects or programs aimed at solutions to or the prevention of important problems, either through research or the application of existing knowledge and capabilities, will be favored, rather than those which deal with the consequences of problems or merely react to "needs." Also favored are proposals which address critical priorities of regional or national, rather than local, significance. Of major concern are endeavors which expand man's knowledge of himself and his world and which promote those values and activities of society leading to a happier, healthier, freer, and more productive life. The trust's primary function is to provide "up-front" or venture capital, along with that of other donors and the applicant's own resources, in the testing and validation of promising concepts and in the launching of well thought-out programs which have the potential to thrive beyond the initial stage of funding.

Sample Grants Toward new facilities, $200,000 to Museum of the Rockies, Bozeman, MT (1984). For start-up costs, $30,000 to Advertising Museum, Portland, OR (1986). For construction of air and space museum, $150,000 to Museum of Flight Foundation, Seattle, WA (1986). For construction costs of Center on the Spirit of the West, $750,000 to Oregon High Desert Museum, Bend, OR (1986). For construction of Asian Elephant Forest, $75,000 to Seattle Zoological Society, Seattle, WA (1986).

Eligibility/Limitations Applications for grants are considered only from organizations which have been ruled tax-exempt under Section 501(c)(3) of the Internal Revenue Code and which are not private foundations as defined in Section 509(a) of the code. Most of the grant funds awarded have been for the support of projects and programs conducted within five states of the Pacific Northwest: Washington, Oregon, Idaho, Montana, and Alaska. The trust does not encourage proposals which merely deal with ongoing general financial needs, minor organizational objectives or projects common to many similar organizations without distinguishing merit. The following kinds of applications are not considered: for the benefit of specific individuals; by individuals acting on behalf of, but without the authority of, qualified tax-exempt organizations; for grants to conduit organizations; by institutions which in policy or practice unfairly discriminate against race, ethnic origin, sex, or creed; by sectarian or religious organizations; for projects requiring financial obligation by the trust over a period of several years; for loans; for grants to organizations which are organized and operate outside any state or territory of the United States.

Fiscal Information Grants awarded in 1986 totaled over $10.4 million.

Application Information Application information and additional information are available in "Grant Proposal Guidelines," available from the foundation. Foundation staff are available to answer specific inquiries by letter or telephone.

Deadline(s) There are no specific deadlines for receipt of proposals.

316. Museum of Comparative Zoology
Harvard University
26 Oxford Street
Cambridge, MA 02138
(617) 495-2466

Ernst Mayr Grants

Program Description The Museum of Comparative Zoology at Harvard University is pleased to announce that a generous gift permits them to endow a program for grants in systematics, to be known as Ernst Mayr Grants. These grants will be awarded to systematists who need to make short visits to museums in order to undertake research needed for the completion of taxonomic revisions and monographs.

Eligibility/Limitations The grants are particularly designed for scientists who might otherwise have difficulty in obtaining access to museum specimens that are necessary for their research. Preference will be given to studies that use the MCZ collections, although applications to work at other museums will also be considered.

Fiscal Information Typical expenses that may be covered by these grants include travel, lodging, and meals for up to a few months while conducting research at the museums; services purchased from the host institution; and research supplies, etc.

Application Information Application and correspondence related to these grants should be addressed to the director of the museum. Applications should consist of a short proposal, budget, curriculum vitae, and three letters of support. Applications should be submitted in triplicate.

Deadline(s) Applications will be reviewed biannually. Deadlines for submissions are September 15 and April 15.

317. The Nalco Foundation
One Nalco Center
Naperville, IL 60566-1024
(312) 961-9500

Grants

Program Description Grants by The Nalco Foundation are made in the following fields: community and civic affairs, culture and arts, and education and health.

Eligibility/Limitations Grants are typically limited to the following geographic areas: Illinois, mainly the Chicago metropolitan area including DuPage County; Carson, California; Cleveland, Ohio; Garyville, Louisiana; Jackson, Michigan; Jonesboro, Georgia; Paulsboro, New Jersey; Sugar Land, Texas. Grants are made to cover operating and capital expenditure needs. In general, the foundation does not support: individuals; state-supported colleges or universities; endowment funds; advertising in charitable publications; or purchase of tickets for fund-raising banquets.

Fiscal Information Grants are generally made in one payment. Some long-term (three-year and five-year) grants are made in exceptional cases. Grants approved in 1986 totaled over $1.4 million, including $178,153 in the culture and arts category.

Application Information Applications for grants should be made in writing to Joanne C. Ford of the foundation. A one- or two-page letter is preferred. The letter should contain the legal name of the organization plus the following: summary of specified project or need; history of the organization; intended use of funds; latest financial statement and/or budget; documentation of federal tax-exempt status under Section 501(c)(3) of the Internal Revenue Code; list of members of the board of directors, their affiliations or addresses; and list of corporate/foundation contributions.

Deadline(s) Proposals for grants are considered continuously throughout the year, except proposals received after October 1, which will not be considered until the following calendar year.

318. NASA Headquarters
Elementary and Secondary Programs Branch, Code LEE
400 Maryland Avenue, SW
Washington, DC 20546
(202) 453-8388

Aerospace Education Services Project

CFDA Program Number 43.001

Program Description The objectives of this program are to provide information about U.S. aeronautics and space research, development activities and their results, to enhance the knowledge of students and teachers and motivate them in science education and careers, to enrich the regular curricula, and to assist with in-service teacher training.

Eligibility/Limitations Eligible applicants include schools, teacher training institutions, colleges, universities, civic groups, museums and planetaria.

Fiscal Information Funds available in FY 1988 are estimated at $2 million.

Application Information Preapplication coordination is not necessary, but it may be helpful for applicants to contact the educational programs office at any NASA Field Center or headquarters or the science supervisor of the respective state department of education. Applications consist of letters to NASA Field Centers. Application guidelines are available in a brochure "NASA Aerospace Education Services Project," available from the program.

Deadline(s) There are no deadlines.

319. National Archives and Records Administration

Office of the National Archives
National Archives Building
Washington, DC 20408
(202) 523-3032

National Archives Reference Services

CFDA Program Number 89.001

Program Description The objective of this program is to provide reference services to the general public and the federal government on records of the federal government and on historical materials in presidential libraries.

Eligibility/Limitations The general public is eligible to apply.

Application Information To see records in person, NARA Form 14003, Researcher Application, is required. To obtain information or copies by mail, contact the depository; if a form is required, applicant will be notified. Requests for Federal Records Centers records should be addressed directly to the agency having legal custody.

Deadline(s) Requests are accepted at any time.

320. National Endowment for the Arts

Advancement Program
1100 Pennsylvania Avenue, NW
Washington, DC 20506
(202) 682-5436

Advancement Program

Program Description The Advancement Program is designed to help organizations of artistic excellence develop strategies to eliminate deficiencies in organizational management practice, and to take carefully planned steps toward the achievement of long-range goals. The program consists of two phases—Phase One: Planning/Technical Assistance and Phase Two: Advancement Grants which must be matched at least three-to-one during the 30-month maximum grant period.

Sample Grants Support for the preparatory stage of an advancement grant, $10,000 to Albany Museum of Art, Inc., Albany, GA (1986). Support for the preparatory stage of an advancement grant, $10,000 to Museum of American Folk Art, New York, NY (1986).

Eligibility/Limitations Current program plans call for eligibility in fiscal year 1989 to include: Arts in Education, Expansion Arts, Inter-Arts, Museums, Music and Theater.

Fiscal Information Advancement grants generally range from $25,000 to $75,000 and must be matched on a three-to-one basis.

Application Information Application information and guidelines are available from the program.

Deadline(s) The deadline for submitting a "Notice of Intent to Apply" card is May 5. The deadline for Phase One is June 2, 1988; all material must be received by close of business on this date. Deadline for submitting the complete application with all required attachments to receive an Advancement Grant, Phase Two of the Advancement Program, is June 15, 1990.

321. National Endowment for the Arts

Arts in Education Program, Room 602
1100 Pennsylvania Avenue, NW
Washington, DC 20506
(202) 682-5426

Arts in Education: Special Projects

Program Description The Arts in Education Program is designed to address the following objectives: to encourage state and local arts agencies to develop long-term strategies to encourage and assist relevant state and local education authorities to establish the arts as basic in education; to encourage state and local education agencies to develop and implement sequential arts education curricula; to encourage the involvement of arts and cultural organizations in enhancing arts in education for a broad segment of the population; to encourage enhancement of the educational process by assisting the career development of excellent teachers and professional artists involved in education; to encourage accountability for quality arts education programs through short, intermediate, and long-range planning and evaluation; and to encourage collection and dissemination of information about current and past successful arts education programs. The Special Projects category of funding is designed to: a) support projects from the field which advance progress toward the arts becoming a basic part of education, K-12; and b) provide for endowment leadership initiatives.

Sample Grants To support "Evenings for Educators," a series of education programs for teachers, $20,400 to Museum Associates, Los Angeles, CA (1986).

Eligibility/Limitations Grants are available to a wide variety of not-for-profit organizations—educational institutions, arts institutions, local arts agencies, etc.—which are undertaking high quality arts education projects of regional or national significance. Grants are project oriented rather than for general operating support. Grants do not fund exhibits of student work, performing group tours, or artist residency activities.

Fiscal Information The minimum grant amount is $5,000. Grants will generally not exceed $50,000. In rare instances, the program may consider applications exceeding this amount. Grant funds may not pay more than one-half of the project costs. Each grantee must match the funds on a least a one-to-one basis.

Application Information Organizations, institutions, and agencies interested in applying for a Special Projects grant are encouraged to send a letter to the Arts in Education Program indicating their intent to apply. Letters should be no more than one page in length and should indicate the nature of the proposed project. No budget information is necessary. Please do not attach any supplementary material. Descriptions are reviewed and the potential applicants notified as to whether or not a project appears to be wholly or partially eligible for funding.

Deadline(s) Letters for fiscal year applications should be postmarked no later than January 4. Applicants must submit the formal application package no later than March 1.

322. National Endowment for the Arts
Challenge Grant Program
1100 Pennsylvania Avenue, NW
Washington, DC 20506
(202) 682-5436

Challenge III Grants

Program Description Challenge III Grants are designed to assist projects with long-term potential to help move the nation forward in achieving excellence in the arts, and provide access to, and appreciation of such excellence, both directly and through nonfederal mechanisms for the arts. The program will assist institutions to undertake new or substantially augmented projects that work to achieve the goals of the program, specifically: to assist nationally significant artistic achievement of the highest quality in one or more of the art forms; to assist improved and broader access to the arts of quality; to assist deeper and broader education in and appreciation of the arts of the highest quality; and to assist nonfederal public and private support systems for the arts to address any or a combination of the above objectives.

Sample Grants A challenge grant award of $1 million to Museum of Fine Arts, Boston, MA (1986). A challenge grant award of $131,000 to International Museum of Photography at George Eastman House, Rochester, NY (1986). A challenge grant award of $800,000 to Whitney Museum of American Art, New York, NY (1986). A challenge grant award to augment an endowment of $200,000 to Contemporary Arts Museum, Houston, TX (1986). A challenge grant award to augment an endowment of $1 million to the Los Angeles County Museum of Art, Los Angeles, CA (1986).

Eligibility/Limitations Institutions, including arts institutions, state and local arts agencies, regional and other organizations, and consortia of such institutions that can further the objectives of the program and meet the legal requirements for applicant organizations are eligible.

Fiscal Information Grant amounts will generally range from $50,000 to $1 million. The matching requirements are a minimum of three-to-one (four-to-one for capital improvements) generally in new and increased monies. Generally, grant periods may be from one to four years.

Application Information Prospective applicants should notify the Challenge Grant Program in writing of their intent to apply by mailing the Intent to Apply Card included on the back of the program guidelines, which are available on request.

Deadline(s) The Intent to Apply Card should be mailed by June 2. Application packages must be received by the program no later than July 2.

323. National Endowment for the Arts
Dance Program
1100 Pennsylvania Avenue, NW
Washington, DC 20506
(202) 682-5435

Dance Program: General Services to the Field

Program Description The Dance Program offers assistance to choreographers and to companies and organizations that present or serve dance. Services to the Field grants assist organizations and individuals who provide services to dance companies, dancers, and choreographers. The program is particularly interested in projects which: increase communication and information exchange within the dance community; increase visibility and public awareness of dance; provide performance and rehearsal space and services to companies and individuals; and increase financial and managerial stability of dance companies, individual dancers, and choreographers. Projects involving the provision of documentation services are eligible for funding through this category.

Sample Grants To support a staff position to provide continued access to materials in the Dance Collection, $30,400 to New York Public Library—Astor, Lenox and Tilden Foundations (1986).

Eligibility/Limitations Individuals and organizations are both eligible. Applicant organizations must meet legal requirements and must usually have: been in continuous operation for at least three years at the time of application; paid professional administrative staff; and demonstrated ability to raise private and/or other public funds. Please note that grant funds are not awarded for an organization's general operating support.

Fiscal Information Matching grants to organizations rarely exceed $50,000; most are substantially less, ranging from $2,000 to $25,000. Grants to individuals rarely exceed $15,000 and may be non-matching.

Application Information Application guidelines and forms are available from the program. Site visits may be made to applicant organizations.

Deadline(s) Application postmark deadline is May 18.

324. National Endowment for the Arts
Design Arts Program, Room 625
1100 Pennsylvania Avenue, NW
Washington, DC 20506
(202) 682-5437

Design Arts Program: Design Advancement

Program Description The Design Arts Program Design Advancement category supports grants that advance the state of the art through design practice, theory and research, media, and education about design. The category encompasses and welcomes applications in all design disciplines: architecture, landscape architecture; urban design, historic preservation and planning; interior design; industrial design; and fashion design. The purpose of Design Advancement is to focus on design itself. Proposals are invited for projects that involve a single design discipline, several design disciplines, or collaborations between designers and other artists. Special subjects, such as the exploration of design issues relating to the 500th anniversary in 1992 of Christopher Columbus' first voyage of discovery to the New World—the Quincentenary—will also be considered.

Sample Grants To support an exhibition exploring the image of city in science fiction films, $10,000 to an individual (1987). To support development, design, and production of three "exhibits in a kit," a product that other museums may purchase in order to replicate Boston Children's Museum exhibits, $29,950 to Children's Museum, Boston, MA (1987). To support a symposium, "Architecture and Landscape in the Twentieth Century: A Critical Assessment," which will be documented in an illustrated publication, $20,000 to Museum of Modern Art, New York, NY (1987).

Eligibility/Limitations The category is open to individuals and organizations. Grants for individuals are open to professional designers and other individuals working in design. Awards are made only to U.S. citizens or permanent residents of the U.S. Applicants for grants to organizations (including local and state governments, community or neighborhood organizations, colleges and universities, and independent nonprofit groups and institutions) must meet NEA legal requirements for applicant organizations outlined in program guidelines.

Fiscal Information Grants for organizations are generally available in amounts up to $50,000. The minimum grant generally will not be less than $5,000. Each grantee must match the funds on at least a one-to-one basis. Grants for individuals are available in amounts up to $15,000. The minimum grant generally will not be less than $5,000. Grants for individuals do not require matching funds.

Application Information Application information, guidelines and application packets are available from the program.

Deadline(s) Design Advancement Project Grants for Organizations application postmark deadlines are April 11 and October 3. Project Grants for Individuals application postmark deadlines are September 1 and March 10. Completed applications, including all required materials, must be postmarked by the deadline dates.

325. National Endowment for the Arts

Design Arts Program, Room 625
1100 Pennsylvania Avenue, NW
Washington, DC 20506
(202) 682-5437

International Exchange Fellowships: France

Program Description The Design Arts Program International Exchange Fellowships are awarded for work and study in France to American artists from the various discipline programs and to museum curators. Project descriptions must reflect activities for which residence in France would be advantageous.

Eligibility/Limitations Awards are made only to U.S. citizens or permanent residents of the U.S. Fellowships are awarded to outstanding mid-career professionals.

Fiscal Information Fellowships cover residencies of up to one year in France.

Application Information For more information contact the Design Arts Program.

Deadline(s) Application postmark deadlines are September 1 and March 10. Completed applications, including all required materials, must be postmarked by the deadline dates.

326. National Endowment for the Arts

Expansion Arts Program
1100 Pennsylvania Avenue, NW
Washington, DC 20506
(202) 682-5443

Expansion Arts Organizations

CFDA Program Number 45.010

Program Description The Expansion Arts Program supports professionally-directed arts organizations of high artistic quality which are deeply rooted in and reflective of the culture of a minority, inner city, rural, or tribal community. These organizations must have a fundamental relationship to their community, and the provision of art to their community must be the organization's primary programmatic activity. Organizations that fit these criteria are referred to by the endowment as "expansion arts organizations." These characteristics distinguish expansion arts organizations from mainstream institutions that offer outreach programs at the communities described as an aspect of their overall activities. The program encourages original and promising works of art; performances of the classic repertoire of a particular culture; exhibitions of new artists or of important artists within a community; and provision of access to quality art of all types. The program also promotes the career development of artists from minority, inner city, rural, or tribal communities through support of professional training of serious and talented individuals.

Sample Grants To support the "Jazz Live" series, which presents monthly performance evenings of local and national groups, and the "Larry Neal" Cultural Series, an annual dramatic reading and discussion event which focuses on black poets, to Afro-American Historical and Cultural Museum, Inc., Philadelphia, PA and "The Sounds of This City: Afro-American Music in Philadelphia," $10,000 (1987). To support the Satellite Gallery program emphasizing exhibition opportunities for minority artists, $15,000 to Bronx Museum of the Arts, Inc., Bronx, NY (1986). To support "In the Tradition: A Celebration of Black Storytelling," and workshops to showcase and document the work of Black writers, $10,000 to DuSable Museum of African American History, Inc., Chicago, IL (1986). To support the exhibition activities of the museum's two major extension facilities in Johnstown and Blair serving the artistic needs of these rural communities, $11,000 to Southern Alleghenies Museum of Art, Lorreto, PA (1986). To support the artists-in-residence program offering fellowships for studio space and art supplies to outstanding emerging artists, the intern program in museology, and administrative costs, $50,000 to Studio Museum in Harlem, Inc., New York (1986).

Eligibility/Limitations Expansion arts organizations may apply in *one* of the following subcategories: performing arts, including dance, theater, music, or a combination; visual, media, or design arts, including visual arts, media arts (film, video, television, radio), design arts, or a combination; literary arts; or interdisciplinary arts. Applicant organizations usually must meet all of the following requirements: be arts organizations; employ professional artists; have been in existence for at least three years. In addition, former grantees must have submitted a final report for the most recently completed Expansion Arts Program grant with an ending date more than ninety days before the application deadline of October 14.

Fiscal Information Grants generally range from $5,000 to $30,000 and generally will not exceed 20 percent of an organization's annual total fiscal activity. Grants must be matched on at least a one-to-one basis.

Application Information Application guidelines, instructions, and additional information are available from the Expansion Arts Program.

Deadline(s) Application postmark deadline is October 14.

327. National Endowment for the Arts

Expansion Arts Program
1100 Pennsylvania Avenue, NW
Washington, DC 20506
(202) 682-5443

Services to the Field

CFDA Program Number 45.010

Program Description This program aids organizations of regional or national scope whose primary function is to offer technical assistance and services to expansion arts organizations. There will be very few grants awarded in this category. Only organizations of exceptional quality with an established national or regional orientation and ongoing working relationships with expansion arts organizations should apply. This program funds regional or national service activities, such as: preparation of arts directories; newsletters; workshop programs leading to economic development of artists and arts organizations; loans of equipment; public relations; audience development; and management assistance.

Sample Grants To support resource information programs for and about Black museums, including a monthly newsletter and a brochure listing Black museums and AAMA services, $11,300 to African American Museums Association, Inc., Washington, DC (1986). To amend a previous grant to support Phase II of the "Black Colleges Collections: Our Commonwealth," a multiphase project for the conservation and study of the art holdings of Black colleges, $28,400 to African American Museums Association, Inc., Washington, DC (1986).

Eligibility/Limitations Applicant organizations usually must meet all of the following requirements: have as their primary function service to expansion arts organizations; employ professional administrators; have an established regional or national service program which has been functional for at least two years. In addition, former grantees must have submitted a final report for the most recently completed Expansion Arts Program grant with an ending date more than ninety days before the application deadline of December 2.

Fiscal Information Grants generally range from $5,000 to $30,000. Grants must be matched on at least a dollar-for-dollar basis and generally will not exceed 20 percent of an organization's total annual fiscal activity. The program generally does not fund local, state, or regional arts agencies.

Application Information Application guidelines, instructions, and additional information are available from the Expansion Arts Program.

Deadline(s) Application postmark deadline is December 2.

328. National Endowment for the Arts
Folk Arts Program
1100 Pennsylvania Avenue, NW
Washington, DC 20506
(202) 682-5449

Folk Arts Grants to Organizations: Media Preservation and Presentation of Traditional Arts

CFDA Program Number 45.015

Program Description It is the purpose of the Folk Arts Program to honor and make visible the stylistic and cultural variety that has made life in the United States an exciting challenge and an adventure in human understanding. Within this purpose, the special responsibility of the Folk Arts Program is to encourage those community and family-based arts that have endured through several generations, that carry with them a sense of community aesthetic, and that demonstrate the highest degree of artistic excellence. The objectives of the program are positive: to identify, assist, and honor those local men and women who demonstrate the highest traditional artistic knowledge and skills; to support the cultural activities of traditional communities in which such artists flourish; and to make the sophistication, vivacity, and significance of our multicultural artistic heritage more available to the wider public. The skills, repertoires, and performance styles of many folk artists may often reach a wider public and may be preserved for future generations through carefully conceived and well executed media documentation. Matching grants are available to organizations for radio or television programs or series, recordings, small publications such as tune books, still photographs, and films that preserve or present traditional arts.

Sample Grants To support an exhibition, catalogue, and demonstrations involving contemporary Central Californian Indian Basketmakers of the Yokuts, Mono, and Miwok tribes, $24,600 to Fresno Metropolitan Museum of Art, History and Science, Fresno, CA (1987).

Eligibility/Limitations Applicant organizations must meet the legal requirements for organizations as outlined in the program guidelines, available from the endowment.

Fiscal Information Amounts requested should reflect a realistic budget for the particular project. Funding will depend upon the significance of the proposed project and the availability of money. Ordinarily, organizational grants will range between $2,500 and $30,000 and will be made on a one-to-one matching basis. The program encourages cash contributions from other sources, but also allows in-kind contributions as part of the match. The program does not fund general operating expenses; start-up costs for institutes, regional centers, or service agencies; research, except as a necessary part of a presentation or documentation project; foreign travel; construction or major repair of buildings or other facilities; the purchase of major equipment; book publishing; historical presentations; theater or dance companies that dramatize or re-create the traditional folk dance and music of many lands; or contemporary studio crafts.

Application Information Application guidelines and additional information are available from the program.

Deadline(s) Application deadlines are October 1 and January 5.

Additional Information Additional programs within the division are Services to the Field, the State Apprenticeship Program, and National Heritage Fellowships.

329. National Endowment for the Arts
Folk Arts Program
1100 Pennsylvania Avenue, NW
Washington, DC 20506
(202) 682-5449

Folk Arts Grants to Organizations: Presentation of Traditional Arts and Artists

CFDA Program Number 45.015

Program Description It is the purpose of the Folk Arts Program to honor and make visible the stylistic and cultural variety that has made life in the United States an exciting challenge and an adventure in human understanding. Within this purpose, the special responsibility of the Folk Arts Program is to encourage those community and family-based arts that have endured through several generations, that carry with them a sense of community aesthetic, and that demonstrate the highest degree of artistic excellence. The objectives of the program are positive: to identify, assist, and honor those local men and women who demonstrate the highest traditional artistic knowledge and skills; to support the cultural activities of traditional communities in which such artists flourish; and to make the sophistication, vivacity, and significance of our multicultural artistic heritage more available to the wider public. Matching grants are available for local or regional celebrations, exhibits, workshops, concerts, residencies, and tours that present traditional arts and artists of the highest excellence.

Sample Grants To support artist and consultant fees for a month-long festival of Indo-American folk art in the greater Washington, DC, area, $18,000 to Capital Children's Museum, Washington, DC (1986). To support a regional folk arts survey and traveling exhibition, including public presentations, $24,800 to Columbia Art League, Columbia, MO (1986). To support a survey of Danish-American traditions of the upper Midwest and the presentation of a selection of these traditions at the annual Tivoli Fest, $9,900 to Danish Immigrant Museum, Elk Horn, IA (1986). To support a concert series featuring outstanding Native American performers of New Mexico and Arizona, including Zuni, San Juan Pueblo, Navajo, and Apache singers, $10,300 to Museum of New Mexico Foundation, Santa Fe, NM (1987). To support an exhibition of Afro-American quilts from the San Francisco Bay area, $8,000 to San Francisco Crafts and Folk Art Museum, San Francisco, CA (1987).

Eligibility/Limitations Applicant organizations must meet the legal requirements as outlined in the program guidelines, available from the endowment.

Fiscal Information Amounts requested should reflect a realistic budget for the particular project. Funding will depend upon the significance of the proposed project and the availability of money. Ordinarily, organizational grants will range between $2,500 and $30,000 and will be made on a one-to-one matching basis. The program encourages cash contributions from other sources, but also allows in-kind contributions as part of the match. The program does not fund general operating expenses; start-up costs for institutes, regional centers, or service agencies; research, except as a necessary part of a presentation or documentation project; foreign travel; construction or major repair of buildings or other facilities; the purchase of major equipment; book publishing; historical presentations; theater or dance companies that dramatize or re-create the traditional folk dance and music of many lands; or contemporary studio crafts.

Application Information Application guidelines and additional information are available from the program.

Deadline(s) Application deadlines are October 1 and January 5.

330. National Endowment for the Arts
Inter-Arts Program, Room 710
1100 Pennsylvania Avenue, NW
Washington, DC 20506
(202) 682-5444

Grants to Presenting Organizations

Program Description The Inter-Arts Program provides support to arts institutions to commission and produce interdisciplinary collaborations between visual artists and artists in other disciplines. Support is also available for organizations which present multidisciplinary art series of national or regional significance on an ongoing annual basis. These grants are designed to improve the ability of professional multidisciplinary presenting organizations to present diverse arts programming of high quality and national or regional significance to their communities.

Sample Grants To support artist's fees and production costs for performance/discussion programs during the 1986-1987 presentation season, $10,000 to Exploratorium, San Francisco, CA (1986). To support "Performance Parameters," a series of collaborative arts events during the 1986-1987 presentation season, $7,500 to La Jolla Museum of Contemporary Art, La Jolla, CA (1986). To support the 1986-1987 presentation of the MAPROOM, $10,000 to Museum of Contemporary Art, Los Angeles, CA (1986). To support the continuation of "fast/forward," a performing arts series that focuses on experimental work in dance, music, and performance art, $11,000 to Virginia Museum of Fine Arts, Richmond, VA (1987).

Eligibility/Limitations Individual presenting organizations and consortia of presenting organizations are eligible. All applicants must meet legal requirements outlined in the program guidelines available from NEA.

Fiscal Information Grant amounts are determined by the quality and merit of the project, the number of requests, and the funds available in this category. Grants generally range between $5,000 and $50,000. Most range between $7,500 and $20,000. Grants may be used to pay no more than half the cost of any project. Each grantee is encouraged to raise the match through cash contributions or earned income.

Application Information Application packages, program guidelines, and additional information are available from the program.

Deadline(s) Applicants should send the Intent to Apply Card to the program by May 8. Completed application packages must be postmarked no later than June 5. Late applications will be rejected.

331. National Endowment for the Arts
Inter-Arts Program, Room 710
1100 Pennsylvania Avenue, NW
Washington, DC 20506
(202) 682-5444

Interdisciplinary Arts Projects

Program Description The Interdisciplinary Arts Projects category supports artists' projects of the highest artistic quality that explore non-traditional formats and processes and that fuse, cross, or transcend distinct arts disciplines. Interdisciplinary work exhibits a sensibility of experimentation that challenges set notions of separate disciplines. At the same time, the interdisciplinary/collaborative arts process has generated a substantial body of work so that new works can be evaluated according to criteria intrinsic to the field itself. This category also supports projects designed to widen the availability of interdisciplinary work to the public. All projects should be of national or regional significance.

Sample Grants To support the creation of a series of works through collaboration between emerging artists-in-residence and the Exploratorium's staff of artists, scientists, technicians, and computer programmers, $20,000 to Exploratorium, San Francisco, CA (1986).

Eligibility/Limitations To be eligible, a project must: be submitted by an organization meeting NEA legal requirements; involve more than one arts discipline; and pay professional artists.

Fiscal Information Grant amounts are determined by the quality and merit of the project, the number of requests, and the funds available in this category. Grants normally range between $7,500 and $15,000, although some grants are made in higher amounts rarely exceeding $35,000. Grants may be used to pay no more than half the cost of any project.

Application Information Before starting the application process, applicants are encouraged to consider carefully whether or not their proposed project does indeed fuse or transcend the traditional disciplines, and that the proposed project and supporting materials reflect an interdisciplinary and/or collaborative focus. Additional information and application guidelines are available from the program.

Deadline(s) Applicants should send the Intent to Apply Card to the program by June 26. Complete application packages must be postmarked no later than July 31.

332. National Endowment for the Arts

Inter-Arts Program, Room 710
1100 Pennsylvania Avenue, NW
Washington, DC 20506
(202) 682-5444

Services to Presenting Organizations

Program Description These grants assist state and regional arts agencies and service organizations that help presenters improve their ability to present diverse, high quality arts programming in their communities.

Eligibility/Limitations Eligible organizations include presenter membership organizations, regional arts organizations, state arts agencies, and consortia of presenting organizations with projects or services that substantially assist presenters. Applicants must meet the legal requirements listed in program guidelines and must have: at least two years' experience at the time of application in providing services to presenters of more than one art form; paid professional staff; and national, regional, and/or state-wide impact.

Fiscal Information Grant amounts are determined by the quality and merit of the project, the number of requests, and the funds available in this category. Grants generally range between $5,000 and $20,000, although on rare occasions grants are made in higher amounts. Grants may be used to pay no more than half the cost of any project. Priority will be given to applicants that can provide a cash match.

Application Information Application packets, including guidelines, and additional information are available from the program.

Deadline(s) Applicants should send the Intent to Apply Card on the back cover of program guidelines to Inter-Arts by May 8. Complete application packages must be postmarked no later than June 5. Late applications will be rejected.

333. National Endowment for the Arts
Inter-Arts Program, Room 710
1100 Pennsylvania Avenue, NW
Washington, DC 20506
(202) 682-5444

Services to the Arts

Program Description Arts service organizations assist artists and arts organizations that create, produce, present, exhibit, or preserve the arts. Their mission is to provide services that individuals or organizations could not otherwise afford or that would not otherwise exist. This category supports exemplary projects that provide professional artists and arts organizations with resources essential to artistic growth and development. These projects must have significant national or regional impact and affect a broad variety of arts disciplines. The category supports service projects that result in a clear benefit to the arts as a whole or to a significant segment of the arts community and which are (a) not otherwise available or affordable from other sources, (b) are provided more evidently through a single source, (c) relate to new or specialized needs or artists and arts organizations, or (d) address areas of long-term importance to the arts community.

Sample Grants To support the Arts Hazards Information Center's work as a national clearinghouse on health hazards in museums and performing arts facilities, $20,000 to Center for Occupational Hazards, Inc., New York, NY (1986).

Eligibility/Limitations Applicant organizations must: meet NEA legal requirements; provide services of national or regional impact to constituents in more than one arts discipline; and have a full-time, year-round paid professional staff.

Fiscal Information Grant amounts are determined by the quality and merit of the project, the number of requests, and the funds available in this category. Grants generally range from $5,000 to $15,000, although some grants are made in higher amounts rarely exceeding $35,000. Grants may be used to pay no more than half the cost of any project.

Application Information Additional information, application forms, and special application requirements are available from the program.

Deadline(s) Applicants should send the Intent to Apply Card to the program by September 4. Complete application packages must be postmarked no later than November 6.

334. National Endowment for the Arts
International Activities
1100 Pennsylvania Avenue, NW
Washington, DC 20506
(202) 682-5562

The Fund for U.S. Artists at International Festivals and Exhibitions

Program Description The fund has three goals: to make possible appropriate U.S. representation at more international festivals and exhibitions; to permit more of the best of United States artists and art works to be seen at these events; and to support the participation of American artists, particularly minority artists, at festivals and exhibitions throughout the world, especially in areas where they have rarely been seen.

Eligibility/Limitations Performing artists and performing arts groups invited to participate in major international festivals who need additional support to make their performances possible are eligible to apply.

Fiscal Information This fund will make available $325,000 for 1988 to support performing artists invited to international festivals abroad. Support from this fund will usually be provided directly to the artists invited and not to the festival.

Application Information Eligible applicants should write to Beverly Kratochvil, Program Officer, International Activities, at the address listed above. The letter should include the dates of the festival and specific information on what the artist has been asked to do. In addition, a copy of the festival's letter of invitation and budget which indicates specifically what support the festival will provide and what the overall costs to the individual or group will be, including fees, transportation, per diem and other costs should be enclosed.

Deadline(s) In order to allocate funds in a timely fashion, requests from artists and organizations who have been invited to festivals abroad will be reviewed four times a year. Deadlines for applications are April 1, July 1, and October 1.

335. National Endowment for the Arts
Literature Program
1100 Pennsylvania Avenue, NW
Washington, DC 20506
(202) 682-5451

Audience Development Projects

CFDA Program Number 45.004

Program Description These grants are designed to promote and develop audiences for contemporary creative writing of the highest quality. A few grants are awarded for a variety of projects, including: cooperative literary promotion projects; regional small press book fairs; traveling exhibits of literary works; permanent exhibits of literary works; projects which distribute review materials; and other innovative projects, in print or other media, which promote literature or literary publishing.

Eligibility/Limitations Applicant organizations must meet legal requirements as defined by NEA in program guidelines.

Fiscal Information In general, grants will range between $2,000 and $20,000. No grant will exceed half of the cash costs of the project. Applicants are encouraged to match grants with cash and to include in their budgets cash salaries for key personnel. In addition, in-kind contributions may be designated as part of the match. However, no grant may be matched entirely with in-kind contributions.

Application Information Application forms, guidelines, and additional information are available from the Literature Program.

Deadline(s) Application postmark deadline is January 16.

336. National Endowment for the Arts
Literature Program
1100 Pennsylvania Avenue, NW
Washington, DC 20506
(202) 682-5451

Literary Publishing: Assistance to Literary Magazines

CFDA Program Number 45.004

Program Description The Literature Program of the National Endowment for the Arts assists individual creative writers of excellence or promise, encourages wider audiences for contemporary literature, and helps support nonprofit organizations that foster literature as a professional pursuit. Grants in this category provide assistance to the nation's noncommercial literary journals and are awarded for publication projects. Examples include: payments to authors and contributors for their work; production, design, and related costs of issues; efforts to improve distribution and to increase readership; purchase of technical assistance; and development of local and private sources of financial support.

Eligibility/Limitations Literary magazines which have published at least three issues in the two years prior to the application deadline may apply. State arts agencies may apply on behalf of literary magazines in their states (one application per magazine). Also, individual literary magazine editors may apply for matching fellowships. Review journals which include as a substantial portion of their regular format reviews and discussion of contemporary literature and literary publications are eligible. Magazines dedicated to special viewpoints or directed toward special audiences are eligible only if they publish substantial amounts of contemporary creative writing or literary reviewing. To be eligible, former grantees must have submitted required final reports for all completed Literature Program grants since (and including) fiscal year 1983. Magazines with time extensions on more than one grant are not eligible to apply.

Fiscal Information Grants will range between $2,000 and $10,000. Grants are awarded on the condition that at least 10 percent of grant funds received are earmarked for writers. Grants may be used to pay only such direct costs as royalties, printing, binding, paper, supplies, proofreading, editing, postage, distribution, and promotion. Applicants are encouraged to match grants with cash. While in-kind contributions may be used as match, no grant should be matched entirely with in-kind contributions. The program prefers that all grants over $5,000 be matched in cash on at least a dollar-for-dollar basis.

Application Information Application forms, guidelines, and additional information are available from the program.

Deadline(s) Application postmark deadline is August 11.

337. National Endowment for the Arts
Literature Program
1100 Pennsylvania Avenue, NW
Washington, DC 20506
(202) 682-5451

Literary Publishing: Small Press Assistance

CFDA Program Number 45.004

Program Description The Literature Program of the National Endowment for the Arts assists individual creative writers of excellence or promise, encourages wider audiences for contemporary literature, and helps support nonprofit organizations that foster literature as a professional pursuit. Grants in this category assist the nation's noncommercial literary small presses and university and college presses with a substantial history of publishing contemporary creative literature of the highest quality. Presses must have developed a distribution and sales strategy. Grants may be used to assist in the publication, promotion, and distribution of books and anthologies of contemporary creative writing and translation, to implement organizational development plans, to purchase technical assistance, and to secure continuing local and private sources of financial support.

Eligibility/Limitations Small presses, and university and college presses which have published at least four volumes (of twenty-four pages or more each) of fiction, poetry, plays, or other creative prose in the past three years may apply. Books of 40,000 or more words will count as the equivalent of two volumes. State arts agencies may apply on behalf of small presses in their states.

Fiscal Information Grants generally ranging from $2,000 to $12,000 are available to all presses which meet the eligibility requirements. Grants generally ranging from $12,000 to $25,000 are available only to small presses which published six or more volumes of forty-eight or more pages (books of 40,000 or more words will count as the equivalent of two volumes) in the year prior to application. Presses which apply to publish a volume of literary prose of 40,000 or more words in a press run of 2,500 or more are eligible for up to $5,000 for that volume. This amount may be in addition to the grant amounts specified above. Applicants are encouraged to match grants with cash, including anticipated sales. While in-kind contributions such as the services of the publishing staff, outside editorial assistance, use of facilities, and materials may be used as part of the match, no grant should be matched entirely with in-kind contributions. The program prefers that all grants over $7,500 be matched in cash on at least a one-to-one basis. State and local arts agencies may provide non-federal funds for a full or partial match.

Application Information Application forms, guidelines, and additional information are available from the program.

Deadline(s) Applications must be postmarked no later than September 11 for projects scheduled to begin after May 1. Late applications will be rejected.

Additional Information The program does not fund books to which the author is required to make a financial contribution toward publication cost. In addition, the program does not fund reprints of titles supported under previous grants. Grants are awarded on the condition that the author(s) of an endowment-supported publication receive a minimum of 10 percent of the sales income in cash (or the equivalent in copies) as at least partial payment of royalties. Preference will be given to presses which pay cash advances or royalties.

338. National Endowment for the Arts
Media Arts: Film/Radio/Television Program
1100 Pennsylvania Avenue, NW
Washington, DC 20506
(202) 682-5452

Film/Video Production Grants

CFDA Program Number 45.006

Program Description The Media Arts: Film/Radio/Television Program of the National Endowment for the Arts recognizes the central role the individual artist plays in the distinctive and innovative use of media. The media arts include documentary, experimental, and narrative works, as well as electronic manipulations, animated film, and audio art. Film/Video Production grants are designed to encourage and support artworks in film and video of the the highest quality. Irrespective of subject or genre, productions must emphasize creative use of media, fulfilling, and, on occasion, extending their artistic possibilities. Grants are generally made for single film and video productions which exemplify the use of these media as art forms.

Sample Grants To support a video installation project by Nam June Paik, $35,000 to American Museum of the Moving Image, Astoria, NY (1987).

Eligibility/Limitations Applicant organizations must have existed at least one year. Individuals must have substantial professional experience and must be U.S. citizens or permanent residents of the United States. Former grantees must have submitted required final reports and interim reports in order to be eligible for subsequent funding.

Fiscal Information Matching grants for organizations generally range from $20,000 to $50,000. A limited number of nonmatching grants to individuals generally range from $10,000 to $25,000. Projects should be completed within two years of the starting date.

Application Information Application forms, guidelines and special application requirement instructions are available from the program.

Deadline(s) Applications must be postmarked no later than November 13. Late applications will be rejected.

339. National Endowment for the Arts
Media Arts: Film/Radio/Television Program
1100 Pennsylvania Avenue, NW
Washington, DC 20506
(202) 682-5452

Media Arts Centers

CFDA Program Number 45.006

Program Description The Media Arts: Film/Radio/Television Program of the National Endowment for the Arts recognizes the central role the individual artist plays in the distinctive and innovative use of media. The media arts include documentary, experimental, and narrative works, as well as electronic manipulations, animated film, and audio art. The purpose of these grants is to advance the arts of film and video and to encourage their wider appreciation and practice. The Media Arts Program assists a limited number of Media Arts Centers of the highest quality and of national or regional importance.

Sample Grants For film and video exhibition series, Saturday screenings for children, lecture series, workshops, and a research collection at the American Museum of the Moving Image, $6,700 to Astoria Motion Picture and Television Center Foundation, Inc., Astoria, NY (1986). For film and video exhibitions, visiting artists programs, a film research collection, and publications at Anthology Film Archives, $9,600 to Film Art Fund, Inc., New York, NY (1986). For a film exhibition program with visiting artists, a research center which includes a film study collection, a film stills collection, video exhibitions, installations, and distribution, $52,000 to Museum of Modern Art, New York, NY (1987). For extensive exhibition program, installations, access to production and post-production facilities workshops, visiting artists, and a videotape library, $31,000 to Long Beach Museum of Art Foundation, Long Beach, CA (1987). For television and radio exhibition programs, retrospectives with extensive program notes, seminars, publication of catalogues, and educational programs, $6,000 to Museum of Broadcasting, New York, NY (1987).

Eligibility/Limitations A Media Arts Center may be an independent organization, or it may be affiliated with a university, museum, city or state arts agency, or other tax-exempt body. Each Media Arts Center must identify itself as *one* of the following: a multipurpose center which provides a variety of services, e.g., exhibitions, workshops, production facilities; an exhibition center which provides a variety of services, e.g., seminars, study collections, publications, with an emphasis on the ongoing exhibition of film and video art; or a production/post-production center which provides a number of services, e.g., workshops, distribution, with an emphasis on making available production and post-production facilities. Applicant organizations must have a record of demonstrated excellence in carrying out two or more of the eight following activities: (1) exhibition to wider audiences of high quality film and video art, with accompanying program notes and visiting filmmakers, videomakers, and critics; (2) making available production and post-production facilities for filmmakers and videomakers; (3) workshops and residency programs involving filmmakers, videomakers, and critics; (4) making available study materials, research facilities, and film or video collections; (5) collection and dissemination of information about media activities on a local, regional, and national basis; (6) distribution of high quality film and video art; (7) conducting seminars, symposia, and conferences; and (8) publication of catalogs, magazines, newsletters, and critical journals. In addition, former grantees must have submitted required final and interim reports in order to be eligible for subsequent funding.

Fiscal Information Matching grants generally range from $10,000 to $50,000.

Application Information Application forms, guidelines, and special application requirements are available from the program.

Deadline(s) Applications must be postmarked no later than April 24. Late applications will be rejected.

340. National Endowment for the Arts
Media Arts: Film/Radio/Television Program
1100 Pennsylvania Avenue, NW
Washington, DC 20506
(202) 682-5452

National Services

CFDA Program Number 45.006

Program Description These grants support a limited number of exemplary activities which provide professional media artists and media arts organizations with resources essential for artistic growth and development. These activities must have significant national impact and/or serve as a model for the field as a whole. Activities which may be funded include: conferences, seminars, and workshops; distribution; publications; circulating exhibitions.

Sample Grants Tc support the touring of "The First Decade: Ethnograpic Art Documentaries from the Margaret Mead Film Festival," a retrospective film program, $7,900 to American Federation of Arts, New York, NY (1986).

Eligibility/Limitations Organizations must meet NEA legal requirements; have been in existence for at least one year; be major organizations of national import, which provide the most significant and far-reaching services of their type. Universities, museums, professional societies, and established service organizations are among those eligible.

Fiscal Information Matching grants generally range from $10,000 to $50,000.

Application Information Additional information, application forms, and special application requirements are available from the program.

Deadline(s) The application postmark deadline is May 13.

341. National Endowment for the Arts
Media Arts: Film/Radio/Television Program
1100 Pennsylvania Avenue, NW
Washington, DC 20506
(202) 682-5452

Radio Production

CFDA Program Number 45.006

Program Description The Media Arts: Film/Radio/Television Program of the National Endowment for the Arts recognizes the central role the individual artist plays in the distinctive and innovative use of media. The Radio Section of the Media Arts Program supports outstanding single productions and series for radio broadcast. Radio production projects may include: documentaries, classic or experimental drama, audio art, children's programming, and the presentation of literature and music. Projects should emphasize the creative use of the radio medium.

Sample Grants To support provision of facilities to radio producers, residencies by independent producers, workshops for children, and museum radio exhibitions, $10,000 to Capital Children's Museum, Washington, DC (1986). To support "The Invisible Museum," a series of stereo exhibitions, $5,000 to an independent producer (1987).

Eligibility/Limitations Applicant organizations must have existed at least one year. Individual radio producers must have substantial professional experience and must be U.S. citizens or permanent residents of the United States. Joint applications from individual producers are eligible; however, only one producer should sign, and accept legal responsibility for, the application. Only one application per project may be submitted.

Fiscal Information Matching grants for organizations generally range from $3,000 to $50,000. Nonmatching grants for individual radio producers generally range from $3,000 to $15,000.

Application Information Application forms, guidelines, special application requirements, and additional information are available from the Media Arts Program.

Deadline(s) Application postmark deadline is October 8.

342. National Endowment for the Arts
Museum Program, Room 624
1100 Pennsylvania Avenue, NW
Washington, DC 20506
(202) 682-5442

Care of Collections: Collection Maintenance

CFDA Program Number 45.012

Program Description These awards are designed to help museums preserve collections primarily of artistic significance through solving problems in the areas of climate control, security, and storage. Grants are available for two types of projects: (1) *Surveys*: for surveys identifying problems and recommending solutions, including a specific renovation plan and cost estimates; and (2) *Implementation*: for renovation projects for which careful plans and cost estimates have been developed.

Sample Grants To support a survey of existing museum space, with a view toward renovation to provide new housing for the textile and works on paper collection, $5,100 to Allentown Art Museum, Allentown, PA (1986). To support the installation of closed-circuit television security systems and the purchase of a two-way portable radio system used by museum guards, $20,700 to Cincinnati Museum Association, Cincinnati, OH (1986). To support the upgrading and renovation of the museum's climate-control system, $15,000 to Museum of Contemporary Art, Chicago, IL (1986). To support the renovation of 5,000 square feet and the installation of an HVAC system, $50,000 to Allentown Art Museum, Allentown, PA (1987). To support the purchase of archival materials and the upgrading of storage facilities, $4,000 to Franklin Furnace Archive, Inc., New York, NY (1987).

Eligibility/Limitations While accreditation by the American Association of Museums is not an eligibility requirement, the endowment generally uses the definition of museums developed by the AAM "...a nonprofit institution essentially educational or aesthetic in purpose with professional staff, which owns or utilizes tangible objects, cares for them, and exhibits them to the public on some regular schedule." In addition to museums, organizations that serve museums, organizations that perform museum functions, state arts agencies, and regional arts organizations are also eligible to apply. Applicant organizations must submit a copy of the Internal Revenue Service determination letter for tax-exempt status or the official document identifying the applicant as a unit of state or local government. In general, organizations should be in operation two years prior to submitting an application. Renovation of galleries may be supported only when directly related to climate control, security systems, or storage facilities. Museums applying for implementation grants must have fully developed plans and cost estimates at the time of application.

Fiscal Information Up to $15,000 is available for surveys; grant awards must be matched at least one-to-one and the minimum grant generally will not be less than $2,500. Up to $200,000 is available for implementation projects. Implementation project awards of $50,000 or less require at least a one-to-one match; grant awards between $50,000 and $100,000 require a two-to-one match; and grant awards of $100,000 or more require a three-to-one match. The minimum implementation grant generally will not be less than $5,000. A grant period of up to one year is allowed for survey projects. A grant period of up to two years is allowed for implementation projects. Grants in this category are not awarded for new construction or for collection maintenance projects in new facilities.

Application Information Application guidelines, application forms, special application requirements, and additional information are available from the museum program.

Deadline(s) Application postmark deadline is September 19.

343. National Endowment for the Arts

Museum Program, Room 624
1100 Pennsylvania Avenue, NW
Washington, DC 20506
(202) 682-5442

Care of Collections: Conservation

CFDA Program Number 45.012

Program Description These awards are designed to help museums conserve collections primarily of artistic significance. Works undergoing conservation treatment must be wholly owned by the applicant institution. Grants are available for: (1) *Conservation*

Planning: to help museums and other organizations plan conservation programs or plan specific treatment of collections; (2) *Conservation of Collections*: for treatment projects executed within a museum's own conservation facilities or by an outside facility and for the purchase of major equipment for a conservation laboratory at a museum or regional conservation center (each institution may submit no more than one application for treatment and one for equipment purchase under this program); and (3) *Conservation Training*: for student stipends at existing university-based training centers, for master-apprentice internship programs (generally of at least one year's duration), to support new or existing professional training programs for the conservation of ethnographic or archaeological works of art, and for seminars and workshops to familiarize museum professionals with current methods used in the handling, packing, examination, conservation, and stabilization of works of art.

Sample Grants To support the purchase of microscope equipment for the museum's conservation laboratory, $20,000 to American Museum of Natural History, New York, NY (1986). To support an advanced, one-year internship in ethnographic conservation, $14,800 to Bernice P. Bishop Museum, Honolulu, HI (1986). For the conservation of archaeological metals from the Andean regions of South America for display in the new Hall of South American Peoples, $25,000 to the American Museum of Natural History, New York, NY (1984). To support conservation treatment of more than forty percent of the center's puppet collection, $3,700 to Center for Puppetry Arts, Inc., Atlanta, GA (1986). To support the conservation treatment of selected books from the Missouri Botanical Garden Library's Rare Book Collection, $10,000 to Missouri Botanical Garden Board of Trustees, St. Louis, MO (1986). To support conservation treatment of selected objects in the museum's Pacific Ethnology Collection, $14,800 to Bernice P. Bishop Museum, Honolulu, HI (1987). To support two master-apprentice internships in the conservation of contemporary art, $40,000 to San Francisco Museum of Art, San Francisco, CA (1987).

Eligibility/Limitations While accreditation by the American Association of Museums is not an eligibility requirement, the endowment generally uses the definition of museums developed by the AAM "...a nonprofit institution essentially educational or aesthetic in purpose with professional staff, which owns or utilizes tangible objects, cares for them, and exhibits them to the public on some regular schedule." In addition to museums, organizations that serve museums, organizations that perform museum functions, state arts agencies, and regional arts organizations are also eligible to apply. Applicant organizations must submit a copy of the Internal Revenue Service determination letter for tax-exempt status or the official document identifying the applicant as a unit of state or local government. In general, organizations should be in operation two years prior to submitting an application. Individuals are not eligible to apply.

Fiscal Information All grants must be matched at least one-to-one. Up to $10,000 is available for conservation planning. Up to $25,000 is available for conservation of collections; the minimum grant in this category generally will not be less than $2,500. Institutions may request: up to $100,000 for student stipends at existing university-based training centers; up to $40,000 for master-apprentice internship programs; up to $150,000 to support new or existing professional training programs for the conservation of ethnographic or archaeological works of art; and up to $20,000 for seminars and workshops. A grant period of up to eighteen months is allowed, except for conservation internships (under Conservation Training) where a longer period of support is possible. Requests for equipment purchases should be submitted in a separate application from requests for treatment projects. Equipment costs are the only allowable expenses in equipment purchase applications.

Application Information Application guidelines, application forms, special application requirements, and additional information are available from the Museum Program.

Deadline(s) Applications should be received by September 19.

344. National Endowment for the Arts
Museum Program, Room 624
1100 Pennsylvania Avenue, NW
Washington, DC 20506
(202) 682-5442

Museum Purchase Plan

Program Description This program category is designed to encourage museums to build and expand their permanent collections through the purchase of works by living American artists. Grants help museums: develop their permanent collections of contemporary American art; raise new funds for acquisitions; increase public awareness of contemporary American art; and support the work of living American artists.

Eligibility/Limitations While accreditation by the American Association of Museums is not an eligibility requirement, the endowment generally uses the definition of museums developed by the AAM "...a nonprofit institution essentially educational or aesthetic in purpose with professional staff, which owns or utilizes tangible objects, cares for them, and exhibits them to the public on some regular schedule." Eligibility requirements under this category of funding are listed in the Museum Program guidelines, available from the endowment.

Fiscal Information Grants of $5,000, $10,000, $15,000, $20,000, and $25,000 are available. A museum must match its grant dollar-for-dollar with new money raised specifically for the acquisitions mentioned in its application. This money must be raised after the application is submitted. Funds raised from the de-accessioning of works are not eligible as matching monies.

Application Information The special application requirements for this program, additional information, and application guidelines are available in program guidelines upon request.

Deadline(s) The grant period for this category will be April 1, 1989 to March 31, 1990. Applications for the program must be postmarked no later than October 17, 1988.

345. National Endowment for the Arts
Museum Program, Room 624
1100 Pennsylvania Avenue, NW
Washington, DC 20506
(202) 682-5442

Professional Development: Fellowships for Museum Professionals

CFDA Program Number 45.012

Program Description This award allows museum professionals to conduct arts-related independent study or to travel, write, engage in community projects, or otherwise improve their professional qualifications. This program is designed to encourage museums to develop and implement programs of regular leave for professional staff members.

Sample Grants To support travel to Latin America to conduct a feasibility study of an exhibition of contemporary Latin American art, $5,000 (1986). To support travel to several West African countries to visit museums of art and ethnography and to travel to tribal villages, $8,440 (1986). To support travel in Japan to study materials, techniques, and conservation of Ukiyo-e prints, $15,000 (1986). To support travel throughout the deep South to study southern-made textiles—types of fabrics, techniques, and styles unique to this region—and to develop a broader understanding of the impact of imports on this art, $11,230 (1986). To support travel to New York to complete research for a book on fiber art, $2,500 (1987). To support travel for study at conservation workshops in China, Korea, and Japan, $6,500 (1987).

Eligibility/Limitations Only currently employed professionals who have served on a museum staff for at least one year may apply. Applicants must be citizens or permanent residents of the United States. Organizations are not eligible. Fellowships are not awarded to cover study or research directed toward a graduate degree or expenses incurred in formal courses of study, workshops, seminars, or conferences. These fellowships are not intended to support research or development of projects eligible elsewhere in the museum program, but rather to encourage independent work.

Fiscal Information Fellowships will not exceed $25,000. Amounts will be based on travel requirements, salary support, and need for materials. Although the fellowships may extend for up to a full year, salary support may be included for only a period of up to three months. Fellowships need not be matched. The minimum grant generally will not be less than $2,500.

Application Information Application guidelines, application forms, and further information are available from the Museum Program.

Deadline(s) Applications should be received by February 16.

346. National Endowment for the Arts
Museum Program, Room 624
1100 Pennsylvania Avenue, NW
Washington, DC 20506
(202) 682-5442

Professional Development: Museum Training

CFDA Program Number 45.012

Program Description These grants are awarded to support arts-related formal training programs, internships, and apprenticeships. Priority will be given to programs for minorities and to efforts to improve staff in geographic areas where there is a demonstrated need to improve professionalism. Grants are awarded for: (1) *Formal Training*: formal education programs, including workshops and seminars directed to mid-career professional training and development, and graduate-level programs in curatorial training, museum administration, exhibit preparation and design, or museum education, conducted jointly by museums and universities, in which courses in art history form an integral part of the program; (2) *Internships*: internships provided by a museum—priority will be given to those at the graduate and post-graduate level; and (3) *Apprenticeships*: apprenticeships to prepare students or staff for positions such as installer, preparator, framer, packer, or carpenter.

Sample Grants To support the Fine Arts Museums of San Francisco's year-long curatorial internship in American art, $12,000 to Fine Arts Museums Foundation, San Francisco, CA (1987). To support a curatorial internship program at Smith College Museum of Art, $10,000 to Smith College, Northampton, MA (1986). To support internship stipends for students in their third year of the Museum Studies Program, $10,000 to University of Southern California, Los Angeles, CA (1987).

Eligibility/Limitations All grants go directly to institutions, not individuals. While accreditation by the American Association of Museums is not an eligibility requirement, the endowment generally uses the definition of museums developed by the AAM "...a nonprofit institution essentially educational or aesthetic in purpose with professional staff, which owns or utilizes tangible objects, cares for them, and exhibits them to the public on some regular schedule." In addition to museums, organizations that serve museums, organizations that perform museum functions, state arts agencies, and regional arts organizations are also eligible to apply. Applicant organizations must submit a copy of the Internal Revenue Service determination letter for tax-exempt status or the official document identifying the applicant as a unit of state or local government.

Fiscal Information Grant awards of up to $60,000 are available for formal training programs. The minimum grant generally will not be less than $5,000. Grant awards of up to $20,000 are available for support of internships and apprenticeships. Endowment funds may be used for stipend support and travel only. The minimum grant generally will not be less than $3,000. Grant awards of $30,000 or less require at least a one-to-one match; grant awards over $30,000 require at least a two-to-one match. A grant period of up to two years is allowed for training programs. A grant period of up to one year is allowed for other types of projects.

Application Information Application forms and additional information are available from the Museum Program.

Deadline(s) Applications should be received by February 16.

347. National Endowment for the Arts

Museum Program, Room 624
1100 Pennsylvania Avenue, NW
Washington, DC 20506
(202) 682-5442

Special Exhibitions

CFDA Program Number 45.012

Program Description These awards are designed to help museums and other organizations develop, tour, or participate in exhibitions of borrowed works of artistic significance.

Sample Grants To support an exhibition of Japanese Buddhist art from the Todai-Ji monastery-temple complex, $140,000 to Art Institute of Chicago, Chicago, IL (1986). To support an exhibition of the work of contemporary artist Scot Burton, $35,000 to Baltimore Museum of Art, Inc., Baltimore, MD (1986). To support an exhibition of works by artists experimenting with computers as a means to find and create new images, $25,000 to Bronx Museum of the Arts, Bronx, NY (1986). To support an exhibition and accompanying catalogue of contemporary ceramic sculpture, $10,000 to Seattle Art Museum, Seattle, WA (1987). To support the planning phase of an exhibition of Polish Jewish art $10,000 to Spertus Museum of Judaica, Chicago, IL (1987).

Eligibility/Limitations Exhibitions of privately owned collections generally will not be funded. Nor will exhibitions that include works by the exhibition's curator, organizers, or applicant's staff, paid or unpaid. While accreditation by the American Association of Museums is not an eligibility requirement, the endowment generally uses the definition of museums developed by the AAM "...a nonprofit institution essentially educational or aesthetic in purpose with professional staff, which owns or utilizes tangible objects, cares for them, and exhibits them to the public on some regular schedule." In addition to museums, organizations that serve museums, organizations that perform museum functions, state arts agencies, and regional arts organizations are also eligible to apply. Applicant organizations must submit a copy of the Internal Revenue Service determination letter for tax-exempt status or the official document identifying the applicant as a unit of state or local government.

Fiscal Information All grants go directly to institutions, not individuals. There is no grant maximum for organizing an exhibition. Grants of up to $20,000 are available to help institutions borrow exhibitions. Grants of $50,000 or less require a one-to-one match; grant awards between $50,000 and $100,000 require a two-to-one match; and grant awards of $100,000 or more require a three-to-one match. Grants may be used to pay for: planning and organizing an exhibition; services of an outside specialist; shipping, insurance, and related costs; installation; catalogues; documentation; related events such as education programs, performing arts activities, and film and lecture series; publicity; or regional touring of exhibitions by regional arts organizations and service organizations. Organizations requesting funds to borrow exhibitions may not include rental fees in their applications if the exhibition was initially funded by the endowment. Grants may not be used to pay for opening receptions. A grant period of more than one year is allowed. The period of support should span the amount of time necessary to plan, execute, and close out the project.

Application Information Application guidelines, application forms special application requirements, and additional information are available from the Museum Program.

Deadline(s) Applications must be received by November 14.

348. National Endowment for the Arts

Museum Program, Room 624
1100 Pennsylvania Avenue, NW
Washington, DC 20506
(202) 682-5442

Special Projects

CFDA Program Number 45.012

Program Description These awards are designed to respond to innovative and exemplary projects which will have a broad impact on the museum field and that are not eligible under other categories. Projects must be consistent with the policies of the Museum Program. Only a limited number of projects of national or regional significance will be supported.

Sample Grants To support the production of an instructional videotape, *Basic Art Handling*, $13,150 to Gallery Association of New York State, Inc., Hamilton, NY (1986). To support the Toledo Museum of Art in efforts to involve underrepresented populations in the museum, $29,650 to the Toledo Museum of Art, Toledo, OH (1986).

Application Information Interested organizations must contact the Museum Program before application.

349. National Endowment for the Arts
Museum Program, Room 624
1100 Pennsylvania Avenue, NW
Washington, DC 20506
(202) 682-5442

Utilization of Museum Resources: Catalogue Program

CFDA Program Number 45.012

Program Description This program is designed to support the cataloguing of permanent collections of artistic significance. Works to be catalogued must be wholly owned by the applicant institution. Grants are available for: (1) *Documentation*: for the documentation of uncatalogued or inadequately documented permanent collections, whether or not a publication will result. The services of an outside consultant may be included in the project, if appropriate. (2) *Preparation of Manuscript*: for research and preparation of catalogue copy for publication. The services of an outside consultant may be included. (3) *Publication*: For publication of catalogues, handbooks, or brochures related to permanent collections. Applicants should indicate readiness of manuscript for publication.

Sample Grants To support the publication by the Taylor Museum of a catalogue documenting approximately 250 pieces of pottery made by the Pueblo Indians of New Mexico in the historic period circa 1600-1940, $30,400 to Colorado Springs Fine Arts Center, Colorado Springs, CO (1986). To support the cataloguing of the university's medieval collection of approximately 280 objects dating from early 11th century through the late 16th century, $8,200 to Duke University, Durham, NC (1986). To support the publication of the first handbook of the museum's Asian art collection, $15,000 to Birmingham Museum of Art, Birmingham, MA (1986). To support the research to produce a catalogue of the William S. Glazer Collection of illuminated manuscripts to replace an earlier out-of-print edition, $25,000 to Pierpont Morgan Library, New York, NY (1986). To support the publication of a scholarly catalogue of the museum's Wedgewood collection, known as the Beeson Collection, $30,000 to Birmingham Museum of Art, Birmingham, MA (1987). To support a full-time researcher for eighteen months to document and catalogue a recent gift of 19th-century French lithographs, $20,000 to Santa Barbara Museum of Art, Santa Barbara, CA (1987).

Eligibility/Limitations While accreditation by the American Association of Museums is not an eligibility requirement, the endowment generally uses the definition of museums developed by the AAM "...a nonprofit institution essentially educational or aesthetic in purpose with professional staff, which owns or utilizes tangible objects, cares for them, and exhibits them to the public on some regular schedule." In addition to museums, organizations that serve museums, organizations that perform museum functions, state arts agencies, and regional arts organizations are also eligible to apply. Applicant organizations must submit a copy of the Internal Revenue Service determination letter of tax-exempt status or the official document identifying the applicant as a unit of state or local government. In general, applicant organizations should be in operation two years prior to submitting an application. Applicants seeking support for the production of a catalogue of the permanent collection should request aid for either research *or* publication, but not both. Applicants may apply for publication support in a subsequent year, whether or not funding was received for research. Generally, no more than one grant will be awarded for the research phase, and no more than one grant will be awarded for publication. Applicants seeking support under Presentation and Education should include costs of accompanying catalogues in those applications. Applicants seeking support for catalogues to accompany special exhibitions should apply under Special Exhibitions.

Fiscal Information Grant requests of up to $75,000 will be considered. Grant awards of $50,000 or less require at least a one-to-one match, and grant awards of more than $50,000 require at least a two-to-one match. The minimum grant generally will not be less than $5,000. A grant period of two years is allowed.

Application Information Application guidelines, application forms, and additional information are available from the Museum Program.

Deadline(s) Applications must be received by June 27.

350. National Endowment for the Arts
Museum Program, Room 624
1100 Pennsylvania Avenue, NW
Washington, DC 20506
(202) 682-5442

Utilization of Museum Resources: Presentation and Education

CFDA Program Number 45.012

Program Description This award is designed to help organizations make greater use of museum collections and other resources primarily of artistic significance. Grants are available for: (1) *Presentation: Reinstallation* awards to help museums install works from their permanent collections in semi-permanent or long-term displays and prepare and publish exhibition catalogues directly related to these activities; *Exhibition* awards to mount temporary exhibitions from their permanent collections, generally for a period of at least three months, or mount a coherent sequence of exhibitions drawn from their permanent collections, to present temporary exhibitions from their permanent collections development in conjunction with loan exhibitions, or to develop related programs and events that enrich these presentations, including the preparation and publication of exhibition catalogues; and *Collection Sharing* awards to support extended loans to or from one or more museums or other organizations (planning as well as implementation grants are available), to support touring exhibitions of an organization's own permanent collection, and support for exhibition catalogues and educational programs directly related to these activities; and (2) *Education*: for innovative projects which interpret permanent collections of works of art and demonstrate effective collaboration between education and curatorial staff; for specific programs that make a museum's own permanent collection more widely available to the public, including museum education and outreach programs (this can include the use of video, film, television, and other media); and for outreach and education projects undertaken by exhibition spaces, museums, and other organizations without permanent collections (this can include the use of video, film television, and other media).

Sample Grants To support the reinstallation of the Southeast Asian Gallery and accompanying educational programs, $50,000 to Asian Art Museum Foundation of San Francisco, San Francisco, CA (1987). To support installation of the Greek art collection in a newly renovated gallery space, $64,000 to Museum of Fine Arts, Boston, MA (1987).

Eligibility/Limitations All grants go directly to institutions, not individuals. While accreditation by the American Association of Museums is not an eligibility requirement, the endowment generally uses the definition of museums developed by the AAM "...a nonprofit institution essentially educational or aesthetic in purpose with professional staff, which owns or utilizes tangible objects, cares for them, and exhibits them to the public on some regular schedule." In addition to museums, organizations that serve museums, organizations that perform museum functions, state arts agencies, and regional arts organizations are also eligible to apply. Applicant organizations must submit a copy of the Internal Revenue Service determination letter for tax-exempt status or the official document identifying the applicant as a unit of state or local government.

Fiscal Information Presentation grants for reinstallment are up to $75,000; the minimum grant generally will not be less than $7,500. Grants for exhibitions are up to $75,000; the minimum grant generally will not be less than $7,500. Grants for collection sharing are up to $75,000; the minimum grant generally will not be less than $10,000. Presentation grant awards of $50,000 or less require at least a one-to-one match, and grant awards of more than $50,000 require at least a two-to-one match. Education grants for innovative projects which interpret permanent collections of works of art are up to $50,000; the minimum grant generally will not be less than $20,000. Other education programs and projects awards are up to $25,000; the minimum grant generally will not be less than $2,500. All education grant awards must be matched at least one-to-one. Presentation and education grants may be used to purchase material needed for installation. They may not, however, be used to pay for major structural modifications to a building. A grant period of more than one year is allowed. The period of support should span the amount of time necessary to plan, execute, and close out the project.

Application Information Application guidelines, application forms, special application requirements, and additional information are available from the Museum Program.

Deadline(s) Applications should be received by June 27.

351. National Endowment for the Arts
Museum Program, Room 624
1100 Pennsylvania Avenue, NW
Washington, DC 20506
(202) 682-5442

Utilization of Museum Resources: Special Artistic Initiatives

CFDA Program Number 45.012

Program Description These awards are designed to support special long-term initiatives by museums to define or redefine their mission and artistic direction through a carefully coordinated series of exhibitions, reinstallations, educational programs, publications, and interdisciplinary projects of the highest artistic level and of national or regional significance. These exhibitions and programs should be primarily concerned with the use and interpretation of the permanent collection. Grants may be used for: planning and organizing a series of special exhibitions, exhibitions primarily from the permanent collection, and/or reinstallations of the permanent collection, conceived within a larger contextual framework; publications, media productions, and education programs; and projects that involve more than one art form, particularly where performing arts and artists are integrated into the visual exhibitions.

Sample Grants To support an initiative by the McKissick Museum to strengthen its programming in the area of Southern Folk art, $100,000 to University of Southern California at Columbia (1987).

Eligibility/Limitations While accreditation by the American Association of Museums is not an eligibility requirement, the endowment generally uses the definition of museums developed by the AAM "...a nonprofit institution essentially educational or aesthetic in purpose with professional staff, which owns or utilizes tangible objects, cares for them, and exhibits them to the public on some regular schedule." In addition to museums, organizations that serve museums, organizations that perform museum functions, state arts agencies, and regional arts organizations are also eligible to apply. Applicant organizations must submit a copy of the Internal Revenue Service determination letter for tax-exempt status or the official document identifying the applicant as a unit of state or local government. Projects funded under this program are not eligible for funding under other categories in the Museum Program.

Fiscal Information Planning and implementation grants will be available. Planning grants will range from $15,000 to $25,000 and will require at least a one-to-one match. Implementation grants will range from $50,000 to $250,000. Implementation grants will require at least a two-to-one match. Applicants are expected to spend the first eight months of the grant period in planning and organization. The subsequent projects should be scheduled over a period of at least two years.

Application Information Museums interested in applying under this category should contact the Museum Program before applying. Application guidelines, application forms, and additional information are available from the Museum Program.

Deadline(s) The application postmark deadline is April 3.

Additional Information A *limited* number of grants are available in this category.

352. National Endowment for the Arts
Music Program
1100 Pennsylvania Avenue, NW
Washington, DC 20506
(202) 682-5445

Music Presenters and Festivals

Program Description The Music Program of the NEA assists creative and performing artists of exceptional talent. The program also awards grants to music performing, presenting, and service organizations of the highest artistic level and of national or regional significance. The Music Presenters and Festivals category of this program is designed to: encourage performance opportunities for American artists, ensembles, conductors, and musical organizations of the highest artistic level and of national or regional significance; increase the availability of music performances of the highest artistic level to the widest possible public; improve the quality of music performances; and encourage the presentation of a wide variety of musical genres and styles including music of our time, especially American music, where appropriate.

Sample Grants To support the presentation of emerging chamber music, jazz, and new music ensembles during the 1986-1987 season, $3,500 to Hudson River Museum at Yonkers, Inc., Yonkers, NY (1986). To support the presentation of chamber music, new music, and jazz ensemble performances during the 1986-1987 season, $20,000 to Walker Art Center, Minneapolis, MN (1986). To support performances of new expressions in music and related costs during the 1986-1987 season, $2,900 to Newport Harbor Art Museum, Newport Beach, CA (1986). To support artists' fees and related costs for the concert series, "Early Music from the Newberry Library," $3,900 to Newberry Library, Chicago, IL (1986).

Eligibility/Limitations Applicants may include presenting organizations, consortia of presenters, music festivals, state arts agencies, and regional arts organizations. In order to apply as a presenter, an organization must meet legal requirements and: provide music of the highest artistic level and of national or regional significance; have a minimum of two years' experience in presenting paid professional musicians or musical groups to the general public; and generally, have paid administrative staff responsible for presenting professional artists. Presenter applicants may include, but are not limited to, performing arts centers, independent and university presenting organizations, jazz organizations, museums, and orchestras.

Fiscal Information Grants will generally range from $3,000 to $50,000. Most grants will be between $5,000 and $10,000. Organizations must match grants on at least a one-to-one basis. Grants of $25,000 or more may require a three-to-one match and may be made as Treasury Fund grants.

Application Information Application forms, guidelines and special application requirements are available from the program.

Deadline(s) Application postmark deadline is April 30.

353. National Endowment for the Arts
Visual Arts Program
1100 Pennsylvania Avenue, NW
Washington, DC 20506
(202) 682-5448

Art in Public Places

Program Description These grants are designed to make the best contemporary art accessible in public places and to provide new challenges and opportunities for living American artists of exceptional talent and achievement. In recent years, grants have supported innovative projects for spaces previously unexplored as sites for artworks, both interior and exterior, and have encouraged an increasing number of young visual artists. Applicants are encouraged to consider imaginative approaches to possible sites: rivers, waterfronts, parks, recreation facilities, airports, subways, roadsides, and public buildings.

Sample Grants To support a commission for an artist to create a series of works for the Drannert Art Museum's new wing, $20,000 to University of Illinois Urbana-Champaign, Champaign, IL (1986). To support six artists' participation in the planning stages for the redesign of a former zoo site at Crandon Gardens in Miami, $15,000 to Metropolitan Dade County, Miami, FL (1986).

Eligibility/Limitations State and local government units and nonprofit tax-exempt organizations meeting NEA legal requirements are eligible to apply.

Fiscal Information The minimum grant in this category is generally $5,000. Grants for planning activities generally will not exceed $15,000. If an organization receives both a planning grant and a final implementation grant, the combined grant amount generally will not exceed $50,000. All grants must be matched at least one-to-one.

Application Information Application forms, guidelines, and special application requirements are available from the program.

Deadline(s) The application postmark deadline for letters of intent is May 29. The application postmark deadline for final application is December 11.

354. National Endowment for the Arts
Visual Arts Program
1100 Pennsylvania Avenue, NW
Washington, DC 20506
(202) 682-5448

Special Projects

Program Description These grants are designed to respond to new and creative ideas that will have a broad impact on the visual arts field and are not eligible under the other Visual Arts Program categories. Projects must be consistent with the purposes of the program. Only a very limited number of projects of national or regional significance will be supported.

Application Information Organizations interested in applying must contact the Visual Arts Program before applying.

Deadline(s) Applications will be accepted at any time during the year, but no later than April 1.

355. National Endowment for the Arts
Visual Arts Program
1100 Pennsylvania Avenue, NW
Washington, DC 20506
(202) 682-5448

Visual Artists Forums

Program Description The grants support projects of national or regional significance that promote discourse regarding the visual arts. Funding is available for a variety of projects which enable visual artists, critics, curators, and other visual arts professionals to communicate with peers and the public about visual arts ideas and issues or allow them to create and present new work in a context which stimulates discussion about contemporary art. Support is also available for non-commercial publications that contribute to the national dialogue on contemporary art.

Sample Grants To support the *Dialogue* Criticism Workshop at the Taft Museum and the Contemporary Arts Center in Cincinnati, $3,000 to Opportunities for the Arts, Inc., Columbus, OH (1986). To support *The Archive*, a serial publication which presents 20th-century photography from the Center for Creative Photography's permanent collection, $7,000 to University of Arizona, Tucson, AZ (1986). To support a three-day symposium in which nationally known writers/critics will work with regional critics to develop regional criticism, $7,100 to Museum of New Mexico, Santa Fe, NM (1987).

Eligibility/Limitations Applicant organizations must meet NEA legal requirements and must represent at least one of the following areas of activity: visiting artists programs, symposia, and conferences (and documentation thereof); projects which allow visual artists to create and present new work in a format or situation which encourages discourse and/or greater public awareness of contemporary art; and critical and theoretical art journals and publications that serve as alternative presenting forums for original works by professional artists.

Fiscal Information The maximum grant amount in this category is $25,000. Most grants range between $5,000 and $15,000. All grant funds must be matched at least one-to-one.

Application Information Application forms, guidelines and special application procedures are available from the program.

Deadline(s) Application postmark deadline is November 2.

356. National Endowment for the Arts
Visual Arts Program
1100 Pennsylvania Avenue, NW
Washington, DC 20506
(202) 682-5448

Visual Artists Organizations

Program Description These grants support organizations which encourage individual artistic development, experimentation, and dialogue between visual artists and the public. Visual Artists Organizations' primary purpose is to serve the needs of, and enhance opportunities for, visual artists, and assure them an integral role in policy development and programming. Priority will be given to organizations that provide professional fees to artists and whose programs are of national or regional significance. Funds may be requested for programming in one or more of the following areas: (1) exhibitions of contemporary visual art, including static and non-static work, temporary installations, and other experimental and innovative activities; (2) working facilities that provide visual artists with the space, equipment, and means to experiment and produce new work and with access to technical assistance; (3) and services that have a direct and immediate effect on the professional lives of a broad community of visual artists, such as information, resource, and advisory services; financial, legal and technical assistance; and lectures, seminars and conferences.

Sample Grants To support Video Data Bank's production and distribution of video documentation on contemporary art, artists, and original video works, $38,000 to Art Institute of Chicago, Chicago, IL (1986). To support exhibitions, lectures and workshops at Clayspace, $10,000 to Erie Art Museum, Erie, PA (1986). To support a program of installations related to book arts and presentations of performance art, $30,000 to Franklin Furnace Archive, Inc., New York, NY (1986). To support exhibitions and services for contemporary visual artists at the Museum of Contemporary Hispanic Art, $12,000 to Friends of Puerto Rico, New York, NY (1986).

Eligibility/Limitations Organizations may apply that: are originated by or for visual artists or to further their interests; generate interaction and dialogue among visual artists and between artists and the public; encourage and support the production and presentation of contemporary art which reflects continued, serious, and exceptional aesthetic investigation; have been in continuous operation for at least one year; and meet NEA legal requirements.

Fiscal Information The maximum grant amount in this category is $50,000. Most grants range between $5,000 and $30,000. All grant funds must be matched at least one-to-one.

Application Information Application forms, guidelines, and special application requirements are available from the program.

Deadline(s) Application postmark deadline is June 15.

357. National Endowment for the Humanities
1100 Pennsylvania Avenue, NW
Washington, DC 20506
(202) 786-0438

Special Initiative: Foundations of American Society

Program Description Within its existing programs, the endowment continues to encourage study, research, and discussion about the history, culture, and principles of the founding period, an emphasis which began with the initiative on the bicentennial of the U.S. Constitution. Proposals may deal directly with the events and achievements of the founding period, including the ratification of the new Constitution, the establishment of the federal government, and the birth of the Bill of Rights. Proposals may also deal with the works of philosophy, politics, literature, and art that were produced during this founding period; and they may treat later events, achievements, and works that have resulted or developed from the founding period or that reflect or respond to its concerns and principles.

Application Information A special initiative is an undertaking by the endowment to encourage proposals in all grant-making categories for projects relating to a specific subject or event. Contact the appropriate division/program for further information about this initiative.

358. National Endowment for the Humanities
Division of Education Programs, Room 302
1100 Pennsylvania Avenue, NW
Washington, DC 20506
(202) 786-0377

Elementary and Secondary Education in the Humanities: Collaborative Projects

CFDA Program Number 45.127

Program Description Collaborative projects are designed to promote ongoing partnerships between schools and institutions of higher education. They bring scholars together with teachers, often for a two- or three-year period, to study materials central to their disciplines, to revise curricula, and to address problems in humanities education common to the schools of a given area. Collaborative projects should focus on specific curricular or educational issues, and they should address these issues in light of the best scholarship available. Collaborative projects may include seminars, colloquia, conferences, meetings, or working groups to address issues in humanities education. They should involve school administrators, curriculum specialists, and other educational leaders responsible for educational policy in the subjects under consideration. Above all else, they should establish relationships that promise to continue after the conclusion of the activities supported by the grant.

Sample Grants To support a collaborative curricular development and teacher training program on Chinese art, combining the expertise of university scholars, museum educators, school administrators, and teachers, $36,000 to Indianapolis Museum of Art, Indianapolis, IN (1986).

Eligibility/Limitations Applicants may be individual schools, school systems, colleges, universities, or groups of institutions working in collaboration.

Fiscal Information The cost of a project will depend on a number of variables. Potential applicants should contact the program for additional information on budget preparation.

Application Information To request guidelines and application forms, write or call the program in which you are interested. Guidelines and application forms are generally available two months in advance of an application deadline. One of the institutions involved in the project should be designated as the applicant organization with responsibility for administering the project.

Deadline(s) Application postmark deadlines are May 16 and January 8.

Additional Information A new NEH program supports planning grants. Some projects are of such scope and complexity that they require extensive planning. The endowment provides funds in modest amounts to support meetings, consultant services, and other planning activities. Endowment support may not be requested solely for the purpose of designing grant proposals. Planning grants must have intrinsic value independent of any subsequent requests for endowment support. The award of an NEH planning grant does not imply that the endowment will necessarily provide support for implementation of the full project.

359. National Endowment for the Humanities
Division of Education Programs, Room 302
1100 Pennsylvania Avenue, NW
Washington, DC 20506
(202) 786-0377

Elementary and Secondary Education in the Humanities: Conferences

CFDA Program Number 45.127

Program Description Conference grants are available for institutions and associations that wish to address important issues in humanities education. Conferences may be local, state, or national in scope. They may involve a single meeting or a series of meetings. Their participants may be teachers, professors, school administrators, or other educational leaders. They may be sponsored by colleges, school systems, professional associations, or other kinds of educational or cultural institutions. A proposal for a conference should be addressed to specific issues in humanities education and should reflect the highest standards of scholarship. The proposal should include a plan for disseminating the results of the conference.

Sample Grants To conduct two regional conferences for thirty educators and two summer institutes, each for twenty participants, designed to improve teachers' understanding of native American tribal history, $250,000 (outright funds) and $10,000 (federal match) to Newberry Library, Chicago, IL (1986).

Eligibility/Limitations Applicants must be individual schools, school systems, colleges, universities, museums, libraries, or groups of institutions working in collaboration.

Fiscal Information The cost of a conference will depend on a number of variables. Potential applicants should contact the program for additional information on budget preparation.

Application Information To request guidelines and application forms, write or call the program in which you are interested. Guidelines and application forms are generally available two months in advance of an application deadline.

Deadline(s) Application postmark deadlines are May 16 and January 8.

360. National Endowment for the Humanities
Division of Education Programs, Room 302
1100 Pennsylvania Avenue, NW
Washington, DC 20506
(202) 786-0377

Elementary and Secondary Education in the Humanities: Institutes for Teachers and Administrators

CFDA Program Number 45.127

Program Description One of the most effective ways of improving humanities instruction is to provide opportunities for teachers and educational leaders to increase their knowledge and understanding of the disciplines they impart to their students. To achieve this goal, the endowment sponsors institutes for teachers and administrators which provide an opportunity for intensive summer residential study, promote collegial exchange, and foster the kind of intellectual renewal that leads to revitalized teaching. An institute should focus on important works, topics, and ideas in the humanities and on the most effective ways to teach them. It should provide a rigorous intellectual program that includes reading and writing about major works under the guidance of leading scholars. Its schedule should provide ample time for thorough treatment of the selected subject and its plan should include follow-up activities to ensure that the summer's work is applied to the school setting.

Eligibility/Limitations Typically, an institute is organized by two or more faculty in higher education and one or more master teachers in elementary and secondary education. They plan the program together, secure commitments from other faculty and from visiting lecturers, and make arrangements for such details as meeting space and housing for participants. Usually an institute is conducted by a college or university, but school systems and cultural institutions are also encouraged to apply.

Fiscal Information The cost of an institute will depend on a number of variables. Potential applicants should contact the program for additional information on budget preparation.

Application Information To request guidelines and application forms, write or call the program in which you are interested. Guidelines and application forms are generally available two months in advance of an application deadline.

Deadline(s) Application postmark deadlines are May 16 and January 8.

361. National Endowment for the Humanities
Division of Education Programs, Room 302
1100 Pennsylvania Avenue, NW
Washington, DC 20506
(202) 786-0380

Higher Education in the Humanities: Collaborative Projects

Program Description Two or more institutions may request support for collaborative activities that will benefit the teaching of the humanities. Such projects may be proposed by cultural institutions such as libraries and museums, schools, universities, or any combination of institutions.

Sample Grants To support a three-year project to improve scholarship and teaching about Native Americans through a fellowship program, three working conferences, and publications on current literature on Indian history, $200,000 to Newberry Library, Chicago, IL (1986).

Eligibility/Limitations Proposals for collaborative projects may be submitted either by existing consortia or by institutions that come together for the purpose of a particular endeavor. A proposal should provide evidence that all of the participating institutions are fully involved in and committed to the project.

Fiscal Information The cost of a project will depend on a number of variables. Potential applicants should contact the program for additional information on budget preparation.

Application Information To request guidelines and application forms, write or call the program in which you are interested. Guidelines and application forms are generally available two months in advance of an application deadline.

Deadline(s) Application postmark deadlines are October 1 and April 1.

362. National Endowment for the Humanities
Division of Education Programs, Room 302
1100 Pennsylvania Avenue, NW
Washington, DC 20506
(202) 786-0380

Higher Education in the Humanities: Conferences

Program Description The endowment provides support for conferences that have as their goal the improvement of teaching in the humanities in particular disciplines or in particular types of institutions. The goals of conferences should be clear and specific, the materials under consideration should be substantial, and as many as possible of the participants should be identified.

Sample Grants To support a series of institutes, seminars, and workshops in various areas of Renaissance studies, $255,089 to Newberry Library, Chicago, IL (1986).

Eligibility/Limitations The applicant for a conference may be an academic or cultural institution, an association, or a group of associations.

Fiscal Information The cost of a conference will depend on a number of variables. Potential applicants should contact the program for additional information on budget preparation.

Application Information To request guidelines and application forms, write or call the program in which you are interested. Guidelines and application forms are generally available two months in advance of an application deadline.

Deadline(s) Application postmark deadlines are October 1 and April 1.

363. National Endowment for the Humanities
Division of Education Programs, Room 302
1100 Pennsylvania Avenue, NW
Washington, DC 20506
(202) 786-0380

Higher Education in the Humanities: Institutes for College and University Faculty

Program Description An effective means for improving the quality of humanities instruction is to provide college and university faculty with opportunities for intensive study of important materials in the humanities under the guidance of leading scholars in a field. For this purpose, the endowment supports national and regional institutes in which college and university faculty come together to study texts related to a theme, issue, major figure, period, or cultural movement. The topic of the institute should be clearly focused, and it should be broadly applicable to subjects frequently taught at the undergraduate level.

Eligibility/Limitations An institute can be sponsored by a university or college, a research library, a museum, a professional association, or any other cultural institution with research facilities and collections appropriate to the institute topic. Institutes may vary in length, but each should allow sufficient time for a thorough examination of the topic. Typically, institutes involve twenty to thirty participants who come together for four to eight weeks during the summer or meet at regular intervals during an academic year. The distinguished scholars who serve as faculty for an institute may be drawn from throughout the country and, where appropriate, from abroad. An individual institution or group of institutions may also employ the institute format for internal use in preparing their own faculty to teach an improved curriculum.

Fiscal Information The cost of an institute will depend on a number of variables. Potential applicants should contact the program for additional information on budget preparation.

Application Information To request guidelines and application forms, write or call the program in which you are interested. Guidelines and application forms are generally available two months in advance of an application deadline.

Deadline(s) Application postmark deadlines are October 1 and April 1.

364. National Endowment for the Humanities

Division of Education Programs, Room 302
1100 Pennsylvania Avenue, NW
Washington, DC 20506
(202) 786-0373

Special Initiatives: The Columbian Quincentenary

Program Description In commemoration of the 500th anniversary of the voyages of Columbus, the Division of Education Programs invites proposals for projects that would enhance humanities education at any level on the historical, political, philosophical, and cultural ramifications of the voyages of Columbus and his contemporaries. The division will be especially receptive to proposals that bring scholars and teachers together to explore the larger contexts of the voyages: e.g., the medieval and Renaissance cultural assumptions that led to and conditioned the voyages of discovery, the "transatlantic encounters" that resulted from them, and the effects that the voyages have had on the world since the fifteenth century. Proposals may be submitted under any of the division's program headings.

Eligibility/Limitations Strengthening the teaching of the humanities in schools, colleges, and universities is the purpose of this division. Projects to improve the teaching of the history of precolonial America or to promote excellence in a Latin American studies curriculum are examples of proposals appropriate to this division under the Columbian Quincentenary initiative. An institute for college and university faculty members on the origins of the New World could be proposed, for example. The institute might focus on recent research from Spanish and Portuguese archives related to expeditions to the Americas. It could be devoted to improving the participants' understanding of particular developments during the colonial period in this hemisphere and to providing the participants with a broader understanding of the transatlantic world in the early modern period.

Application Information Applicants who are not certain where to direct an inquiry about this special initiative should call or write the director of the Division of Education Programs.

365. National Endowment for the Humanities

Division of Fellowships and Seminars, Room 316
1100 Pennsylvania Avenue, NW
Washington, DC 20506
(202) 786-0466

Faculty Graduate Study Program for Historically Black Colleges and Universities

Program Description Grants provide support for faculty to undertake one year of full-time study leading to a doctoral degree in the humanities with preference given to those individuals who are at the dissertation stage of their work. This is the only NEH program that supports work leading to a graduate degree.

Eligibility/Limitations Teachers in historically Black colleges and universities are eligible to apply. Grants are made through the applicant's institution.

Application Information For additional information write or call the program.

Deadline(s) The deadline for receipt of applications is March 15.

366. National Endowment for the Humanities
Division of Fellowships and Seminars, Room 316
1100 Pennsylvania Avenue, NW
Washington, DC 20506
(202) 786-0466

Fellowships for College Teachers and Independent Scholars
CFDA Program Number 45.143

Program Description These fellowships provide opportunities for individuals to pursue independent study and research that will enhance their capacities as teachers, scholars, or interpreters of the humanities and that will enable them to make significant contributions to thought and knowledge in the humanities. Fellowships enable people to devote extended periods of uninterrupted time to investigation, reflection, and often writing. The program is intended for a range of people, from those who have made significant contributions to the humanities to those who stand at the beginning of their careers. Projects, too, may cover a range of activities from general study to specialized research.

Eligibility/Limitations The program of Fellowships for College Teachers and Independent Scholars, including special NEH initiatives within this program, is open to faculty members, either full-time or part-time, of two-year, four-year, and five-year colleges; faculty members of university departments, interdepartmental programs, and central graduate schools that do not grant the Ph.D.; individuals affiliated with institutions other than colleges and universities; and scholars and writers working independently. Individuals who have such positions on terminating contracts are eligible for this program as long as they do not take appointments in departments or programs that grant the Ph.D. before the January following the application deadline. Retired faculty members who had such positions are also eligible for this program. Although applicants need not have advanced degrees, those whose professional training includes a degree program must have received their degrees or completed all official requirements for them by June 1, the application deadline. If a prospective applicant has completed all of the official requirements for the degree and is awaiting only the formal award, certification that all requirements for the degree have been met by the application deadline must be submitted by the dean of the school awarding the degree. Persons seeking support for work leading to a degree are not eligible to apply, nor are active candidates for degrees, even if they expect to have finished all work for their degree by the time they would begin tenure of the fellowship and the work proposed is not related to the degree program. Persons who have recently held major fellowships or grants are not eligible to apply for an NEH fellowship. Specifically, three years must have elapsed between the conclusion of tenure of the fellowship or grant and the proposed beginning date of tenure for an NEH fellowship. For the endowment, a "major fellowship or grant" is a postdoctoral award or its equivalent which provides a continuous period of released time covering at least one term of the academic year; which enables the recipient to pursue scholarly research, personal study, professional development, or writing; which provides a stipend of at least $6,000; and which comes from sources other than the recipient's employing institution. Thus, sabbaticals and grants from an individual's own institution are not considered major fellowships, nor are stipends and grants from other sources supporting study and research during the summer academic recess, such as NEH Summer Stipends and NEH Summer Seminar awards. An applicant for an NEH fellowship should be a U.S. citizen, a native resident of a U.S. territorial possession, or a foreign national who has been residing in the United States or its territories for at least the three years immediately preceding the application deadline.

Fiscal Information Fellowships normally support full-time work and are awarded for continuous periods of six to twelve full months of tenure. The stipend is intended primarily to replace salary lost through the taking of leave. The maximum amount of the NEH stipend for tenure periods of between nine and twelve months, which for teachers encompass the full academic year, is $27,500. The maximum for periods of between six and nine months is prorated by months or, for teachers, by academic year terms. Some assistance may be provided within the stipend limit to help defray the costs of necessary travel, but no allowance is given for any other expense. Fellows may supplement their awards with small grants from other sources but may not hold other major fellowships or grants during fellowship tenure, except sabbaticals and grants from their own institutions. Successful applicants who receive offers of fellowships from other foundations after June 1 must hold the NEH fellowship first.

Application Information Guidelines and application materials are available from the Division of Fellowships and Seminars. When contacting NEH include the name of the program for which you are applying.

Deadline(s) Applications must be postmarked by June 1.

367. National Endowment for the Humanities
Division of Fellowships and Seminars, Room 316
1100 Pennsylvania Avenue, NW,
Washington, DC 20506
(202) 786-0466

Fellowships for University Teachers

CFDA Program Number 45.142

Program Description These fellowships provide opportunities for individuals to pursue independent study and research that will enhance their capacities as teachers, scholars, or interpreters of the humanities and that will enable them to make significant contributions to thought and knowledge in the humanities. Fellowships enable people to devote extended periods of uninterrupted time to investigation, reflection, and often, writing. The program is intended for a range of people, from those who have made significant contributions to the humanities to those who stand at the beginning of their careers. Projects, too, may cover a range of activities from general study to specialized research. Fellowships for University Teachers are for faculty members of departments and programs in universities that grant the Ph.D. and faculty members of post-graduate professional schools.

Eligibility/Limitations The program of fellowships for university faculty, including special NEH initiatives within this program, is open only to faculty members of departments in universities that grant the Ph.D., faculty members with appointments to interdepartmental programs and central graduate schools that grant the Ph.D., and faculty members of post-graduate professional schools. Individuals who have such appointments either part-time or full-time or on terminating contracts are eligible only for this program. Retired faculty members who had such positions are normally eligible for this program. Although applicants need not have advanced degrees, those whose professional training includes a degree program must have received their degrees or completed all official requirements for them by June 1, the application deadline. If a prospective applicant has completed all of the official requirements for the degree and is awaiting only the formal award, certification that all requirements for the degree have been met by the application deadline must be submitted by the dean of the school awarding the degree. Persons seeking support for work leading to a degree are not eligible to apply, nor are active candidates for degrees, even if they expect to have finished all work for their degree by the time they would begin tenure of the fellowship and the work proposed is not related to the degree program. Persons who have recently held major fellowships or grants are not eligible to apply for an NEH fellowship. Specifically, three years must have elapsed between the conclusion of tenure of the fellowship or grant and the proposed beginning date of tenure for an NEH fellowship. For the endowment, a "major fellowship or grant" is a postdoctoral award or its equivalent which provides a continuous period of released time covering at least one term of the academic year; which enables the recipient to pursue scholarly research, personal study, professional development, or writing; which provides a stipend of at least $6,000; and which comes from sources other than the recipient's employing institution. Thus, sabbaticals and grants from an individual's own institution are not considered major fellowships, nor are stipends and grants from other sources supporting study and research during the summer academic recess, such as NEH Summer Stipends and NEH Summer Seminar awards. An applicant for an NEH fellowship should be a U.S. citizen, a native resident of a U.S. territorial possession, or a foreign national who has been residing in the United States or its territories for at least the three years immediately preceding the application deadline.

Fiscal Information Fellowships normally support full-time work and are awarded for continuous periods of six to twelve full months of tenure. The stipend is intended primarily to replace salary lost through the taking of leave. The maximum amount of the NEH stipend for tenure periods of between nine and twelve months, which for teachers encompass the full academic year, is $27,500. The maximum for periods of between six and nine months is prorated by months or, for teachers, by academic year terms. Some assistance may be provided within the stipend limit to help defray the costs of necessary travel, but no allowance is given for any other expense. Fellows may supplement their awards with small grants from other sources but may not hold other major fellowships or grants during fellowship tenure, except sabbaticals and grants from their own institutions. Successful applicants who receive offers of fellowships from other foundations after June 1 must hold the NEH fellowship first.

Application Information Guidelines and application materials are available from the Division of Fellowships and Seminars. When contacting NEH include the name of the program for which you are applying.

Deadline(s) Applications must be postmarked by June 1.

368. National Endowment for the Humanities
Division of Fellowships and Seminars, Room 316
1100 Pennsylvania Avenue, NW
Washington, DC 20506
(202) 786-0458

Special Initiatives: The Columbian Quincentenary

Program Description As part of the international observance of the 500th anniversary of Christopher Columbus's voyage of discovery to the New World, NEH invites proposals for original scholarship on related topics, the dissemination of original scholarship on related topics, and the dissemination of both new and existing scholarship. This division supports individual scholarship within the humanities and provides opportunities for the collegial study of topics and texts. All programs of the division welcome applications to conduct projects related to the Columbian Quincentenary.

Eligibility/Limitations A scholar wishing to explore a topic in early Latin American colonial history or a researcher describing the effect of the discovery of the New World upon a particular artistic or literary tradition might submit a proposal for a Fellowship for University Teachers, a Fellowship for College Teachers and Independent Scholars, or a Summer Stipend. A historian of Renaissance technology might wish to organize a Summer Seminar for College Teachers to examine the cultural and historical foundations underlying the Columbian adventure.

Application Information Applicants who are not certain where to direct an inquiry about this special initiative should call or write the director of the Division of Fellowships and Seminars.

369. National Endowment for the Humanities
Division of Fellowships and Seminars, Room 316
1100 Pennsylvania Avenue, NW
Washington, DC 20506
(202) 786-0463

Summer Seminars for College Teachers

CFDA Program Number 45.116

Program Description Summer seminars for college teachers are offered for teachers at undergraduate and two-year colleges who wish to deepen and enrich their knowledge of the subjects they teach. The purpose of the seminars is to provide college teachers with opportunities to work with distinguished scholars in their teaching or research fields; to work with other college teachers who share similar interests; and to undertake individual projects (e.g., intensive reading, scholarly research, or writing) of their own choosing at institutions with libraries suitable for advanced work. The seminars offered in the program deal with significant works and subject matter of central concern to the humanities. Proposals to direct summer seminars for college teachers are encouraged from professors who are not only recognized scholars in their fields but who are also well qualified by virtue of their interest and ability in undergraduate teaching or the pertinence of their work to the interests of undergraduate teachers.

Eligibility/Limitations College teachers wishing to participate in the seminars should be persons who are well qualified to do the work of the seminar, who are able and committed teachers, and who can make significant contributions to the seminar. The program is intended primarily for individuals teaching undergraduate courses, full- or part-time, at two-year, four-year, or five-year colleges and universities, but other persons who are qualified to do the work of the seminar and make a contribution are also eligible to apply. Preference will be given to those who have been teaching at least three years and who have not recently had the resources of a major library readily available to them. Faculty members of departments with doctoral programs in the humanities are not eligible as participants in this program.

Fiscal Information Participation in each seminar is limited to twelve college teachers, each of whom receives a stipend of $3,500 for the eight-week seminar. The selection of participants and the awarding of stipends is the responsibility of seminar directors, acting in consultation with their selection committees and within the guidelines established by the endowment. Funds are officially awarded to the institution hosting the NEH summer seminar (in most instances the institution with which the selected seminar director is affiliated). The grant will include stipends for the participants, salary for the seminar director, secretarial support, and direct and indirect costs to the host institution. General grant provisions, narrative and financial reporting requirements and forms, payment information, and applicable conditions and special provisions are provided within the award notification. Institutional fiscal personnel and the seminar director will be expected to comply with normal grant procedures.

Application Information After the decisions are made on the seminars to be offered, the complete list of seminars will be publicized by the endowment. College teachers wishing to participate in the seminars apply directly to the seminar director.

Deadline(s) The deadline for receipt of applications is March 1.

370. National Endowment for the Humanities

Division of Fellowships and Seminars, Room 316
1100 Pennsylvania Avenue, NW
Washington, DC 20506
(202) 786-0466

Summer Stipends

CFDA Program Number 45.121

Program Description The Summer Stipends program provides support for faculty members in universities and in two-year and four-year colleges, and for others working in the humanities so that they can devote two consecutive months of full-time study and research to a project. The proposed project should be not only an immediate contribution to learning in a particular field, but also a contribution to the advancement of knowledge in the humanities more generally, and to the applicant's development as a scholar, teacher, and interpreter of the humanities. Each college and university in the United States and its territorial possessions may nominate three members of its faculty for the Summer Stipend competition. No more than two of the nominees may be in the early stages of their careers, i.e., junior nominees; no more than two may be at a more advanced stage, i.e., senior nominees.

Sample Grants Summer stipends were awarded for: a catalogue of early Demotic papyri in the British Museum (1986); a catalogue of Ezra Pound Papers in the Olga Rudge Collection (1986); study of the cuneiform tablets in the Emory University Museum (1986); study of Ice Age art and ornamentation in the Beloit College collections (1986).

Eligibility/Limitations An applicant for an endowment fellowship should be a U.S. citizen, a native resident of a U.S. territorial possession, or a foreign national who has been residing in the United States or its territories for at least the three years immediately preceding the application deadline. Although applicants need not have advanced degrees, those whose professional training includes a degree program must have received their degrees, or completed all official requirements for them by October 1. If a prospective applicant has completed all of the official requirements for the degree and is awaiting only the formal award, certification that all requirements have been met by the application deadline must be submitted by the dean of the school awarding the degree. Persons seeking support for work leading toward degrees are not eligible to apply, nor are active candidates for degrees, even if they expect to have finished all work for their degree by the time they would begin tenure of the summer stipend and the work proposed is not related to their degree program. Preference is given to persons who have not received major fellowships or other leave-providing grants, except sabbaticals or grants from their own institutions, within the last five years. The more recent the grant, the more heavily it weighs in the endowment's decision.

Fiscal Information Each summer stipend provides $3,500 for two consecutive summer months of full-time study or research. Recipients of summer stipends may not hold major fellowships or grants during the tenure of their awards, and they must devote full time to their projects for the two months of their tenure.

Application Information Application forms and additional information and guidelines are available from the Division of Fellowships and Seminars. When contacting NEH include the program for which you are applying.

Deadline(s) Applications must be postmarked by October 1.

371. National Endowment for the Humanities
Division of Fellowships and Seminars, Room 316
1100 Pennsylvania Avenue, NW
Washington, DC 20506
(202) 786-0463

Travel to Collections

CFDA Program Number 45.152

Program Description The purpose of the Travel to Collections program is to enable American scholars to travel to use the research collections of libraries, archives, museums, or other repositories to consult research materials of fundamental importance for the progress of their scholarly work. This grant program is intended to help scholars meet the costs associated with a research trip anywhere in the world. The research proposed must fall within the scope of the humanities. Projects in the social sciences which are historical or philosophical, or which attempt to cast light on questions of interpretation or criticism traditionally in the humanities are eligible, as are historical or philosophical studies of the natural sciences. Projects that involve critical, historical, and theoretical studies of the arts are eligible for support. The program is designed for scholars whose research could not progress satisfactorily without consultation of materials at a specific location.

Sample Grants Travel to Collections grants have been awarded: to support study of the conservation of Japanese folded sheet books (1986); to support study of California feather blankets in European museums (1986); to support research in the archives of Dr. William Menninger at the Menninger Foundation (1986); for archival studies on the Gold Coast war experience, 1939-1945, at Rhodes House Library, Oxford, England (1986); to study archaeological collections in Frankfurt, West Germany (1986).

Eligibility/Limitations Applicants should be citizens of the United States, native residents of U.S. territorial possessions, or foreign nationals who have lived in the United States or its territories for three years immediately prior to submitting an application. Applicants need not have academic affiliations to be eligible. Although applicants need not have advanced degrees, candidates for degrees and persons seeking support for work leading to degrees are not eligible. Applications that are focused on pedagogical theory, research in educational methods, tests and measurements, or cognitive psychology are not eligible.

Fiscal Information Applicants recommended for awards will receive an award of $750 in one payment. The award is to be used exclusively to help defray the scholar's expenses in undertaking the specific research trip, including travel costs, subsistence and lodging, reproduction and photoduplication costs, and other associated research expenses. Applications for research travel to locations easily accessible to the applicant on a regular basis will not be considered. Applicants are expected to undertake the research travel during the period proposed in the application. The expenditures proposed may not include salary support or replacement or support for released time from the applicant's regular employment.

Application Information Application forms and additional information and guidelines are available from the Division of Fellowships and Seminars. When contacting NEH include the program for which you are applying.

Deadline(s) To be eligible for consideration an application must be postmarked no later than July 15 or January 15.

372. National Endowment for the Humanities

Division of Fellowships and Seminars, Room 316
1100 Pennsylvania Avenue, NW
Washington, DC 20506
(202) 786-0463

Younger Scholars Program

CFDA Program Number 45.115

Program Description Awards for younger scholars provide the nation's students with opportunities to conduct noncredit independent research and writing projects during the summer months. Under the close supervision of advisers who are humanities scholars, individuals pursue their own humanities projects during a concentrated period of time not normally available during the school year. This program enables grantees to enhance their intellectual development by producing research papers on a specific humanities topic. In both subject matter and methodology, projects must be firmly grounded in one of the disciplines of the humanities. Applicants are expected to discuss the way in which their projects engage one or more of the following areas of emphasis: the interpretation of cultural works; the study of historical ideas, figures, and events; and understanding the disciplines of the humanities.

Eligibility/Limitations Applicants must be twenty-one years of age or under throughout the entire calendar year in which the application is submitted; or, if they are over twenty-one, they must be full-time college students pursuing an undergraduate degree at the time of application. Applicants must be either U.S. citizens or foreign nationals who have lived in the United States for at least three consecutive years at the time of application. Proposed projects require a project adviser with knowledge and qualifications in an appropriate humanities discipline and must result in a substantial research paper. Individuals who will have received or expect to receive a bachelor's degree by October 1 are not eligible to apply. No project activities may take place outside the United States during the grant period. Joint projects by two or more individuals may not be submitted.

Fiscal Information College students (or high-school graduates at the time of application) may apply for $2,200, of which $400 is allotted to the adviser. High-school students (at the time of application) may apply for $1,800, of which $400 is allotted to the adviser. All grants involve nine weeks of full-time work by an individual on a specific humanities project during the summer months. Grantees may not be enrolled in a credit course during the grant period, and projects may not be used for academic credit.

Application Information Application forms and additional information are available from the Division of Fellowships and Seminars. When contacting NEH include the program for which you are applying.

Deadline(s) Applications should be received by November 1.

373. National Endowment for the Humanities
Division of General Programs
1100 Pennsylvania Avenue, NW, Room 420
Washington, DC 20506
(202) 786-0271

Humanities Projects in Libraries

CFDA Program Number 45.137

Program Description Through Humanities Projects in Libraries, the endowment supports programs that are designed to increase public understanding of the humanities through the discovery, interpretation, and greater appreciation of books and other resources in library collections. Projects should involve the active collaboration of scholars from the appropriate disciplines of the humanities and the professional staff of libraries during both the planning and implementation of programs. The Humanities Projects in Libraries program encourages public, academic, or special libraries to plan and present programs in the humanities. The program also encourages the development of cooperative projects between public, academic, or special libraries, as well as between libraries, museums, historical societies, and other cultural institutions. Programs may also take place at locations other than a library, but the primary objective of using the resources of libraries to enhance the understanding and appreciation of the humanities must be evident in the design of any project. Applicants for these grants are expected to address the manner in which their projects deal with one or more of the following areas: the appreciation and interpretation of cultural works; the illumination of historical ideas, figures, and events; and an understanding of the disciplines of the humanities.

Sample Grants To support public programs on southern folk art in which folk artists are introduced as the creators of art and the recorders of history, $5,000 to Museum of American Folk Art, New York, NY (1986). To plan an interpretive exhibition of unpublished manuscripts and incunabula from public and private collections in western Pennsylvania, $15,000 to the University of Pittsburgh, Pittsburgh, PA (1987).

Eligibility/Limitations Eligible applicants include nonprofit public, academic, special, or institutional libraries; local, state-wide or regional library systems; and state, regional, or national library associations. The following types of projects are not eligible for support: projects to create musical composition, dance, painting, sculpture, poetry, short stories or novels, and projects providing for performance or training in these arts; projects from profit-making organizations or institutions, or from individuals without an organizational or institutional base; projects whose primary function is to mount exhibitions from the collections of museums or historical societies; projects that have as their primary focus a media production; projects for renovation, restoration, rehabilitation, construction, establishment of historic markers and plaques or historic preservation; projects that have as their primary focus organizing, cataloguing, indexing, microfilming, or preserving collections; projects that consist primarily of research activities; individual fellowships and stipends, support for graduate education, or projects that require participants to register for academic credit; projects for training of personnel or individual requests for travel to professional meetings; the publication or editorial costs of articles or monographs for scholarly audiences; and projects directed at persuading an audience to a particular political, philosophical, religious, or ideological point of view or that advocate a particular program of social action or change.

Fiscal Information Humanities Projects in Libraries offers planning and implementation grants. Planning grants are awarded to support the collaborative efforts of scholars and an institution's administrative staff to design programs. Planning grants generally last no longer than six months and usually range from $5,000 to $15,000. Support may occasionally exceed $15,000 if such activities are regional or national in scope or involve more than one type of institution. Requests for funds in excess of $15,000 should be discussed with the program's staff before an application is made. Implementation grants support the presentation of fully developed public programs in the humanities. Such grants are normally funded for periods of one to three years. These grants usually range from $15,000 to $200,000. Requests for funds in excess of $200,000 should be discussed with the program's staff before an application is submitted. Cost sharing of at least 20 percent of a project's total budget is recommended for an implementation grant.

Application Information Application forms and additional information are available from the Division of General Programs.

Deadline(s) Applications must be received by August 5 for planning grants and by September 16 for implementation grants.

374. National Endowment for the Humanities
Division of General Programs, Room 420
1100 Pennsylvania Avenue, NW
Washington, DC 20506
(202) 786-0278

Humanities Projects in Media

CFDA Program Number 45.104

Program Description The Media Program seeks to transmit work in scholarship and learning in the humanities, to convey the best in thought and culture, and to engage the public in critical analysis and interpretation through quality television, film, and radio programming. The program expects high standards, not only of technical quality but also of intellectual depth and rigor. Other public and private agencies support media projects, but the endowment funds only those that centrally involve the disciplines of the humanities. This is accomplished by collaboration between scholars in the humanities and media professionals. Humanities scholars are expected to participate in each project at every stage: planning, script preparation, and production. Proposals must reflect the knowledge of scholars and teachers as well as the expertise and talent of producers, directors, and writers. Scholars ensure that the programs reflect the critical and reflective work of the humanities in content and approach and that the information presented in the programs is conceptually sound and factually accurate. Producers, directors, and writers help the scholars translate materials from their research into effective and interesting programs. Constructive collaboration is the basis and the key to high quality programs that are aesthetically and intellectually stimulating. The Media Program encourages applicants to select the media format and the program length best suited for the material—dramatization, documentary, talk show, animation, or other. In order to reach the largest number of adults and children, all television projects supported through the program should be designed for broadcast to national audiences or, if cable is selected, have demonstrable value for a national audience. Radio projects may be designed for local, regional, or national distribution and broadcast on public and commercial stations or distributed on cable audio systems. Applicants are expected to discuss the manner in which their projects embody one or more of the division's three categories of special concern: the appreciation and interpretation of cultural works; the illumination of historical ideas, figures, and events; and an understanding of the disciplines of the humanities.

Sample Grants To support planning for a feature-length film for television on the major fiction and autobiography of the American-Jewish author Ludwig Lewisohn (1882-1955), examining these works as literature and for the light they shed on key American issues: ethnicity and assimilation, marriage and family, $19,540 to American Jewish Archives, Cincinnati, OH (1986).

Eligibility/Limitations Any private, nonprofit organization, college or university, or branch of state or local government may apply for a Media Program grant. In addition, any group of scholars or professionals with experience in media and the humanities may form their own nonprofit group to apply for funding. Applicants are not required to be incorporated or to have 501(c)(3) status with the Internal Revenue Service although obtaining such status is recommended, especially for larger projects. In any case, applicants must have the ability to administer the project in compliance with federal regulations as well as generally accepted accounting principles. The Media Program does not provide support for the following projects: projects to create musical composition, dance, painting, sculpture, poetry, short stories, novels, or projects providing for performance or training in these arts; projects directed at persuading an audience to a particular political, philosophical, religious, or ideological point of view or projects that advocate a particular program of social action or change; projects that are designed exclusively to preserve information for deposit in archives; projects that require the permanent acquisition of facilities or equipment or the establishment of training programs in film, radio, or television productions; projects aimed at technological experimentation in the development of electronic media; and instructional projects primarily designed for classroom use.

Fiscal Information The endowment provides three types of funding for projects: matching grants, outright grants, and a combination of the two.

Application Information Early contact with Media Program staff can be helpful and is strongly recommended. Either a letter describing the project or a draft proposal may be submitted (no later than six weeks before the deadline to allow time for a response). A staff member will be able to determine if the basic idea fits within the general guidelines of the program and, if time permits, can help anticipate some questions that reviewers and panelists may later raise. In preparing the application, applicants should remember that it will be read by both authorities in the subject area and professionals in the broadcast industry. The more precise an applicant can be about a proposal's concept, its importance in the humanities, the way it will be developed, how the medium will be used to enhance it, and the roles of key participants, the more likely it is that evaluators will have confidence in the quality of the project, in the applicant's control of it and ability to carry it out.

Deadline(s) Applications should be received by March 18 and September 16.

Additional Information The Media Program has three funding categories—planning, scripting, and production—which are designed to help applicants produce high quality programs, following appropriate stages and steps. However, the applicant may apply in any category depending on the status and needs of the project in question.

375. National Endowment for the Humanities
Division of General Programs, Room 420
1100 Pennsylvania Avenue, NW
Washington, DC 20506
(202) 786-0284

Humanities Projects in Museums and Historical Organizations

CFDA Program Number 45.125

Program Description The goal of this program is to help make possible exhibitions that "speak" to people today, exhibitions that give visitors an understanding and appreciation of an object itself and also of its relationship to ideas, events, and aesthetics. The endowment seeks to facilitate the groundwork of research and collections management that is the foundation for any intellectually substantial public exhibition, and it seeks to help in the planning and implementation of the exhibitions themselves. The spectrum of endowment support extends from an inventory of permanent collections, to the preparation of catalogues, to the sharing of collections among several museums. The endowment supports projects designed especially for children as well as those designed for adults. It supports the preparation of publications related to permanent collections and to both temporary and permanent exhibitions. In addition, the endowment can assist in the conservation of objects used in an exhibition or, under some circumstances, objects that are part of the permanent collection.

Sample Grants To plan a permanent exhibition interpreting the planetarium's collection of historical scientific instruments by illuminating the social, political, economic, and philosophical aspects of the development of science, $30,000 to the Adler Planetarium, Chicago, IL (1986). To plan a major exhibition on Mexican masquerade emphasizing the history of masking and costume from the Spanish conquest to the present day, $40,000 to the International Folk Art Museum, Santa Fe, NM (1987). To support part of the permanent exhibition of films, video excerpts, and archival materials interpreting the impact of the moving image media on American audiences from 1900-1929, $182,000 to American Museum of the Moving Image, Astoria, NY (1986). To support planning a temporary exhibition and catalogue of the art and culture of the Mangbetu peoples of northeastern Zaire, based on materials collected by the Chapin and Lang expedition of 1909-1915, $34,458 to American Museum of

Natural History, New York, NY (1986). To support the implementation of a temporary, traveling exhibition of 100 sculptures and 200 miniature paintings that will interpret for the general public the concept of *rasa* that underlies the philosophy of aesthetic appreciation in India, $225,000 to Asian Art Museum Foundation, San Francisco, CA (1986). To support reinstallation of the exhibition at the Sears Hall of Human Ecology, which will interpret traditional and modern societies in the diverse habitats in which they function, $100,000 to Cleveland Museum of Natural History, Cleveland, OH (1986). To support a self-study to examine and evaluate the center's plans for interpretive exhibitions and educational programs, $14,961 to Hawaii Maritime Center, Honolulu, HI (1986). To support an exhibition and brochure exploring the environments, history, and lifeways of the New Jersey Pinelands, $69,248 to New Jersey State Museum, Trenton, NJ (1986). To support computerized documentation of the photo archives at the museum, $25,000 to Southwest Museum, Los Angeles, CA (1986).

Eligibility/Limitations Eligible applicants include museums, historical societies, and other nonprofit organizations and institutions.

Fiscal Information Project costs can be supported by (1) endowment funds and (2) cash and noncash contributions, such as donated services and goods, which are contributed to the project by the applicant and nonfederal third parties. Contributions from the applicant and third parties constitute the applicant organization's "cost sharing." While the program for museums and historical organizations does not have established requirements for levels of cost sharing, all applicants are encouraged to participate in the support of the expenses related to carrying out a project, especially for large projects. More specific information on cost sharing is available from the program. The endowment provides three types of funding for projects: matching grants, outright grants, and a combination of the two. The program for museums and historical organizations does not provide support for the following activities: projects in the creative or performing arts; establishment of a new institution; general operating expenses; architectural preservation; acquisition of artifacts, works of art, or documents; purchase of permanent equipment for general operation purposes (filing cabinets, office equipment, or furniture); capital improvements of buildings; attendance at professional meetings; and projects that focus on current affairs or events for the purpose of eliciting a specific public response or advocating a particular program of social action or change.

Application Information Additional information and specific guidelines are available from the program.

Deadline(s) Applications should be received by June 10 and December 9.

376. National Endowment for the Humanities
Division of General Programs, Room 426
1100 Pennsylvania Avenue, NW
Washington, DC 20506
(202) 786-0271

Public Humanities Projects

CFDA Program Number 45.113

Program Description This program offers support to a wide variety of projects designed to increase public understanding of the humanities. Through this program the endowment recognizes exemplary public programs and promotes model projects that may have national significance. The program is especially interested in identifying new opportunities for calling the public's attention to the work of humanities scholars. This program does not restrict its grant-making to any one type of project, and applicants may make use of a number of formats—including public symposia, community forums, debates, interpretive pamphlets, or audiovisual materials—to reach segments of the general public with humanities scholarship.

Sample Grants To support planning for a series of noncredit courses exploring the cultural significance of the architecture and interior design of the American home, $15,000 to Indianapolis Museum of Art, Indianapolis, IN (1986). To support an oral history project and archive documenting the lives of residents active in the South

Bronx from 1960 to the present, $2,431 to CUNY Research Foundation, Lehman College, Bronx, NY (1986).

Eligibility/Limitations Eligible applicants include colleges and universities, professional organizations or associations, cultural and community organizations, agencies of state and local governments, and various nonprofit community groups. In many cases, an applicant will be a consortium of such groups or an ad-hoc group formed to mount special, one-time events such as the commemoration of an anniversary. As a general rule, priority is given to applications which promise to reach a national and regional audience, but well-conceived local projects are frequently competitive. All projects should feature the participation of scholars from one or more disciplines of the humanities.

Fiscal Information The program offers both planning grants and implementation awards. Normally, planning grants range from $5,000 to $20,000 and last no longer than six months. Cost sharing is not required for planning grants. Implementation grants may range from $15,000 to $150,000 and are funded for periods of one to three years. Normally, the endowment will support no more than 80 percent of the total costs of an implementation project.

Application Information Applicants should submit a preliminary proposal six to eight weeks before a deadline, and this draft should include a tentative budget to enable the program staff to determine eligibility and competitiveness. Contact the program for guidelines and application forms.

Deadline(s) The program runs two competitions each year; deadlines are March 18 and September 16.

377. National Endowment for the Humanities
Division of General Programs, Room 426
1100 Pennsylvania Avenue, NW
Washington, DC 20506
(202) 786-0267

Special Initiatives: The Columbian Quincentenary

Program Description As part of the international observance of the 500th anniversary of Christopher Columbus's voyage of discovery to the New World, NEH invites proposals for original scholarship on related topics and for the dissemination of both new and existing scholarship. Topics may include the expansion of European civilization through the efforts of the Spanish and Portuguese crowns; the establishment of new societies and new forms of cultural expression through encounters among native American, European, and African peoples; and the ideas—political, religious, philosophical, scientific, technological, and aesthetic—that shaped the processes of exploration, settlement, and cultural conflict and transformation set into motion by Columbus's momentous voyage. Proposals related to this initiative are welcome in any of the grant categories of the Division of General Programs. Of particular interest are projects that will result in a deeper appreciation and understanding of important works of literature and the arts; a heightened understanding of significant historical figures, events, and ideas; and a greater comprehension of the disciplines or methodology of the humanities.

Sample Grants Support for an exhibition tracing the variety of interpretations of ancient Mayan culture offered by scholars in different centuries and different disciplines, using architectural drawings, maps, prints, and other materials to document the theories put forward by explorers, archaeologists, and scholars (1986).

Eligibility/Limitations The division supports projects intended to increase public understanding of the humanities. To achieve this end, the division makes grants for the planning and implementation of traveling and permanent exhibitions at museums, historical organizations, and libraries; planning, scripting, and production of humanities programming for television and radio; and lectures, conferences, symposia, discussion groups, and related activities held at libraries, colleges, universities, and other institutions and organizations. All projects receiving awards must reflect an active collaboration among scholars in the humanities and professionals with knowledge of humanities programming for the general public.

Application Information For further information about the Columbian Quincentenary and for application guidelines, contact the Division of General Programs.

378. National Endowment for the Humanities

Division of Research Programs, Room 318
1100 Pennsylvania Avenue, NW
Washington, DC 20506
(202) 786-0210

Interpretive Research: Humanities, Science, and Technology

CFDA Program Number 45.133

Program Description In this program the endowment supports research that employs the theories and methods of humanities disciplines to study science and technology as well as research that broadens and deepens understanding of the fundamental concerns that lie behind current issues about the conduct and applications of science and technology. The endowment encourages studies that promote the collaboration of scientists or engineers with humanities scholars as well as projects that promise to improve interdisciplinary research methods. Support is available for collaborative or coordinated research in many areas of inquiry that include, but are not limited to, the form, content, and purposes of scientific knowledge; the processes through which scientific knowledge is developed; the invention, innovation, and transfer of technology; the social, moral, and legal meaning of specific scientific and technological innovations; the interaction among sciences, technology, and other elements of culture; and the methods and concepts that the humanities use to study science and technology. The endowment supports projects that involve historical and philosophical approaches to the social sciences but does not support empirical social scientific research, specific policy studies, or technical impact assessments.

Eligibility/Limitations Institutions in the United States engaged in the humanities and individual United States citizens or foreign nationals who have been living in the United States or its territories for at least three years at the time of application are eligible to apply. Support may also be given to any individual or organization whose work promises significantly to advance knowledge and understanding of the humanities in the United States. Foreign nationals who do not meet the residence requirement may apply if they are formally affiliated with a United States educational institution and in these cases must apply through the institution. In exceptional circumstances, the endowment may also provide support to a foreign institution or foreign national not meeting the eligibility criteria mentioned above when a project promises to advance knowledge and understanding of the humanities in the United States to an unusually large extent. The endowment does not support research in pursuit of an academic degree.

Fiscal Information Awards can support full- or part-time activities for up to three years. Although requests for grants may be of any size, each project budget should be appropriate to the scope and magnitude of the proposed activities. The average grant is $50,000 per year. Applicants proposing complex projects or projects that are likely to involve large budget requests should consult with a member of the program staff before final application is submitted. Normally, the endowment's contribution to a project will not exceed 80 percent of the project's total costs. For all types of projects, applicants are encouraged to consider seeking support through federal matching funds.

Application Information Program guidelines are available upon request. After reading these guidelines, the prospective applicant should draft a brief description (no more than five pages) of the proposed project. This description should be sent to the program officer. So that staff members have sufficient time to give the project thorough attention, this correspondence should begin at least two or three months prior to the formal application deadline. Applicants should not attempt to prepare a full proposal using only general guidelines. Upon receipt of the brief description, endowment staff will assess the eligibility and competitiveness of the project and will contact the applicant about the proposal. If the project is eligible, the endowment staff member will send application forms and instructions. If sufficient time before the deadline remains, the applicant may submit a draft of the proposal for further informal comment. After this additional consultation with the staff, the applicant should prepare a full application using the appropriate forms.

Deadline(s) Deadline for receipt of applications is October 1.

379. National Endowment for the Humanities
Division of Research Programs, Room 318
1100 Pennsylvania Avenue, NW
Washington, DC 20506
(202) 786-0210

Interpretive Research: Projects

CFDA Program Number 45.140

Program Description Grants in this category are intended to support major collaborative or coordinated projects that will be influential in and important for humanities scholarship. The endowment encourages applications that are grounded in the individual disciplines of the humanities as well as those that cross disciplinary boundaries. Applicants must make a convincing case for the importance of the project as well as for the choice of the proposed methodology. Applicants must also demonstrate that the proposed personnel and institutional resources are available and appropriate to the project's goals. Projects supported in this program include biographies; historical and analytical studies in literature and the arts; research in history, philosophy, and other basic humanities disciplines; focused interdisciplinary studies; humanistic research in political science, sociology, and cultural anthropology; and other major collaborative or cooperative undertakings that promise to advance research methods or the means of interpretation in the humanities. In this category, the endowment also supports archaeological projects that promise to strengthen scholarly knowledge and understanding of history and culture. Support is available for foreign and American archaeology, including survey, excavation, materials analysis, laboratory research, artifact preservation, and preparation of archaeological monographs.

Sample Grants To prepare a data base, the *Corpus Maya Hieroglyphic Inscriptions*, which will serve the needs of cultural and art historians, epigraphists, and archaeologists, $135,000 to Harvard University (1987). To support the study of English ceramics in the late 18th and 19th century, providing a classification system useful for American studies and material culture, $49,986 to Colonial Williamsburg Foundation, Williamsburg, VA (1986). To provide continuing support for the first of two phases of analysis and preparation for publication on materials from salvage excavations at Gritille, Turkey, $24,640 to Bryn Mawr College, Bryn Mawr, PA (1986). To support a collaborative study of stained glass panels and panes in American museums and private collections, one component of the international *Corpus Vitrearum*, $70,000 to Tufts University, Medford, MA (1986).

Eligibility/Limitations Institutions in the United States engaged in the humanities and individual United States citizens or foreign nationals who have been living in the United States or its territories for at least three years at the time of application are eligible to apply. Support may also be given to any individual or organization whose work promises significantly to advance knowledge and understanding of the humanities in the United States. Foreign nationals who do not meet the residence requirement may apply if they are formally affiliated with a United States educational institution and in these cases must apply through the institution. In exceptional circumstances, the endowment may also provide support to a foreign institution or foreign national not meeting the eligibility criteria mentioned above when a project promises to advance knowledge and understanding of the humanities in the United States to an unusually large extent. The endowment does not support research in pursuit of an academic degree.

Fiscal Information Awards can support full- or part-time activities for up to three years. Although requests for grants may be of any size, each project budget should be appropriate to the scope and magnitude of the proposed activities. The average grant is $50,000 per year. Applicants proposing complex projects or projects that are likely to involve large budget requests should consult with a member of the program staff before final application is submitted. Normally, the endowment's contribution to a project will not exceed 80 percent of the project's total costs. For all types of projects, applicants are encouraged to consider seeking support through federal matching funds. Applicants who seek funding for major archaeological expeditions should already have completed preliminary survey work. If a survey has not been made, the applicant may request an initial grant to fund a preparatory investigation. Support is available for materials analysis only if the analysis is an integral part of a larger project that focuses on problems of research and interpretation in the humanities.

Application Information Program guidelines are available upon request. After reading these guidelines, the prospective applicant should draft a brief description (no more than five pages) of the proposed project. This description should be sent to the program officer. So that staff members have sufficient time to give the project thorough attention, this correspondence should begin at least two or three months prior to the formal application deadline. Applicants should not attempt to prepare a full proposal using only general guidelines. Upon receipt of the brief description, endowment staff will assess the eligibility and competitiveness of the project and will contact the applicant about the proposal. If the project is eligible, the endowment staff member will send application forms and instructions. If sufficient time before the deadline remains, the applicant may submit a draft of the proposal for further informal comment. After this additional consultation with the staff, the applicant should prepare a full application using the appropriate forms.

Deadline(s) Deadline for receipt of applications is October 1.

380. National Endowment for the Humanities
Division of Research Programs, Room 318
1100 Pennsylvania Avenue, NW
Washington, DC 20506
(202) 786-0358

Reference Materials: Access

CFDA Program Number 45.124

Program Description In this category the endowment supports projects that promise to increase the availability of important research collections and other significant source material in all fields of the humanities. Support is provided for such activities as archival arrangement and description projects; bibliographies; records surveys; cataloguing projects involving print, graphic, film, sound, and artifact collections; indices; and other guides to humanities documentation. Under certain circumstances, oral histories are also eligible. In addition, support is provided for the development of national standards for access to different types of scholarly resources and for projects that promise to improve significantly the ways in which libraries, archives, and other repositories make research documentation available. Archival arrangement and description projects that involve the microfilming of unique materials are also eligible for support in the access category, as are projects to microfilm important collections in foreign repositories that are largely inaccessible to American scholars. An applicant must demonstrate that the level and form of description proposed is an appropriate and cost-effective means of gaining bibliographic control over the collection or collections involved. In standard archival arrangement and description projects, support is normally limited to the preparation of finding aids to the box and folder level. Applicants who propose to organize non-textual collections are urged to employ minimal level cataloguing.

Sample Grants To support the arrangement and description of records and papers of individuals who formed new churches or institutions during the 1970s schism in the Lutheran Church-Missouri Synod, $28,710 to Archives of the Lutheran Church in America, Chicago, IL (1986). To support the development of a computerized catalogue of photographic collections which will offer a means for subject access to a major photographic archives documenting native American history and culture in North and South America, $14,824 to the Museum of the American Indian, New York, NY (1985). To support the arrangement and description of records held by the Hagley Museum and Library of the Penn Central Corporation and its predecessor companies, $60,000 to Hagley Museum and Library, Wilmington, DE (1986). To support cataloguing 18,000 monographs and 500 manuscript collections on the ethnology, archaeology, and history of Native Americans, $100,000 to Southwest Museum, Los Angeles, CA (1986).

Eligibility/Limitations Institutions in the United States engaged in the humanities and individual United States citizens or foreign nationals who have been living in the United States or its territories for at least three years at the time of application are eligible to apply. Support may also be given to any individual or organization whose work promises significantly to advance knowledge and understanding of the humanities in the United States. Foreign nationals who do not meet the residence requirement may apply if they are formally affiliated with a United States educational institution and in these cases must apply through the institution. In exceptional circumstances, the endowment may also provide support to a foreign institution or foreign national not meeting the eligibility criteria mentioned above when a project promises to advance knowledge and understanding of the humanities in the United States to an unusually large extent. The endowment does not support research in pursuit of an academic degree.

Fiscal Information Awards can provide up to three years of support and usually range from $20,000 to $150,000, depending upon the size and scope of the project. Applicants whose projects are complex in organization or are likely to involve large budget requests should consult with a member of the program staff before a final application is submitted. Normally, the endowment's contribution to projects that are focused chiefly on an applicant institution's own holdings will not exceed 60 percent of the project's total costs. Endowment support of projects that do not primarily benefit the applicant institution will usually not exceed 80 percent of the project's total costs. All applicants are encouraged to seek full or partial support through federal matching funds.

Application Information Program guidelines are available upon request. After reading these guidelines, the prospective applicant should draft a brief description (no more than five pages) of the proposed project. This description should be sent to the program officer. So that staff members have sufficient time to give the project thorough attention, this correspondence should begin at least two or three months prior to the formal application deadline. Applicants should not attempt to prepare a full proposal using only general guidelines. Upon receipt of the brief description, endowment staff will assess the eligibility and competitiveness of the project and will contact the applicant about the proposal. If the project is eligible, the endowment staff member will send application forms and instructions. If sufficient time before the deadline remains, the applicant may submit a draft of the proposal for further informal comment. After this additional consultation with the staff, the applicant should prepare a full application using the appropriate forms.

Deadline(s) Deadline for receipt of applications is November 1.

381. National Endowment for the Humanities
Division of Research Programs, Room 318
1100 Pennsylvania Avenue, NW
Washington, DC 20506
(202) 786-0358

Reference Materials: Tools

CFDA Program Number 45.145

Program Description Grants in this category support the creation of dictionaries, historical or linguistic atlases, encyclopedias, concordances, *catalogues raisonnes*, linguistic grammars, descriptive catalogues, data bases, and other materials that serve to codify information essential to research in the humanities. Applicants must make a convincing case for the project's editorial and administrative procedures and for the importance of the final product to scholars in several fields. In addition, applicants must demonstrate that the form chosen for the proposed research tool (printed volume, microform, on-line data base, etc.) represents the most effective means of disseminating the information.

Sample Grants To support preparation of a detailed analytical index and statistical analysis of the diaries, commonplace books, and family sketches written by Thomas Thistlewood, an Anglo-Jamaican plantation owner, from 1748 through 1786, $45,000 to the College of William and Mary, Williamsburg, VA (1985). To support preparation of a computerized index and related subject indices to the documents of the Provincias Internas branch of the General Archive of Mexico, $153,155 to University of Arizona, Tucson, AZ (1986).

Eligibility/Limitations Institutions in the United States engaged in the humanities and individual United States citizens or foreign nationals who have been living in the United States or its territories for at least three years at the time of application are eligible to apply. Support may also be given to any individual or organization whose work promises significantly to advance knowledge and understanding of the humanities in the United States. Foreign nationals who do not meet the residence requirement may apply if they are formally affiliated with a United States educational institution and in these cases must apply through the institution. In exceptional circumstances, the endowment may also provide support to a foreign institution or foreign national not meeting the eligibility criteria mentioned above when a project promises to advance knowledge and understanding of the humanities in the United States to an unusually large extent. The endowment does not support research in pursuit of an academic degree.

Fiscal Information Awards can be made for periods extending from one to three years, and typically range from less than $10,000 to more than $150,000, depending upon the scope of the project. Applicants whose projects are complex in organization or are likely to involve large budget requests should consult with a member of the program staff before final application is submitted. Normally, the endowment's contribution to a project will not exceed 80 percent of the project's total costs. All applicants are encouraged to seek full or partial support through federal matching funds.

Application Information Program guidelines are available upon request. After reading these guidelines, the prospective applicant should draft a brief description (no more than five pages) of the proposed project. This description should be sent to the program officer. So that staff members have sufficient time to give the project thorough attention, this correspondence should begin at least two or three months prior to the formal application deadline. Applicants should not attempt to prepare a full proposal using only general guidelines. Upon receipt of the brief description, endowment staff will assess the eligibility and competitiveness of the project and will contact the applicant about the proposal. If the project is eligible, the endowment staff member will send application forms and instructions. If sufficient time before the deadline remains, the applicant may submit a draft of the proposal for further informal comment. After this additional consultation with staff, the applicant should prepare a full application using the appropriate forms.

Deadline(s) Deadline for receipt of applications is November 1.

382. National Endowment for the Humanities
Division of Research Programs, Room 318
1100 Pennsylvania Avenue, NW
Washington, DC 20506
(202) 786-0204

Regrants: Centers for Advanced Study

CFDA Program Number 45.122

Program Description Through grants in this category, the endowment supports coordinated research in well-defined subject areas at independent centers for advanced study, overseas research centers, independent research libraries, and research museums. In assessing an application from a center, the endowment emphasizes the intrinsic importance of the work to be undertaken at the center, the relation of this work to the center's collections and other facilities, and the degree to which arrangements at the center will promote collegial exchange. The regrants awarded by the centers enable individual scholars to pursue their own research for periods ranging from six to twelve months and to participate in the interchange of ideas among the center's scholars.

Sample Grants To support postdoctoral fellowships in the fields of the library's collections, $90,500 to Henry E. Huntington Library and Art Gallery, San Marino, CA (1986). To support postdoctoral fellowships in the fields of the library's collections, $30,000 to John Carter Brown Library, Providence, RI (1986).

Eligibility/Limitations Awards are made to colleges and universities and to organizations such as learned societies, federations and committees of scholarly associations, and major independent research libraries and centers.

Application Information Centers, libraries, museums, or other appropriate institutions that wish to apply to this program should write to the endowment to request more detailed information and application instructions. Individuals interested in pursuing research at any of the centers receiving endowment support should apply directly to the centers. A list of currently funded centers is available from the endowment on request.

Deadline(s) Applications should be received by December 1.

383. National Endowment for the Humanities
Division of Research Programs, Room 318
1100 Pennsylvania Avenue, NW
Washington, DC 20506
(202) 786-0204

Regrants: Conferences

CFDA Program Number 45.134

Program Description Grants in this category support conferences that enable both American and foreign scholars to advance the current state of research on topics of major importance in the humanities. These conferences should be designed to accomplish objectives that cannot be achieved by other means. Normally, presenters at the conference number from ten to twenty and include both junior and senior scholars. Other conference participants number from 30 to 200 and should draw junior and senior faculty from a wide range of institutions and fields of specialty.

Sample Grants To support a conference on introducing quantitative methods to the study of the history of American Indians, $15,000 to Newberry Library, Chicago, IL (1986). To conduct an international conference on the role of books in the Americas, especially in the development of colonial Latin American society and culture, $10,000 to the John Carter Brown Library, Providence, RI (1986).

Eligibility/Limitations Awards are made to colleges and universities and to organizations such as learned societies, federations and committees of scholarly associations, and major independent research libraries and centers.

Fiscal Information In addition to the costs of organizing and publicizing the conference, endowment funds awarded to the sponsoring institution or organization support travel and other expenses for the presenters as well as stipends to participants for partial travel and per diem expenses. Support is also available for the publication of conference results, but such publication costs are frequently contributed by the applicant as cost sharing. Normally, the endowment's contribution to the total costs of a conference will range from $6,000 to $40,000, depending upon the number of participants. All applicants are encouraged to seek full or partial support through federal matching funds.

Application Information Centers, libraries, museums, or other appropriate institutions that wish to apply to this program should write to the endowment to request more detailed information and application instructions.

Deadline(s) Applications should be received by February 15 and July 1.

384. National Endowment for the Humanities
Division of Research Programs, Room 318
1100 Pennsylvania Avenue, NW
Washington, DC 20506
(202) 786-0204

Regrants: International Research

CFDA Program Number 45.148

Program Description Through this category, the endowment awards funds to national organizations and learned societies to enable American scholars to pursue research abroad, to attend or participate in international conferences, and to engage in collaborative work with foreign colleagues. The regranting organizations also sponsor international scholarly exchange and collaborative international research endeavors.

Eligibility/Limitations National organizations and learned societies are eligible to apply.

Application Information Organizations and societies that wish to apply to this program should write to the endowment to request more detailed information and application instructions. Individuals interested in applying for support should write directly to the funded organization or society; a list of currently funded organizations and societies is available from the endowment upon request.

Deadline(s) Applications should be received by March 15.

385. National Endowment for the Humanities
Division of Research Programs, Room 318
1100 Pennsylvania Avenue, NW
Washington, DC 20506
(202) 786-0200

Special Initiatives: The Columbian Quincentenary

Program Description As part of the international observance of the 500th anniversary of Christopher Columbus's voyage of discovery to the New World, NEH invites proposals for original scholarship on related topics and for the dissemination original scholarship on related topics and for the dissemination of both new and existing scholarship. Topics may include the expansion of European civilization through the efforts of the Spanish and Portuguese crowns; the establishment of new societies and new forms of cultural expression through encounter among native American, European, and African peoples; and the ideas—political, religious, philosophical, scientific, technological, and aesthetic—that shaped the processes of exploration, settlement, and cultural conflict and transformation set into motion by Columbus's momentous voyage. Proposals related to this initiative are welcome in any of the grant categories of the Division of Research Programs.

Sample Grants Support to the University of Florida to establish a research center at its Institute for Early Contact Period Studies, where historians, archaeologists, and anthropologists conduct coordinated research on the settlements established by Columbus and other early explorers in the Florida and Caribbean region—an endowment grant supports four main projects at the center: a search for Columbus's first settlement in Haiti; an excavation and analysis of Puerto Real, Haiti, fourth oldest site in the New World; editing of documents related to Columbus's third voyage; and a international conference on early explorations (1984).

Application Information Applicants who are not certain where to direct an inquiry about this special initiative should call or write the director of the Division of Research Programs.

386. National Endowment for the Humanities
Division of Research Programs, Room 318
1100 Pennsylvania Avenue, NW
Washington, DC 20506
(202) 786-0207

Texts: Editions

CFDA Program Number 45.146

Program Description Grants in this category support various stages of the preparation of authoritative and annotated editions of sources of significant value to humanities scholars and general readers. Support is provided for projects that make available important texts and documents that have been either previously unavailable or accessible only in seriously flawed editions. All printed editions supported by the endowment are accompanied by critical introductions and annotations that provide essential information about the form, transmission, and historical and intellectual context of the texts and documents involved. Since complete editions in printed volumes are expensive to produce, endowment reviewers frequently recommend selected editions, microform editions, and editions that combine printed volumes and microform. Consequently, applicants must demonstrate that the form proposed for the edition represents the most effective means of disseminating the material involved. Applicants for microform editions must also demonstrate that the project will make available materials dispersed among a number of widely scattered repositories.

Sample Grants To support a multi-volume edition of selected documents from the National Archives illustrating the transformation of the lives of Black people in the wake of emancipation, 1861-1867, $75,000 to University of Maryland, College Park, MD (1986). To support a twelve-volume print edition of *The Papers of Dr. Martin Luther King, Jr.*, $75,000 to Martin Luther King, Jr. Center, Atlanta, GA (1986). To support work on a comprehensive microfilm edition and a selected print edition of the papers of Black Americans active in the antislavery movement, 1830-1865, $15,000 to Florida State University, Tallahassee, FL (1986).

Eligibility/Limitations Institutions in the United States engaged in the humanities and individual United States citizens or foreign nationals who have been living in the United States or its territories for at least three years at the time of application are eligible to apply. Support may also be given to any individual or organization whose work promises significantly to advance knowledge and understanding of the humanities in the United States. Foreign nationals who do not meet the residence requirement may apply if they are formally affiliated with a United States educational institution and in these cases must apply through the institution. In exceptional circumstances, the endowment may also provide support to a foreign institution or foreign national not meeting the eligibility criteria mentioned above when a project promises to advance knowledge and understanding of the humanities in the United States to an unusually large extent.

Fiscal Information Awards in the Editions category are made for up to three years and range from $25,000 to $100,000 per year, with the amount of the award dependent on the scope and importance of the project. Applicants whose projects are complex in organization or are likely to involve large budget requests should consult with a member of the program staff before a final application is submitted. Normally, the endowment's contribution to a project will not exceed 80 percent of the project's total costs. All applicants are encouraged to seek full or partial support through federal matching funds.

Application Information Program guidelines are available upon request. After reading these guidelines, the prospective applicant should draft a brief description (no more than five pages) of the proposed project. This description should be sent to the program officer. So that staff members have sufficient time to give the project thorough attention, this correspondence should begin at least two or three months prior to the formal application deadline. Applicants should not attempt to prepare a full proposal using only general guidelines. Upon receipt of the brief description, endowment staff will assess the eligibility and competitiveness of the project and will contact the applicant about the proposal. If the project is eligible, the endowment staff member will send application forms and instructions. If sufficient time before the deadline remains, the applicant may submit a draft of the proposal for further informal comment. After this additional consultation with the staff, the applicant should prepare a full application using the appropriate forms.

Deadline(s) Deadline for receipt of application is June 1.

387. National Endowment for the Humanities

Division of Research Programs, Room 318
1100 Pennsylvania Avenue, NW
Washington, DC 20506
(202) 786-0207

Texts: Publication Subvention

CFDA Program Number 45.132

Program Description Grants in this category are intended to assist the publication and dissemination of distinguished scholarly works in all fields of the humanities. In all cases, the scholarly work for which an application is being made must have been formally accepted for publication by the appropriate editor or editorial board. All applications for subvention will be judged on the basis of the quality and scholarly importance of the work to be published as well as on the appropriateness of the budget and publishing plan. In this category, the endowment will also consider applications for projects designed to diminish the need for individual publication subventions by introducing cost-effective mechanisms, such as computerized typesetting machines, into the operation of a press.

Sample Grants To support the publication of detailed epigraphic and architectural surveys of two Egyptian temples from the 15th century B.C. in Semna and Kumma in Sudanese Nubia, $4,000 to Egypt Exploration Society, London, England (1986).

Eligibility/Limitations Applicants must be established publishers or scholarly publishing entities; applications from individual scholars are not accepted.

Fiscal Information Awards in this category average $6,000 per volume; no award for a single volume will exceed $10,000 in outright funds. All applicants are encouraged to seek support through federal matching funds. In a federal fiscal year a single publisher may not receive more than $50,000 in outright and federal matching funds or support for more than five works, whichever is less.

Application Information Program guidelines are available upon request. After reading these guidelines, the prospective applicant should draft a brief description (no more than five pages) of the proposed project. This description should be sent to the program officer. So that staff members have sufficient time to give the project thorough attention, this correspondence should begin at least two or three months prior to the formal application deadline. Applicants should not attempt to prepare a full proposal using only general guidelines. Upon receipt of the brief description, endowment staff will assess the eligibility and competitiveness of the project and will contact the applicant about the proposal. If the project is eligible, the endowment staff member will send application forms and instructions. If sufficient time before the deadline remains, the applicant may submit a draft of the proposal for further informal comment. After this additional consultation with the staff, the applicant should prepare a full application using the appropriate forms.

Deadline(s) Deadlines for receipt of applications are April 1 and September 1.

388. National Endowment for the Humanities

Division of Research Programs, Room 318
1100 Pennsylvania Avenue, NW
Washington, DC 20506
(202) 786-0207

Texts: Translations

CFDA Program Number 45.147

Program Description In this category the endowment supports the translation into English of works that will provide insight into the history, literature, philosophy, and artistic achievements of other cultures and that will make available the thought and learning of their civilizations. Applicants may propose to translate from any language, and the texts to be translated may be either primary sources or secondary works. Every applicant must make a convincing case for the importance of the translation to those scholars and general readers who do not command the language of the original text. All translations supported by the endowment must provide critical introductions and explanatory annotations that clearly establish the historical and intellectual contexts of the work involved. Where an authoritative text in the original language does not exist, applicants may apply for support to establish one. Applicants proposing to retranslate works that already exist in English must provide a strong argument for a new version or for an emendation of the existing version.

Sample Grants To support work on the translation and editing of archives of New Netherland, a major source for the study of the early history and culture of the middle Atlantic states, $35,588 to University of the State of New York, Albany, NY (1986).

Eligibility/Limitations Institutions in the United States engaged in the humanities and individual United States citizens or foreign nationals who have been living in the United States or its territories for at least three years at the time of application are eligible to apply. Support may also be given to any individual or organization whose work promises significantly to advance knowledge and understanding of the humanities in the United States. Foreign nationals who do not meet the residence requirement may apply if they are formally affiliated with a United States educational institution and in these cases must apply through the institution. In exceptional circumstances, the endowment may also provide support to a foreign institution or foreign national not meeting the eligibility criteria mentioned above when a project promises to advance knowledge and understanding of the humanities in the United States to an unusually large extent.

Fiscal Information Grant awards in this category usually range from $3,500 to $75,000, depending upon the scope and magnitude of the project. Applicants are encouraged to seek support from appropriate foreign governments and from foundations and are also encouraged to apply for federal matching funds.

Application Information Program guidelines are available upon request. After reading these guidelines, the prospective applicant should draft a brief description (no more than five pages) of the proposed project. This description should be sent to the program officer. So that staff members have sufficient time to give the project thorough attention, this correspondence should begin at least two or three months prior to the formal application deadline. Applicants should not attempt to prepare a full proposal using only general guidelines. Upon receipt of the brief description, endowment staff will assess the eligibility and competitiveness of the project and will contact the applicant about the proposal. If the project is eligible, the endowment staff member will send application forms and instructions. If sufficient time before the deadline remains, the applicant may submit a draft of the proposal for further informal comment. After this additional consultation with the staff, the applicant should prepare a full application using the appropriate forms. All translation applications must be accompanied by a seven-page sample of the translation to be undertaken during the course of the grant.

Deadline(s) Deadline for receipt of applications is June 1.

389. National Endowment for the Humanities
Division of State Programs, Room 411
1100 Pennsylvania Avenue, NW
Washington, DC 20506
(202) 786-0254

Special Initiatives: The Columbian Quincentenary

Program Description Humanities councils in each state, the District of Columbia, Puerto Rico, and the U.S. Virgin Islands make grants for humanities projects to engage the citizens of these states in the texts, disciplines, and methods of the humanities. The state councils are uniquely positioned to bring to localities the benefits of the latest humanities scholarship on the 1492 voyages and their global consequences. Since the beginning of the program in 1971, state councils have sponsored and funded scholarly symposia, museum exhibitions, book discussion projects, local media productions, and an array of other programming vehicles to present the humanities to general audiences. The Columbian Quincentenary is an initiative well suited for projects that invite public consideration of the events of 1492. In recent years, many of the councils have supported projects designed to strengthen elementary and secondary education. This grant category has included workshops, institutes, and seminars for teachers in connection with the Quincentenary. A summer institute on the place of Italian maritime exploration in the development of European commerce would be as likely in this category as, for example, a project intended to produce a traveling exhibition for school libraries.

Eligibility/Limitations Nonprofit agencies, cultural and educational institutions, civic organizations or groups may apply to the council in their states, the District of Columbia, Puerto Rico, or the Virgin Islands.

Application Information Each state council establishes its own grant guidelines and application deadlines. Contact the endowment for addresses of all councils.

390. National Endowment for the Humanities

Office of Challenge Grants, Room 429
1100 Pennsylvania Avenue, NW
Washington, DC 20506
(202) 786-0361

Challenge Grants

CFDA Program Number 45.130

Program Description The endowment developed the Challenge Grants program to join federal and major nonfederal support for the humanities and to improve financial stability and program quality within those institutions and organizations in which teaching, learning, and research in the humanities occur. Endowment challenge grants offer support for a variety of purposes so that institutions or organizations performing meritorious work within the context of their missions and resources may improve the quality of their work and achieve greater financial stability and an appropriate growth of their resources. Challenge grant applicants must demonstrate that the funds will sustain or develop a high quality of work which will contribute significantly to the promotion of the humanities.

Sample Grants To support conversion of the main museum building for office, archival, library, and conservation use, and to establish an endowment for museum operations and a development office, $50,000 to Calvert Marine Museum, Solomons, MD (1986). To support building expansion and to establish an endowment for humanities programs, $38,569 to Children's Museum of Oak Ridge, Inc., Oak Ridge, TN (1986). To support renovation and establishment of a humanities program endowment, $100,000 to Fraunces Tavern Museum, New York, NY (1986). To support an endowment for basic research in the cultural anthropology and archaeology of the Colorado plateau and curation of anthropological collections, $265,000 to Museum of Northern Arizona, Flagstaff, AZ (1986).

Eligibility/Limitations With the exception of public and private elementary and secondary schools, any nonprofit institution or organization working wholly or in part within the humanities may apply for a challenge grant. Such institutions and organizations include junior and community colleges, four-year colleges, universities, museums, historical societies, research libraries, public libraries, advanced study centers, media organizations, university presses, professional societies, and educational, cultural, or community groups.

Fiscal Information Endowment challenge grants in the last three years have ranged from $5,000 to $1 million. These amounts are the federal portion of the total challenge grant. Because each challenge grant recipient must raise three times the amount of the offer in nonfederal funds from new or increased contributions, the federal portion is 25 percent of the total proposed fund-raising campaign goal. The amount requested for a challenge grant should be reasonable and yet sufficient to accomplish the applicant's proposed aims. Any endowment challenge offer exceeding $1 million is rare (less than one percent of all grants offered). Although there have been a few such offers in the history of the program, there has been none in recent years. Anyone intending to request funding in excess of $1 million should discuss the proposal with the staff of the Office of Challenge Grants.

Application Information Application information and guidelines are available upon request. The office encourages potential applicants to discuss an institution's or organization's proposal plans with the staff before submitting the formal application and also to submit a draft application for staff review. Draft applications should be sent to the office at least six weeks prior to the formal application deadline.

Deadline(s) The deadline for receipt of applications is May 1. There are no extensions or exceptions.

391. National Endowment for the Humanities
Office of Challenge Grants, Room 429
1100 Pennsylvania Avenue, NW
Washington, DC 20506
(202) 786-0361

Special Initiatives: The Columbian Quincentenary

Program Description Challenge grants stimulate long-range institutional planning and financial development. A challenge grant is intended to improve the financial stability of a college, university, museum, historical organization, research or public library, public media station, or university press so that it may reach or sustain excellence in its humanities programs, collections, and research. Challenge grants may be used to develop long-term support for institutional needs in areas related to the Columbian Quincentenary.

Sample Grants Renovation of buildings used to house Columbian Quincentenary exhibitions, collections, or archives (1984). The development of acquisition funds for books or other collections related to the period of discovery, to studies of the Americas, or to ethnocultural fields (1984).

Eligibility/Limitations Nonprofit educational and cultural institutions and organizations working in the humanities are eligible to apply.

Fiscal Information Recipients must raise three times the offered federal funds in the form of new or increased contributions from nonfederal sources.

Application Information Additional information is available from the office.

392. National Endowment for the Humanities
Office of Preservation, Room 802
1100 Pennsylvania Avenue, NW
Washington, DC 20506
(202) 786-0570

Preservation

Program Description Grants in this category support projects that address the problem of the disintegration of significant humanities materials, particularly books and newspapers, but also other media such as journals, manuscripts, documents, maps, drawings, plans, photographs, film and tapes. Eligible activities include cooperative and selective microfilming, professional training in preservation management, and the improvement of preservation technology.

Sample Grants To conduct preservation activities leading to microfilming and conservation of critical parts of the Stewart Culin Library Collection, a critical resource for the study of ethnohistory, museological history, anthropology, and art history, $48,259 to Brooklyn Museum, New York, NY (1987). To conduct a series of five regional workshops on the care and preservation of two-dimensional materials held by museums, historical societies, and other historical organizations, $91,699 to American Association for State and Local History, Nashville, TN (1987). To edit and produce a manual on the duplication of photographic negatives, $10,000 to Northeast Document Conservation Center, Andover, MA (1987). To conduct a preservation survey and consultation activities for a three-year period for institutions in the mid-Atlantic states, $11,028 (outright funds) and $3,000 (federal match) to Conservation Center for Art and Historic Artifacts, Philadelphia, PA (1987).

Eligibility/Limitations Eligible applicants include individuals and institutions. Any nonprofit institution or organization may apply. Such institutions include, but are not limited to, research or public libraries, historical societies, archives, museums, regional organizations, library consortia, and scholarly or professional societies.

Fiscal Information The endowment provides three types of funding: federal matching funds, outright funds, and a combination of the two. The program emphasizes the use of federal matching funds in making awards. Federal matching funds are awarded on a one-for-one basis when an applicant raises gifts from third parties that will be used to support project activities during the grant period. Most of the endowment's awards for preservation will be made on a matching basis. An outright grant is one in which the award of endowment funds is not contingent on the applicant's raising gifts for the project.

Application Information One of the major responsibilities of staff in the Office of Preservation is to counsel prospective applicants about the program and their proposals. Potential applicants are strongly encouraged to discuss their proposal plans with program staff before submitting a formal application. Program staff will review draft applications, and applicants are also strongly encouraged to submit a draft application for staff review well in advance of an application deadline. Program staff provide the majority of counsel by telephone or letter.

Deadline(s) Application deadlines are June 1 and December 1.

393. National Endowment for the Humanities

Office of Preservation, Room 802
1100 Pennsylvania Avenue, NW
Washington, DC 20506
(202) 786-0570

Special Initiatives: The Columbian Quincentenary

Program Description Projects funded through the Office of Preservation address the problem of the physical deterioration of humanities resources—books, photographs, drawings, film, audio and video tapes, recordings, pamphlets, maps, charts, and manuscripts. The office welcomes applications concerned with the preservation of scholarly materials relating to the Quincentenary.

Sample Grants Support to the Art Institute of Chicago for the production of a microfiche-use copy of the final report of the 1893 Chicago World's Columbian Exposition, issued by Burnham and Root, the architectural firm in charge of planning and construction for the exposition (1984).

Eligibility/Limitations Grants support projects that address national preservation needs of research documentation in the humanities.

Application Information Contact the office for additional information.

394. National Endowment for the Humanities
Office of Preservation, Room 802
1100 Pennsylvania Avenue, NW
Washington, DC 20506
(202) 786-0570

U.S. Newspapers Program

Program Description Grants support projects in states and U.S. territories for the bibliographic control and preservation of U.S. newspapers, the planning of statewide projects, the cataloguing of newspapers, and the entry of bibliographic data and holding records in the Library of Congress CONSER data base. Applicants may request support for microfilm preservation of newspapers when bibliographic control is complete.

Sample Grants To conduct a second stage of cataloguing newspapers in Texas repositories as part of the U.S. Newspapers program; records for 2,500 titles will be entered into the OCLC/CONSER data base, $173,975 (outright funds) and $25,000 (federal match) to Panhandle-Plains Historical Museum, Canyon, TX (1988).

Eligibility/Limitations Eligible applicants include state agencies, organizations, institutions, and libraries. Projects must be tailored to the circumstances of each state.

Application Information Endowment staff work closely with applicants to ensure that technical and organizational criteria for project activities are met. Inquiries about this program should be made directly to Office of Preservation staff.

Deadline(s) The deadlines for applications are June 1 and December 1.

395. National Gallery of Art
Department of Extension Programs
Washington, DC 20565
(202) 842-6273

National Gallery of Art Extension Service

CFDA Program Number 68.001

Program Description The objective of this program is to provide educational material (slide programs, videocassettes, and films) on the gallery's collections and exhibitions, free of charge except for transportation costs, to schools, colleges, and libraries across the nation.

Eligibility/Limitations Eligible applicants include schools, colleges, libraries, clubs, museums, community organizations, and individuals.

Fiscal Information In fiscal year 1986, audiovisual art education materials relating to the nation's collection of paintings and sculptures were shown 85,145 times.

Application Information Write to the headquarters office for a list of available materials. Order forms are provided.

Deadline(s) Requests are accepted at any time.

396. National Geographic Society
Committee for Research and Exploration
Seventeenth and M Streets, NW
Washington, DC 20036
(202) 857-7439

Research Grants

Program Description Grants-in-Aid support basic research in the sciences pertinent to geography. These sciences include but are not limited to projects in anthropology, archaeology, astronomy, biology, botany, ecology, physical and human geography, geology, oceanography, paleontology, and zoology.

Sample Grants Continuation support for a study of Jurassic and Cretaceous terrestrial vertebrates (Patagonia), $10,800 to Museo Argentino de Ciencias Naturales, Buenos Aires, Argentina (1985). To support study of hybrid origin of unisexual shiny lizards of South America, $3,080 to Department of Herpetology, American Museum of Natural History, New York, NY (1986). Continuation support for study of paleontology and paleomagnetics, Late Cretaceous to Mid-Tertiary, Canadian high arctic, $27,872 to Carnegie Museum of Natural History, Pittsburgh, PA (1986). To support a study of Swahili ethnoarchaeology: the social uses of houses and artifacts, $14,000 to Lowie Museum of Anthropology, University of California, Berkeley, CA (1986). Continuation support for collecting Chisocheton in Malesian rain forests, $5,300 to Fairchild Tropical Gardens, Miami, FL (1986). Continuation support for East African Early Man Program, $63,500 to National Museums of Kenya, Nairobi, Kenya (1986).

Eligibility/Limitations Investigators who have earned doctoral degrees and are associated with institutions of higher learning or other scientific and educational nonprofit organizations, such as museums, are eligible to apply. Occasionally, grants are awarded to exceptionally well qualified graduate students or scientific workers who do not have research degrees or who are not associated with a university but who do have full qualifications for research on a scientific project of significance. Citizens of any country are eligible.

Fiscal Information Grants vary in amount, depending upon the need and nature of the projects. Recent awards ranged from $1,200 to $49,000. The society's annual budget for its research program is currently $3.9 million. Grants will be considered for up to three years when a project requires more than one year. Society policy does not permit the payment of overhead to any individual or institution. Except under the most unusual circumstances, payment of salary to the principal investigator is not approved; it is also unusual to make a grant that involves the payment of salaries to research associates, especially those having faculty status or other similar institutional connections or who are candidates for the Ph.D. degree. The society does not provide fellowships or pay tuition at any level. The Committee for Research and Exploration is reluctant to provide funds for capital equipment. In cases where funds are made available for such purposes, it is always with the stipulation that the equipment or its salvage value shall be returned to the society when the project is complete. If still or motion picture film or equipment is necessary to the research, it should be included in the budget. The society does not provide funds for publication or for travel to scientific meetings.

Application Information Official application forms are available upon request. Applications will not be considered unless submitted on this standard form. It is suggested that the investigator in writing for application forms state the nature of the program briefly. This may help a candidate avoid loss of time required for completing an application for a grant that is outside the stated interests of the society.

Deadline(s) Applications may be submitted at any time. The society's Committee for Research and Exploration usually meets every month.

Additional Information Grants are normally made only for field research. Museum or archival research may occasionally qualify as field research. Laboratory work is supported only to the extent that it may be necessary follow-up to field research.

397. National Historical Publications and Records Commission

National Archives Building
Washington, DC 20408
(202) 724-1090

Publications Program

CFDA Program Number 89.003

Program Description The publications program is intended to ensure the dissemination and more general availability of documentary source material important to the study and understanding of U.S. history. Projects should therefore be based upon material of widespread interest among scholars, students, and informed citizens. Documents should have historical value and interest that transcends local and state boundaries. Grants in the program include: (1) book publication projects that reproduce in print the text of the papers of outstanding U.S. citizens and other documents that may be important for an understanding and appreciation of U.S. history (projects involve collecting, compiling, editing, and publishing such papers or documents); and (2) microfilm publications projects that involve the arrangement and microcopying (in roll microfilm, microfiche, etc.) of papers of national significance.

Eligibility/Limitations Nonprofit organizations and institutions and federal, state, and local government agencies may apply to the commission for assistance in funding appropriate publications projects. Grants are made only to institutional sponsors of projects. Private scholars are eligible for support if a sponsoring institution agrees to submit the grant application and administer the grant funds.

Fiscal Information An application for an outright grant requests the commission to recommend support for the entire cost of a project, minus the share of costs borne by the sponsoring institution. Any direct or indirect costs relating to the project that are contributed by the applicant's institution may be included as cost sharing. As a rule, the institution's share of the costs should be at least one-half of the entire cost. A matching grant may be awarded as a supplement to an outright grant or as the sole form of commission support. When a matching grant is offered, the grantee is authorized to raise gifts up to a level approved by the NHPRC and have that amount matched by the commission. For example, a $50,000 matching offer means that a grantee must raise $25,000 in nonfederal funds to secure the maximum match. Gifts cannot be submitted from an applicant's immediate family or academic institution nor from another federal agency. Matching funds are not to be confused with the cost-sharing requirement noted above.

Application Information Application information and guidelines are available upon request.

Deadline(s) The commission usually meets in February, June, and October to consider grant applications. Except for certain types of microfilm proposals that must meet earlier records program deadlines, new publications program proposals should reach the commission offices by November 15, March 15, and July 15 in order to be considered at the next commission meeting.

Additional Information The commission considers applications from university and other nonprofit presses for subvention for printing and manufacturing costs in book publications that have been formally endorsed by the commission. Grants not exceeding $10,000 per volume are recommended in order to reduce the amount of financial losses anticipated by the presses in publishing volumes considered essential to the commission's programs. The granting of a subvention is intended to encourage the highest standards in the production of volumes, particularly the quality of paper and binding materials. Only a limited number of subvention grants are available annually. Applications for subvention should be submitted by the press. The applications should include the press estimate of editorial, design, manufacturing, warehousing, and distribution costs, as well as anticipated sales price and income. The difference between costs and projected income is the amount eligible for subvention support.

398. National Historical Publications and Records Commission
National Archives Building
Washington, DC 20408
(202) 523-5384

Records Program
CFDA Program Number 89.003

Program Description Through its national historical records program, the National Historical Publications and Records Commission encourages a greater effort by private organizations and government to preserve and make available for use those records that further an understanding and appreciation of American history. In the public sector, these historical records document significant activities of state, county, municipal, and other units of government. In the private sector, historical records include manuscripts, personal and family papers, and organizational and corporate archives that are maintained by a variety of repositories, as well as materials in special collections relating to particular fields of study. In addition to supporting projects relating directly to a body of records, the commission also supports projects to advance the state of the art, to promote cooperative efforts among institutions and organizations, and to improve the knowledge, performance, and professional skills of those who work with historical records.

Eligibility/Limitations Nonprofit organizations and institutions, state and local government agencies, and most federal agencies are eligible for grants and allocations.

Fiscal Information The commission makes funds available as outright or matching grants or as grants combing these two types of funding. Applicants may request the funding arrangement best suited to their needs, although occasionally the commission will decide to offer a different mixture of funding. Institutional cost sharing in the form of cash and in-kind contributions is also an important part of each project's funding. The commission suggests that cost sharing equal approximately fifty percent of the total cost of the project, although it prefers to see even greater cost sharing.

Application Information A brochure containing application guidelines and additional information is available from the commission.

Deadline(s) Applications should be received by February 1, June 1, and October 1.

399. National Park Service
Cultural Resources, Department of the Interior
Washington, DC 20240
(202) 343-7625

Historic Preservation Grants-in-Aid

CFDA Program Number 15.904

Program Description These grants are designed to expand and maintain the National Register of Historic Places, the nation's listing of districts, sites, buildings, structures, and objects significant in American history, architecture, archaeology, engineering, and culture at the national, state, and local levels; to provide matching grants-in-aid for the identification, evaluation, and protection of historic properties by such means as survey, planning, technical assistance, acquisition, development, and certain tax incentives available for historic properties; and to provide matching grants-in-aid to the National Trust for Historic Preservation for its Congressionally-chartered responsibilities to preserve historic resources.

Eligibility/Limitations Eligible applicants are the National Trust for Historic Preservation, and states and territories as defined in the National Historic Preservation Act operating programs administered by a State Historic Preservation Officer appointed by the governor or according to state law and which are otherwise in compliance with the requirements of the act. States and the National Trust may hold subgrants with public and private parties, including local governments, federally recognized Indian tribal governments, nonprofit and for-profit organizations, and/or individuals, to accomplish program objectives. State and local governments, public and private organizations, and private owners of properties listed on the National Register of Historic Places can apply for subgrants according to procedures established by the states and the National Trust.

Fiscal Information In fiscal 1986, grant awards ranged in amount (for states) from $44,000 to $544,000 with an average award of $351,000.

Application Information Application is made by the states and National Trust for Historic Preservation for an annual grant in the form of planned activities and projects. OMB Circular No. A-102 applies to awards to states. OMB Circular No. A-110 applies to the National Trust. Contact the program for additional information and application guidelines.

Deadline(s) Deadlines are set dependent upon the date of enactment of appropriations for the fiscal year for which assistance is requested.

400. National Park Service
Department of the Interior, Historic American Buildings Survey/Historic
 American Engineering Record
P.O. Box 37127
Washington, DC 20013
(202) 343-9606

Historic American Buildings Survey/Historic American Engineering Record

CFDA Program Number 15.909

Program Description The objectives of this program are to assemble a national archive
of historic architecture, engineering, and industrial sites, and assist cooperating public
and private organizations in documenting structures of historical and architectural
merit and producing inventories and documentation of historically significant engineering structures, industrial archaeological sites, and National Park Service owned and/or
maintained properties. The program offers specialized services, advisory services and
counseling, and dissemination of technical information to eligible applicants.

Eligibility/Limitations Eligible applicants include state and local governments, private
institutions and organizations, educational institutions, historical and related organizations.

Fiscal Information Estimated project funds available in fiscal year 1988 total $862,000.
Normally, 100 percent of the cost of the project is paid by the cooperator.

Application Information Application procedure is by letter to headquarters office.

Deadline(s) There are no deadlines.

401. National Science Foundation
1800 G Street, NW
Washington, DC 20550
(202) 357-7806

Doctoral Dissertation Research Improvement

Program Description The foundation awards grants to improve the scientific quality of
doctoral dissertation research. Awards are made to allow doctoral candidates opportunities for greater creativity in the gathering and analysis of data than would otherwise
be possible. Dissertation improvement awards are available only in certain disciplines.
These include the social and behavioral sciences and certain of the biological, earth,
atmospheric, and ocean sciences. No dissertation improvement awards are made in the
mathematical and physical sciences, engineering, cellular and molecular biology, or
physiology.

Sample Grants For dissertation research in systematic biology on the phylogeny and
evolution of South American Quaternary Tayassuidae (Mamalia), $5,500 to a student
from the University of Massachusetts, Amherst (1986).

Eligibility/Limitations Doctoral students in appropriate disciplines are eligible to apply.

Fiscal Information Grants generally do not exceed $10,000 and are intended to cover
research related expenses. These include expenses for field equipment and supplies and
for travel to and from research sites. These awards are not fellowships and no stipend
is included. However, the student may concurrently receive support from other
sources.

Application Information Each NSF division that administers grants treats applications
in a different way. Doctoral students who wish to apply for a dissertation improvement grant should write directly to the appropriate research division(s).

402. National Science Foundation
Directorate for Biological, Behavioral, and Social Sciences, Division of
  Behavioral and Neural Sciences
1800 G Street, NW
Washington, DC 20550
(202) 357-7804

Anthropology Program

CFDA Program Number 47.051

Program Description The Division of Behavioral and Neural Sciences is responsible for
the support of research on nervous systems and human and animal behavior. The
division's goals are to advance understanding of the biological, environmental, and
cultural factors that underlie the behavior of humans and animals, with explicit
emphasis on nervous system structure and function. The Anthropology Program
supports research in cultural and social anthropology, archaeology, and physical anthropology. It provides support for scientific research on all topics, techniques, and
geographic areas. Support is also provided for preserving and increasing research
accessibility of systematic anthropological collections, and for archaeometric research
and laboratories.

Eligibility/Limitations The most frequent recipients of support for research are academic institutions and nonprofit research groups. In special circumstances, grants are
also awarded to other types of institutions and to individuals. In these cases, preliminary inquiry should be made to the appropriate program officer before a proposal is
submitted. Support may be provided for projects involving a single scientist or a
number of scientists. Awards are made for projects confined to a single disciplinary
area and for those that cross or merge disciplinary interests.

Fiscal Information Level of support varies from project to project. Grant awards range
from $700 to $1,574,000 with an average award of $61,458. Although most grants are
for much shorter periods, up to five years of support may be requested. Grant funds
may be used for paying direct and indirect costs necessary to conduct research or
studies. Institutions are required to share in the cost of each research project. This may
be accomplished by a contribution to any cost element, direct or indirect.

Application Information Address inquiries to the program director. Guidelines are
contained in the publication *Grants for Scientific and Engineering Research.*

Deadline(s) The target dates for the submission of senior research proposals in archaeology, social/cultural and physical anthropology are July 1 and December 1.
Proposals received by July 1 may receive support as early as January 1, while
December 1 submissions may receive funding as early as June 1. The target date for
archaeometry is October 31 and for Systematic Anthropological Collections proposals
is January 1. Proposals for doctoral dissertation support may be submitted at any time
during the year.

Additional Information The Division of Behavioral and Neural Sciences also provides
funds for doctoral dissertation research, research conferences, publication costs, acquisition of specialized research equipment and materials, construction of specialized
research facilities, and special projects such as data banks and preservation of anthropological collections. Special funds are also available for small college personnel
whose research is related to ongoing NSF-supported projects.

403. National Science Foundation
Directorate for Biological, Behavioral, and Social Sciences, Division of Biotic
  Systems and Resources
1800 G Street, NW
Washington, DC 20550
(202) 357-9734

Biological Research Resources

CFDA Program Number 47.051

Program Description The Biological Research Resources program provides operational and refurbishment support for biological research resources—including living organism stock centers, biological field research facilities, and systematic research collections—to enhance the use of these resources by U.S. scientists.

Sample Grants Foreign travel and activity support of a study of the biogeography and evolution of the lomas formations of Peru and Chile, $46,703 to the Field Museum of Natural History (1986). Foreign travel and activity support of the administration, maintenance and development of La Selva Biological Station, Puerto Viejo de Sarapiqui, Costa Rica, $255,000 to Duke University (1986).

Eligibility/Limitations The most frequent recipients of support for research are academic institutions and nonprofit research groups. In special circumstances, grants are also awarded to other types of institutions and to individuals. In these cases, preliminary inquiry should be made to the appropriate program officer before a proposal is submitted. Support may be provided for projects involving a single scientist or a number of scientists. Awards are made for projects confined to a single disciplinary area and for those that cross or merge disciplinary interests.

Fiscal Information Level of support varies from project to project. Although most grants are for much shorter periods, up to five years of support may be requested. Grant funds may be used for paying direct and indirect costs necessary to conduct research or studies. Institutions are required to share in the cost of each research project. This may be accomplished by a contribution to any cost element, direct or indirect.

Application Information Address inquiries to the program director. Guidelines are contained in the publication *Grants for Scientific and Engineering Research.*

Deadline(s) Deadlines and target dates for receipt of proposals are published in the NSF *Bulletin.*

404. National Science Foundation

Directorate for Biological, Behavioral, and Social Sciences, Division of Biotic
 Systems and Resources
1800 G Street, NW
Washington, DC 20550
(202) 357-9588

Systematic Biology Program

CFDA Program Number 47.051

Program Description The Systematic Biology Program supports comparative and experimental research on the characterization, affinities, adaptations, and evolutionary histories of all groups of organisms. Emphasis is on description and analysis of biotic diversity using modern methods of comparative morphology/physiology, biochemical and numerical systematics, experimental hybridization, biogeography, floristics, and faunistics; elements of paleobiology, except studies that deal with humans or that are primarily ecological or stratigraphic, are also pertinent. Practical and theoretical aspects of classification at all taxonomic levels are included in the scope of the program.

Sample Grants For support of "Projecto Flora Amazonica—Phase IV," $164,132 to the New York Botanical Garden (1986). Foreign travel and activity support of systematic investigations on Philodendron Sect. Pteromischum (Araceae), $54,583 to Missouri Botanical Garden (1986).

Eligibility/Limitations The most frequent recipients of support for research are academic institutions and nonprofit research groups. In special circumstances, grants are also awarded to other types of institutions and to individuals. In these cases, preliminary inquiry should be made to the appropriate program officer before a proposal is submitted. Support may be provided for projects involving a single scientist or a number of scientists. Awards are made for projects confined to a single disciplinary area and for those that cross or merge disciplinary interests.

Fiscal Information Level of support varies from project to project. Although most grants are for much shorter periods, up to five years of support may be requested. Grant funds may be used for paying direct and indirect costs necessary to conduct research or studies. Institutions are required to share in the cost of each research project. This may be accomplished by a contribution to any cost element, direct or indirect.

Application Information Address inquiries to the program director. Guidelines are contained in the publication *Grants for Scientific and Engineering Research.*

Deadline(s) Deadlines and target dates for receipt of proposals are published in the NSF *Bulletin.*

Additional Information Proposals for specialized research equipment, doctoral dissertation support, and research conferences and workshops will also be considered.

405. National Science Foundation

Directorate for Science and Engineering Education, Division of Materials
  Development, Research and Informal Science Education
1800 G Street, NW
Washington, DC 20550
(202) 357-7075

Informal Science Education

Program Description This program provides support for projects that strengthen and enhance the scientific and technical understanding of the public outside the formal education environment—both young people and adults, and such target groups as women, minorities, and the physically disabled. The program seeks to encourage a rich environment for recreational learning, where both children and adults can acquire a substantial measure of science literacy and awareness while satisfying a natural curiosity. Appropriate activities include, but are not limited to: science programs broadcast by television or radio which reach large and varied audiences; museum exhibitions, both permanent and traveling, that provide direct involvement and "hands on" experience with science and technology; recreational learning activities that encourage interaction with the resources and staff of museums, science/technology centers, nature centers, zoos, aquariums and planetariums; and innovative science programs and projects by organizations and clubs, which reach significant target audiences and provide recreational opportunities to learn about science and technology.

Sample Grants To support the development and replication of science exhibits to circulate to a group of eight science centers, $423,900 to Impressions 5 Museum, Lansing, MI (1987). To build an 11,000 square foot permanent exhibit using the American tropical rain forest as the core teaching and learning experience, $163,750 to Milwaukee Public Museum (1987). To support a survey of science museums, $58,297 to Association of Science-Technology Centers, Washington, DC (1987).

Eligibility/Limitations Organizations with a scientific or educational mission are eligible to submit proposals. Among these are: colleges and universities; state and local education agencies; publishers; professional societies; science museums and zoological parks; research laboratories; media associations, whether print or electronic; private foundations; private industries; and other public and private organizations, whether for profit or nonprofit. Proposers are strongly encouraged to involve participation from more than one of these areas. Proposals may relate to any field of science in which NSF supports research.

Application Information The division employs a two-stage proposal process. First, a preliminary proposal is required. After it has been reviewed by the foundation staff and a response has been received, a formal proposal may be submitted. The written preliminary proposal should sketch, in broad strokes, the essential features of the project, its purpose and design, the evaluation plan (if appropriate), the plan or potential for achieving widespread impact, the key personnel and their duties, and a rough estimate of cost and duration. Preliminary proposals may not exceed six pages (single-spaced) in length. Preliminary proposals should be addressed to the program.

Deadline(s) Target dates for receipt of applications are April 1, August 1, and December 1.

406. National Trust for Historic Preservation
Office of Financial Service
1785 Massachusetts, NW
Washington, DC 20036
(202) 673-4000

Preservation Services Fund

Program Description Grants are intended to increase the flow of information and ideas in the field of preservation. They help stimulate public discussion, enable local groups to gain technical expertise needed for particular projects, introduce students to preservation concepts and crafts and encourage participation by the private sector in preservation. Activities eligible for Preservation Services Fund grants include: hiring consultants to undertake preservation planning or design projects; obtaining professional advice to strengthen management capabilities; sponsoring preservation conferences; designing and implementing innovative preservation education programs targeted to a specific audience; and undertaking other planning activities that will lead to implementation of a specific preservation project.

Eligibility/Limitations PSF grants most often are used to enable nonprofit organizations or public agencies to obtain professional advice for specific preservation projects. To be considered for a grant award, applicants must be members of the National Trust at the organizational level or above.

Fiscal Information Maximum grant awards are $5,000, but because of strong competition and limited resources, most will be $1,000 to $1,500. All grants must be matched on at least a dollar-for-dollar basis, primarily using cash contributions.

Application Information Grant applications and National Trust membership information are available from regional offices of the National Trust. Applications should be mailed to the appropriate National Trust regional office.

Deadline(s) There are three funding rounds each year. Applications must be postmarked by February 1, June 1, or October 1.

407. The New York Community Trust
415 Madison Avenue
New York, NY 10017
(212) 758-0100

Grants

Program Description As the trust is a community foundation for the greater New York City area, the distribution committee gives priority to grant proposals which deal with the problems of this metropolitan region. Giving categories include: arts and culture; arts in education; education; environment; film; and neighborhood revitalization.

Sample Grants To help meet an increasing operating budget, to expand its gift shop and explore the idea of selling reproductions of pieces in the collection, $30,000 to The Jewish Museum, New York (1985). To help preserve its important collections and make them available for research and exhibition, $55,000 to the Central Research Library of The New York Public Library (1985).

Eligibility/Limitations No grants are made to individuals. The trust rarely makes grants for endowments, building campaigns, deficit financing, films, general operating support, or religious purposes. Grants are concentrated in the New York City area.

Fiscal Information Grants awarded in 1986 totaled over $42 million.

Application Information Specific grantmaking guidelines are available for each category of funding. Contact the trust in writing for these guidelines and additional information.

Deadline(s) No deadlines are announced.

408. The New York Times Company Foundation, Inc.
229 West 43rd Street
New York, NY 10036
(212) 556-1091

Grants

Program Description The major areas in which the foundation entertains applications for grants are education, journalism, cultural affairs, community services, and environmental concerns. Although urban affairs rank high among the foundation's interests, grants are not usually made on the neighborhood level. Some national and international activities receive contributions, but the majority of grants are concentrated in the greater New York area and in localities served by affiliates of The New York Times Company.

Sample Grants Toward support of its Gallery of Arms and Armors, $200,000 (first installment of a total pledge of $500,000) to the Metropolitan Museum of Art, New York (1986). For the education program, $25,000 to the New York Zoological Society, New York (1986). In support of Frick Museum concerts, $10,000 to WYNC Foundation, New York (1986).

Eligibility/Limitations No grants are made to individuals, to sectarian religious institutions, or for health related purposes.

Fiscal Information In 1986, the foundation made grants totaling over $4.3 million. Cultural affairs, including museums and libraries and performing arts, constituted the largest category of grants, a total of over $1.5 million.

Application Information Appeals for grants should be addressed to the president of the foundation. In order not to tax grant seekers' resources unnecessarily, the foundation discourages investment of excessive time and money in the preparation of requests and proposals. A letter describing the purpose for which funds are requested and providing information concerning the funds involved in the specific venture, including details of other potential sources of support, is sufficient. Submission of a copy of a determination by the IRS that the applicant enjoys tax-exempt status under the Internal Revenue Code is required.

Deadline(s) The board meets at least twice annually, within the first and third quarter of each calendar year, to review the president's recommendations and authorize grants to be disbursed. In extraordinary circumstances, decisions may be made outside that schedule.

409. New York Zoological Society
Wildlife Conservation International
Bronx, NY 10460
(212) 220-5090

Grants

Program Description Grants support specific conservation concerns for a particular species or assemblage of species, or more broadly conceived topics in conservation biology.

Eligibility/Limitations Any individual affiliated with an institution, or an institution itself is eligible to apply. WCI does not usually support conferences, airfares to scientific meetings, legal actions, erection of permanent field stations, salaries at institutions, or overhead costs. Expensive laboratory analyses are also outside grant guidelines.

Fiscal Information Grants in the recent past have ranged from $150 to over $100,000 (for a two-year project). Grants average under $20,000, and the median grant is $5,000.

Application Information Applicants are strongly urged to send a brief letter of inquiry before making formal application. Applicants should not submit identical proposals to other organizations simultaneously; in such cases WCI usually awaits the outcome of others' deliberations, thus delaying consideration of the proposal.

Deadline(s) The WCI Conservation Committee meets twice a year and the closing dates for applications are January 1 and July 1.

410. The Newberry Library
60 West Walton Street
Chicago, IL 60610
(312) 943-9090

American Society for Eighteenth-Century Studies Fellowships

Program Description The Newberry Library, founded in 1887, is a privately endowed independent research library located on the near north side of Chicago. Comprising more than one million volumes and five million manuscripts, it has a strong general collection embracing history and the humanities within Western civilization from the late Middle Ages to the early twentieth century. Bibliographic holdings are extensive, and certain special collections are internationally noted. ASECS/Newberry Library Fellowships are available for one to three months in residence at the Newberry for studies in the period 1660-1815.

Eligibility/Limitations Applicants must be postdoctoral scholars no more than ten years from receipt of their Ph.D., and members in good standing of the American Society for Eighteenth Century Studies at the time of application.

Fiscal Information Stipends are $750 per month.

Application Information For additional information and application forms, write to the Committee on Awards, The Newberry Library.

Deadline(s) Completed applications are due by March 1 or October 15.

411. The Newberry Library
60 West Walton Street
Chicago, IL 60610
(312) 943-9090

Columbian Quincentennial Fellowships

Program Description The Newberry Library, founded in 1887, is a privately endowed independent research library located on the near north side of Chicago. Comprising more than one million volumes and five million manuscripts, it has a strong general collection embracing history and the humanities within Western civilization from the late Middle Ages to the early twentieth century. Bibliographic holdings are extensive, and certain special collections are internationally noted. Columbian Quincentennial Fellowships are offered for work in residence on topics related to the transatlantic exchange of ideas, products, and peoples in the period 1450-1650. Projects must be synthetic or interdisciplinary in approach, or represent new fields of study for the applicant, or aim at the creation of new classroom materials, teaching units, or courses.

Sample Grants Support to an Assistant Professor of Foreign Languages, Arizona State University, for research on the metalinguistic theme in Columbian documents (1986-1987).

Fiscal Information Stipends are $800 per month for periods up to four months.

Application Information For information write the Transatlantic Encounters Program at the Newberry, or call (312) 943-9090, extension 475.

Additional Information The fellowships are offered in conjunction with a program of summer institutes on the *Transatlantic Encounters* theme, but prior participation in an institute is not required for application.

412. The Newberry Library
60 West Walton Street
Chicago, IL 60610
(312) 943-9090

The Hermon Dunlap Smith Center for the History of Cartography Fellowships

Program Description The Newberry Library, founded in 1887, is a privately endowed independent research library located on the near north side of Chicago. Comprising more than one million volumes and five million manuscripts, it has a strong general collection embracing history and the humanities within Western civilization from the late Middle Ages to the early twentieth century. Bibliographic holdings are extensive, and certain special collections are internationally noted. These fellowships support short-term or long-term research in the history of cartography.

Eligibility/Limitations Applicants for long-term fellowships must be established scholars.

Fiscal Information Short-term fellowships carry a stipend of $750 per month for periods not exceeding three months. Long-term fellowships are available for six to twelve months' research in residence (maximum stipend $27,500).

Application Information For additional information and application forms, write to the Committee on Awards, The Newberry Library.

Deadline(s) Applications for long-term fellowships will be considered once a year, with a deadline of March 1. Applications for short-term fellowships will be considered twice a year, with deadlines of March 1 and October 15.

413. The Newberry Library
60 West Walton Street
Chicago, IL 60610
(312) 943-9090

Joint Fellowships with the American Antiquarian Society

Program Description The Newberry Library, founded in 1887, is a privately endowed independent research library located on the near north side of Chicago. Comprising more than one million volumes and five million manuscripts, it has a strong general collection embracing history and the humanities within Western civilization from the late Middle Ages to the early twentieth century. Bibliographic holdings are extensive, and certain special collections are internationally noted. Scholars who desire to use collections both at the Newberry and the American Antiquarian Society may apply for a joint fellowship via a single application.

Eligibility/Limitations Applicants must have the Ph.D. or have completed all requirements except the dissertation.

Fiscal Information Awards are available for up to two months at the Newberry, and from one to three months at the American Antiquarian Society. Stipends at the Newberry are $750 per month.

Application Information For additional information and application forms, write the Committee on Awards, The Newberry Library.

Deadline(s) Completed applications are due by January 31 or October 15.

Additional Information Decisions will be made independently at each institution.

414. The Newberry Library
60 West Walton Street
Chicago, IL 60610
(312) 943-9090

Monticello College Foundation Fellowship for Women

Program Description The Newberry Library, founded in 1887, is a privately endowed independent research library located on the near north side of Chicago. Comprising more than one million volumes and five million manuscripts, it has a strong general collection embracing history and the humanities within Western civilization from the late Middle Ages to the early twentieth century. Bibliographic holdings are extensive, and certain special collections are internationally noted. The Monticello College Foundation Fellowship is designed primarily for women at an early stage in their professional careers whose work gives clear promise of scholarly productivity and whose career would be significantly enhanced by six months of research and writing. Preference will be given to applicants whose scholarship is particularly concerned with the study of women, but study may be proposed in any field appropriate to the Newberry's collections.

Eligibility/Limitations Applicants must have the Ph.D. at the time of application, and must be U.S. citizens or permanent residents.

Fiscal Information The six-month fellowship for work in residence at the Newberry carries a stipend of $8,500.

Application Information For additional information and application forms, write to the Committee on Awards, The Newberry Library.

Deadline(s) Completed applications are due by January 15.

415. The Newberry Library
60 West Walton Street
Chicago, IL 60610
(312) 943-9090

National Endowment for the Humanities Fellowships

Program Description The Newberry Library, founded in 1887, is a privately endowed independent research library located on the near north side of Chicago. Comprising more than one million volumes and five million manuscripts, it has a strong general collection embracing history and the humanities within Western civilization from the late Middle Ages to the early twentieth century. Bibliographic holdings are extensive, and certain special collections are internationally noted. NEH/Newberry Fellowships are designed not only to encourage the individual scholar's research, but also to deepen and enrich the opportunities for serious intellectual exchange through the active participation of fellows in the Newberry community. Fellowships are available for research in residence in any field appropriate to the Newberry's collections.

Eligibility/Limitations These grants are for established scholars at the postdoctoral level or its equivalent. Awards are open to United States citizens or nationals, and to foreign nationals who have been living in the United States for at least three years. Preference is given to applicants who have not held major fellowships or grants for three years preceding the proposed period of residency.

Fiscal Information Fellowships are available for six to eleven months' research and provide a maximum of $27,500 for eleven months' residency.

Application Information For additional information and application forms, write to the Committee on Awards, The Newberry Library.

Deadline(s) Completed applications are due by January 15.

416. The Newberry Library
60 West Walton Street
Chicago, IL 60610
(312) 943-9090

Resident Fellowships for Unaffiliated Scholars

Program Description The Newberry Library, founded in 1887, is a privately endowed independent research library located on the near north side of Chicago. Comprising more than one million volumes and five million manuscripts, it has a strong general collection embracing history and the humanities within Western civilization from the late Middle Ages to the early twentieth century. Bibliographic holdings are extensive, and certain special collections are internationally noted. These fellowships support unaffiliated scholars working on a specific research project in a field appropriate to the Newberry's collections.

Eligibility/Limitations Applicants must have held the Ph.D. at least two years and not be employed professionally as scholars. Applicants must anticipate spending at least six to eight hours a week in residence and participating fully in the intellectual life of the Newberry.

Fiscal Information The fellowships carry stipends of $250 per calendar quarter. Stipends may be renewed quarterly up to one year; after the first year fellowship status may be renewed annually, but without stipend.

Application Information For additional information and application forms, write to the Committee on Awards, The Newberry Library.

Deadline(s) Completed applications are due March 1 or October 15.

417. The Newberry Library

60 West Walton Street
Chicago, IL 60610
(312) 943-9090

Short-Term Resident Fellowships for Individual Scholars

Program Description The Newberry Library, founded in 1887, is a privately endowed independent research library located on the near north side of Chicago. Comprising more than one million volumes and five million manuscripts, it has a strong general collection embracing history and the humanities within Western civilization from the late Middle Ages to the early twentieth century. Bibliographic holdings are extensive, and certain special collections are internationally noted. Short-term fellowships are designed primarily to help provide access to Newberry resources for people who live beyond commuting distance. Preference is given accordingly to applicants from outside the greater Chicago area.

Eligibility/Limitations Applicants must have the Ph.D. or have completed all requirements except the dissertation.

Fiscal Information Fellowships carry stipends of $750 per month, for periods of up to two months, or when travel from a foreign country is involved, three months.

Application Information For additional information and application forms, write to the Committee on Awards, The Newberry Library.

Deadline(s) Completed applications are due by March 1 or October 15.

418. Edward John Noble Foundation

32 East 57th Street
New York, NY 10022
(212) 759-4212

Grants

Program Description The foundation's principal interests lie in the arts, education, conservation, and health. In arts, the foundation's priorities are to assist major cultural organizations in New York City and their educational programs; in conservation, priorities are to support the several conservation projects on St. Catherine's Island and selected other programs which help preserve the natural environment. Consideration in conservation is generally limited to organizations in the eastern states.

Sample Grants For development of the Classical Music Collection, including publication of a catalogue, $58,350 to The Museum of Broadcasting, New York (1985-1986). For the creation of a group reception and orientation area and an Education Center in the new museum building, $750,000 to The Museum of Modern Art, New York (1985-1986). For ethnobotanical research in the Amazonian rain forest, $56,000 to The New York Botanical Garden, Bronx, NY (1985-1986).

Eligibility/Limitations Applicants should note that the foundation generally does not consider support for buildings or equipment, publications, performances, films or television projects, and it does not make grants to individuals. Applicant organizations must be tax-exempt.

Fiscal Information Grants authorized for payment in 1987-1989 total over $3.5 million, including over $2 million in the arts category and over $1 million for conservation projects.

Application Information Applications should be initiated by letter, describing the project for which support is requested. Included or attached should be: a brief description of the nature and purpose of the organization; a concise statement of the need for and objectives of the project, the methods by which it will be carried out, and its anticipated duration; the qualifications of the key personnel involved; a program budget; a list of other sources of support assured and being sought; a copy of the organization's most recent 501(c)(3) tax-exemption certification from the IRS; a copy of the organization's most recent annual audit or financial statement. If the foundation is able to give further consideration to a proposal, additional information will be requested as needed.

Deadline(s) No deadlines are announced.

419. Norfolk Southern Foundation

P.O. Box 3040
Norfolk, VA 23514-3040
(804) 629-2650

Grants

Program Description The foundation exists solely to make charitable donations as the philanthropic arm of Norfolk Southern Corporation. The foundation has no formal guidelines or descriptive materials. Foundation giving essentially is divided into three categories: health and human services; colleges and universities; and cultural and artistic organizations in the areas the foundation serves.

Eligibility/Limitations The foundation considers only those organizations qualified as tax-exempt by the Internal Revenue Service Code 501(c)(3).

Application Information Requests generally outline the purpose and objectives of the organization, sources of funding, intended use of the funds requested, along with an explanation of why Norfolk Southern was approached. Generally, a copy of the IRS determination letter is required.

Deadline(s) No deadlines are announced.

420. Northwestern Bell Foundation

1314 Douglas On-The-Mall, Fifth Floor
Omaha, NE 68102
(402) 422-4242

Grants

Program Description Four categories continue to characterize foundation giving: health and human services; cultural; education; and civic and community.

Eligibility/Limitations The foundation will contribute only to organizations which provide written proof of their tax-exempt status. Foundation giving is limited to organizations headquartered or operating primarily within the territory served by Northwestern Bell Telephone Company. This includes large portions of the states of Iowa, Minnesota, Nebraska, North Dakota, and South Dakota. The foundation excludes certain organizations and types of giving from support, including: political campaigns; sectarian religious causes; activities which primarily benefit an individual or a very narrow segment of the company's overall stakeholder groups; tax-supported organizations; contributions to schools below the college level; labor or labor-sponsored organizations; endowment portions of any fund-raising campaigns; goodwill advertising.

Fiscal Information In 1986, the foundation contributed more than $2.2 million in grants.

Application Information The foundation's board of directors and staff seek the recommendation of the company's local management team regarding proposed contributions. Applications for grants may be directed to Northwestern Bell managers or to the company's state headquarters locations in Des Moines, Iowa; Minneapolis, Minnesota; Omaha, Nebraska; Fargo, North Dakota; and Sioux Falls, South Dakota.

Deadline(s) No deadlines are announced.

421. Norton Company
Social Investments
1 New Bond Street
Worcester, MA 01606
(617) 795-5000

Contributions

Program Description The goal of the Norton Company contributions program is to support organizations, institutions, and programs which significantly contribute to the improved quality of life in communities where company employees reside and enhance Norton's business. Support is directed in four areas: civic and community activities; culture and the arts; health and welfare; and education. Within the culture and the arts category, support is available for special projects for the visual and performing arts, libraries, museums, cultural centers, councils, and the like which specifically address at least one of the criteria of giving; for basic operating support to cultural institutions which have traditionally had a major impact on the cultural life of the community; for arts education projects, especially in collaboration with schools; and for selected public radio and television stations.

Eligibility/Limitations Support is ordinarily restricted to institutions, organizations and programs located in communities where Norton has plant facilities. Ordinarily, Norton will not contribute: to organizations which are not tax-exempt and covered by the IRS code Section 501(c)(3); for fund-raising dinners or courtesy or journal advertising; to individuals; for capital/endowment drives (exceptions are made for selected institutions which make extraordinary contributions to Norton communities and/or Norton Company); to support a project or organization for which Norton is the only donor.

Fiscal Information 1986 contributions totaled over $1.2 million.

Application Information An application for a contribution should include: a brief description of the organization or project; evidence of the organization's tax-exempt status; a brief description of the budget and plan for funding; identification of the need to be met; and a list of the board of directors. From this information, Norton determines if the organization or project falls within funding guidelines. If necessary, Norton will contact the applicant for further information. Requests for contributions within communities where Norton has a plant, except Worcester, MA, should go to the plant manager. Worcester requests and all others should be sent to the company at the address listed above.

Deadline(s) No deadlines are announced.

Additional Information Requests for contributions other than cash such as products and services of Norton Company should be directed to the Manager of Social Investments.

422. Norwest Foundation
1200 Peavey Building
Minneapolis, MN 55479
(612) 372-8847

Contributions

Program Description Norwest's giving program reflects a balance among education, social service, civic, and cultural activities; the foundation recognizes that the proper balance will vary among the many communities it serves.

Eligibility/Limitations Grants are restricted to nonprofit, tax-exempt organizations under section 501(c)(3) of the Internal Revenue Code. Grants are generally restricted to programs having a direct impact on Norwest's primary trade areas.

Fiscal Information Contributions in 1986 totaled over $3.8 million.

Application Information Proposals should be in the form of a letter with accompanying documentation that includes the following: a brief description of the organization, its history and purpose; a summary letter describing the request or project, its purpose, and how it will be accomplished; a complete budget for the requestor project; a list of officers and board of directors; a donor list showing individual, corporate, and foundation support during the past year, and planned contribution support for the future; an audited financial statement, if available, for the organization's previous fiscal year; and letter of tax-exempt status. Organizations serving a specific neighborhood or city should apply directly to the nearest Norwest affiliate in that area; organizations or programs serving the entire seven-county Minneapolis-St. Paul metro area should apply to the Norwest Foundation—Metro at the above address; organizations serving the state of Minnesota, the Upper Midwest region, or that are national in scope—and do not have local chapters—should submit proposals to the foundation at the above address.

Deadline(s) No deadlines are announced.

423. Pacific Northwest Bell Telephone Company

1600 Bell Plaza, Room 3203
Seattle, WA 98191
(206) 345-5500

Contributions

Program Description One of the ways in which Pacific Northwest Bell demonstrates a sense of responsibility to the communities it serves is through financial and other material support for charitable, educational, and general welfare purposes in these communities. The company is particularly interested in support for broad based, action oriented programs which fall within the scope of stated priorities: educational, social and economic, health and welfare, and cultural. Within the cultural category, the company recognizes that vital institutions in the arts and cultural affairs add significantly to the quality of American life. In providing support for arts and culture, decisions will be made in such a way as to distinguish carefully among those forms of support that serve the company's promotional objectives and those that are clearly contributions. In this latter category, the company supports: arts organizations which promise to enlarge the audience for cultural presentations; arts service organizations that provide distinct and identifiable services to more than one type of arts organization; umbrella organizations that reduce overall administrative costs to solicit and provide funds to a number of arts organizations; significant local arts organizations that serve the communities in which the company has a major presence.

Eligibility/Limitations The company's emphasis on funding is primarily on local and regional matters in those states the company serves: Washington, Oregon, and part of Idaho. The company will consider requests for capital fund drives as well as operating and program funds. Contributions, as a general rule, will not be made to individuals or in support of the following: organizations that the IRS rulings would render ineligible for tax-deductible contributions; organizations which discriminate; special occasion goodwill advertising; foundations that are themselves strictly grant making bodies; trips or tours; endowment funds.

Fiscal Information Contributions in 1987 totaled over $5 million.

Application Information For more information or to submit a grant request, call: in Oregon, (503) 242-6594; in Washington and Idaho, (206) 345-4764.

Deadline(s) The corporate contributions committee meets monthly. Organizations seeking support should submit applications as early as possible, especially when a major contribution involving an annual budget is involved. The company operates on a calendar fiscal year.

424. Pacific Telesis Foundation

Pacific Telesis Center
130 Kearny Street, Room 3351
San Francisco, CA 94108
(415) 882-8000

Grants

Program Description Contributions are made in the areas of education, human services, community and civic programs, and arts and culture. Within the arts and culture category, the foundation recognizes that vital cultural institutions add significantly to the quality of people's lives, and makes grants to performing and visual arts programs and organizations. Priority is given to programs that: reach out to special audiences which do not ordinarily have easy access to the arts; have demonstrated artistic and managerial excellence; promote the unique artistic traditions and expressions of different cultures (e.g., Hispanics, Blacks, Asians); offer statewide, national, or international exposure; and directly support arts institutions rather than service agencies or umbrella groups.

Sample Grants To support Campaign II, aimed at raising $35 million to create an endowment and to purchase a permanent contemporary collection, $50,000 (two-year pledge of $25,000) to Museum of Contemporary Art, Los Angeles, CA (1986-1987). Sole sponsorship of an exhibition of Goya's works at the National Gallery of Art, $50,000 to National Gallery of Art, Washington, DC (1986). To develop a special brochure in conjunction with the Ansel Adams exhibition at the San Diego Museum of Art, $7,500 to San Diego Museum of Art, San Diego, CA (1986). To underwrite the museum's school and free return admission programs for one year, $25,000 to San Francisco Museum of Modern Art, San Francisco, CA (1986).

Eligibility/Limitations It is the policy of the foundation not to make grants: to organizations that do not have current 501(c)(3) tax-exempt status; to private foundations; to "flow-through" organizations; for endowment funds; to individuals; for general operating purposes; to organizations that practice discrimination; for emergencies; for special occasion goodwill advertising; or in the form of products and services.

Fiscal Information Grants awarded in 1986 totaled over $5.1 million, including $793,180 in the cultural category.

Application Information Requests should include: a description of the organization's purpose and scope, as well as its short-term and long-range objectives; evidence of how the request fits foundation guidelines; standards by which the success of the program will be evaluated; the current total budget of the organization; a budget for the specific project for which support is requested; current IRS documentation of tax-exempt status; a copy of most recent audited financial statement and the most recent federal tax return; a list of members of the board of directors, including their business, governmental, or educational affiliations; a list of current corporate and foundation funders and funding levels; evidence of strategies to develop earned income and to avoid over-dependence on any single source of contributed income.

Deadline(s) There is no specific deadline for submission of grant requests. However, because of the high volume of grant requests considered by the foundation, grant seekers should allow six to eight weeks for a decision.

Additional Information In addition to the Pacific Telesis Foundation, two of Pacific Telesis Group's subsidiaries, Pacific Bell and Nevada Bell, manage their own separate local contributions programs under the direction of community relations organizations throughout California and Nevada. Inquiries about these giving programs should be directed to area managers.

425. The David and Lucile Packard Foundation
330 Second Street, Suite 200
Los Altos, CA 94022
(415) 948-7658

Ancient Studies and Archaeology Program

Program Description The foundation has provided long-term support for the creation of computer databases of literature and other texts, primarily ancient Greek. Smaller foundation grants support similar projects in other languages, not all of them ancient; for example, cuneiform texts from the ancient Near East, the ancient Greek text of the Bible, classical Latin, commentaries on Dante's *Divine Comedy*, and modern French texts.

Eligibility/Limitations Applications for grants are accepted only from qualified tax-exempt charitable organizations. Applications cannot be accepted for the benefit of individuals or religious purposes.

Fiscal Information In 1986, the foundation awarded $460,401 to projects in ancient studies and $80,000 to projects in archaeology.

Application Information Foundation staff is willing, whenever possible, to offer assistance through advice and contacts, in addition to the review of proposals. Additional information and application guidelines are available on request.

Deadline(s) Although proposals shall be accepted throughout the year, applicants wishing to be considered at quarterly board meetings should forward their proposals by the following deadlines: January 1 for the March meeting; April 1 for the June meeting; July 1 for the September meeting; and October 1 for the December meeting.

426. The David and Lucile Packard Foundation
330 Second Street, Suite 200
Los Altos, CA 94022
(415) 948-7658

Conservation Program

Program Description The conservation program reflects the foundation's local, national and international interests in the major areas of land use planning, the purchase of open space, wildlife and wildlife habitat preservation, and a small program concerning water conservation on agricultural land.

Sample Grants To help pay travel costs for speakers at the Second International Conference on the Monarch Butterfly, $6,000 to Natural History Museum of Los Angeles County, Los Angeles, CA (1986). For water management and an irrigation project, $10,000 to Pacific Tropical Botanical Garden, Lawai, Kauai, Hawaii (1986).

Eligibility/Limitations Applications for grants are accepted only from qualified tax-exempt charitable organizations. Applications cannot be accepted for the benefit of individuals or religious purposes.

Fiscal Information In 1986, the foundation authorized grants totaling $801,612 in this program area.

Application Information Foundation staff is willing, whenever possible, to offer assistance through advice and contacts, in addition to the review of proposals. Additional information and application guidelines are available on request.

Deadline(s) Although proposals shall be accepted throughout the year, applicants wishing to be considered at quarterly board meetings should forward their proposals by the following deadlines: January 1 for the March meeting; April 1 for the June meeting; July 1 for the September meeting; and October 1 for the December meeting.

427. The David and Lucile Packard Foundation
330 Second Street, Suite 200
Los Altos, CA 94022
(415) 948-7658

Film Preservation Program

Program Description The preservation of American films of the first half of this century, both newsreels and feature films, continues to be of interest to the foundation. The foundation is currently providing funding for the UCLA film archives to preserve Hearst Metrotone Newsreels from 1919 to 1955, including major material never shown in theaters, and to preserve the very best picture and sound quality of certain classic films of the "Golden Age" of American cinema. A related goal is to make it possible for theaters to show high quality prints of these films and to publish a complete list and description of films made from 1900 to 1960.

Eligibility/Limitations Applications for grants are accepted only from qualified tax-exempt charitable organizations. Applications cannot be accepted for the benefit of individuals or religious purposes.

Fiscal Information In 1986, the foundation awarded $263,131 to projects in this category of funding.

Application Information Foundation staff is willing, whenever possible, to offer assistance through advice and contacts, in addition to the review of proposals. Additional information and application guidelines are available on request.

Deadline(s) Although proposals shall be accepted throughout the year, applicants wishing to be considered at quarterly board meetings should forward their proposals by the following deadlines: January 1 for the March meeting; April 1 for the June meeting; July 1 for the September meeting; and October 1 for the December meeting.

428. The Parker Foundation
1200 Prospect Street, Suite 575
La Jolla, CA 92037
(619) 456-3038

Grants

Program Description Grants support organizations and programs in adult and youth services, visual and performing arts, museums and zoos, education, and community activities.

Sample Grants For assistance with the acquisition of an Apollo space vehicle, $4,000 to San Diego Aerospace Museum, San Diego, CA (1987).

Eligibility/Limitations The foundation is limited to the funding of grants to organizations organized exclusively for charitable purposes and operating in San Diego County, CA. Grants are not made to individuals.

Fiscal Information Grants paid in 1987 totaled $607,609.

Application Information The foundation has no formal grant request format, but a request for grant support must: specify the dollar amount of the grant requested; include tax-exempt verification; describe the specific use proposed for the requested funds; provide a detailed budget for the organization and the specific project; contain, in addition to the original, six copies of the grant request. The foundation considers initial grant applications in written form only.

Deadline(s) Since the board of directors of the foundation meets frequently throughout the year, no deadlines for grant requests are needed.

429. William Penn Foundation
1630 Locust Street
Philadelphia, PA 19103-6305
(215) 732-5114

Grants

Program Description The foundation awards grants in the following categories: culture; environment; human development; community fabric; national and policy grants; international peace and international development. Within the culture program, the foundation acknowledges that the life and vitality of a community are enhanced by its cultural quality and diversity, and the lives of individuals at all economic levels are enriched when they have ready access to the arts. The foundation will continue nurturing, making more accessible, and protecting the Philadelphia region's cultural assets by seeking to support projects which promote high quality in performances and exhibits, increase access to the arts, and promote conservation of cultural artifacts. In its environmental grants, the foundation retains a strong interest in the urban environment and will support work on issues of urban growth and development within the six counties of the Philadelphia metropolitan area, as well as on issues that pertain to the larger region. Grants will continue to be made for projects which promote urban open space, parks, and sound planning.

Sample Grants For the "Sensorium" exhibit at the Elmwood Park Zoo, $25,000 to Norristown Zoological Society, Norristown, PA (1986). For a three-year grant to help implement the institutional self-study in the areas of management and development of the collection and establishment of a development office, $345,400 to Afro-American Historical and Cultural Museum, Inc., Philadelphia, PA (1986-1987). For a two-year grant to produce a guidebook on museums on behalf of the Museum Council of Philadelphia and the Delaware Valley, $98,850 to Atwater Kent Museum, Philadelphia, PA (1985-1986). For a two-year grant for an assistant curator to register, catalog, and conserve the collection, $48,250 to Please Touch Museum, Philadelphia, PA (1985-1986). For a two-year grant to develop public programing and marketing, $75,000 to Rosenbach Museum and Library, Philadelphia, PA (1985-1986).

Eligibility/Limitations Grants are limited to organizations which are defined as tax-exempt under Section 501(c)(3) of the Internal Revenue Code and which are not private foundations. Foundation grants are almost always limited to organizations in the five southeastern Pennsylvania counties and Camden County, New Jersey. In the case of grants made to protect the environment, the foundation will consider proposals from a geographic area which encompasses a radius of approximately fifty miles from Philadelphia. No grants will be made to institutions which, in policy or practice, unfairly discriminate. The foundation does not fund grants to individuals or for scholarships, fellowships, or travel; grants to organizations wishing to distribute funds at their own discretion; recreational programs; or films.

Fiscal Information Grant payments in 1986 totaled over $19.1 million, including over $3.7 million in the culture category.

Application Information The foundation has no standard application form. Only proposals submitted in writing will be considered. Proposals for grants should include a complete and detailed narrative statement. Brevity is appreciated. A complete application should have the following elements; a one-page summary outline; information about the agency making the request; complete description of the project proposed; a copy of the IRS letter stating tax-exempt status; a list of officers and directors of the organization making application; a copy of the organization's most recent annual program report; and a copy of the most recent financial statement.

Deadline(s) The foundation accepts and reviews written requests for grants throughout the year. There are no formal deadlines.

430. Pennzoil Company
Community Relations and Contributions
Pennzoil Place, P.O. Box 2967
Houston, TX 77252-8200
(713) 546-8535

Corporate Contributions

Program Description Pennzoil Company seeks to be a good corporate citizen and neighbor in the communities where it lives and works. One of the ways the company demonstrates corporate citizenship is through the support of organizations which work to improve the quality of life and the general welfare of employees and the citizens of home communities. The company contributes in the following principal categories: social betterment and welfare; education; health; cultural; civic; and unclassified causes. Within the cultural category, Pennzoil recognizes the value of arts and cultural activities and therefore will contribute to organizations engaged in the performing or visual arts, museums, zoos, libraries, and other cultural endeavors which enjoy broad community support and which benefit a large segment of the population in communities where the company has significant operations.

Eligibility/Limitations To be considered for support, an organization must have a ruling of tax-exemption from the U.S. Treasury Department as an educational, charitable, health, or social betterment organization. Causes to be supported should fulfill a corporate obligation to the communities in which Pennzoil has a presence and benefit a wide segment of the population. Primary consideration is given at the local level to communities in which the company has plants, refineries or offices. Pennzoil will not generally support strictly sectarian or denominational religious activities, individual testimonial dinners, secondary schools, donations which are not tax deductible, charitable advertising, or the donation of products.

Fiscal Information Contributions in 1985 totaled approximately $2 million.

Application Information Requests for support should be sent to the manager of Pennzoil's Community Relations and Contributions department along with a copy of the organization's 501(c)(3) statement from the IRS and an audited financial report.

Deadline(s) Applicants should be advised that Pennzoil's contributions budget is completed in the fall of each year. Organizations making proposals following the completion of the budgeting process are not likely to be considered for funding during the following year.

431. The Pew Charitable Trusts
Three Parkway, Suite 501
Philadelphia, PA 19102-1305
(215) 568-3330

Conservation and Environment Grants

Program Description The Pew Charitable Trusts represent seven individual philanthropic funds established between 1948 and 1979 by the four surviving sons and daughters of Joseph N. Pew, founder of the Sun Oil Company. Reflecting the broad concerns and interests of the founders, the trusts provide support in the areas of conservation and the environment, culture, education, health and human services, public policy, and religion. Conservation and environment grants are made to advance the field of conservation through development of its human and information resources. Support is given for research and training which will help strengthen the field's infrastructure and enhance its capacity to cope with the changing and complex challenges of managing finite resources.

Sample Grants In support of the pilot "sister zoo" technology transfer program with Zoo Aurora, Guatemala, $27,000 to The Dallas Zoological Society, Dallas, TX (1986). For Wildlife Conservation International in support of the local training component of seventeen field research projects in Africa and Asia, $140,000 to New York Zoological Society, New York, NY (1986).

Eligibility/Limitations The trusts make grants to nonprofit organizations that are not classified as private foundations under section 509(a) of the IRS code. Grants are made to individuals only as part of specific programs initiated by the trusts.

Fiscal Information Conservation grants totaled $3.7 million in 1986.

Application Information There are no application forms, and only one copy of a proposal with supporting documents is required. Before submitting a formal proposal, organizations may wish to contact a member of the trusts' staff or submit a brief summary of their project for initial review and discussion. Those who wish to send in full proposals without prior contact may do so, however, they should be sure to include all the information set out in the proposal checklist available from the trusts.

Deadline(s) Requests for funding are reviewed throughout the year. Grants are awarded five times a year in February, April, June, September, and December.

432. The Pew Charitable Trusts
Three Parkway, Suite 501
Philadelphia, PA 19102-1305
(215) 568-3330

Culture Grants

Program Description The Pew Charitable Trusts represent seven individual philanthropic funds established between 1948 and 1979 by the four surviving sons and daughters of Joseph N. Pew, founder of the Sun Oil Company. Reflecting the broad concerns and interests of the founders, the trusts provide support in the areas of conservation and the environment, culture, education, health and human services, public policy, and religion. Culture grants are made primarily in the Philadelphia area to foster cultural activities of the highest quality and an environment that encourages artistic and institutional advancement. Of particular interest are projects designed to heighten awareness and appreciation of Philadelphia's diverse cultural resources. The trusts also support significant cultural and artistic advancement nationally.

Sample Grants In support of the ceramics and glass conservation lab and program, over three years, $130,000 to The Henry Francis duPont Winterthur Museum, Winterthur, DE (1986). Toward the installation of an open study storage center in the American Wing, over two and one-half years, $1.1 million to Metropolitan Museum of Art, New York, NY (1986). Toward the computer cataloging and videodisc mastering of the Rosenfeld Collection of Maritime Photography, over two years, $90,000 to Mystic Seaport Museum, Mystic, CT (1986). In support of educational programs, $180,000 to Philadelphia Museum of Art, Philadelphia, PA (1986).

Eligibility/Limitations The trusts make grants to nonprofit organizations that are not classified as private foundations under section 509(a) of the IRS code. Grants are made to individuals only as part of specific programs initiated by the trusts.

Fiscal Information Culture grants totaled over $22.1 million in 1986.

Application Information There are no application forms, and only one copy of a proposal with supporting documents is required. Before submitting a formal proposal, organizations may wish to contact a member of the trusts' staff or submit a brief summary of their project for initial review and discussion. Those who wish to send in full proposals without prior contact may do so, however, they should be sure to include all the information set out in the proposal checklist available from the trusts.

Deadline(s) Proposals for museums and the visual arts are due by April 1.

433. The Philadelphia Center for Early American Studies
3808 Walnut Street
Philadelphia, PA 19104
(215) 898-9251

Dissertation Fellowships

Program Description The Philadelphia Center for Early American Studies was established by the University of Pennsylvania in order to marshal the vast scholarly and archival resources of Philadelphia's libraries, museums, colleges, and universities in an interdisciplinary research program focused on the history and culture of the American nation to 1850. A consortium of eight Philadelphia area institutions—the University of Pennsylvania, the American Philosophical Society, the Library Company of Philadelphia, Temple University, Bryn Mawr, Swarthmore, and Haverford Colleges—the center has a special mission to increase scholarly and public awareness of the historic heritage of the Delaware Valley. The center expects to appoint one or several dissertation fellows, who are either working on doctoral dissertations dealing with the early history or culture of the Delaware Valley or whose research on other topics is concentrated primarily in Philadelphia area archives.

Eligibility/Limitations Advanced graduate students in relevant disciplines from any university are eligible to apply.

Fiscal Information Each dissertation fellow will receive a stipend of $8,500. Appointment is for a term of nine months, beginning September 1.

Application Information Applicants should send credentials to the center. Credentials should include curriculum vitae, at least two letters of recommendation, a three-to-five page statement of purpose, and a sample of work.

Deadline(s) The application deadline is February 15.

434. The Philadelphia Center for Early American Studies
3808 Walnut Street
Philadelphia, PA 19104
(215) 898-9251

Independent Research Fellowships

Program Description The Philadelphia Center for Early American Studies was established by the University of Pennsylvania in order to marshal the vast scholarly and archival resources of Philadelphia's libraries, museums, colleges, and universities in an interdisciplinary research program focused on the history and culture of the American nation to 1850. A consortium of eight Philadelphia area institutions—the University of Pennsylvania, the American Philosophical Society, the Library Company of Philadelphia, Temple University, Bryn Mawr, Swarthmore, and Haverford Colleges—the center has a special mission to increase scholarly and public awareness of the historic heritage of the Delaware Valley. The center expects to appoint one or several research fellows, either faculty members on leave or independent scholars. Each research fellow will pursue at the center a research project of his or her own design. Preference will be given to projects that analyze significant new problems or explore previously neglected materials.

Eligibility/Limitations Scholars whose research would benefit from residence at the center are eligible to apply.

Fiscal Information The center has attempted to limit its stipends to $10,000, but works with fellowship recipients to obtain additional support either from their home institutions or other granting agencies.

Application Information Applicants should send credentials to the center. Credentials should include curriculum vitae, at least two letters of recommendation, a three-to-five page statement of purpose, and a sample of work.

Deadline(s) The application deadline is February 15.

Additional Information The center is also pleased to announce a fellowship available to either pre- or postdoctoral applicants for the study of the American Revolution. A detailed description of the fellowship appointment is available upon request.

435. The Philadelphia Center for Early American Studies
3808 Walnut Street
Philadelphia, PA 19104
(215) 898-9251

Sponsored Research Fellowships

Program Description The Philadelphia Center for Early American Studies was established by the University of Pennsylvania in order to marshal the vast scholarly and archival resources of Philadelphia's libraries, museums, colleges, and universities in an interdisciplinary research program focused on the history and culture of the American nation to 1850. A consortium of eight Philadelphia area institutions—the University of Pennsylvania, the American Philosophical Society, the Library Company of Philadelphia, Temple University, Bryn Mawr, Swarthmore, and Haverford Colleges—the center has a special mission to increase scholarly and public awareness of the historic heritage of the Delaware Valley. For the next several years, the Philadelphia Center will be awarding postdoctoral fellowships to scholars with special interests and talents relevant to its project on "The Transformation of Philadelphia and the Delaware Valley, 1750-1850." In 1987-1988, the Transformation Project explored the topic of gender and family life in the city and region during this period. The project welcomes applications for fellowships from scholars whose work promises to illuminate the ways in which male-female relations and family structure changed significantly during this one hundred year period.

Eligibility/Limitations Scholars whose areas of specialization or interest would contribute the center's ongoing projects are encouraged to apply.

Application Information Applicants should send credentials to the center. Credentials should include curriculum vitae, at least two letters of recommendation, a three-to-five page statement of purpose, and a sample of work.

Deadline(s) The application deadline is February 15.

Additional Information The center also welcomes applications for formal affiliation with both the center and the University of Pennsylvania from scholars who are capable of providing their own financial support. Interested individuals should write directly to the center for more information.

436. Ellis L. Phillips Foundation
13 Dartmouth College Highway
Lyme, NH 03768
(603) 795-2790

Grants

Program Description The Ellis L. Phillips Foundation makes grants in the fields of religion, education, the arts, social service, conservation/historic preservation, professional development, and health care.

Sample Grants To help fund research, indexing, and preservation of their Portrait Collection, $2,000 to Harvard University, Fine Arts Library, Cambridge, MA (1987). Toward construction of a Historical Archives building, $5,000 to Greenwich Historical Society, Greenwich, CT (1987). Toward restoration of the glass and iron canopy over the main entrance of this building, built in 1915 as the Union Railroad Station, $3,000 to Brattleboro Museum and Art Center, Brattleboro, VT (1987).

Eligibility/Limitations The foundation makes grants to institutions rather than individuals. All applicants must show that they are tax-exempt under Section 501(c)(3) of the Tax Reform Act of 1969 and "not a private foundation" as defined in Section 509(a) of the Internal Revenue Code.

Fiscal Information Grants awarded in 1987 totaled $340,776.

Application Information The foundation suggests application by a one- to three-page letter describing applicant organization and the program for which the grant is sought. Enclose a copy of the organization's annual report or similar descriptive material, information on plans for future funding, and details of current sources of support.

Deadline(s) The foundation's board of directors meets three times a year, in October, February, and May.

437. The Pillsbury Company
Community Relations, M.S. 3775
Pillsbury Center
Minneapolis, MN 55402-1464
(612) 330-4629

Grants

Program Description The Pillsbury Company seeks to respond to needs in communities where it does business with creative problem solving in partnership with those who seek it. In addition to supporting health and welfare, educational, cultural, art and civic organizations, the company focuses its foundation resources on the most urgent needs of particular interest to the company: hunger and youth. Within the categories of culture and art, grants include donations to historical societies, museums, libraries, performing arts groups and other cultural organizations in communities where Pillsbury operates.

Eligibility/Limitations The company does not fund: organizations operating for profit; support of individuals; endowment campaigns; capital campaigns, with limited exceptions; appeals for product donations; projects of religious denominations or sects; propaganda or lobbying efforts to influence legislation; fund-raising events or advertising associated with such events; or support of travel for individuals or groups.

Fiscal Information During fiscal 1987, the company and the company foundation contributed $7.5 million, addressing the needs of local communities and a broad spectrum of social and economic issues.

Application Information All proposals should be typewritten and include: a brief description of the requesting organization's history of service and a statement of its purpose and objectives; a definition of the project, including an explanation of community need and the specific goals and objectives which the project is designed to meet; specific activities or methods to reach the project goals and a plan of evaluation should be included; an itemized budget and a list of sources of financial support, both committed and pending; a request for a specific amount of money, date by which the funds are needed and timeline of the project. The proposal should also include: a copy of the IRS ruling of the organization's tax-exempt status under Section 501(c)(3); a copy of the most recent audited financial statements; a detailed organizational budget for the current operating year; a donor's list, showing private, corporate and foundation support during the past twelve months; a list of the board of directors, officers and their affiliations; a copy of Form 990-Income Tax Return.

Deadline(s) Pillsbury tries to acknowledge proposals within thirty days of receipt. For careful investigation and assessment of proposals, however, notification of final action may take up to 120 days.

438. The Pittsburgh Foundation

301 Fifth Avenue, Suite 1417
Pittsburgh, PA 15222-2494
(412) 391-5122

Grants to the Arts

Program Description The foundation supports arts and arts organizations in the Pittsburgh area. Initiatives of special interest include: retaining artistic talent; supporting the small arts community; enhancing public awareness of the arts; strengthening education in the arts; creating joint marketing programs between the art community and tourist-related businesses; and networking among art organizations. Grants in the arts may be awarded from two sources: discretionary funds from which grants are awarded to arts organizations which have demonstrated significant artistic and administrative competence; and the A.W. Mellon Educational and Charitable Trust Fund from which grants are made to small arts organizations with budgets of less than $250,000 or to arts/education programs of local schools or colleges. Arts/education programs must include performance or exhibition components which are open to the general public.

Sample Grants Toward support of "The Urbanization of Pittsburgh" exhibit, $40,000 to The Carnegie Museum (1986). For a brochure describing the activities of the Greater Pittsburgh Museum Council's twenty-one area museums, $10,000 to The Pittsburgh Trust for Cultural Resources (1986).

Eligibility/Limitations Grants are limited to organizations located in Allegheny County, except as provided in the terms of a particular trust fund. The following types of grants are preferred: special projects which are not part of the ongoing operations of an organization; seed money grants for new programs; grants which generate additional funding; grants for capital and equipment needs; research grants of an administrative, evaluative, or nontechnical nature. The foundation does not normally make grants to annual campaigns, endowments, operating or maintenance grants (except in exceptional circumstances), loans or assistance to individuals, scholarships, fellowships, or travel grants.

Fiscal Information Grants awarded in 1986 totaled over $4.7 million, including $574,232 in the arts category.

Application Information Grant requests may be submitted either by letter or in the form of a full proposal. After receipt of application, an initial decision will be made to determine if the proposal fits the foundation's guidelines and funding practices. If this decision is favorable, additional information will be requested by means of a grant application form.

Deadline(s) The distribution committee meets four times a year for the purpose of approving grants: March, June, September, and December. Proposals should be submitted sixty days prior to the meeting at which consideration is requested.

439. Polaroid Foundation
28 Osborn Street
Cambridge, MA 02139
(617) 577-4035

Grants

Program Description The Polaroid Foundation makes contributions from funds and photographic products made available by its parent company, Polaroid Corporation. The foundation responds to a range of issues and needs. Its work is done primarily within Massachusetts and/or specifically within greater Boston and Cambridge. The foundation's cultural subcommittee provides support to a wide range of cultural activities including matching gift programs for employees, fine arts organizations, and community-based groups with an interest in grass roots cultural activities. Institutions belonging to the Massachusetts Cultural Alliance are assisted through the Cultural Matching Gifts Program. Exceptional photographic collections, exhibitions, and filmmaking are supported program areas. The foundation will consider funding outside the Commonwealth of Massachusetts in the area of higher education benefiting minorities and in support of photographic acquisition, exhibition, and filmmaking. Its donation of photographic products is nationwide.

Sample Grants To support an exhibit, $2,000 to the Chinese Culture Institute, Boston, MA (1982). For corporate membership, $5,000 to Museum of Fine Arts, Boston, MA (1985). For a capital campaign, $5,000 to Museum of Science, Boston, MA (1985). For general support, $1,000 to New England Aquarium, Boston, MA (1984).

Eligibility/Limitations Eligible institutions are: degree-granting two- and four-year colleges, universities, graduate or professional schools; primary and secondary schools; and primary and secondary schools of special education. All of these schools must be located in the U.S. or its possessions and recognized by the U.S. Treasury Department as schools to which contributions are deductible by donors for federal income tax purposes. All cultural organizations that are members of the Massachusetts Cultural Alliance are eligible to apply.

Fiscal Information The foundation makes grants in the range of $100 to $10,000. Product grants are also awarded.

Application Information Requests for grants should be submitted on organization letterhead and include: a brief history of the program; a description of the population served; an outline of the program or project for which support is requested; the annual budget for the specific project or for the overall program if general support is requested; a copy of the organization's 501(c)(3) tax-exempt letter from the IRS. All proposals should be submitted in duplicate. Once received, the funding request passes through a preliminary foundation staff screening. Applicants will receive a grant application form to complete and return.

Deadline(s) Contributions are approved by an operating committee that meets monthly.

440. PPG Industries Foundation
One PPG Place
Pittsburgh, PA 15272
(412) 434-2970

Grants

Program Description The objectives of the foundation continue to be the enhancement of the quality of life in those communities within the United States where PPG Industries has a major presence, and the development of human potential. In fulfillment of these objectives, five areas receive nearly all of the foundation's grants: human services, health and safety, education, civic and community affairs, and culture. Cultural activities supported by the foundation favor projects that provide access to the public and include grants for music, art, theater, public radio and television, libraries, and museums.

Eligibility/Limitations Normally, only organizations that are designated as public foundations or charities by the IRS are eligible to be considered for funds. Private operating foundations may qualify under certain conditions. In general, the foundation gives priority to applications from local organizations dedicated to enhancing the welfare in communities where PPG is a resident, as well as to those organizations whose activities either enhance individual opportunities or help to strengthen the nation's human services, educational or economic systems on a regional or nationwide basis. In general, the foundation will not award grants to individuals. The foundation will not consider grant applications for less than $100.

Fiscal Information Grants awarded in 1986 totaled over $4.3 million, including $366,805 in support of cultural activities.

Application Information No specific application form is required. Initial inquiries about foundation interest are normally made in the form of a one- or two-page letter that briefly outlines the purpose of the organization, the population it serves, and how the requested funds will be used. Organizations located in the Pittsburgh area and organizations of national scope should direct their inquiries to the executive director of the foundation. Organizations serving communities where PPG facilities are located should direct their initial inquiries to the local PPG Industries Foundation agent in their area. If the response to an initial inquiry is favorable, a formal proposal will be invited.

Deadline(s) The foundation does not have an application deadline, although proposals to be considered for the following calendar year's budget must be received by September 1.

441. Primerica Foundation
American Lane, P.O. Box 3610
Greenwich, CT 06836
(203) 552-2148

General Grants Program

Program Description The Primerica Foundation has announced new policy directions recently adopted by its board of directors. In the present era, when public funding for social and human services and cultural needs is shrinking, the concept of corporate responsibility has acquired fresh meaning. The foundation acknowledges this responsibility and recognizes the need to focus contributions more sharply in order to promote a healthier and more vital society. The foundation therefore joins a movement among major American corporations to set clear priorities for social investments. The foundation also affirms its bias in favor of encouraging innovative management of our major institutions, and supporting projects which test fresh policies and concepts. In pursuing its broader mission, the foundation will concentrate on these basic elements in the General Grants Program: health and human services, education, culture and the arts, civic concerns, and international giving.

Eligibility/Limitations Grants will be made only to nonprofit organizations and institutions possessing a 501(c)(3) federal tax-exempt status. Awards will not be made to individuals, political organizations, religious bodies, labor organizations, or organizations whose sole purpose is recreation. Tax-supported institutions, including schools, colleges, and health care facilities are eligible for foundation grants. The foundation encourages applications from organizations which have obtained, or are seeking, matching public or private funds for its proposed projects.

Fiscal Information Grant awards in 1986 totaled over $3.7 million.

Application Information Applicants may wish to send a brief description (one or two pages) of the program for which funding is sought, including a clear statement of goals and objectives. Or, applicants may send a full proposal which should contain: description of the nature and purpose of the organization; clear description of the project for which funding is sought, including a line-item budget; a list of recent contributors; a description of the methodology to be used in evaluating the effectiveness of the project; list of members of the organization's governing board and brief description of organization staff; financial information, including a copy of most recent annual report and budget; copy of 501(c)(3) IRS letter of determination of tax-exempt status; and proof that the organization's services are non-discriminatory.

Deadline(s) Proposals will be accepted at any time.

442. The Prospect Hill Foundation
420 Lexington Avenue, Suite 3020
New York, NY 10170
(212) 370-1144

Grants

Program Description The foundation has a broad range of philanthropic interests. In 1986, grants primarily addressed arms control, environmental conservation, family planning, and youth and social services issues and also supported selected arts, cultural, and educational institutions.

Sample Grants For general support, $4,000 to The Brooklyn Children's Museum, Brooklyn, NY (1986). For general support ($25,000) and for the Fund of the Met Campaign ($25,000), $50,000 to Metropolitan Museum of Art, New York, NY (1986). For general support, $25,000 to The New York Botanical Garden, Bronx, NY (1986). For first installment of a $50,000 pledge to the snow leopard habitat, $25,000 to New York Zoological Society, New York, NY (1986). Toward preparation of *Wild Mammals in Captivity: A Guide to Management*, $25,000 to Smithsonian Institution, Washington, DC (1986).

Eligibility/Limitations The foundation does not consider grants for individuals, scholarly research, or sectarian religious activities. The foundation favors project support over general support requests. Only a limited number of new applications for grant requests from arts, cultural, and educational institutions receive favorable consideration and such institutions are cautioned that applications for grants should be made only upon invitation.

Fiscal Information Grants in 1986 totaled over $1.4 million and were awarded to fifty-five organizations for sixty-one projects.

Application Information Grant requests may be in the form of a letter (three pages maximum) that summarizes the applicant organization's history and goals; the project for which funding is sought; the contribution of the project to other work in the field or to the organization's own development; the organization's total budget and staff size; the project budget; the organization's board of directors. All material is reviewed by the executive director and one or more members of the board. If there is interest in the proposal, more detailed information will be requested.

Deadline(s) Applicants may submit grant requests to the executive at any time of the year.

443. The Prudential Foundation
Prudential Plaza
Newark, NJ 07101
(201) 877-7354

Grants

Program Description The Prudential Foundation makes grants in the following categories: health and human services, education, urban and community development, business and civic affairs, and culture and the arts. Culture and the arts grants are awarded to projects, programs, or organizations that: offer cultural opportunities to the economically disadvantaged and other individuals who would not normally have access to major arts and cultural institutions; and that provide a diversity of cultural experiences through support of local and national cultural organizations.

Sample Grants To fund capital improvements, $25,000 to Newark Museum, Newark, NJ (1984). To fund capital improvements, $55,000 to Newark Museum, Newark, NJ (1986).

Eligibility/Limitations Priority will be assigned to programs with potential impact in those areas in which the company has a major economic presence, with a special emphasis on Newark, NJ. Grants are not generally made to organizations that are not tax-exempt under section 501(c)(3) of the Internal Revenue Code.

Fiscal Information Grants awarded in 1986 totaled over $10.4 million, including $530,300 in the culture category.

Application Information Initial contact with the foundation should consist of a letter or brief abstract of the funding proposal. If the foundation subsequently requires additional information, it will be requested.

Deadline(s) Proposals are accepted and reviewed on a continuing basis and, based on scope and amount, may be held over until the next meeting of the board of trustees. The board meets three times a year, in April, August, and December

444. The Regenstein Foundation
3450 North Kimball Avenue
Chicago, IL 60618
(312) 463-4355

Grants

Program Description The foundation's primary interests are in the arts, music, and education in the Chicago metropolitan area.

Eligibility/Limitations Any charitable organization other than private foundations may apply for a grant for exempt purposes. No grants are made to individuals or for the benefit of designated individuals.

Fiscal Information Grants awarded in 1986 totaled over $2.4 million.

Application Information All applications must be in writing. It is suggested that they be brief and in letter form. The application should briefly describe the organization, explain the proposed use of the funds, the hoped-for results from their expenditure, and the source of other funds, if any, to be used for the project. All applicants not well known to the foundation should send copies of their letters of determination from the IRS indicating that their organization is tax-exempt and not a private foundation. A great many, if not most, of the foundation's grants are made on the initiative of the trustees themselves.

Deadline(s) There are no deadlines for applications.

445. Reynolds Metals Company Foundation
6601 Broad Street Road
Richmond, VA 23261
(804) 281-2222

Grants

Program Description The major areas of foundation interest listed in order of priority are: health and welfare, education, youth activities, civic, and culture/arts. A main objective of the grants program is to support the maintenance or improvement of the quality of life in the geographic areas served by the foundation.

Eligibility/Limitations The foundation awards grants to organizations that are tax-exempt. Generally, the foundation does not support: causes and organizations outside designated geographic areas served by the foundation; conferences, trips, or tours; operating expenses of organizations receiving United Way support; advertising, tickets, or tables for benefits; duplicating funds; nor will it support an organization acting as an agent for another.

Application Information A request for contribution should include: statement of requesting organization's purpose; history of achievement; a description of program activities and goals for the current year; a letter from the IRS showing tax-exempt status as described in section 501(c)(3); current budget information showing income and expenditures; a list of the board of directors; a description of the use of requested funds. If the grant request is $5,000 or more, a Grant Application Form (R-3-2) should be secured from the foundation's office.

Deadline(s) The deadline for receipt of applications is September 1 to be considered for the ensuing year.

446. The Rockefeller Foundation
1133 Avenue of the Americas
New York, NY 10036
(212) 869-8500

Bellagio Study and Conference Center

Program Description The Rockefeller Foundation maintains the Bellagio Study and Conference Center, located in northern Italy on Lake Como. Each year, the center is host to approximately thirty-five conferences that focus on topics of international importance relating to one of the foundation's areas of interest. In addition, the foundation offers approximately eighty residencies of about four weeks each to scholars, writers, and composers engaged in major projects that relate in some way to the foundation's own program interests.

Application Information Additional information on these programs can be obtained by writing to the conference coordinator.

447. The Rockefeller Foundation
1133 Avenue of the Americas
New York, NY 10036
(212) 869-8500

Grants

Program Description The foundation largely concentrates its efforts in selected areas with well-defined goals. It tries to keep its overall program flexible and dynamic through periodic reappraisals and changes in the light of new needs and opportunities. At present, interest in the arts and humanities focuses on aspects of American cultural life reflected in the three major program components in this category: (1) support for the creative person, which has given priority to a number of national programs that address the needs of artists and scholars; (2) strengthening secondary school education, which supports a national network of collaborating school systems, universities, and cultural organizations engaged in teacher training and enrichment programs in languages, history, and other disciplines of the humanities; and (3) enhancing the public's understanding of international affairs, which supports projects which increase understanding across cultural boundaries. In 1986, an appropriation was approved for a major museum initiative which will aim at helping American museums promote better understanding of the cultures of sub-Saharan Africa. This program focus will include funds for exhibitions, an international conference and publications.

Sample Grants For a resident fellows program in "Media Culture: New Technology and the Arts," $94,500 to Whitney Museum of American Art, New York, NY (1986). For organizing and mounting the first national exhibition of contemporary Hispanic-American art, $150,000 to Museum of Fine Arts, Houston, TX (1986). For its public radio series, "The Territory of Art," $35,000 to Museum of Contemporary Art, Los Angeles, CA (1986). For the Afro-American Editing Consortium, $25,000 to National Archives Trust Fund Board, Washington, DC (1986). For an exhibition and conference on "Women in the Progressive Era" at the National Museum of American History, $25,000 to Smithsonian Institution, Washington, DC (1986).

Eligibility/Limitations To accomplish lasting results with finite resources, the foundation must necessarily concentrate its support on projects that fall within defined program areas. As a matter of policy, the foundation does not undertake to give or lend money for personal aid to individuals; appraise or subsidize cures or inventions; contribute to the establishment of local schools or libraries, or to their building or operating funds. The foundation does not normally provide general institutional support or endowment.

Fiscal Information Grants awarded in 1986 totaled over $59.8 million.

Application Information No special form is required in making a request for foundation aid. An application should be addressed to the assistant secretary of the foundation. It should include a description of the project; a comprehensive plan for the total funding of the project; and a listing of the applicant's qualifications and accomplishments. Additional information and application guidelines are available upon request.

Deadline(s) Grant appropriations are approved by an independent board of trustees which meets three times a year, in April, September, and December.

448. Helena Rubinstein Foundation

405 Lexington Avenue
New York, NY 10174
(212) 986-0806

Grants

Program Description The foundation supports programs in education, the arts, community services, health care, and medical research, with an emphasis on projects which benefit women and children. The largest percentage of the grants, particularly for the arts and community services, is made to organizations in New York City.

Sample Grants Support for a participatory museum for young people and art education programs for New York City elementary school children and teachers, $20,000 to Children's Museum of Manhattan, New York, NY (1986). For partial tuition scholarships for Master's of Arts candidates in the decorative arts program, $10,000 to Cooper-Hewitt Museum, New York, NY (1986). For educational exhibitions in the Youth Wing of the Israel Museum, Jerusalem, $10,000 to The Israel Museum, American Friends, New York, NY (1986). For education department programs for children, $15,000 to The Jewish Museum, New York, NY (1986). For an independent study program to train college and graduate students for careers as museum curators, $50,000 to Whitney Museum of American Art, New York, NY (1986).

Eligibility/Limitations Grants are made only to federally tax-exempt, nonprofit organizations. Grants are not offered to individuals, or for film or video projects. Grants are rarely made to endowment funds and capital campaigns.

Fiscal Information Grants awarded in 1986 totaled over $3.4 million.

Application Information There is no application form. Organizations seeking funds are asked not to make telephone inquiries, but to submit a brief letter outlining the project, its aims, budget, amount requested, other funding sources, and a short history of the organization. If the proposal is one the foundation is able to consider, more detailed information will be requested.

Deadline(s) Proposals are accepted throughout the year.

449. SAFECO Insurance Companies
SAFECO Plaza
Seattle, WA 98185
(206) 545-5000

Corporate Contributions

Program Description SAFECO demonstrates its commitment to maintaining vital communities by annually setting aside corporate funds to make contributions to nonprofit organizations in the areas of civic, culture, education, health, social concerns, United Way, and matching gifts. In the civic category, emphasis is on programs which reduce crime, promote neighborhood improvement and economic development, and support zoos and parks. In the culture category, support is provided for the performing arts, museums, and public radio and television. In thirteen branch offices, funding decisions are guided by employee community involvement committees. These committees, in Atlanta, Cincinnati, Chicago, Dallas, Denver, Los Angeles, Fountain Valley and Pleasanton, CA, Nashville, Portland, St. Louis, Spokane, and Mississauga, Ontario, review requests and administer contributions budgets. Because SAFECO is headquartered in Seattle, the majority of corporate contributions are channeled to organizations in the Pacific Northwest.

Eligibility/Limitations To be eligible for contributions, organizations must be tax-exempt under Internal Revenue Service Code 501(c)(3), or have a Revenue Canada tax-exempt registration number. As a general rule, the company does not make contributions for: funds to individuals; projects of a political nature; general fund-raising events and advertising associated with such events; projects or programs operating outside the U.S. or Canada; national programs; endowment funds.

Fiscal Information Contributions in 1986 totaled over $2 million.

Application Information If an organization meets eligibility requirements, a cover letter should be submitted of no more than two pages, and include the following: description of the organization, its name, address, telephone number, and name of the contact person; statement of purpose or objectives; request for a specific grant amount with an explanation of how funds will be spent; description of the geographic area and people to be served; description of how the project will be evaluated. To each letter, please attach: a copy of the organization's most recent tax-exempt ruling or documentation; a list of the board of directors and their affiliations; financial report showing overall budget of the organization, including income and expenses for the past two years and for the year in which the contribution is being sought; donors for the last twelve months.

Deadline(s) Organizations will be notified within six weeks of the action taken on their request.

450. The San Francisco Foundation
500 Washington Street, Eighth Floor
San Francisco, CA 94111
(415) 392-0600

Grants

Program Description The San Francisco Foundation was established in 1948 to improve the quality of life, promote equality of opportunity, and assist those in need or at risk. It is a community trust for the Bay Area counties of Alameda, Contra Costa, Marin, San Francisco, and San Mateo. Grants are made in the areas of arts and humanities, community health, education, environment and urban affairs.

Sample Grants For capital costs related to exhibit design and construction of a new experiential museum for children, $180,000 to Children's Discovery Museum, San

Anselmo (1986). To develop exhibits and identify a site for the new children's museum, $120,000 to Children's Discovery Museum, San Anselmo (1986). To retain an executive recruitment firm to identify candidates for the position of director, $29,800 to the Exploratorium, San Francisco (1986). To support expansion of fund-raising and management capacity to advance a four-year organizational plan, $15,000 to Mexican Museum, San Francisco (1986).

Eligibility/Limitations The foundation funds tax-exempt, nonprofit organizations that are legally constituted with appropriate financial records and controls.

Fiscal Information Grants awarded in 1985 totaled over $38.2 million.

Application Information To apply for a grant, submit a letter of intent, not a full proposal. The letter of intent should be no longer than three pages and should cover the following: what is the proposed project; why is the project important; who is the applicant? Address all letters of intent to the intake coordinator at the address listed above. Upon review of the program staff, a full proposal may be invited.

Deadline(s) Letters of intent are accepted throughout the year.

451. Santa Fe Southern Pacific Foundation
224 South Michigan Avenue
Chicago, IL 60604-2401
(312) 786-6204

Grants

Program Description The foundation contributes to educational, health and human services, cultural, civic, and other charitable organizations. Within the category of culture and the arts, the foundation awards support for the performing arts, art centers, museums, and other cultural organizations and activities.

Eligibility/Limitations Most contributions are made to nonprofit organizations in communities served by the company and its operating components. Grants to cultural and art organizations that are national in scope are rarely considered. The foundation generally will not contribute to: individuals; tax-supported educational institutions or governmental agencies; tours, conferences, seminars, or workshops; purchase of tables, tickets or advertisements; endowment funds; or programs beyond stated geographic areas of interest.

Fiscal Information Contributions in 1986 totaled over $3.1 million.

Application Information Initial inquiries and proposals should be handled by mail. Proposals should include: a brief covering letter that describes the organization, summarizes the proposal and specifies the amount requested; a copy of IRS tax-exempt letter; a current audited financial statement and budget data; other sources of support during the most recent year; list of organization's officers and directors; a narrative explaining the organization's history, purpose, geographic area of concern and accomplishments; the kind and amount of grant requested and how it will be used. When funds are requested for special programs, indicate the program's objectives and how it will be accomplished and evaluated. Plans for future funding of ongoing projects should be outlined.

Deadline(s) Proposals will be accepted and reviewed continuously, except that major requests in excess of $20,000 will be reviewed annually in the fall, if received prior to September 1. All proposals received after September 1 will be considered in the following year.

452. Sara Lee Foundation
Three First National Plaza
Chicago, IL 60602-4206
(312) 558-8448

Grants

Program Description Sara Lee has developed general principles that guide its efforts in the area of employee and public responsibility. To provide a focus for giving, corporate contributions concentrate on programs affecting the disadvantaged, and on those supporting cultural activities. To emphasize involvement with local communities, contributions programs support projects in the areas of company operations. To maximize resources and improve expertise, programs stress not only financial support, but also the personal involvement of company employees.

Sample Grants For operating support for the Planetarium's exhibits, $2,500 to Adler Planetarium (1987). Operating grant for the Brookfield Zoo's educational, research and conservation actions, $2,500 to Chicago Zoological Society (1987). To underwrite the "Treasures of the Field Museum" fund-raising benefit, $50,000 to Field Museum of Natural History (1987). For general operating support for the Aquarium's programs, $1,500 to John G. Shedd Aquarium (1987). For support as a founding member of the only museum devoted to the work of women artists, $5,000 to National Museum of Women in the Arts (1987).

Eligibility/Limitations Organizations must be duly certified by the state in which they operate and be in receipt of an IRS ruling that they are classified as a 501(c)(3) organization. The following are not eligible for grants: capital and endowment campaigns; individuals; organizations with a limited constituency; organizations which limit their services to members of one religious group or those whose purpose is to propagate a particular religious faith or creed; political organizations; the purchase of tickets to dinners and other fund-raising events as well as goodwill advertising. In general, contributions reflect the geographic mix of company operations. The foundation's cash grants are used primarily to support organizations in the greater Chicago area.

Fiscal Information Foundation programs awarded $3.9 million in fiscal year 1985.

Application Information Application forms and additional information on any foundation program can be obtained by writing the foundation at the address listed above.

Deadline(s) Applications must be received by the first working day of March, June, September, or December to be considered during that quarter. Applications received after these dates will be held for a subsequent meeting. The foundation's fiscal year begins July 1.

453. School of American Research
P.O. Box 2188
Santa Fe, NM 87504
(505) 982-3583

Resident Scholar Fellowship Program

Program Description The Resident Scholar Fellowship Program at the School of American Research provides support for scholars pursuing advanced study in anthropology and related fields. While the program stresses southwestern studies, scholars in other areas are urged to apply. The major benefit of the resident scholar program is an opportunity to work with no other responsibilities and with the stimulus of intellectual interaction with fellow resident scholars, visiting anthropologists, and SAR staff.

Eligibility/Limitations Funding for this program is provided by the Weatherhead Foundation and NEH. Weatherhead scholarships are awarded to Ph.D. candidates, postdoctoral scholars, and retired scholars. NEH fellowships are awarded only to postdoctoral scholars.

Fiscal Information The length of tenure is usually eleven months and begins on September 15. Preference will be given to those whose field work is complete. Additional benefits of the program include: a furnished apartment for Weatherhead scholars and a rental allowance for NEH scholars; a $650 stipend for each month in residence; a separate office on the school campus; medical insurance; and assistance from the school's part-time librarian in obtaining books to supplement the school's limited anthropological collection.

Application Information For additional information contact the school.

454. Scott Paper Company Foundation
Scott Plaza
Philadelphia, PA 19113
(215) 522-5000

Grants

Program Description The foundation has identified several key priorities which fall into four broad giving categories: education, human services and community development, arts and culture, and United Way. Within the arts and culture category, contributions are targeted to cultural organizations such as museums, public broadcasting stations and performing arts groups that are accessible to the general public and have a significant positive impact on community life. In addition, priority is given to projects that seek to build an organization's earned income base, multiply the impact of contributions and build the capability of staff to achieve management excellence.

Eligibility/Limitations For the most part, support is restricted to organizations that are located in company plant, headquarters, or woodlands communities. Applicant organizations must have evidence of IRS 501(c)(3) status. Requests for support must demonstrate that the program/organization is addressing a clear and important need in the community. The foundation does not generally provide unrestricted operating support to organizations; requests should be for specific projects and initiatives that address a target need and population. In general, support is not directed toward capital campaign efforts. As a matter of policy, the foundation does not provide support to the following types of organizations: organizations that do not have nonprofit tax-exempt status; organizations based outside the U.S.; endowment funds; national organizations; individuals; or special events such as walk-a-thons.

Fiscal Information Contributions in 1986 totaled over $1.6 million, including $209,000 in the arts and culture category.

Application Information The following information must be provided to the foundation when applying for a grant. The information may be presented in any format, but should be as concise as possible: name of organization, address, contact person, telephone number, and date of application; brief history and general purpose of the organization; general three-year budget and current budget of the organization; purpose of this request, including a history of the organization's involvement in concept, needs assessment, proposed achievement, goals and benefits; detailed project budget; amount of request; description of how project will be funded on an ongoing basis, if pertinent; description of project cooperation with other similar agencies; explanation of how project will be evaluated; list of board of directors; and evidence of tax-exempt status.

Deadline(s) Applications are accepted throughout the year.

455. Security Pacific Foundation HC-4
Mrs. Carol E. Taufer, President & CEO
Terminal Annex, P.O. Box 2097
Los Angeles, CA 90051
(213) 345-6688

Grants

Program Description The Security Pacific Foundation was created to support the efforts of Security Pacific Corporation and particularly Security Pacific National Bank to provide support to broad based community groups working to improve the well-being of local communities and dealing with major social service, education, cultural and civic concerns throughout the state of California. Recognizing the need for continuing improvement in the quality of life, the foundation provides limited support to key cultural organizations in major population centers.

Sample Grants For capital support, $32,500 to the California Museum of Science & Industry (1986). For capital support of the Fresno Metropolitan Museum, $10,000 (1986). For capital support, $20,000 to the Greater Los Angeles Zoo Association (1986). For operating support, $1,500 to the Dallas Museum of Fine Arts (1986). For operating support, $1,750 to the Field Museum of Natural History, Chicago (1986). For operating support, $6,000 to the Hunting Library, Pasadena (1986).

Eligibility/Limitations Recipient organizations must qualify on a professional level. To be considered for a grant, an organization must have an Internal Revenue Service designation as a nonprofit, tax-exempt public charity. Areas which are not considered for grants include: individuals; veterans, military, fraternal, or professional organizations or service clubs; trips or tours for individuals or groups; direct support of churches or religious groups; scholarships; advertising in charitable publications; private foundations or private operating foundations; any marathon-type fund-raising activity; political organizations or programs; unsolicited ticket sales; conferences, seminars, or workshops; research or study projects; or advocacy organizations. Grants to agencies receiving in excess of 50 percent of their funding from government agencies will not be considered.

Fiscal Information Average annual unrestricted grants fall in a range from $250 to $1,500. In 1986, the foundation awarded grants totaling over $4.7 million, including over $770,000 in the culture category. The foundation makes only unrestricted operating grants and capital grants for major building projects.

Application Information Requests for grants should include: a brief description of the organization's purpose, objectives, and programs; a copy of the Internal Revenue Service 501(c)(3) determination letter designating the organization as a nonprofit, tax-exempt public charity; a list of the board of directors with their business affiliations; a copy of the current year's operating budget and, if the proposal is for capital funds, a detailed statement of the total project cost; a statement of the current financial position and the most recent audited financial statement; a copy of the most recent 990 report to the Internal Revenue Service; and a list of current contributions with giving levels.

Deadline(s) Requests for unrestricted operating grants are considered on an ongoing basis through the year. Capital grants are handled once a year. Request for capital grant consideration must be in the foundation's office by 5:00 pm on July 15th (the following Monday when the 15th falls on a weekend) for consideration in the current year.

Additional Information The foundation cannot directly support all areas of cultural interest. Through a matching gift program for employees of Security Pacific Corporation, cultural organizations qualify for matching gift program funds. Qualified organizations include: arboretums; arts councils or funds; historical villages or cultural preservation efforts open to the public; museums of art, science, or history; performing arts companies; planetariums; public libraries; public radio and TV stations; theaters; and zoos. The minimum gift matched is $25 and the maximum is $2,500 per employee per year.

456. Shell Oil Company Foundation

Two Shell Plaza, P.O. Box 2099
Houston, TX 77252
(713) 241-3617

Culture and the Arts Grants

Program Description The foundation has for some time offered support to cultural and arts activities both nationally and in communities where Shell people live. At the national level, contributions go to a limited number of organizations building broad-based strength in the visual, performing, and literary arts. The foundation believes that within the limits of its available funds, this is the most effective way to help arts organizations in the country at large. At the local level, the foundation concentrates its culture and arts funding in a few cities where significant numbers of Shell people are located. Here, the activities of such organizations as libraries, museums, and major performing arts groups are supported.

Eligibility/Limitations Most of the foundation's contributions are made through planned, continuing programs in support of education and charitable activities in communities where Shell people are located. The foundation prefers not to contribute in certain areas, including: capital campaigns of national organizations; endowment or development funds and special requests of colleges and universities; college fund-raising associations; direct donations to individuals and individual community organizations; and hospital operating expenses.

Fiscal Information In 1987, support for culture and the arts totaled more than $13.2 million.

Application Information There is no formal application procedure. Requests may be made by letter and should include the following information: a description of the structure, purpose, history, and program of the organization; a summary of the need for support and how it will be used; detailed financial data on the organization such as an independent financial audit, budget, sources of income, breakdown of expenditures by program, administration, and fund-raising; and a copy of the IRS rule, dated after 1969, classifying the organization as tax-exempt under section 501(c)(3) and not a private foundation under section 509(a) of the code; a copy of the organization's most recent Form 990; and a list of corporate donors and their level of support.

Deadline(s) Contributions are planned a year in advance and based on a calendar year budget. Interim donations are rarely made.

457. The L. J. Skaggs and Mary C. Skaggs Foundation
1330 Broadway, 17th Floor
Oakland, CA 94612
(415) 451-3300

Grants

Program Description The foundation presently makes grants under six program categories: performing arts; social and community concerns; projects of historic interest; folklore/folklife; international grants; and special projects. Where necessary, as new program areas arise, new funding categories may be opened.

Sample Grants To support the salary of the registrar of the museum, $3,000 to the Mexican Museum, San Francisco, CA (1985). To support the completion and equipping of a library/office area for this museum, $10,000 to Mingei International Museum of World Folk Art; La Jolla, CA (1985). Second year subvention of a two-year $20,000 grant for publications, $10,000 to the Museum of International Folk Art, Santa Fe, NM (1985). To support a computerized folklore archive, $5,000 to the Vermont Folklife Center, Vermont Council on the Arts, Montpelier, VT (1985).

Eligibility/Limitations The foundation makes grants to qualified tax-exempt charitable organizations. No grants are made to individuals, or for capital, endowment, or annual fund drives, sectarian, or religious purposes. With very special exceptions, grants to programs in the social and community concerns category will only be made in Northern California.

Fiscal Information In 1985, the foundation awarded 292 grants for a total of over $1.9 million. Grants ranged in size from $300 to $150,000.

Application Information Telephone inquiries regarding program eligibility are not encouraged. Requests for grants are initiated by a brief letter of intent to apply for funding during the following calendar year. This letter should briefly describe the applying organization and the purpose for which funds are sought. Information concerning the organization's income and expenses, and material outlining the experience and expertise of key personnel should also be included. When a letter of intent is received, the foundation's staff determines whether the proposed project meets current guidelines and interests. The foundation then invites a full proposal.

Deadline(s) Letters of intent must be received by the foundation no later than June 1; full proposals, if invited, must be received by the foundation no later than September 1.

458. Smithsonian Institution
Office of Fellowships and Grants
3300 L'Enfant Plaza
Washington, DC 20560
(202) 287-3271

Academic Internships

Program Description An internship at the Smithsonian Institution is a prearranged, structured learning experience scheduled within a specific time frame. The experience must be relevant both to the intern's stated academic or professional goals and to disciplines and research and museum professions represented at the institution. An internship is essentially a tutorial situation and is performed under direct supervision of Smithsonian staff. Academic internships offering research related experience can be arranged for students and other qualified applicants in most of the bureaus and programs of the institution. However, they are not intended to provide training for museum professions. For the most part, internships are arranged individually.

Eligibility/Limitations Students and other qualified individuals are eligible to apply.

Application Information Applications can be made by contacting a bureau internship coordinator.

Deadline(s) Applications may be made at any time.

459. Smithsonian Institution
Office of Fellowships and Grants
3300 L'Enfant Plaza
Washington, DC 20560
(202) 287-3271

Conservation Analytical Laboratory—Postgraduate Internships

Program Description An internship at the Smithsonian Institution is a prearranged, structured learning experience scheduled within a specific time frame. The experience must be relevant both to the intern's stated academic or professional goals and to disciplines, research, and museum professions represented at the institution. An internship is essentially a tutorial situation and is performed under direct supervision of Smithsonian staff. The Conservation Analytical Laboratory (CAL) makes a number of postgraduate internships in conservation available for recent graduates of academic conservation programs or conservators with equivalent training and experience.

Eligibility/Limitations Graduates of academic conservation training programs are eligible to apply.

Fiscal Information The internships are for a period of one year, and usually start in the fall.

Application Information For information, contact the Intern Coordinator, Conservation Analytical Laboratory, Museum Support Center, Smithsonian Institution, Washington, DC 20560.

Additional Information CAL also provides one-year internships for advanced students at academic conservation training programs, as well as summer internships for less advanced students.

460. Smithsonian Institution
Office of Fellowships and Grants
3300 L'Enfant Plaza
Washington, DC 20560
(202) 287-3271

Daniel and Florence Guggenheim Fellowship

Program Description Through the support of a fund established by the Daniel and Florence Guggenheim Foundation, a residential appointment for graduate research is offered at the National Air and Space Museum. One fellowship may be awarded annually for research related to technology transfer, planetary exploration, or the history of aviation.

Eligibility/Limitations Applicants for a predoctoral award should have completed preliminary coursework and examinations and be engaged in dissertation research.

Postdoctoral applicants preferably should have received the Ph.D. degree within the past seven years.

Fiscal Information The stipend amount and allowances are subject to change.

Application Information For further information and application materials, write: Guggenheim Fellowship, Office of the Deputy Director, National Air and Space Museum, Smithsonian Institution, Washington, DC 20560.

Deadline(s) January 15 is the deadline for applications each year.

461. Smithsonian Institution
Office of Fellowships and Grants
3300 L'Enfant Plaza
Washington, DC 20560
(202) 287-3271

Faculty Fellowships

Program Description Faculty fellowships are awarded to provide opportunities for minority faculty members to conduct research in association with members of the Smithsonian professional research staff, using facilities and collections of the institution.

Fiscal Information Awards may be for two to four months. Stipends are determined by the appointee's faculty status.

Application Information Additional information is available from the Office of Fellowships and Grants.

Deadline(s) The deadline for application is February 15.

462. Smithsonian Institution
Office of Fellowships and Grants
3300 L'Enfant Plaza
Washington, DC 20560
(202) 287-3271

Fellowships: Graduate Student Fellowships

Program Description The Smithsonian Institution offers in-residence fellowships for support of research and study in fields pursued at the Smithsonian. At present, these fields are: anthropology, including archaeology; astrophysics and astronomy; ecology, behavioral and environmental sciences; evolutionary and systematic biology; history of science and technology; history of art; social and cultural history, and folklife of the United States. Graduate student fellowships are offered to students to study and conduct research in residence under the guidance of Smithsonian staff members.

Eligibility/Limitations Applicants must be students actively engaged in graduate study at any level, and submit a proposal for research in a discipline which is pursued at the Smithsonian.

Fiscal Information Graduate student fellowships are awarded for ten weeks and carry a stipend of $2,500.

Application Information Potential applicants should write directly to the Office of Fellowships and Grants for further information and application materials. In so doing, indicate the academic degrees held or expected and the dates of their conferral, as well as the field of interest at the Smithsonian.

Deadline(s) The deadline for receipt of applications is January 15.

463. Smithsonian Institution

Office of Fellowships and Grants
3300 L'Enfant Plaza
Washington, DC 20560
(202) 287-3700

Fellowships in Materials Analysis

Program Description Fellowships are available for research in the applications of techniques of the physical sciences to problems of art history, anthropology, archaeology, and the history of technology. The offering reflects a joint interest in such problems by the staff of the Conservation Analytical Laboratory and other Smithsonian conservation facilities, and the Departments of Anthropology and Mineral Sciences at the National Museum of Natural History.

Eligibility/Limitations Predoctoral and postdoctoral fellowships are available; applications will also be accepted from persons with a degree or certificate of advanced training in the conservation of artifacts or art objects.

Application Information It is recommended that applicants first contact the appropriate member of the Conservation Analytical Laboratory research staff before making formal application. Additional information and application guidelines are available from the Office of Fellowships and Grants.

Deadline(s) The deadline for receipt of applications is January 15.

464. Smithsonian Institution

Office of Fellowships and Grants
3300 L'Enfant Plaza
Washington, DC 20560
(202) 287-3271

Fellowships: Postdoctoral Fellowships

Program Description The Smithsonian Institution offers in-residence fellowships for support of research and study in fields pursued at the Smithsonian. At present, these fields are: anthropology, including archaeology; astrophysics and astronomy; ecology, behavioral and environmental sciences; evolutionary and systematic biology; history of science and technology; history of art; social and cultural history, and folklife of the United States. Postdoctoral fellowships are offered to investigators who wish to conduct research in areas in which the Smithsonian institution has particular research strengths.

Eligibility/Limitations Applicants must have completed the doctoral degree less than seven years before the application deadline. The applicant must submit a detailed proposal including a justification for conducting the research in residence at the institution. Candidates with the equivalent of the doctorate in experience, training, and accomplishment may be considered for postdoctoral fellowships.

Fiscal Information Postdoctoral fellowships are awarded for not less than six months and not more than twelve months, and carry a stipend of $19,000 per year plus allowances.

Application Information Potential applicants should write directly to the Office of Fellowships and Grants for further information and application materials. In so doing, indicate the academic degrees held or expected and the dates of their conferral, as well as the field of interest at the Smithsonian.

Deadline(s) The deadline for receipt of applications is January 15.

465. Smithsonian Institution

Office of Fellowships and Grants
3300 L'Enfant Plaza
Washington, DC 20560
(202) 287-3271

Fellowships: Predoctoral Fellowships

Program Description The Smithsonian Institution offers in-residence fellowships for support of research and study in fields pursued at the Smithsonian. At present, these fields are: anthropology, including archaeology; astrophysics and astronomy; ecology, behavioral and environmental sciences; evolutionary and systematic biology; history of science and technology; history of art; social and cultural history, and folklife of the United States. Predoctoral fellowships are offered to investigators who have completed preliminary coursework and examinations and are engaged in dissertation research.

Eligibility/Limitations Applicants must have the approval of their universities to conduct their doctoral research at the Smithsonian Institution.

Fiscal Information Predoctoral fellowships are awarded for not less than six months and not more than twelve months, and carry a stipend of $12,000 per year plus allowances.

Application Information Potential applicants should write directly to the Office of Fellowships and Grants for further information and application materials. In so doing, indicate the academic degrees held or expected and the dates of their conferral, as well as the field of interest at the Smithsonian.

Deadline(s) The deadline for receipt of applications is January 15.

466. Smithsonian Institution
Office of Fellowships and Grants
3300 L'Enfant Plaza
Washington, DC 20560
(202) 287-3271

Fellowships: Senior Postdoctoral Fellowships

Program Description The Smithsonian Institution offers in-residence fellowships for support of research and study in fields pursued at the Smithsonian. At present, these fields are: anthropology, including archaeology; astrophysics and astronomy; ecology, behavioral and environmental sciences; evolutionary and systematic biology; history of science and technology; history of art; social and cultural history, and folklife of the United States. Senior Postdoctoral Fellowships are offered to scholars who have held the degree for more than seven years.

Eligibility/Limitations The applicant must submit a detailed proposal including a justification for conducting research in residence at the institution.

Fiscal Information The term of the fellowship is three to twelve months and carries a stipend of $25,000 per year plus allowances.

Application Information Potential applicants should write directly to the Office of Fellowships and Grants for further information and application materials. In so doing, indicate the academic degrees held or expected and the dates of their conferral, as well as the field of interest at the Smithsonian.

Deadline(s) The deadline for receipt of applications is January 15.

467. Smithsonian Institution
Office of Fellowships and Grants
3300 L'Enfant Plaza
Washington, DC 20560
(202) 287-3271

Graduate Internships at the National Museum of American Art

Program Description An internship at the Smithsonian Institution is a prearranged, structured learning experience scheduled within a specific time frame. The experience must be relevant both to the intern's stated academic or professional goals and to disciplines and research and museum professions represented at the institution. An internship is essentially a tutorial situation and is performed under direct supervision of Smithsonian staff. Graduate internship appointments are available at the National

Museum of American Art for students of art history, studio art, American history, and/ or American studies. Unlike the summer program, students move from office to office, spending the first semester in two different departments and the second semester in the office of their choice. Graduate interns are required to spend twenty hours weekly at the museum. The program includes an extensive reading list, special workshops and lectures, an evaluation and grade at the end of each semester, and a comprehensive oral exam at the end of the second semester.

Eligibility/Limitations Students who have completed twelve semester hours in art history, studio art, American history, and/or American studies are eligible to apply. Although this program is designed for graduate students, it will accept outstanding college seniors.

Application Information For further information, contact: Committee on Professional Training Programs, National Museum of American Art, Smithsonian Institution, 8th and G Streets, NW, Washington, DC 20560, telephone (202) 357-2714.

Deadline(s) The deadline for applications is March 15.

468. Smithsonian Institution

Office of Fellowships and Grants
3300 L'Enfant Plaza
Washington, DC 20560
(202) 287-3271

International Fellowships

Program Description The National Air and Space Museum has established a program of international fellowships. These fellowships are intended to foster historical and scientific studies with an international scope, carried out at the museum by researchers from countries other than the U.S. The fellows will work in residence at the museum on subjects of their own interest that are related to the museum's collections, staff research, exhibitions, or other resources.

Fiscal Information Fellowships are for up to one year.

Application Information Potential candidates are encouraged to contact the museum before applying to discuss their research interests. Applications may be made by writing to: International Fellowships, Office of the Deputy Director, National Air and Space Museum, Smithsonian Institution, Washington, DC 20560.

469. Smithsonian Institution

Office of Fellowships and Grants
3300 L'Enfant Plaza
Washington, DC 20560
(202) 287-3271

Internships at the National Air and Space Museum

Program Description An internship at the Smithsonian Institution is a prearranged, structured learning experience scheduled within a specific time frame. The experience must be relevant both to the intern's stated academic or professional goals and to disciplines and research and museum professions represented at the institution. An internship is essentially a tutorial situation and is performed under direct supervision of Smithsonian staff. Internships are offered throughout the year at the National Air and Space Museum for students who have an interest in aviation, space sciences, or museum programs. Projects are tailored to the individual student's background, and each student is assigned to one or more departments of the museum under the supervision of staff members.

Eligibility/Limitations Applicants should be enrolled in undergraduate or graduate school.

Fiscal Information Intern appointments are for a minimum of six weeks and may last up to a year.

Application Information For information on stipends, application procedures, and deadlines, write: Intern Program, Office of Volunteer Service, National Air and Space Museum, Smithsonian Institution, Washington, DC 20560.

Deadline(s) Applications are considered on a semester basis; interested persons should inquire about exact deadlines.

470. Smithsonian Institution
Office of Fellowships and Grants
3300 L'Enfant Plaza
Washington, DC 20560
(202) 287-3271

Internships at the National Museum of African Art

Program Description An internship at the Smithsonian Institution is a prearranged, structured learning experience scheduled within a specific time frame. The experience must be relevant both to the intern's stated academic or professional goals and to disciplines and research and museum professions represented at the institution. An internship is essentially a tutorial situation and is performed under direct supervision of Smithsonian staff. Internships are offered at the National Museum of African Art to persons interested in museum work and the research opportunities available at the museum. Applicants should be students with a major in art history, anthropology, or a humanities discipline related to the study of African culture.

Eligibility/Limitations Applicants should be either undergraduate juniors or seniors, college graduates, or graduate students.

Fiscal Information Interns work in one of several museum departments, usually for two to six months.

Application Information For further information, contact: Internship Coordinator, National Museum of African Art, Smithsonian Institution, Washington, DC 20560, telephone (202) 357-4600.

Deadline(s) The application deadlines for these internships are: for the fall semester, July 15; for winter semester or for a mid-semester internships, October 15; for summer, April 1.

471. Smithsonian Institution
Office of Fellowships and Grants
3300 L'Enfant Plaza
Washington, DC 20560
(202) 287-3271

Internships in Museum Practices

Program Description An internship at the Smithsonian Institution is a prearranged, structured learning experience scheduled within a specific time frame. The experience must be relevant both to the intern's stated academic or professional goals and to disciplines and research and museum professions represented at the institution. An internship is essentially a tutorial situation and is performed under direct supervision of Smithsonian staff. The Office of Museum Programs administers an internship program which focuses on various aspects of museum operations and practices at the Smithsonian.

Eligibility/Limitations Internship opportunities are offered to undergraduate and graduate students and museum professionals from the U.S. and abroad.

Fiscal Information Internships may vary in length according to the needs of the individual; usual residency is from two to six months. Appointments are made without stipend.

Application Information For further information and application forms, contact: Internship Program, Office of Museum Programs, Arts and Industries Building, Room 2235, Smithsonian Institution, Washington, DC 20560.

472. Smithsonian Institution
Office of Fellowships and Grants
3300 L'Enfant Plaza
Washington, DC 20560
(202) 287-3271

James E. Webb Fellowships

Program Description In 1982, the Smithsonian established a new fellowship program in honor of James E. Webb, for many years a Smithsonian Regent and chairman of the Regents' Executive Committee. The Webb Fellowships are designed to promote excellence in the management of cultural and scientific not-for-profit organizations by recognizing and developing the management ability of individuals with career aspiration in this field.

Eligibility/Limitations Eligibility extends to students in graduate level management degree programs in the United States.

Application Information For program description, application guidelines, and other information, contact the Office of Fellowships and Grants.

473. Smithsonian Institution
Office of Fellowships and Grants
3300 L'Enfant Plaza
Washington, DC 20560
(202) 287-3271

James Renwick Fellowships in American Crafts Since 1930

Program Description The Office of Fellowships and Grants administers funds provided by the James Renwick Alliance for fellowships in residence at the Renwick Gallery of the National Museum of American Art. Proposals are sought for scholarly research in American crafts since 1930. Topics may relate to the Renwick's collections and/or initiate scholarly symposia, exhibitions, or other major museum activities.

Eligibility/Limitations Graduate, masters, predoctoral, or postdoctoral scholars are eligible to apply.

Fiscal Information Fellowships are for up to twelve months in residence at the Renwick Gallery.

Application Information For more information and application forms, write to the Office of Fellowships and Grants, Suite 7300, Smithsonian Institution at the address listed above.

474. Smithsonian Institution
Office of Fellowships and Grants
3300 L'Enfant Plaza
Washington, DC 20560
(202) 287-3271

Minority Internship Program

Program Description An internship at the Smithsonian Institution is a prearranged, structured learning experience scheduled within a specific time frame. The experience must be relevant both to the intern's stated academic or professional goals and to disciplines and research and museum professions represented at the institution. An internship is essentially a tutorial situation and is performed under direct supervision of Smithsonian staff. The Office of Fellowships and Grants offers a number of opportunities to increase minority participation in the Smithsonian scholarly programs.

Eligibility/Limitations Minority junior and senior undergraduates and graduate students are invited to apply.

Fiscal Information Internships are available for periods of nine to twelve weeks and carry a stipend of $200 per week for undergraduates and $250 per week for graduate students. A travel allowance is provided.

Application Information Students should contact the Office of Fellowships and Grants for application information.

Deadline(s) Application deadlines are July 1, October 1, and March 1 of each year.

475. Smithsonian Institution

Office of Fellowships and Grants
3300 L'Enfant Plaza
Washington, DC 20560
(202) 287-3271

Native American Community Scholars Awards

Program Description The Office of Fellowships and Grants offers awards to Native Americans, who are formally or informally affiliated with a Native American community, to undertake projects which are related to a Native American topic and require the use of the Native American resources of the Smithsonian.

Fiscal Information Appointments are available for up to six weeks.

Application Information For application and program guidelines contact the Office of Fellowships and Grants.

476. Smithsonian Institution

Office of Fellowships and Grants
3300 L'Enfant Plaza
Washington, DC 20560
(202) 287-3271

Native American Internships

Program Description An internship at the Smithsonian Institution is a prearranged, structured learning experience scheduled within a specific time frame. The experience must be relevant both to the intern's stated academic or professional goals and to disciplines and research and museum professions represented at the institution. An internship is essentially a tutorial situation and is performed under direct supervision of Smithsonian staff. Appointments are offered to Native American students to pursue internship projects related to Native American topics and requiring use of Native American resources at the Smithsonian.

Eligibility/Limitations Native American junior and senior undergraduates and graduate students are invited to apply.

Fiscal Information The appointment is for periods of from nine to twelve weeks and carries a stipend of $200 per week for undergraduates and $250 per week for graduate students and a travel allowance is also provided.

Application Information Write the Office of Fellowships and Grants for further information.

Deadline(s) Deadlines for applications are May 1, June 1, and September 15.

477. Smithsonian Institution

Office of Fellowships and Grants
3300 L'Enfant Plaza
Washington, DC 20560
(202) 287-3271

Office of Architectural History and Historic Preservation Internship Program

Program Description An internship at the Smithsonian Institution is a prearranged, structured learning experience scheduled within a specific time frame. The experience must be relevant both to the intern's stated academic or professional goals and to disciplines and research and museum professions represented at the institution. An internship is essentially a tutorial situation and is performed under direct supervision of Smithsonian staff. The Office of Architectural History (OAHP) offers internships for the study of the architectural history of various Smithsonian buildings. The focus of this internship is the use of primary research materials. The goal will be to integrate original documentation, such as correspondence and memoranda, architectural drawings, photographs, and other archival materials into the architectural history of the Smithsonian.

Eligibility/Limitations The internship program is provided for both undergraduates and graduate students. Preference is given to those who have previously completed course work in either art history or architectural history.

Application Information Applicants should send their resumes with a personal letter and two recommendations to the Office of Architectural History and Historic Preservation, Room SI-T238, Smithsonian Institution, Washington, DC 20560.

Deadline(s) Deadlines for application submissions are July 15 for the fall, October 16 for the winter/spring, and April 1 for the summer.

478. Smithsonian Institution
Office of Fellowships and Grants
3300 L'Enfant Plaza
Washington, DC 20560
(202) 287-3271

Research Traineeships at the National Zoological Park

Program Description An internship at the Smithsonian Institution is a prearranged, structured learning experience scheduled within a specific time frame. The experience must be relevant both to the intern's stated academic or professional goals and to disciplines and research and museum professions represented at the institution. An internship is essentially a tutorial situation and is performed under direct supervision of Smithsonian staff. The National Zoological Park sponsors research traineeships during the summer. This program is funded by the Friends of the National Zoo and is intended to provide opportunities for students to practice research and clinical methods in several program areas of the zoo. Students participate in projects at the zoo's facilities in Washington, DC, and at the Department of Conservation in Front Royal, VA.

Fiscal Information Internships are available for a period of three months beginning sometime between mid-May and early June. A stipend is provided to appointees under the program.

Application Information Information about eligibility requirements, deadlines, and applications procedures may be obtained by contacting: Research Traineeship Program, Friends of the National Zoo, National Zoological Park, Washington, DC 20008, telephone (202) 673-4955.

479. Smithsonian Institution
Office of Fellowships and Grants
3300 L'Enfant Plaza
Washington, DC 20560
(202) 287-3271

Rockefeller Foundation Residency Program in the Humanities

Program Description The Office of Fellowships and Grants administers a grant program provided by the Rockefeller Foundation for postdoctoral fellowships in residence at the National Museum of African Art, the Arthur M. Sackler Gallery, and the Freer Gallery of Art.

Eligibility/Limitations Proposals are sought from postdoctoral scholars in African art history and anthropology with an emphasis on material culture and in Asian art history for research in the collections and/or topics that could initiate scholarly symposia, exhibitions, or other major museum activities.

Application Information For more information and application forms, write to the Office of Fellowships and Grants, Rockefeller Residency Program, Suite 7300, L'Enfant Plaza, Washington, DC 20560.

Additional Information This program differs from existing fellowship programs in that it will also allow the fellows direct involvement in the programmatic pursuits of the museums.

480. Smithsonian Institution
Office of Fellowships and Grants
3300 L'Enfant Plaza
Washington, DC 20560
(202) 287-3271

Short-Term Appointments at the Smithsonian Tropical Research Institute

Program Description The Smithsonian Tropical Research Institute occasionally offers short-term awards to visiting researchers for work on any aspect of tropical biology and such allied subjects as the climates, ecology, and paleoecology of human populations and the geology, paleobotany, and paleozoology of tropical regions.

Application Information Inquiries about these limited appointments should be addressed to: Director, Smithsonian Tropical Research Institute, Box 2072, Balboa, Republic of Panama.

481. Smithsonian Institution
Office of Fellowships and Grants
3300 L'Enfant Plaza
Washington, DC 20560
(202) 287-3271

Short-Term Visits

Program Description Support for investigators wishing to conduct research projects at Smithsonian facilities is sometimes offered by individual bureaus of the institution. The specific museum, research facility, or bureau in which research might be undertaken can provide further information about these opportunities. Limited financial support through the Office of Fellowships and Grants is available to scholars and students seeking access to Smithsonian facilities and staff members for short periods of time.

Application Information Applications (available from the Office of Fellowships and Grants) should be directed to an appropriate member of the institution's professional research staff.

Deadline(s) Applications are accepted throughout the year.

482. Smithsonian Institution
Office of Fellowships and Grants
3300 L'Enfant Plaza
Washington, DC 20560
(202) 287-3271

Summer Internships at the Hirshhorn Museum and Sculpture Garden

Program Description An internship at the Smithsonian Institution is a prearranged, structured learning experience scheduled within a specific time frame. The experience must be relevant both to the intern's stated academic or professional goals and to disciplines and research and museum professions represented at the institution. An internship is essentially a tutorial situation and is performed under direct supervision of Smithsonian staff. Five internships are offered at the Hirshhorn Museum and

Sculpture Garden to work on special departmental projects. They also participate in a series of seminars on the museum's collection and organizations.

Eligibility/Limitations Undergraduate students who have completed their junior or senior year by June and have at least twelve semester hours in art history are eligible to apply.

Fiscal Information Academic credit may be arranged on an individual basis and a small stipend is provided for interns. In addition, a few non-stipended internships may be available.

Application Information For further information, please contact: Education Department, Hirshhorn Museum and Sculpture Garden, Smithsonian Institution, Washington, DC 20560, telephone (202) 357-3235.

Deadline(s) The application deadline is usually February 1 each year.

483. Smithsonian Institution
Office of Fellowships and Grants
3300 L'Enfant Plaza
Washington, DC 20560
(202) 287-3271

Summer Internships at the National Museum of American Art

Program Description An internship at the Smithsonian Institution is a prearranged, structured learning experience scheduled within a specific time frame. The experience must be relevant both to the intern's stated academic or professional goals and to disciplines and research and museum professions represented at the institution. An internship is essentially a tutorial situation and is performed under direct supervision of Smithsonian staff. A maximum of six internship appointments at the National Museum of American Art are offered to students interested in concentrating on one aspect of museum work. Applicants should have a strong background in art history, studio art, or American studies.

Eligibility/Limitations Applicants must have completed their junior or senior year of undergraduate work.

Fiscal Information The intern will spend a period of nine weeks working in the department of the museum appropriate to the intern's individual interest. Interns appointed to this program may receive a small stipend.

Application Information For further information, contact: Committee on Professional Training Programs, National Museum of American Art, Smithsonian Institution, 8th and G Streets, NW, Washington, DC 20560, telephone (202) 357-2714.

Deadline(s) The application deadline is February 28.

484. Smithsonian Institution
Office of Fellowships and Grants
3300 L'Enfant Plaza
Washington, DC 20560
(202) 287-3271

Summer Internships for High School Seniors

Program Description An internship at the Smithsonian Institution is a prearranged, structured learning experience scheduled within a specific time frame. The experience must be relevant both to the intern's stated academic or professional goals and to disciplines and research and museum professions represented at the institution. An internship is essentially a tutorial situation and is performed under direct supervision of Smithsonian staff. The Office of Elementary and Secondary Education sponsors an annual summer internship program for high school students finishing their senior year. Interns participate in projects related to the ongoing work of Smithsonian staff members in the institution's bureaus in the Washington, DC area. The program is divided into two five-week sessions of twenty students each.

Eligibility/Limitations High school students finishing their senior year are eligible to apply.

Fiscal Information A small allowance is provided; in addition, round-trip transportation and lodging are provided for students outside the Washington, DC area.

Application Information Contact the Office of Fellowships and Grants for additional information.

485. Smithsonian Institution
Office of Fellowships and Grants
3300 L'Enfant Plaza
Washington, DC 20560
(202) 287-3271

Verville Fellowship

Program Description The National Air and Space Museum has established the A. Verville Fellowship to honor the memory of Alfred V. Verville, a noted aircraft designer. The Verville is intended to assist scholars interested in the analysis of major trends, developments, and accomplishments in aviation or space studies.

Fiscal Information The fellowship is supported by a stipend.

Application Information For further information and application materials, write: Verville Fellowship, Office of the Deputy Director, National Air and Space Museum, Smithsonian Institution, Washington, DC 20560.

Deadline(s) January 15 is the deadline for applications each year.

486. Smithsonian Institution
Office of Fellowships and Grants, Foreign Currency Program
3300 L'Enfant Plaza
Washington, DC 20560
(202) 357-4795

Special Foreign Currency Program

Program Description The Foreign Currency Program awards grants to U.S. institutions of higher learning, including the Smithsonian Institution, for studies in countries where the U.S. holds foreign currencies. The program welcomes proposals from senior scholars in the fields of anthropology and archaeology; culture and history; astrophysics and earth sciences; and museum programs.

Eligibility/Limitations All American institutions of higher learning are eligible.

Fiscal Information The awards are in local currency and may cover international and local travel, living allowance, and research expenses.

Application Information Proposals should provide a summary and description of the research including methodology, bibliography, biographical information on major participants, and a detailed budget. Further information on the program and application instructions may be obtained from the program manager.

Deadline(s) The deadline for receipt of proposals is November 1.

487. Social Science Research Council
605 Third Avenue
New York, NY 10158
(212) 661-0280

Grants for Area Studies Research

Program Description Grants for advanced international research are offered to scholars whose competence for research in the social sciences or humanities has been demonstrated by previous work. These programs are designed to support research in one country, comparative research between countries in any area, and comparative research between areas. Research under these program grants may be conducted in Africa, China, Eastern Europe, Japan, Korea, Latin America and the Caribbean, the Near and Middle East, South Asia, Southeast Asia, the Soviet Union, and Indochina Studies.

Sample Grants 1988 grants have been awarded: to a Mellon fellow, Department of Primitive Art, Metropolitan Museum of Art, for a comparative study of political disputes in Ghana; to a curator, Art of Africa, the Americas, and Oceania, Baltimore Museum of Art, for archival research on the Baga of Guinea.

Eligibility/Limitations Eligibility requirements vary from country to country. Generally, applicants must be citizens or permanent residents of the United States and must hold the Ph.D. or demonstrate equivalent professional experience. These grants are not for training and candidates for academic degrees are not eligible.

Fiscal Information Grants are normally for periods of two months to one year, and awards range up to $25,000. Grants may be used for travel and research expenses as well as for partial maintenance.

Application Information Application forms are furnished in response to written requests. In requesting forms, the applicant should give the following information: a brief statement of the proposed research; geographical area or areas of interest; proposed site of research; occupation or current activity; university or other affiliation; country of citizenship and/or permanent residence; academic degrees, specifying disciplines or fields of study; proposed date for beginning tenure of the award and the duration requested; and the approximate amount needed. Application forms will be sent after preliminary determination of eligibility by council staff.

Deadline(s) The application deadline is December 1.

Additional Information Fellowship awards are available for doctoral research. Contact the council for additional information.

488. Southwestern Bell Foundation
One Bell Center, Room 38-K-8
Saint Louis, MO 63101
(314) 235-7040

Contributions

Program Description The Southwestern Bell companies have an obligation to the quality of life in the communities where they operate. The Southwestern Bell Foundation was formed in 1984 with that responsibility in mind. The foundation receives funds from the Southwestern Bell Corporation to support two major objectives: to encourage innovative programs which promote voluntarism, which provide services directly to those in need, and which have the potential of multiplying the effect of the contributed dollar; and to help find solutions for those problems the foundation has identified as areas of concern in the communities served by Southwestern Bell Corporation and its subsidiaries. The foundation contributes to many types of nonprofit organizations, but concentrates on specific areas of interest within the general categories of education, civic affairs, health and welfare, and culture and the arts. Within the general category of culture and the arts, the foundation is particularly interested in performing arts and cultural programs in major metropolitan serving areas, especially those with outreach potential and which are enjoyed by a broad spectrum of the public, and performing arts and cultural programs that promise to increase public interest and support for cultural presentations.

Sample Grants To the Dallas Arboretum and Botanical Society, Inc., Dallas, TX $13,333 (1986). To the National Gallery of Art Georgia O'Keeffe Exhibition, Washington, DC, $450,000 (1986). To the Friends of the St. Louis Art Museum, Saint Louis, MO, $25,000 (1986).

Eligibility/Limitations The foundation does not make contributions to: organizations without 501(c)(3) tax-exempt status, although in some circumstances, the foundation will consider organizations which qualify as government instrumentalities; organizations that practice discrimination by race, color, creed, sex, age, or national origin; hospital operating funds or capital funds, unless a unique community need can be demonstrated; major operating expenses for organizations supported by the United Way; individuals; political activities or organizations; religious organizations; fraternal, veterans, or labor groups, when serving only their membership; or special goodwill advertising and ticket/dinner purchases.

Fiscal Information In 1986, the foundation awarded grants totaling over $11.8 million. The foundation made 410 grants, totaling $2.6 million, to cultural and arts organizations in 1986.

Application Information Local or statewide nonprofit organizations whose programs meet foundation guidelines should seek contributions from the foundation by sending a written request to the local Southwestern Bell manager. National or regional organizations should send their requests directly to the foundation. Appropriate titles and addresses, additional application procedures, and contributions guidelines are published in a brochure available directly from the foundation at the address above.

Deadline(s) The foundation or the appropriate subsidiary manager will respond to all requests within four to six weeks after receipt.

489. Steele-Reese Foundation
c/o Morgan Guaranty Trust Company of New York
9 West 57th Street
New York, NY 10019
(212) 826-7607

Grants

Program Description The foundation tends to devote its available income in the following categories: scholarships, education, health, welfare, and humanities. The categories are broad, while the welfare category is especially diverse. In the past, it has included projects ranging from youth ranches to conservation.

Sample Grants For the endowment fund and an Appalachian Arts project, $100,000 (of which $50,000 was paid during the year) to Children's Museum of Oak Ridge, Inc., Oak Ridge, TN (1987). For the completion of the visitors' area and for furthering the education program in the Tropical Raptor Building, $40,000 (of which $20,000 was paid during the year) to The Peregrine Fund, Inc., Boise, ID (1987). For a final payment of $40,000 toward a grant of $200,000 for the educational functions of the museum, $40,000 to Oregon High Desert Museum, Bend, OR (1987).

Eligibility/Limitations The foundation generally confines its grants to operating charities in Southern Appalachia (particularly Kentucky) and in the Northwest (particularly Idaho). No grants are made to individuals, virtually none for research or planning, and few for construction. The foundation has a strong preference for projects benefiting rural areas.

Fiscal Information Grants paid (including scholarships) for the financial year ended August 31, 1987 totaled $684,500. Grants vary in size from a few thousand dollars to about $250,000 (with rare exceptions at both ends of the scale) and the larger ones are generally paid in annual installments over a period of three, four, or five years.

Application Information The foundation has no printed forms for applications. An applicant organization can best serve itself and aid the foundation by (a) reviewing the foundation's policy and criteria in detail, and if a proposal seems warranted (b) by writing a succinct factual letter of not more than a couple of pages. This initial inquiry should be addressed (in the case of southern applicants) to: Dr. John R. Bryden, 760 Malabu Drive, Lexington, KY 40502. In the case of northwest applicants to: Mrs. Christine N. Brady, P.O. Box 23, Carmen, ID 83467. Or, in the case of general matters, to: William T. Buice, III, Esq., Messrs. Davidson, Dawson & Clark, 330 Madison Avenue, New York, NY 10017. Any short printed material that is pertinent to an application should also be included.

Deadline(s) Although grant installments are generally paid in February and August of each year, inquiries and applications for grants may be submitted at any time and will be considered as soon as possible.

490. Doris Jones Stein Foundation
1024 Summit Drive
Beverly Hills, CA 90210
(213) 201-7467

Grants

Program Description The Doris Jones Stein Foundation's exclusive purpose is to provide funding to deserving charitable organizations. The foundation was organized in 1981 and has provided grant support to a great variety of worthy causes with emphasis upon educational, medical, and artistic programs.

Eligibility/Limitations Funding is provided only to qualified organizations and institutions which are tax-exempt by federal law. No grants are ever made to individuals or political campaigns. Funding requests for a special program or project will receive more consideration than an application which seeks support for the general operating budget. Organizations of local, national, and international scope have all been recipients of the foundation's funding.

Fiscal Information Over 200 organizations receive grant assistance from the foundation annually.

Application Information The foundation has a special application form, The Doris Jones Stein Foundation Grant Request Summary, which is available on request. This form must be filled out in its entirety and submitted to the foundation by each applicant.

Deadline(s) Grant applications can be made at any time during the year.

491. Sun Company, Inc.
Director, Social Investment
100 Matsonford Road
Radnor, PA 19087
(215) 293-6192

Corporate Contributions Program

Program Description Sun Company believes that its contributions program is a key part of the company's response to the public's economic and social needs. The purpose of the program, then, is to help improve the intellectual, economic, social, and cultural environments in those communities within the continental United States where the corporation has a major presence. Sun Company prioritizes its contributions efforts into five program areas, each with specific attributes: education; civic, economic development, and employment opportunities; health and human services; arts and culture; and public information and policy research. In the arts and culture program, support is available to museums, symphonies, and other visual and performing arts programs and institutions that have established community acceptance and support; and to other organizations that broaden the cultural experiences available to the public in Sun's communities.

Eligibility/Limitations Sun Company supports nonprofit organizations and institutions which meet the corporation's contributions guidelines. Company contributions programs are primarily local in scope and are focused on those areas where the corporation has a major presence, by virtue of a major installation or large concentration of employees. At the national level, Sun directs its contributions activities to limited program areas which fall within the company's priority funding areas and which are determined to help improve the economic, educational, and social climate throughout the nation in general. Contributions are not directed toward: political parties or political candidates; organizations that are not tax-exempt; nor individuals. Generally, funds are not expended to: veterans, religious, or athletic groups; goodwill advertising or benefit fund-raisers; or funding to cover continuing operating deficits.

Application Information All requests must be submitted in writing. Proposals should be brief but concise and should include a description of the organization as follows: brief history of the organization; copy of tax-exempt status; latest audited financial report; current operating budget and sources of income; listing of the organization's key management and board of directors; annual report or update of activities; and number of employees (paid and volunteer). Information regarding the particular program for which funding is being sought should include: purpose and objective of the program; needs to be addressed; population served; plan of action and time frame for proposed program; qualifications of program's administrators; total funding required and projected sources; amount of funds requested; methods of evaluation; and utilization of results.

Deadline(s) No deadlines are announced.

492. Anne Burnett and Charles Tandy Foundation
1577 Interfirst Tower
Fort Worth, TX 76102
(817) 877-3344

Grants

Program Description The foundation provides grants in the fields of education, the arts, and health and human services. The foundation focuses its resources primarily on the Fort Worth and Dallas area. Occasionally, grants are also made to organizations located in other areas in the state of Texas. Generally grants are not made to organizations located outside the state.

Sample Grants For acquisitions, $800,000 to Fort Worth Art Museum, Fort Worth, TX (1985).

Eligibility/Limitations The foundation provides grants to organizations evidencing tax-exempt status under Internal Revenue Code Section 501(c)(3). No grants are made to individuals.

Application Information Applicants are encouraged to write a letter of inquiry to the foundation briefly describing the organization for which the grant is sought, the specific program or project to be considered, a budget summary and the amount of support requested from the foundation. Following staff review of the letter, a more detailed grant application will be requested by the foundation if the program or project fits within the foundation's guidelines and priorities.

Deadline(s) No deadlines are announced.

493. Tenneco Inc.
Director, Community Affairs
Tenneco Building, P.O. Box 2511
Houston, TX 77252-2511
(713) 757-3930

Grants

Program Description Tenneco does not publish guidelines for proposals. Tenneco operates a decentralized giving program with each division responding to the needs of the communities in which it operates.

Eligibility/Limitations Since Houston is the company's headquarters, a substantial portion of corporate contributions is directed to local organizations. The remaining programs supported are regional and national in scope. Tax-exempt organizations are eligible to apply.

Fiscal Information Contributions in 1986 totaled over $8 million.

Application Information Proposals must be in writing and address a specific program, as the company prefers not to fund general operating expenses. In order to be considered for funding, a proposal must include: current audited financial statement and/or budget data; copy of IRS determination letter; listing of board of directors and corporate supporters.

Deadline(s) Proposals are reviewed quarterly and final recommendations for the ensuing year's budget are submitted to the contributions committee in late September.

494. Texaco Philanthropic Foundation Inc.
2000 Westchester Avenue
White Plains, NY 10650
(914) 253-4000

Grants

Program Description The purpose of the Texaco Philanthropic Foundation Inc. is to enhance the quality of life in the United States by providing financial support to selected, nonprofit, tax-exempt organizations in the areas of education, health and hospitals, social welfare, arts and culture, civic and public interest, environmental protection, and other deserving charitable needs. In general, the foundation will make contributions to national organizations that serve a large segment of the population, and to local organizations in areas where Texaco has a significant presence.

Eligibility/Limitations In general, the foundation will not consider contributions to the following: individuals; private foundations; organizations not tax-exempt under the Internal Revenue Code; social functions, commemorative journals, or meetings; religious, fraternal, social, or veterans organizations; endowments; political or partisan organizations or candidates; organizations established to carry on propaganda, or to attempt to influence legislation; organizations established to influence the outcome of any specific public election, or to carry on any voter registration drive.

Fiscal Information Grant contributions in 1986 totaled over $7.4 million.

Application Information Applications should include the following: description of the overall purpose and objectives of the organization; description of the project or event for which funds are requested, including specific objectives and purposes of the project; specific reason(s) why Texaco Foundation is an appropriate donor; budget for the project or event; size and composition of the population to be served by the project; explanation of how the project does not duplicate the efforts of other agencies/ institutions in the same or related fields; timetable of the project; method of measuring success of the project, and by whom; names of officers and key staff members; list of names and primary professional affiliations of members of the board of trustees; proof of tax-exempt status and certification as a 501(c)(3) charitable organization; most recent audited financial statements; funding sources by category for the organization and, if available, a listing of contributors and the size of gifts; description of how Texaco Foundation support will be acknowledged.

Deadline(s) No deadlines are announced.

495. Textron Charitable Trust
P.O. Box 878
Providence, RI 02091
(401) 421-2800

Grants

Program Description The Textron Charitable Trust has been established and is periodically funded by Textron. The contributions program, administered by the Textron Charitable Trust, is one way the company demonstrates its responsibility to the public interest. Financial support is directed primarily to the following: culture and the arts; education; health care; minorities and women; United Way; and youth groups. Additionally, the trust offers to eligible employees and directors matching gift programs for cultural, educational and hospital institutions.

Eligibility/Limitations The goal of the trust's contributions program is to support organizations, institutions and programs that contribute significantly to the quality of life in the communities where Textron employees live and work. The trust cannot contribute to: organizations which are not determined to be a tax-exempt public charity as defined by the Internal Revenue Code 501(c)(3); individuals; endowment funds; or requests that intend to reduce operating deficits.

Fiscal Information The size and number of grants are directly related to the funding available annually. A unique advantage of the trust is its potential for flexibility.

Multiple-year commitments are kept to a minimum which enables the trust to respond to unforeseen needs and special situations.

Application Information Organizations interested in applying for a grant are encouraged to call or write the trust for assistance in determining eligibility for financial support and clarification of the application process. Grant requests should be submitted in writing to the manager, corporate contributions. Special forms and multiple copies are not required. Each proposal received by the trust will receive careful review. More detailed information may be requested as needed. Proposals should include: a statement of purposes and objectives of the organization; a history of the programs of the organization; a list of the organization's officers, board of directors and staff; an annual operating budget for the organization for the year in which the project will occur; audited financial statements for the most recently completed year; a description of the program or project that is the subject of the proposal; the dollar level of support requested; a copy of tax-exempt determination letter from the IRS; a list of other sources approached for financial assistance with the project.

Deadline(s) The trust processes requests for contributions throughout the year.

496. 3M Foundation, Inc.
3M Center, Building 521-11-01
Saint Paul, MN 55144
(612) 736-3781

Contributions

Program Description 3M's tradition of giving is a coordinated effort of the 3M Foundation and the 3M Corporate Contributions Committee. Support is awarded in the following categories: government, special projects, international; federated; civic/ community; arts, media and culture; health care; and education. 3M's support of artistic and cultural programs is an effort to nurture creative expression in the theaters, museums, and music halls of the communities it serves.

Eligibility/Limitations Organizations applying for contributions must have been in existence for at least one year and have an IRS 501(c)(3) tax-exempt status. The program will not make grants to: individuals; organizations with a limited constituency; religious organizations for religious endeavors; propaganda or lobbying efforts to influence legislation; support of any type of travel or tours for individuals or groups; subsidization of books, magazines; newspapers or articles in professional journals; planning or scripting support for media promotion or direct sponsorship of such projects; advertising for any purpose; for-profit organizations.

Fiscal Information Contribution program gifts in 1986 totaled over $17.5 million, including over $2.5 million in the arts, media, culture category.

Application Information 3M requests that inquiries be made by mail. All written inquiries or requests received from nonprofit 501(c)(3) tax-exempt organizations should be submitted on the organization's letterhead and include: brief organizational history; project description including need, objective and target group; specific contribution requested; program/project timetable; listing of directors and officers and their affiliations. The letter of inquiry will be reviewed to determine general eligibility, guideline conformity, and relation to 3M priorities. If, after the initial review, further consideration is to be given, a grant application will be forwarded to the organization.

Deadline(s) The 3M Corporate Contributions Committee and the 3M Foundation Board meet concurrently at quarterly intervals to review proposals. Meetings are usually scheduled in March, June, September, and December. Grant applications must be received at least six weeks before the month in which the request is to be reviewed.

497. Times Mirror Foundation
Corporate Contributions
Times Mirror Square
Los Angeles, CA 90053
(213) 237-3945

Contributions

Program Description Times Mirror's charitable contributions program emphasizes the support of higher education and the arts with increasing support to community service agencies. Times Mirror's educational giving is directed primarily to supporting liberal arts, communications, and business programs at colleges and universities. Times Mirror's cultural grants provide assistance to museums, libraries, performing arts centers, and arts education institutions.

Sample Grants To help establish the Southern California Collecting Project, $10,000 (three year/$30,000 grant) to Archives of American Art (1986). For annual support, $15,000 to California Museum Foundation (1986). Support for the museum's $75 million expansion program, $250,000 (four year/$1 million grant) to Los Angeles County Museum of Natural History (1986). Toward the capital campaign to establish this major new museum in downtown Los Angeles, $100,000 (five year/$500,000 grant) to Museum of Contemporary Art (1986). Contributions toward the new West Wing of the museum, $25,000 (two year/$50,000 pledge) to Saint Louis Art Museum (1986).

Eligibility/Limitations Times Mirror's contributions program provides grants to national and Southern California organizations, and to organizations in communities served by Times Mirror subsidiaries. Times Mirror will not provide grants for religious or fraternal purposes, publications, conferences, films, or to individuals.

Fiscal Information First-time grants generally range from $1,000 to $5,000 for general operating support and from $2,500 to $25,000 for special projects. Grants from the foundation amounted to more than $4.9 million in 1986. Additionally, during 1986 direct corporate contributions awarded over $1 million in grants.

Application Information Send a two- to three-page letter describing the organization, its purpose, programs, and project to be considered. The following attachments should also be submitted: proof of tax-exempt status; list of current supporting organizations and amount of support; and organizational budget for current and upcoming fiscal years.

Deadline(s) The deadline for submitting grant requests for the first meeting of the foundation will be May 1.

Additional Information Agencies located in communities served by subsidiary companies should submit grant requests to the subsidiary directly.

498. The Travelers Companies Foundation
One Tower Square
Hartford, CT 06183
(203) 277-4178

Grants

Program Description Current priority areas of funding include the following: health care and economic security for older Americans; jobs, education and training programs for youth in the Hartford area; small business development; higher education; community and civic affairs; and arts and culture.

Sample Grants For support of the Science Enrichment Program, $5,000 to Children's Museum of Hartford, West Hartford, CT (1985). For renovation costs, $12,500 ($25,000 over two years) to Wadsworth Atheneum, Hartford, CT (1985). For match of NEH grant to help with the costs for mounting, publicizing, and developing materials for the exhibit "The Great River: Art and Society of the Connecticut Valley," $50,000 (plus $35,000 in 1986) to Wadsworth Atheneum, Hartford, CT (1985).

Eligibility/Limitations Grants will not be considered for: organizations which are not tax-exempt under Section 501(c)(3) of the Internal Revenue Code; mass mail appeals, political organizations, testimonial dinners, or memberships in associations; nor grants to individuals.

Fiscal Information Contributions expended in 1985 totaled over $3.5 million

Application Information Organizations should initially submit a "Request for Consideration." This should include: brief history of the organization, its goals and objectives, and the purpose for which the grant is requested. Additional information will be requested if the application falls within the foundation's areas of interest.

Deadline(s) No deadlines are announced.

499. TRW Foundation
1900 Richmond Road
Cleveland, OH 44124
(216) 291-7164

Grants

Program Description The TRW Foundation makes contributions in the following six categories: education; health, welfare, and youth; United Way, civic and cultural; hospitals; and national and international.

Eligibility/Limitations Grants are limited to organizations defined as tax-exempt under Section 501(c)(3) of the Internal Revenue Code. Grants support organizations serving the needs of the public in TRW's U.S. plant communities, selected educational institutions, and selected national and international groups.

Fiscal Information Foundation grants generally represent 85 percent of the total TRW contributions program.

Application Information A detailed and complete grant proposal should be in the form of a narrative statement. Brevity is appreciated. It is generally not necessary to submit extensive documentation; if it is required, the organization will be notified. The following information should be included with the proposal: brief description of the organization, including its legal name, history, activities, and governing board; purpose for which the grant is requested; amount requested and list of other sources of financial support; copy of the organization's most recent audited financial statement; copy of the latest IRS determination letter indicating organization's status as 501(c)(3) tax-exempt, public foundation; statement of need for and objective of proposed project; fully defined budget, including sources of financial support committed and pending; how the project or organization benefits the community; any additional staffing requirements that may be required if the project is funded; how the success of the project will be evaluated.

Deadline(s) The foundation accepts and reviews grant requests throughout the year.

500. Union Pacific Foundation
345 Park Avenue
New York, NY 10154
(212) 418-7926

Grants

Program Description Union Pacific Foundation grants are made primarily to private institutions of higher education, health, social welfare, science, culture and the arts located in communities served by Union Pacific companies. Within the culture and the arts category, the foundation supports museums, cultural centers, arts service organizations such as arts councils and combined arts drives, as well as performing arts groups.

Eligibility/Limitations The foundation's activities are concentrated in geographic areas where there is a significant Union Pacific presence, which is principally in the west. The foundation does not award grants to organizations not eligible for tax-exempt status under Section 501(c)(3) of the Internal Revenue Code or to individuals.

Application Information Grant request forms may be obtained by writing to the foundation. The letter requesting these forms should include a brief description of the soliciting organization and the purpose for which funds will be sought.

Deadline(s) The board of trustees of the foundation meets annually to act on requests which are considered as they are received throughout the year. Only requests received by August 15 will be considered for the following year's budget.

501. USX Foundation Inc.
USX Tower
600 Grant Street, Room 6284
Pittsburgh, PA 15230
(412) 433-5237

Grants

Program Description The USX Foundation provides financial support in a planned and balanced manner to a variety of selected organizations and projects of benefit to educational, scientific, civic, medical/health, cultural, and charitable activities.

Eligibility/Limitations Grants are generally awarded in areas where USX Corporation and its divisions and subsidiaries operate. The foundation does not make grants to individuals. Additionally, grants are not generally awarded for conferences, seminars, symposia, travel purposes, or for the publishing of books, magazines, films, or television productions.

Fiscal Information Grants awarded in 1987 totaled over $4.9 million.

Application Information There is no standard form which must be used to apply for a grant from the foundation. Requests, however, must be made in writing. A one- to two-page letter should be submitted which concisely and completely explains the request, with all appropriate documentation attached. Requests must include a copy of the IRS notification of tax-exempt status as a public foundation under Section 501(c)(93) of the Internal Revenue Code. Requests for grants must include a copy of the requesting organization's current budget and the most recent audited financial report. To be given full and prompt consideration, requests should include the following information: a description of the project and its goals; the amount requested and the estimated cost of the project with a full and complete explanation of the necessity of funds requested in relation to the total requirements and resources; a statement of other sources of aid in hand (if any) and the amounts of such aid; a statement of other sources of anticipated aid where requests are pending or have yet to be made and the amounts requested; the name of the executive in charge of the organization's activities and the names of the members of the board of directors or trustees. The request must be prepared and signed by an authorized executive of the tax-exempt organization or a statement of approval prepared and signed by the individual in charge of the parent organization, if the application originates in a subdivision of such entity.

Deadline(s) While requests are received throughout the year, it is strongly recommended that requests in the cultural category be received by January 15 to be considered during the current fiscal year.

Additional Information USX Foundation also funds Marathan Oil Foundation, Inc., which awarded grants totaling over $1.9 million in 1987. Requests for support must be made directly to: Marathan Oil Foundaiton, Inc., 539 South Main Street, Findlay, OH, 45840-9980, telephone (419) 422-2121.

502. Valley Bank Charitable Foundation
P.O. Box 29524
Phoenix, AZ 85038
(602) 261-2984

Grants

Program Description The foundation has committed financial resources to a wide variety of health and human service organizations, educational programs, cultural endeavors, and civic projects. The foundation supports broad based organizations and programs that fall within the scope of the stated priorities. Foundation contributions are made to the following categories of giving: health/human services; education; culture/art; civic; and other. Within the culture/art category, the foundation, recognizing the need for continuing improvement in the quality of life, provides operational and capital grants to cultural organizations and activities. Consideration may also be given to specific requests for seed money and outreach programs of these organizations.

Eligibility/Limitations The foundation considers all legitimate requests from organizations that qualify for 501(c)(3) tax-exempt status as prescribed by the IRS code. The foundation does not fund: individuals, out-of-state organizations, endowments or private foundations, trips or tours, or research projects.

Application Information All requests must be submitted in writing using the foundation application procedure. Contact the foundation for required application forms and additional information.

Deadline(s) Effective January 1, 1988, all requests for over $5,000 will be reviewed in December of each year. The deadline for these proposals is October 1 of the same year. All other requests will be considered on a monthly basis.

503. Vatican Film Library

Saint Louis University, The Pius XII Memorial Library
3655 West Pine Boulevard
Saint Louis, MO 63108
(314) 658-3090

The Andrew W. Mellon Fellowship Program

Program Description The Andrew W. Mellon Foundation has made available a grant for a continuing postdoctoral fellowship program to assist scholars wishing to conduct research in the manuscript collections in the Vatican Film Library at Saint Louis University. Projects proposed for support under the fellowship program can be in such areas as classical languages and literature, paleography, scriptural and patristic studies, history, philosophy and sciences in the Middle Ages and the Renaissance, and Romance literature. There are also opportunities for supported research in the history of music manuscript illumination, mathematics and technology, theology, liturgy, Roman and canon law, and political theory.

Eligibility/Limitations Scholars with well defined research projects which require the collections of the library are eligible to apply.

Fiscal Information The program provides travel expenses and a reasonable per diem for periods of research at the library ranging from two full weeks to eight weeks.

Application Information Applications should be submitted in the form of a project description including a precise statement of the project, an account of current research, a bibliography of the applicant's publications in areas related to the project, curriculum vitae, a statement of the length of time for which support is requested, and letters from three persons qualified to judge the applicant's manuscript research skills in the project area.

Deadline(s) Fellowship projects can be scheduled only within one of the following periods: January 15 to May 15, June 1 to July 31, and September 1 to December 22. Persons wishing to apply for research support within one of these periods should first write to indicate the exact dates during which support is desired. These persons will be notified whether facilities are still available for the desired dates; if facilities are available these persons will be given a deadline by which project descriptions must be submitted.

504. Dewitt Wallace-Reader's Digest Fund

1270 Avenue of the Americas, Suite 2118
New York, NY 10020
(212) 489-1540

Grants

Program Description The DeWitt Wallace-Reader's Digest Fund is primarily interested in the following program areas: educational opportunities for disadvantaged youth at the pre-college level; independent secondary education; youth employment training and placement; prevention of adolescent pregnancy and parenthood; and youth leadership. The majority of grants are made to organizations in New York City and the northeast.

Consideration is given to proposals from groups outside this region for foundation-initiated programs or when the project has regional or national impact.

Sample Grants For continued work on the Hemlock Forest study, $100,000 (total approved $250,000) to New York Botanical Garden, New York, NY (1987). For the Explainers program, in which high school students act as museum guides, $20,000 (total approved $60,000) to Exploratorium, San Francisco, CA (1987). For renovation of Theodore Roosevelt Hall, $50,000 (total approved $150,000) to American Museum of Natural History, New York, NY (1987).

Eligibility/Limitations Grants are awarded only to nonprofit, public charitable organizations which are tax-exempt under Section 501(c)(3) of the Internal Revenue Code. The fund does not support individuals, religious or veterans' organizations, or private foundations. In addition, the fund does not presently make grants to support public television, film and media projects, or government and public policy organizations. The fund usually does not consider proposals for capital purposes, operating endowments, or scholarly research. Apart from the New York City area, it does not support local chapters of national organizations.

Fiscal Information In general, the fund does not make grants under $25,000. The fund endeavors to support programs that can make substantial progress toward their goals in a period of three years or less. It is willing to consider renewal of selected grants, but it avoids long-term annual support of organizations.

Application Information Initial support should be by a brief letter of inquiry (no more than three pages) which describes the organization, the proposed project and its goals, an estimated budget, and the names and qualifications of the person in charge of the project. If the request falls within the fund's interests, a formal proposal and more detailed information will be requested.

Deadline(s) No deadlines are announced.

505. Lila Wallace-Reader's Digest Fund
1270 Avenue of the Americas, Suite 2118
New York, NY 10020
(212) 489-1540

Grants

Program Description The Lila Wallace-Reader's Digest Fund is primarily interested in the following program areas: the performing arts; the visual arts; and museums, especially programs designed to increase public access and appreciation.

Sample Grants For the Patrons' Permanent Fund for acquisition of new works, $50,000 (total approved $500,000) to National Gallery of Art, Washington, DC (1987). For operating support, $25,000 to Solomon R. Guggenheim Museum, New York, NY (1987). To complete the Lila Acheson Wallace Wing of 20th Century Art, $3.5 million to Metropolitan Museum of Art, New York, NY (1987). For renovation of Central Park Zoo, $2.5 million to New York Zoological Society, New York, NY (1987).

Eligibility/Limitations Grants are awarded only to nonprofit, public charitable organizations which are tax-exempt under Section 501(c)(3) of the Internal Revenue Code. The fund does not support individuals, religious or veterans' organizations, or private foundations. In addition, the fund does not presently make grants to support public television, film and media projects, or government and public policy organizations. The fund usually does not consider proposals for capital purposes, operating endowments, or scholarly research. Apart from the New York City area, it does not support local chapters of national organizations.

Fiscal Information In general, the fund does not make grants under $25,000. The fund endeavors to support programs that can make substantial progress toward their goals in a period of three years or less. It is willing to consider renewal of selected grants, but it avoids long-term annual support of organizations.

Application Information Initial support should be by a brief letter of inquiry (no more than three pages) which describes the organization, the proposed project and its goals, an estimated budget, and the names and qualifications of the person in charge of the project. If the request falls within the fund's interests, a formal proposal and more detailed information will be requested.

Deadline(s) No deadlines are announced.

506. Wells Fargo Foundation
Mac 0101-111
420 Montgomery Street
San Francisco, CA 94163
(415) 396-3568

Contributions Program

Program Description The Wells Fargo Foundation was established in 1978 to administer grants to worthy undertakings in support of human services, the arts and culture, education, and civic improvement on behalf of Wells Fargo & Company and its subsidiaries. Civic enhancement projects involving parks, zoos, historic museums, and science and industry museums are supported. Within the category of arts and culture, the foundation's primary focus is on leading cultural organizations—art museums, ballet and opera companies, and symphonies—in major metropolitan areas within California. Requests from established cultural organizations in other California communities will be considered where their work is characterized by professionalism, innovation, and quality.

Eligibility/Limitations To be eligible for a contribution an organization must: be previously designated as a nonprofit, tax-exempt organization as defined under Sections 501(c)(3) and 170(b) of the IRS code; show program capability, sound fiscal policies, responsible financial management, evidence of long-range planning and effective use of volunteers; have a competent, active board of directors; produce a budget, financial statements, and a plan for funding beyond the period covered by the proposed contribution, particularly in the case of start-up costs; and show a method of evaluating the results of the proposed project. In general, the foundation does not provide repetitive annual grants or continuing support for organizations or programs. As a general rule, the foundation does not make grants for: individuals; religious organizations; production of videotapes, films, and publications; organizations that discriminate on the basis of race, color, creed, sex, age, or national origin; hospital operating funds, the maintenance of medical facilities, or the purchase of medical equipment; research; direct grants to primary and secondary schools; medical clinics; health organizations; endowment funds; conferences, seminars, or symposia; United Way-supported agencies; consortia and grant-making foundations; programs and organizations outside the U.S.; sports programs and events; environmental organizations; political or lobbying activities; or organizations primarily supported by taxes.

Fiscal Information In 1986, the foundation awarded 598 grants totaling over $4.4 million. In the category of civic enhancement, 80 grants were awarded and totaled over $300,000; in the category of arts and culture, 86 grants were awarded and totaled over $660,000.

Application Information Letters of application, no more than two pages long, should include: a description of the organization, its name, address, telephone number, and name of contact person; a short statement of the purpose or objectives of the organization; and a request for a specific amount of money with an explanation of how the funds will be used. To each letter or request, attach a copy of the organization's most recent tax-exempt ruling statement from the IRS, a list of the board of directors and their affiliations, and a financial report showing the overall budget of the organization.

Deadline(s) Requests are reviewed by the foundation's board of directors at quarterly meetings.

507. Wenner-Gren Foundation for Anthropological Research
1865 Broadway
New York, NY 10023-7596
(212) 957-8750

Developing Country Training Fellowships

Program Description Wenner-Gren's sphere of interest is the support of research in all branches of anthropology and in related disciplines pertaining to the sciences of man. Projects supported use cross-cultural, historical, biological, and linguistic approaches towards understanding man's origins, development, and variation. Special consideration is given to projects integrating two or more subfields of anthropology or related disciplines, particularly when combined with theoretical or methodological issues.

Eligibility/Limitations Developing Country Fellowships are awarded to qualified scholars or students from developing countries. These fellowships are designed primarily to support younger scholars who need training unavailable in their home country and who cannot meet the costs of such training elsewhere.

Fiscal Information Fellowships of up to $12,500 are awarded annually. Foundation aid does not support large-scale projects, salary and/or fringe benefits, tuition, non-project personnel, travel to national meetings, dissertation publication, institutional overhead, intermediary funding agencies, or building materials and construction.

Application Information Additional information and application materials for Developing Country Fellowships are mailed on request. Applicants may submit a brief description of the proposed project, including anticipated starting date and required funding. If a project is considered eligible, a formal application will be invited and the appropriate forms and guidelines supplied.

Deadline(s) Applications must be submitted no less than nine months prior to starting date of training.

508. Wenner-Gren Foundation for Anthropological Research
1865 Broadway
New York, NY 10023-7596
(212) 957-8750

Foundation-Administered Conferences

Program Description Wenner-Gren's sphere of interest is the support of research in all branches of anthropology and in related disciplines pertaining to the sciences of man. Projects supported use cross-cultural, historical, biological, and linguistic approaches towards understanding man's origins, development, and variations. Special consideration is given to projects integrating two or more subfields of anthropology or related disciplines, particularly when combined with theoretical or methodological issues. In addition to awarding direct grants-in-aid for conferences, the foundation accepts proposals from accredited scholars for conferences to be administered by the foundation under its conference program.

Fiscal Information Foundation assistance varies with the size and location of each conference. Foundation aid does not support large-scale projects, salary and/or fringe benefits, tuition, non-project personnel, travel to national meetings, dissertation publication, institutional overhead, intermediary funding agencies, or building materials and construction.

Application Information Additional information and application materials concerning foundation-administered conferences are mailed on request. Applicants may submit a brief description of the proposed project, including anticipated starting date and required funding. If a project is considered eligible, a formal application will be invited and the appropriate forms and guidelines supplied.

Deadline(s) Applications must be submitted at least eighteen (18) months in advance of a conference.

509. Wenner-Gren Foundation for Anthropological Research
1865 Broadway
New York, NY 10023-7596
(212) 957-8750

Postdoctoral Fellowships

Program Description Wenner-Gren's sphere of interest is the support of research in all branches of anthropology and in related disciplines pertaining to the sciences of man. Projects supported use cross-cultural, historical, biological, and linguistic approaches towards understanding man's origins, development, and variations. Special consideration is given to projects integrating two or more subfields of anthropology or related disciplines, particularly when combined with theoretical or methodological issues. Postdoctoral fellowships are intended to allow recent Ph.D.s in the anthropological sciences to train in a related field or fields outside anthropology. The program of study must be designed to broaden interdisciplinary skills relevant to a particular problem or project within the candidate's area of specialization.

Eligibility/Limitations Recent Ph.D.s in the anthropological sciences may apply. Postdoctoral fellowships are not designed to support fieldwork. Formal enrollment or association with a non-anthropological department or research laboratory is required.

Fiscal Information Fellowships carry an award up to $15,000. Foundation aid does not support large-scale projects, salary and/or fringe benefits, tuition, non-project personnel, travel to national meetings, dissertation publication, institutional overhead, intermediary funding agencies, or building materials and construction.

Application Information Application materials for postdoctoral fellowships are mailed on request. Applicants may submit a brief description of the proposed project, including anticipated starting date and required funding. If a project is considered eligible, a formal application will be invited and the appropriate forms and guidelines supplied.

Deadline(s) Applications must be postmarked no later than June 1.

510. Wenner-Gren Foundation for Anthropological Research
1865 Broadway
New York, NY 10023-7596
(212) 957-8750

Senior Scholar Research Stipends

Program Description Wenner-Gren's sphere of interest is the support of research in all branches of anthropology and in related disciplines pertaining to the sciences of man. Projects supported use cross-cultural, historical, biological, and linguistic approaches towards understanding man's origins, development, and variations. Special consideration is given to projects integrating two or more subfields of anthropology or related disciplines, particularly when combined with theoretical or methodological issues. Senior scholar stipends provide support for writing and study integrating a scholar's past research with his/her current interests.

Eligibility/Limitations Scholars who have established records of research and publication may apply. Priority consideration will be given to retired scholars, to those about to retire, or to those who have no facilities at the time of application.

Fiscal Information Stipends up to $15,000 are available. Foundation aid does not support large-scale projects, salary and/or fringe benefits, tuition, non-project personnel, travel to national meetings, dissertation publication, institutional overhead, intermediary funding agencies, or building materials and construction.

Application Information Application materials for senior scholar research stipends are mailed on request. Applicants may submit a brief description of the proposed project, including anticipated starting date and required funding. If a project is considered eligible, a formal application will be invited and the appropriate forms and guidelines supplied.

Deadline(s) Application materials must be postmarked no later than June 1.

511. Wenner-Gren Foundation for Anthropological Research
1865 Broadway
New York, NY 10023-7596
(212) 957-8750

Small Grants Program: Regular Grants

Program Description Wenner-Gren's sphere of interest is the support of research in all branches of anthropology and in related disciplines pertaining to the sciences of man. Projects supported use cross-cultural, historical, biological, and linguistic approaches towards understanding man's origins, development, and variations. Special consideration is given to projects integrating two or more subfields of anthropology or related disciplines, particularly when combined with theoretical or methodological issues. Small grants are available to accredited scholars and to students enrolled for an advanced degree and cover research expenses contemplated by the applicant. Small grants are geared to seeding innovative or untried approaches and ideas, and provide material support to encourage aid from other funding agencies. Regular Grants are awarded to individual scholars from anywhere in the world who are affiliated with an accredited institution or organization.

Eligibility/Limitations Accredited scholars may apply.

Fiscal Information Regular Grant awards usually range from $500 to $7,000 and are primarily for basic research. Foundation aid does not support large-scale projects, salary and/or fringe benefits, tuition, non-project personnel, travel to national meetings, dissertation publication, institutional overhead, intermediary funding agencies, or building materials and construction.

Application Information Applicants are required to submit project description forms, which are available on request. Project description forms will be accepted only in accordance with the current deadline schedule, available from the foundation. Applicants may submit a brief description of the proposed project, including anticipated starting date and required funding. If a project is considered eligible, a formal application will be invited and the appropriate forms and guidelines supplied.

Deadline(s) Applications must be postmarked by June 1.

512. Wenner-Gren Foundation for Anthropological Research
1865 Broadway
New York, NY 10023-7596
(212) 957-8750

Small Grants Program: Richard Carley Hunt Memorial Postdoctoral Fellowships

Program Description Wenner-Gren's sphere of interest is the support of research in all branches of anthropology and in related disciplines pertaining to the sciences of man. Projects supported use cross-cultural, historical, biological, and linguistic approaches towards understanding man's origins, development, and variations. Special consideration is given to projects integrating two or more subfields of anthropology or related disciplines, particularly when combined with theoretical or methodological issues. Small grants are available to accredited scholars and to students enrolled for an advanced degree and cover research expenses contemplated by the applicant. Small grants are geared to seeding innovative or untried approaches and ideas, and provide material support to encourage aid from other funding agencies. The Richard Carley Hunt Memorial Postdoctoral Fellowships are awarded to aid completion of specific studies or for preparation for publication of field manuals.

Eligibility/Limitations Postdoctoral scholars may apply.

Fiscal Information The fellowship carries a stipend of $4,000 and is non-renewable. Foundation aid does not support large-scale projects, salary and/or fringe benefits, tuition, non-project personnel, travel to national meetings, dissertation publication, institutional overhead, intermediary funding agencies, or building materials and construction.

Application Information Applicants are required to submit project description forms, which are available on request. Project description forms will be accepted only in accordance with the current deadline schedule, available from the foundation. Applicants may submit a brief description of the proposed project, including anticipated starting date and required funding. If a project is considered eligible, a formal application will be invited and the appropriate forms and guidelines supplied.

Deadline(s) Applications must be postmarked by June 1.

513. Wenner-Gren Foundation for Anthropological Research
1865 Broadway
New York, NY 10023-7596
(212) 957-8750

Small Grants Program: Student Grants

Program Description Wenner-Gren's sphere of interest is the support of research in all branches of anthropology and in related disciplines pertaining to the sciences of man. Projects supported use cross-cultural, historical, biological, and linguistic approaches towards understanding man's origins, development, and variations. Special consideration is given to projects integrating two or more subfields of anthropology or related disciplines, particularly when combined with theoretical or methodological issues. Small grants are available to accredited scholars and to students enrolled for an advanced degree and cover research expenses contemplated by the applicant. Small grants are geared to seeding innovative or untried approaches and ideas, and provide material support to encourage aid from other funding agencies. Student Grants are awarded to individuals at the advanced predoctoral level for research.

Eligibility/Limitations Students at the advanced predoctoral level are eligible. Anyone enrolled in a degree program at the time of application is considered by the foundation to be in the student category.

Fiscal Information Student Grant awards usually range from $500 to $7,000 and are primarily for basic research. Foundation aid does not support large-scale projects, salary and/or fringe benefits, tuition, non-project personnel, travel to national meetings, dissertation publication, institutional overhead, intermediary funding agencies, or building materials and construction. Whenever possible, student applicants from North America, Western Europe, and Japan should demonstrate the availability of matching funds. However, any worthy project will be taken under consideration despite lack of such funds, regardless of the citizenship of the applicant.

Application Information Applicants are required to submit project description forms, which are available on request. Project description forms will be accepted only in accordance with the current deadline schedule, available from the foundation. Applicants may submit a brief description of the proposed project, including anticipated starting date and required funding. If a project is considered eligible, a formal application will be invited and the appropriate forms and guidelines supplied.

Deadline(s) Applications must be postmarked by June 1.

514. Westinghouse Electric Fund
Westinghouse Electric Corporation
Pittsburgh, PA 15222
(412) 642-6035

Corporate Contributions

Program Description The Westinghouse Electric Fund, established in 1952, is a trust designed to make charitable contributions to tax-exempt, nonprofit organizations primarily in areas where Westinghouse has a significant presence. The emphasis is on unified campaigns that support health and welfare organizations—especially the United Way, hospitals, and youth programs. The fund also supports various educational, cultural, and civic programs initiated by nonprofit, tax-exempt organizations approved by the board of directors. Art and cultural support enhances the quality of life primarily in Westinghouse locations with special attention directed toward access to cultural programming by the economically disadvantaged; support of the development of the arts that focuses on local community involvement; support of those organizations dedicated to supporting and improving the arts nationally. Civic and social support is made to organizations whose efforts in research, program development, publications, and impact on society benefit those special groups of people of most concern to the trustees with a focus on community development.

Eligibility/Limitations The fund provides support to nonprofit organizations and activities at Westinghouse locations throughout the United States. All recipients must be nonprofit, tax-exempt organizations operating primarily in the United States. The fund does not support grants to individuals or organizations outside the U.S. and its territories.

Fiscal Information Grants in 1986 totaled over $9.5 million, including $811,843 to culture and the arts.

Application Information For information on the fund, address correspondence to the executive director at the address listed above.

Deadline(s) No deadlines are announced.

515. Whatcom Museum of History and Art
Melville and Jacobs Research Fund
121 Prospect Street
Bellingham, WA 98225
(206) 676-6981

Jacobs Research Funds: Small Grants Program

Program Description The funds invite application for small grants for research in the field of social and cultural anthropology among living American native peoples. Preference will be given to the Pacific Northwest as an area of study, but other regions of North America will be considered. Field studies which address cultural expressive systems, such as music, language, dance, mythology, world view, plastic and graphic arts, intellectual life, and religion, including studies which propose comparative psychological analysis, are appropriate.

Eligibility/Limitations Grants are made to individuals. Projects in archaeology, physical anthropology, applied anthropology, and applied linguistics are not eligible, nor is archival research supported.

Fiscal Information Grants are usually small, with a maximum of $1,200. Informant fees, supplies, and some travel will be supported, but not salary or general maintenance, although exceptions may be made under unusual circumstances. Grants are made for a maximum of one year and be renewed only on the basis of a new application.

Application Information Additional information and application forms are available on request.

Deadline(s) Completed applications must be received by the Whatcom Museum Foundation by February 15.

516. Woodrow Wilson International Center for Scholars
Smithsonian Institution Building
Washington, DC 20560
(202) 357-2841

History, Culture, and Society

Program Description The center seeks to commemorate through its residential fellowship program of advanced research both the scholarly depth and the public concerns of Woodrow Wilson. The center welcomes from individuals throughout the world outstanding project proposals representing a wide diversity of scholarly interests and approaches. Projects are encouraged from the whole range of the humanities and social sciences. In this program—the largest and most diversified—the center accommodates fellows who work on geographic regions not represented by other programs (e.g., Africa, Europe and the Middle East), comparative studies that cut across several global areas, or international relations. The program is also receptive to projects that study the distant as well as the recent past and to those with theoretical, philosophical, or theological dimensions.

Eligibility/Limitations Applicants from any country are eligible. Men and women with outstanding capabilities and experience from a wide variety of backgrounds (such as academia, journalism, government, labor, business, and the professions) are eligible for support. For academic participants, eligibility is limited to the postdoctoral level, and normally it is expected that academic candidates will have demonstrated their scholarly development by the publication of some major work beyond the Ph.D. dissertation. For participants from other fields, an equivalent degree or professional achievement is expected. While English is the working language of the center, research and writing may be pursued in any language. The center's program is residential in character and fellows are expected to devote full time to the major research project proposed in the application.

Fiscal Information Because the center has a limited amount of fellowship support it strongly encourages applicants to seek concurrent sources of funding, e.g., other fellowships, foundation grants, sabbaticals, or other funding from their home institutions. All center stipends are subject to a ceiling of $35,000 per twelve-month period. For scholars from abroad, the center attempts to approximate, but does not exceed, the salaries of U.S. scholars of comparable experience and position. Certain travel expenses for a fellow and accompanying spouse and younger children may also be provided. Appointments normally extend from four months to one year.

Application Information Additional information and application procedures are available from the center.

Deadline(s) The center holds one round of competitive selection per year. The deadline for receipt of applications and all supporting materials is October 1.

517. Woodrow Wilson National Fellowship Foundation
Box 642
Princeton, NJ 08540
(609) 924-4666

Mellon Fellowships in the Humanities

Program Description The Mellon Fellowships in the Humanities have two objectives: to attract annually 100 to 125 exceptionally promising students into preparation for careers in humanistic teaching and scholarship by providing top-level, competitive, portable awards tenable for as many as three years; and to contribute thereby to the continuity of teaching and research of the highest order in America's colleges and universities. Fields eligible are the traditional humanities disciplines, including history, but not the creative or performing arts. American studies, other area studies, and interdisciplinary programs are also eligible if the emphasis in subject and method is substantially humanistic.

Eligibility/Limitations Any college senior or recent graduate who is a U.S. or Canadian citizen, can present evidence of outstanding academic promise, and wishes to begin graduate work in preparation for a career of teaching and scholarship in a humanistic field of study is eligible for consideration. Individuals who have been candidates in a previous year, however, are normally not eligible.

Fiscal Information The stipend for fellows entering graduate school in the fall will be $8,500 plus payment of tuition and standard fees to their graduate schools. Fellowships will be renewed for a second year on recommendation of the graduate school concerned. In that year, the graduate school is expected to cover one-third of tuition and fees; the Mellon Fellowships will cover the remainder. In addition, fellows who have performed with distinction will be eligible for stipends (but not tuition and fee support) in the final year of work on their dissertations. Normally, the support will not extend beyond the fifth year of graduate study, but in special circumstances it may be available later at the discretion of the director.

Application Information Candidacy must be initiated by nomination from a faculty member to the program's appropriate regional chairman or the central office if the nominee is overseas or expects to be there during January-February.

Deadline(s) Nominations must reach the regional chairman by November 4. Applications must reach the regional chairman by December 9.

518. Winterthur Museum
Office of Advanced Studies
Winterthur, DE 19735
(302) 656-8591 ext. 249

Benno M. Forman Fellowships

Program Description Winterthur is a research center for the study of art and cultural history, as well as a major museum and period display garden. Its resources for advanced study include over 70,000 domestic artifacts from the seventeenth through the nineteenth centuries and a specialized research library of nearly 60,000 bound volumes and over half a million manuscripts, slides, and photographs. The Benno M. Forman Fellowships are designed to promote research in American material culture, particularly the history, theory, or criticism of decorative arts, household furnishings, or domestic environments.

Eligibility/Limitations Applications from scholars in any relevant discipline are welcome, including candidates for degrees and individuals enrolled in degree-granting programs.

Fiscal Information These fellowships provide stipends of $1,000 per month for one to three months.

Application Information Applicants should submit a three- to five-page statement of purpose, curriculum vitae, and at least two letters of recommendation. A separate application must be made for each fellowship and each candidate must specify when during the academic year they expect to be in residence.

Deadline(s) All materials must be received by June 1.

519. Winterthur Museum
Office of Advanced Studies
Winterthur, DE 19735
(302) 656-8591 ext. 249

Beverley R. Robinson Doctoral Research Fellowships

Program Description Winterthur is a research center for the study of art and cultural history, as well as a major museum and period display garden. Its resources for advanced study include over 70,000 domestic artifacts from the seventeenth through the nineteenth centuries and a specialized research library of nearly 60,000 bound volumes and over half a million manuscripts, slides, and photographs. The Beverley R. Robinson Doctoral Research Fellowships are designed to support doctoral research in the fields of seventeenth-, eighteenth-, and nineteenth-century American art, American decorative arts or American material culture.

Eligibility/Limitations These graduate fellowships are designed to support doctoral research at the Winterthur.

Fiscal Information These fellowships provide stipends of $1,000 per month for three to six months.

Application Information Applicants should submit a three- to five-page statement of purpose, curriculum vitae, and at least two letters of recommendation. A separate application must be made for each fellowship and each candidate must specify when during the academic year they expect to be in residence. Supporting materials for this fellowship must include a dissertation prospectus and a letter from the dissertation adviser.

Deadline(s) All materials must be received by June 1.

520. Winterthur Museum
Office of Advanced Studies
Winterthur, DE 19735
(302) 656-8591 ext. 249

Henry Francis du Pont Fellowships

Program Description Winterthur is a research center for the study of art and cultural history, as well as a major museum and period display garden. Its resources for advanced study include over 70,000 domestic artifacts from the seventeenth through the nineteenth centuries and a specialized research library of nearly 60,000 bound volumes and over half a million manuscripts, slides, and photographs. The Henry Francis du Pont Fellowships are designed to promote advanced research and study at Winterthur in the fields of American art, American decorative arts, and American material life.

Eligibility/Limitations Applications from university faculty and museum professionals are welcome; candidates for degrees or persons seeking support for degrees are ineligible.

Fiscal Information These fellowships provide stipends of $2,000 per month for six to twelve months.

Application Information Applicants should submit a three- to five-page statement of purpose, curriculum vitae, and at least two letters of recommendation. A separate application must be made for each fellowship and each candidate must specify when during the academic year they expect to be in residence.

Deadline(s) All materials must be received by June 1.

521. Winterthur Museum
Office of Advanced Studies
Winterthur, DE 19735
(302) 656-8591 ext. 249

Louise du Pont Crowninshield Fellowships

Program Description Winterthur is a research center for the study of art and cultural history, as well as a major museum and period display garden. Its resources for advanced study include over 70,000 domestic artifacts from the seventeenth through the nineteenth centuries and a specialized research library of nearly 60,000 bound volumes and over half a million manuscripts, slides, and photographs. The Crowninshield Fellowships support research for scholarly catalogues in American decorative arts and related fields.

Eligibility/Limitations These fellowships are intended to assist museum professionals actively engaged in producing catalogues for special exhibitions or permanent collections.

Fiscal Information These fellowships provide stipends of $1,000 per month for one to three months.

Application Information Applicants should submit a three- to five-page statement of purpose, curriculum vitae, and at least two letters of recommendation. A separate application must be made for each fellowship and each candidate must specify when during the academic year they expect to be in residence.

Deadline(s) All materials must be received by June 1.

522. Winterthur Museum
Office of Advanced Studies
Winterthur, DE 19735
(302) 656-8591 ext. 249

Winterthur Museum Visiting Scholars

Program Description Winterthur is a research center for the study of art and cultural history, as well as a major museum and period display garden. Its resources for advanced study include over 70,000 domestic artifacts from the seventeenth through the nineteenth centuries and a specialized research library of nearly 60,000 bound volumes and over half a million manuscripts, slides, and photographs. The Winterthur will consider granting visiting scholar status to individuals who have obtained awards from other granting institutions and would like to do research at and be associated with the museum.

Fiscal Information Visiting scholars will be accorded full access to the museum's resources but will receive no stipend from Winterthur. Appointments may be for one to nine months during the academic year.

Application Information Applicants should submit a three- to five-page statement of purpose, curriculum vitae, and at least two letters of recommendation. A separate application must be made for each fellowship and each candidate must specify when during the academic year they expect to be in residence.

Deadline(s) All materials must be received by June 1.

523. The Wortham Foundation, Inc.
2727 Allen Parkway, Suite 2000
Houston, TX 77019

Grants

Program Description The founders are interested in "enriching the lives of the people primarily in the city of Houston," thus, the Wortham Foundation's major interests are in maintaining its cultural arts and enhancing civic beautification. Grants are awarded in the following categories: performing arts, museums, parks/recreation, public interest/civic affairs, youth/social services, and other.

Eligibility/Limitations Requesting organizations must be 501(c)(3) under the Internal Revenue Code. Federal tax laws prohibit private foundations from lending or giving money to individuals.

Fiscal Information Grants awarded in 1987 totaled over $7.4 million.

Application Information One unbound copy of a proposal should be sent, which should include: specific description of program or project for which request is submitted; project budget; amount requested and date needed; copy of all documents from IRS relative to tax-exempt status under Section 170 of the Internal Revenue Code; listing of trustees or directors and principal staff; current fiscal year-to-date and last complete fiscal year financial statements. A formal application will be mailed upon request.

Deadline(s) The fiscal year of the foundation is October 1 to September 30. Grants are awarded in November, February, May, and August each year. Proposals should be received no later than the first week in October, January, April, and July.

524. The Xerox Foundation
P.O. Box 1600
Stamford, CT 06904
(203) 329-8700

Xerox Grants

Program Description Each year, the foundation distributes grants among five general focus areas which together comprise the entire social sphere: higher education, community affairs, national affairs, international affairs, and cultural activities.

Eligibility/Limitations Grants are only made to organizations that are exempted from Federal Income Tax under Section 501(c)(3) and ruled to be publicly supported under Section 509(a) of the Internal Revenue Code.

Fiscal Information Foundation activity in the U.S. totaled approximately $10 million in 1984.

Application Information No specific application form is used. Applications for grants must be submitted in letter form, preferably no longer than two or three pages. This letter should contain the legal name of the organization, the official contact person, its tax-exempt status, a brief description of its activities and programs, the purpose for which the grant is being requested, the benefits expected, the plans for evaluation, the projected budget, and the expected sources and amount of needed funds. Any additional factual material related to the organization or the request that may be useful for evaluation, plus a copy of the latest annual financial statement, should also be included.

Deadline(s) There is no deadline for submitting proposals. The foundation has approximately four committee meetings per year to consider requests qualifying for support.

525. The Yale Center for British Art
Box 2120 Yale Station
New Haven, CT 06520

Visiting Fellowships

Program Description The Yale Center for British Art offers a limited number of short-term fellowships to allow scholars of literature, history, the history of art, or related fields to study the center's holdings of paintings, drawings, prints, and rare books, and to make use of its research facilities (photograph archive and art reference library). The collections reflect the development of English art from the Elizabethan period onward, with particular emphasis on the period between the birth of Hogarth (1697) and the death of Turner (1851).

Eligibility/Limitations Scholars engaged in postdoctoral or equivalent research related to British art are eligible to apply. Recipients of the fellowship will be required to be in residence in New Haven during the bulk of the grant period.

Fiscal Information Grants pay for travel expenses to and from New Haven and provide a living allowance. The length of the grant will depend on the applicant's research proposal and will normally be for periods of four weeks, although grants for shorter or longer periods may be awarded in exceptional cases.

Application Information Typed applications should be mailed to the director of the center and should include: name, address, and telephone number; resume listing educational background, professional experience, and publications; and a brief outline of the research proposal and an indication of the length of time required to complete the project, including preferred dates, not to exceed three pages. Two referees should be asked to send confidential letters to arrive by December 31.

Deadline(s) Applications for fellowships should be submitted before December 31.

Additional Information One of the fellowships is reserved for members of the American Society for Eighteenth-Century Studies; applicants should indicate whether they belong to the society. By arrangement with the Huntington Library, scholars may apply for tandem awards; each institution requires a separate application, but every effort will be made to offer consecutive dates to successful applicants.

Subject Index

Endowment Funds

The Ahmanson Foundation, 4
Blandin Foundation, 88
Borg-Warner Foundation, 92
Edward C. Johnson Fund, 265

Environment

Edward C. Johnson Fund, 265

Equipment

The Ahmanson Foundation, 4
The George I. Alden Trust, 6
Blandin Foundation, 88
Burroughs Corporation, 104
The Champlin Foundations, 122
Adolph Coors Company, 138
Data General, 160
General Services Administration, 195
Hewlett-Packard Company Foundation, 232
IBM Corporation, 241
Indian Arts and Crafts Board, 243
The Kresge Foundation, 275
The J. E. and L. E. Mabee Foundation, Inc., 287
The John D. and Catherine MacArthur Foundation, 289
National Endowment for the Arts, 327, 343
The Pittsburgh Foundation, 438
Polaroid Foundation, 439

Europe, Western

Council for International Exchange of Scholars, 153

Exhibitions

The American Academy and Institute of Arts and Letters, 8
American Express Foundation, 35
Asian Cultural Council, 78
AT&T Foundation, 83
Champion International Corporation, 121
Dayton Hudson Foundation, 161
First Interstate Bank of California Foundation, 183
The Armand Hammer Foundation, 224
Lannan Foundation, 279
Morgan Guaranty Trust Company of New York, 312
National Endowment for the Arts, 326, 329-30, 335, 340, 347, 350-51, 356
National Endowment for the Humanities, 375
National Science Foundation, 405
William Penn Foundation, 429
Polaroid Foundation, 439

The Rockefeller Foundation, 447

Faculty Support *See* Fellowships, Senior/Faculty

Fellowships, Doctoral *See Also* Internships

American Antiquarian Society, 16
American Association of University Women Educational Foundation, 20
American Council of Learned Societies, 24, 27
American Institute of Indian Studies, 40
American Jewish Archives, 48-49
The American Numismatic Society, 55
American Oriental Society, 56-57
American School of Classical Studies at Athens, 62
American Schools of Oriental Research, 68
Asian Cultural Council, 78, 81
Center for Advanced Study in the Visual Arts, 111-17
The Gladys Krieble Delmas Foundation, 162
Dumbarton Oaks Center for Byzantine Studies, 167
Eastern National Park & Monument Association, 171
Eleutherian Mills Historical Library, 175
The Getty Center for the History of Art and the Humanities, 197
The Huntington Library, 240
Institute of International Education, 248
International Research & Exchanges Board, 251-53, 259
National Endowment for the Humanities, 365
National Science Foundation, 401
The Newberry Library, 413, 417
The Philadelphia Center for Early American Studies, 433
Winterthur Museum, 519

Fellowships, Graduate *See Also* Internships

American Council of Learned Societies, 26
American Museum of Natural History, 52
The American Research Center in Egypt, 59
American Research Institute in Turkey, 60
American School of Classical Studies at Athens, 61
Asian Cultural Council, 77
Committee on Scholarly Communication with the People's Republic of China, 133
Early American Industries Association, 169

Management Development

Robert Sterling Clark Foundation, Inc., 127
Institute of Museum Services, 249
National Endowment for the Arts, 320

Matching/Challenge Funds

The Ahmanson Foundation, 4
Best Products Foundation, 86
Borg-Warner Foundation, 92
The J. Paul Getty Trust, 199
James G. Hanes Memorial Fund/
Foundation, 225
IBM Corporation, 241
National Endowment for the Arts, 322
National Endowment for the
Humanities, 390

Material Culture

Center for Advanced Study in the Visual
Arts, 110, 118
Winterthur Museum, 518-20

Media *See* Film/Video; Radio/Television

Medieval Studies

American Academy in Rome, 9

Mediterranean Studies

The Dr. M. Aylwin Cotton Foundation, 140-41
The Metropolitan Museum of Art, 303

Middle East

Council for International Exchange of
Scholars, 151

Middle Eastern Studies

American Schools of Oriental Research,
63-66, 69-71
Social Science Research Council, 487

Mineral Sciences

American Museum of Natural History,
50, 53

Minorities, Eligibility of *See Also* Women, Eligibility of

Indian Arts and Crafts Board, 243
National Endowment for the
Humanities, 365
Smithsonian Institution, 461, 474-76

Museology

American Museum of Natural History,
51
William Hammond Mathers Museum,
290

National Endowment for the Arts, 345-46
Smithsonian Institution, 471-72, 486

Music

National Endowment for the Arts, 352

National Parks

Eastern National Park & Monument
Association, 170-71

Natural History

American Museum of Natural History,
54
The Bristol-Myers Fund, Inc., 96
Mountain Bell Foundation, 314

Near Eastern Studies

The American Research Center in Egypt,
59
American Research Institute in Turkey,
60
Social Science Research Council, 487

Numismatics

The American Numismatic Society, 55

Operating Support *See* General/Operating Support

Ornithology

American Museum of Natural History,
52

Outreach Programs

ARCO Foundation, 75
Citicorp, 126
The Ford Foundation, 187
The John D. and Catherine MacArthur
Foundation, 288
McKesson Foundation, Inc., 293
National Endowment for the Arts, 326,
350
Pacific Telesis Foundation, 424
Southwestern Bell Foundation, 488
Valley Bank Charitable Foundation, 502

Pakistan

American Institute of Pakistan Studies,
44

Postdoctoral Support *See* Fellowships, Postdoctoral

Geographic Restriction Index*

Company Operating Areas (no state preference)

The Abbott Laboratories Fund, 1
Burroughs Corporation, 104
Corning Glass Works Foundation, 139
Data General, 160
Eastman Kodak Company, 172
Eaton Corporation, 173
General Motors Foundation, Inc., 194
Eli Lilly and Company Foundation, 280
Norfolk Southern Foundation, 419
Santa Fe Southern Pacific Foundation, 451
Shell Oil Company Foundation, 456
TRW Foundation, 499
Union Pacific Foundation, 500
Westinghouse Electric Fund, 514

Company Operating Areas (with state preference)

ALABAMA
The William Bingham Foundation, 87
Burlington Northern Foundation, 103
Adolph Coors Company, 138
Reynolds Metals Company Foundation, 445
Scott Paper Company Foundation, 454
Textron Charitable Trust, 495

ALASKA
Adolph Coors Company, 138

ARIZONA
Best Products Foundation, 86
The May Stores Foundation, Inc., 291
Reynolds Metals Company Foundation, 445

ARKANSAS
Burlington Northern Foundation, 103
Adolph Coors Company, 138
The Pillsbury Company, 437
Reynolds Metals Company Foundation, 445
Scott Paper Company Foundation, 454
Southwestern Bell Foundation, 488

CALIFORNIA
Anheuser-Busch Companies, Inc., 74
Best Products Foundation, 86
Burlington Northern Foundation, 103
Adolph Coors Company, 138
The May Stores Foundation, Inc., 291
McGraw-Hill Foundation, Inc., 292
Pennzoil Company, 430
The Pillsbury Company, 437
Reynolds Metals Company Foundation, 445
Sara Lee Foundation, 452
Textron Charitable Trust, 495
USX Foundation Inc., 501

COLORADO
Anheuser-Busch Companies, Inc., 74
Best Products Foundation, 86
Burlington Northern Foundation, 103
Adolph Coors Company, 138
The May Stores Foundation, Inc., 291
McGraw-Hill Foundation, Inc., 292
The Pillsbury Company, 437
Reynolds Metals Company Foundation, 445

CONNECTICUT
Cooper Industries Foundation, 137
Dart & Kraft Foundation, 159
Hallmark Cards, Inc., 223
The May Stores Foundation, Inc., 291
The Pillsbury Company, 437
Reynolds Metals Company Foundation, 445
Sara Lee Foundation, 452
Textron Charitable Trust, 495

DELAWARE
Best Products Foundation, 86
The William Bingham Foundation, 87
Mellon Bank Corporation, 297
Scott Paper Company Foundation, 454

DISTRICT OF COLUMBIA
Best Products Foundation, 86
The William Bingham Foundation, 87
Adolph Coors Company, 138
McGraw-Hill Foundation, Inc., 292
The Pillsbury Company, 437

---

*For further information see "How to Use This Directory"

Sponsor Type Index

Museum/Library

Nonprofit Organization

Listing of Sponsoring Organizations

The Abbott Laboratories Fund
Abbott Park
North Chicago, IL 60064

Aeroquip Foundation
300 South East Avenue
Jackson, MI 49203-1972

Aetna Life & Casualty Foundation
151 Farmington Avenue
Hartford, CT 06156

The Ahmanson Foundation
9215 Wilshire Boulevard
Beverly Hills, CA 90210

Alcoa Foundation
1501 Alcoa Building
Pittsburgh, PA 15219

The George I. Alden Trust
370 Main Street
Worcester, MA 01608

Allstate Foundation
Allstate Plaza
Northbrook, IL 60062

The American Academy and Institute of Arts and Letters
633 West 155th Street
New York, NY 10032-7599

American Academy in Rome
41 East 65th Street
New York, NY 10021

American Antiquarian Society
185 Salisbury Street
Worcester, MA 01609-1634

American Association of University Women Educational Foundation
2401 Virginia Avenue, NW
Washington, DC 20037

American Council of Learned Societies
228 East 45th Street
New York, NY 10017

American Express Foundation
American Express Plaza, 19th Floor
New York, NY 10004

American Historical Association
400 A Street SE
Washington, DC 20003

American Institute of Indian Studies
1130 East 59th Street
Chicago, IL 60637

American Institute of Pakistan Studies
138 Tolentine Hall
Villanova, PA 19085

American Jewish Archives
3101 Clifton Avenue
Cincinnati, OH 45220

American Museum of Natural History
Central Park West at 79th Street
New York, NY 10024

The American Numismatic Society
Broadway at 155th Street
New York, NY 10032

American Oriental Society
329 Sterling Memorial Library, Yale Station
New Haven, CT 06520

American Philosophical Society
104 South Fifth Street
Philadelphia, PA 19106

The American Research Center in Egypt
50 Washington Square South
New York, NY 10003

American Research Institute in Turkey
1155 East 58th Street
Chicago, IL 60637

American School of Classical Studies at Athens
41 East 72nd Street
New York, NY 10021

American Schools of Oriental Research
4243 Spruce Street
Philadelphia, PA 19104

Ameritech Foundation
30 South Wacker Drive, 34th Floor
Chicago, IL 60606

Amoco Foundation
200 East Randolph Drive
Chicago, IL 60601

Anheuser-Busch Companies, Inc.
One Busch Place
Saint Louis, MO 63118-1852

ARCO Foundation
515 South Flower Street
Los Angeles, CA 90071

Asian Cultural Council
280 Madison Avenue
New York, NY 10016

The Vincent Astor Foundation
405 Park Avenue
New York, NY 10022

AT&T Foundation
550 Madison Avenue, Room 2700
New York, NY 10022

Mary Reynolds Babcock Foundation
102 Reynolda Village
Winston-Salem, NC 27106-5123

The Bay Foundation, Inc.
14 Wall Street, Suite 1600
New York, NY 10005

Best Products Foundation
1616 P Street, NW, Suite 100
Washington, DC 20036

The William Bingham Foundation
1250 Leader Building
Cleveland, OH 44114

Blandin Foundation
100 Pokegama Avenue North
Grand Rapids, MN 55744

Bodman Foundation
767 Third Avenue
New York, NY 10017

The Boeing Company
Mail Stop: P.O. Box 3707
Seattle, WA 98124-2207

Boettcher Foundation
1670 Broadway, Suite 3301
Denver, CO 80202

Borg-Warner Foundation
200 South Michigan Avenue
Chicago, IL 60604

The Boston Foundation
One Boston Place
Boston, MA 02109

The Boston Globe Foundation
135 Morrissey Boulevard
Boston, MA 02107

BP America Inc.
200 Public Square
Cleveland, OH 44114-2376

The Bristol-Myers Fund, Inc.
345 Park Avenue
New York, NY 10154

The Brown Foundation, Inc.
2118 Welch Avenue, P.O. Box 13646
Houston, TX 77219

John Carter Brown Library
Box 1894
Providence, RI 02912

Mary Ingraham Bunting Institute of Radcliffe College
10 Garden Street
Cambridge, MA 02138

Burlington Northern Foundation
999 Third Avenue
Seattle, WA 98104-4097

Burroughs Corporation
One Burroughs Place
Detroit, MI 48232

Cabot Corporation Foundation
950 Winter Street, P.O. Box 9073
Waltham, MA 02254-9073

The Morris and Gwendolyn Cafritz Foundation
1825 K Street, NW
Washington, DC 20006

The Louis Calder Foundation
230 Park Avenue
New York, NY 10169

Amon G. Carter Foundation
1212 InterFirst Bank Building, P.O. Box 1036
Fort Worth, TX 76101

Caterpillar Foundation
100 NE Adams
Peoria, IL 61629-1480

Center for Advanced Study in the Visual Arts
Washington, DC 20565

The Center for Field Research
680 Mount Auburn Street, Box 403
Watertown, MA 02172

Center for Italian Renaissance Studies
401 Boylston Hall
Cambridge, MA 02138

Champion International Corporation
One Champion Plaza
Stamford, CT 06921

The Champlin Foundations
P.O. Box 637
Providence, RI 02901

Chevron Corporation
P.O. Box 7753
San Francisco, CA 94120

The Chicago Community Trust
222 North LaSalle Street, Suite 1400
Chicago, IL 60601

Chrysler Corporation Fund
P.O. Box 1919
Detroit, MI 48288

Citicorp
200 South Wacker Drive
Chicago, IL 60606

Robert Sterling Clark Foundation, Inc.
112 East 64th Street
New York, NY 10021

William Andrews Clark Memorial Library
2520 Cimarron Street
Los Angeles, CA 90018

Columbia Foundation
1090 Sansome Street
San Francisco, CA 94111

The Columbus Foundation
1265 Neil Avenue
Columbus, OH 43201

Committee on Scholarly Communication with the People's Republic of China
2101 Constitution Avenue, NW
Washington, DC 20418

Compton Foundation
10 Hanover Square
New York, NY 10005

Cooper Industries Foundation
P.O. Box 4446
Houston, TX 77210

Adolph Coors Company
Golden, CO 80401

Corning Glass Works Foundation
MP-HF-02-1
Corning, NY 14831

The Dr. M. Aylwin Cotton Foundation
P.O. Box 232, Pollet House
The Pollet, St. Peter Port, Guernsey, Channel Islands

Council for International Exchange of Scholars
Eleven Dupont Circle, NW, Suite 300
Washington, DC 20036-1257

The Cowles Charitable Trust
630 Fifth Avenue, Suite 1612
New York, NY 10111-0144

Cummins Engine Foundation
Mail Code 60814, Box 3005
Columbus, IN 47202-3005

Charles and Margaret Hall Cushwa Center
Room 614, Memorial Library
Notre Dame, IN 46556

Dart & Kraft Foundation
2211 Sanders Road
Northbrook, IL 60062

Data General
4400 Computer Drive
Westboro, MA 01580

Dayton Hudson Foundation
777 Nicollet Mall
Minneapolis, MN 55402

The Gladys Krieble Delmas Foundation
40 West 57th Street, 27th Floor
New York, NY 10019

Geraldine R. Dodge Foundation, Incorporated
95 Madison Avenue, P.O. Box 1239R
Morristown, NJ 07960

Dow Chemical Company Foundation
2030 Willard H. Dow Center
Midland, MI 48674

Dresser Foundation, Inc.
P.O. Box 718
Dallas, TX 75221

Dumbarton Oaks Center for Byzantine Studies
1703 32nd Street, NW
Washington, DC 20007

Early American Industries Association
The Winterthur Museum
Winterthur, DE 19735

Eastern National Park & Monument Association
P.O. Box 671
Cooperstown, NY 13326

Eastman Kodak Company
343 State Street
Rochester, NY 14650

Eaton Corporation
Eaton Center
Cleveland, OH 44114

El Pomar Foundation
P.O. Box 158
Colorado Springs, CO 80901

Eleutherian Mills Historical Library
P.O. Box 3630, Greenville
Wilmington, DE 19807

Enron Foundation—Houston
P.O. Box 1188
Houston, TX 77001

Enron Foundation—Omaha
2600 Dodge Street
Omaha, NE 68131

Exxon Education Foundation
111 West 49th Street
New York, NY 10020-1198

Federal Council on the Arts and the Humanities
1100 Pennsylvania Avenue, NW
Washington, DC 20506

Federal Express Corporation
P.O. Box 727
Memphis, TN 38194-1850

Leland Fikes Foundation
3206 Republic Bank Tower
Dallas, TX 75201

First Bank System Foundation
517 Marquette Avenue
Minneapolis, MN 55402

First Interstate Bank of California Foundation
707 Wilshire Boulevard, W15-3
Los Angeles, CA 90017

The Fluor Foundation
3333 Michelson Drive
Irvine, CA 92730

FMC Foundation
200 East Randolph Drive
Chicago, IL 60601

Folger Shakespeare Library
201 East Capitol Street, SE
Washington, DC 20003

The Ford Foundation
320 East 43rd Street
New York, NY 10017

Ford Motor Company Fund
The American Road, P.O. Box 1899
Dearborn, MI 48121-1899

Gannett Foundation, Inc.
Lincoln Tower
Rochester, NY 14604

General Electric Foundations
3135 Easton Turnpike
Fairfield, CT 06431

General Foods
250 North Street
White Plains, NY 10625

General Mills Foundation
P.O. Box 1113
Minneapolis, MN 55440

General Motors Foundation, Inc.
3044 West Grand Boulevard
Detroit, MI 48202-3091

General Services Administration
Federal Supply Service
Washington, DC 20406

The Wallace Alexander Gerbode Foundation
470 Columbus Avenue, Suite 209
San Francisco, CA 94133

The Getty Center for the History of Art and the Humanities
401 Wilshire Boulevard, Suite 400
Santa Monica, CA 90401-1455

The J. Paul Getty Trust
1875 Century Park East, Suite 2300
Los Angeles, CA 90067

Florence J. Gould Foundation
Eighty Pine Street
New York, NY 10005

Graham Foundation
4 West Burton Place
Chicago, IL 60610

Philip L. Graham Fund
1150 Fifteenth Street, NW
Washington, DC 20071

Mary Livingston Griggs and Mary Griggs Burke Foundation
1400 Norwest Center, 55 East Fifth
Street
Saint Paul, MN 55101

GTE Foundation
One Stamford Forum
Stamford, CT 06904

The Daniel and Florence Guggenheim Foundation
950 Third Avenue
New York, NY 10022

The Harry Frank Guggenheim Foundation
527 Madison Avenue
New York, NY 10022-4301

John Simon Guggenheim Memorial Foundation
90 Park Avenue
New York, NY 10016

Hagley Museum and Library
P.O. Box 3630
Wilmington, DE 19807

The Hall Family Foundations
P.O. Box 419580
Kansas City, MO 64141-6580

Hallmark Cards, Inc.
2501 McGee, Box 580
Kansas City, MO 64108

The Armand Hammer Foundation
10889 Wilshire Boulevard
Los Angeles, CA 90024

James G. Hanes Memorial Fund/ Foundation
P.O. Box 3099
Winston-Salem, NC 27150

Hawaiian Electric Industries Charitable Foundation
P.O. Box 730
Honolulu, HI 86808-0730

Charles Hayden Foundation

One Bankers Trust Plaza, 130 Liberty Street
New York, NY 10006

The Hearst Foundations

90 New Montgomery Street, Suite 1212
San Francisco, CA 94105

H. J. Heinz Company Foundation

P.O. Box 57
Pittsburgh, PA 15230

Howard Heinz Endowment

301 Fifth Avenue, Suite 1417
Pittsburgh, PA 15222-2494

The William R. and Flora L. Hewlett Foundation

525 Middlefield Road
Menlo Park, CA 94025

Hewlett-Packard Company Foundation

3000 Hanover Street
Palo Alto, CA 94304

The Hillman Foundation, Inc.

2000 Grant Building
Pittsburgh, PA 15219

Historic Deerfield

Deerfield, MA 01342

The Hitachi Foundation

1725 K Street, NW, Suite 1403
Washington, DC 20006

Hoblitzelle Foundation

1410 Tower 1, First Republic Bank Center
Dallas, TX 75201

Honeywell Foundation

MN12-5259, Honeywell Plaza
Minneapolis, MN 55408

Hoover Presidential Library Association, Inc.

P.O. Box 696
West Branch, IA 52358

The George A. and Eliza Gardner Howard Foundation

42 Charlesfield Street, Box 1867
Providence, RI 02912

The Huntington Library

1151 Oxford Road
San Marino, CA 91108

IBM Corporation

2000 Purchase Street
Purchase, NY 10577

IC Industries, Inc.

One Illinois Center, 111 East Wacker Drive
Chicago, IL 60601

Indian Arts and Crafts Board

Department of the Interior
Washington, DC 20240

Institute of Early American History and Culture

Box 220
Williamsburg, VA 23187

Institute of International Education

809 United Nations Plaza
New York, NY 10017

Institute of Museum Services

1100 Pennsylvania Avenue, NW, Room 609
Washington, DC 20202

International Paper Company Foundation

Two Manhattanville Road
Purchase, NY 10577

International Research & Exchanges Board

126 Alexander Street
Princeton, NJ 08540-7102

The James Irvine Foundation

One Market Plaza, Steuart Street Tower, Suite 2305
San Francisco, CA 94105

Jerome Foundation, Inc.

West 2090 First National Bank Building
Saint Paul, MN 55101

George Frederick Jewett Foundation

One Maritime Plaza, Suite 1340
San Francisco, CA 94111

Johnson Controls Foundation

5757 North Green Bay Avenue, P.O. Box 591
Milwaukee, WI 53201

Edward C. Johnson Fund
82 Devonshire Street
Boston, MA 02109

The Johnson's Wax Fund, Inc.
1525 Howe Street
Racine, WI 53403

The Fletcher Jones Foundation
One Wilshire Building, Suite 1210, 624
    South Grand Avenue
Los Angeles, CA 90017

W. Alton Jones Foundation
433 Park Street
Charlottesville, VA 22901

The J. M. Kaplan Fund, Inc.
330 Madison Avenue
New York, NY 10017

W. M. Keck Foundation
555 South Flower Street, Suite 3230
Los Angeles, CA 90071

Peter Kiewit Foundation
Woodmen Tower, Suite 1145, Farnam
    at Seventeenth
Omaha, NE 68102

**Robert J. Kleberg, Jr. and Helen C.
Kleberg Foundation**
700 North St. Mary's Street, Suite 1200
San Antonio, TX 78205

Knight Foundation
1 Cascade Plaza, 8th Floor
Akron, OH 44308

The Kresge Foundation
3215 West Big Beaver Road, P.O. Box
    3151
Troy, MI 48007-3151

Samuel H. Kress Foundation
221 West 57th Street
New York, NY 10019

Lannan Foundation
12555 West Jefferson Boulevard, Suite
    218
Los Angeles, CA 90066

Eli Lilly and Company Foundation
Lilly Corporate Center
Indianapolis, IN 46285

The Lincoln Electric Foundation
22801 St. Clair Avenue
Cleveland, OH 44117

The Charles A. Lindbergh Fund, Inc.
Box O
Summit, NJ 07901

The Henry Luce Foundation, Inc.
111 West 50th Street
New York, NY 10020

**The J. E. and L. E. Mabee Foundation,
Inc.**
401 South Boston, 30th Floor
Tulsa, OK 74103-4017

**The John D. and Catherine MacArthur
Foundation**
140 South Dearborn Street
Chicago, IL 60603

William Hammond Mathers Museum
601 East Eighth Street
Bloomington, IN 47405

The May Stores Foundation, Inc.
611 Olive Street
Saint Louis, MO 63101

McGraw-Hill Foundation, Inc.
1221 Avenue of the Americas
New York, NY 10020

McKesson Foundation, Inc.
One Post Street
San Francisco, CA 94104

The Mead Corporation Foundation
Courthouse Plaza Northeast
Dayton, OH 45463

The Meadows Foundation
2922 Swiss Avenue
Dallas, TX 75204-5928

The Andrew W. Mellon Foundation
140 East 62nd Street
New York, NY 10021

Mellon Bank Corporation
One Mellon Bank Center, Room 368
Pittsburgh, PA 15258

Metropolitan Life Foundation
One Madison Avenue
New York, NY 10010

The Metropolitan Museum of Art
Fifth Avenue and 82nd Street
New York, NY 10028

The Milwaukee Foundation
1020 North Broadway
Milwaukee, WI 53202

Mobil Foundation, Inc.
150 East 42nd Street
New York, NY 10017

The Moody Foundation
704 Moody National Bank Building
Galveston, TX 77550

Morgan Guaranty Trust Company of New York
23 Wall Street
New York, NY 10015

Philip Morris Companies Inc.
120 Park Avenue
New York, NY 10017

Mountain Bell Foundation
1801 California Street, Room 5050
Denver, CO 80202

M. J. Murdock Charitable Trust
P.O. Box 1618
Vancouver, WA 98668

Museum of Comparative Zoology
26 Oxford Street
Cambridge, MA 02138

The Nalco Foundation
One Nalco Center
Naperville, IL 60566-1024

NASA Headquarters
400 Maryland Avenue, SW
Washington, DC 20546

National Archives and Records Administration
National Archives Building
Washington, DC 20408

National Endowment for the Arts
1100 Pennsylvania Avenue, NW
Washington, DC 20506

National Endowment for the Humanities
1100 Pennsylvania Avenue, NW
Washington, DC 20506

National Gallery of Art
Washington, DC 20565

National Geographic Society
Seventeenth and M Streets, NW
Washington, DC 20036

National Historical Publications and Records Commission
National Archives Building
Washington, DC 20408

National Park Service
Washington, DC 20240

National Science Foundation
1800 G Street, NW
Washington, DC 20550

National Trust for Historic Preservation
1785 Massachusetts, NW
Washington, DC 20036

The New York Community Trust
415 Madison Avenue
New York, NY 10017

The New York Times Company Foundation, Inc.
229 West 43rd Street
New York, NY 10036

New York Zoological Society
Bronx, NY 10460

The Newberry Library
60 West Walton Street
Chicago, IL 60610

Edward John Noble Foundation
32 East 57th Street
New York, NY 10022

Norfolk Southern Foundation
P.O. Box 3040
Norfolk, VA 23514-3040

Northwestern Bell Foundation
1314 Douglas On-The-Mall, Fifth Floor
Omaha, NE 68102

Norton Company
1 New Bond Street
Worcester, MA 01606

Norwest Foundation
1200 Peavey Building
Minneapolis, MN 55479

Pacific Northwest Bell Telephone Company
1600 Bell Plaza, Room 3203
Seattle, WA 98191

Pacific Telesis Foundation
130 Kearny Street, Room 3351
San Francisco, CA 94108

The David and Lucile Packard Foundation
330 Second Street, Suite 200
Los Altos, CA 94022

The Parker Foundation
1200 Prospect Street, Suite 575
La Jolla, CA 92037

William Penn Foundation
1630 Locust Street
Philadelphia, PA 19103-6305

Pennzoil Company
Pennzoil Place, P.O. Box 2967
Houston, TX 77252-8200

The Pew Charitable Trusts
Three Parkway, Suite 501
Philadelphia, PA 19102-1305

The Philadelphia Center for Early American Studies
3808 Walnut Street
Philadelphia, PA 19104

Ellis L. Phillips Foundation
13 Dartmouth College Highway
Lyme, NH 03768

The Pillsbury Company
Pillsbury Center
Minneapolis, MN 55402-1464

The Pittsburgh Foundation
301 Fifth Avenue, Suite 1417
Pittsburgh, PA 15222-2494

Polaroid Foundation
28 Osborn Street
Cambridge, MA 02139

PPG Industries Foundation
One PPG Place
Pittsburgh, PA 15272

Primerica Foundation
American Lane, P.O. Box 3610
Greenwich, CT 06836

The Prospect Hill Foundation
420 Lexington Avenue, Suite 3020
New York, NY 10170

The Prudential Foundation
Prudential Plaza
Newark, NJ 07101

The Regenstein Foundation
3450 North Kimball Avenue
Chicago, IL 60618

Reynolds Metals Company Foundation
6601 Broad Street Road
Richmond, VA 23261

The Rockefeller Foundation
1133 Avenue of the Americas
New York, NY 10036

Helena Rubinstein Foundation
405 Lexington Avenue
New York, NY 10174

SAFECO Insurance Companies
SAFECO Plaza
Seattle, WA 98185

The San Francisco Foundation
500 Washington Street, Eighth Floor
San Francisco, CA 94111

Santa Fe Southern Pacific Foundation
224 South Michigan Avenue
Chicago, IL 60604-2401

Sara Lee Foundation
Three First National Plaza
Chicago, IL 60602-4206

School of American Research
P.O. Box 2188
Santa Fe, NM 87504

Scott Paper Company Foundation
Scott Plaza
Philadelphia, PA 19113

Security Pacific Foundation HC-4
Terminal Annex, P.O. Box 2097
Los Angeles, CA 90051

Shell Oil Company Foundation
Two Shell Plaza, P.O. Box 2099
Houston, TX 77252

The L. J. Skaggs and Mary C. Skaggs Foundation
1330 Broadway, 17th Floor
Oakland, CA 94612

Smithsonian Institution
3300 L'Enfant Plaza
Washington, DC 20560

Social Science Research Council
605 Third Avenue
New York, NY 10158

Southwestern Bell Foundation
One Bell Center, Room 38-K-8
Saint Louis, MO 63101

Steele-Reese Foundation
9 West 57th Street
New York, NY 10019

Doris Jones Stein Foundation
1024 Summit Drive
Beverly Hills, CA 90210

Sun Company, Inc.
100 Matsonford Road
Radnor, PA 19087

Anne Burnett and Charles Tandy Foundation
1577 Interfirst Tower
Fort Worth, TX 76102

Tenneco Inc.
Tenneco Building, P.O. Box 2511
Houston, TX 77252-2511

Texaco Philanthropic Foundation Inc.
2000 Westchester Avenue
White Plains, NY 10650

Textron Charitable Trust
P.O. Box 878
Providence, RI 02091

3M Foundation, Inc.
3M Center, Building 521-11-01
Saint Paul, MN 55144

Times Mirror Foundation
Times Mirror Square
Los Angeles, CA 90053

The Travelers Companies Foundation
One Tower Square
Hartford, CT 06183

TRW Foundation
1900 Richmond Road
Cleveland, OH 44124

Union Pacific Foundation
345 Park Avenue
New York, NY 10154

USX Foundation Inc.
600 Grant Street, Room 6284
Pittsburgh, PA 15230

Valley Bank Charitable Foundation
P.O. Box 29524
Phoenix, AZ 85038

Vatican Film Library
3655 West Pine Boulevard
Saint Louis, MO 63108

Dewitt Wallace-Reader's Digest Fund
1270 Avenue of the Americas, Suite 2118
New York, NY 10020

Lila Wallace-Reader's Digest Fund
1270 Avenue of the Americas, Suite 2118
New York, NY 10020

Wells Fargo Foundation
420 Montgomery Street
San Francisco, CA 94163

Wenner-Gren Foundation for Anthropological Research
1865 Broadway
New York, NY 10023-7596

Westinghouse Electric Fund
Westinghouse Electric Corporation
Pittsburgh, PA 15222

Whatcom Museum of History and Art
121 Prospect Street
Bellingham, WA 98225

Woodrow Wilson International Center for Scholars
Smithsonian Institution Building
Washington, DC 20560

**Woodrow Wilson National Fellowship
Foundation**

Box 642
Princeton, NJ 08540

Winterthur Museum

Winterthur, DE 19735

The Wortham Foundation, Inc.

2727 Allen Parkway, Suite 2000
Houston, TX 77019

The Xerox Foundation

P.O. Box 1600
Stamford, CT 06904

The Yale Center for British Art

Box 2120 Yale Station
New Haven, CT 06520

Bibliography

GENERAL FUNDING AND GRANTSMANSHIP

Printed Source Materials

Academic Research Information Service (ARIS). San Francisco: Academic Research Information System. Monthly newsletters (*Biomedical Sciences Report, Creative Arts and Humanities Report, Social and Natural Sciences Report, The Student Report*) detailing grant information and deadlines of federal programs, foundations, associations, organizations, and universities.

America's Newest Foundations. 2nd ed. Washington, DC: The Taft Group, 1988. A list of new and emerging foundations.

Annual Register of Grant Support 1987-1988. 20th ed. Wilmette, IL: National Register Publishing Co., 1987. Lists 2,679 grant programs offered by the federal government, foundations, and professional and educational associations. Includes support for research, travel, exchanges, and information about prizes and awards.

ARTS REVIEW. Washington, DC: Superintendent of Documents, U.S. Government Printing Office. A quarterly review of NEA programs and deadlines.

The Capital Campaign Handbook: How to Maximize Your Fund Raising Campaign. David J. Hauman. Washington, DC: The Taft Group, 1988. A "how-to" book on managing successful capital campaigns.

Catalog of Federal Domestic Assistance. 22nd ed. Washington, DC: U.S. Office of Management and Budget, 1988. Lists federal grants, loans, technical assistance, programs, and other service and information activities. Includes information on program purpose, eligibility, deadlines, and points of contact for additional information.

Chronicle of Higher Education. Washington, DC: The Chronicle of Higher Education, Inc. A weekly publication which includes grant and fellowship information and deadlines.

Commerce Business Daily. Washington, DC: Superintendent of Documents, Government Printing Office. A daily publication, Monday through Friday, which includes information about grants and contracts from the federal government.

Computer Resource Guide for Nonprofits. 3rd ed. San Francisco: Public Management Institute, 1985. Lists foundations, corporations, and federal agencies that award grants for computer hardware, software, and training.

Corporate 500: The Directory of Corporate Philanthropy. 7th ed. San Francisco: Public Management Institute, 1988. Contains information on corporate direct-giving programs and foundation giving programs. Includes information on funding areas, eligibility, points of contact, and listings of former grant recipients.

Corporate Foundation Profiles. 5th ed. New York: The Foundation Center, 1987. Provides information on 230 of the largest company-sponsored foundations in the United States.

The Corporate Fund Raising Directory. 1985-1986 ed. Hartsdale, NY: Public Service Materials Center, 1984. Lists information on the application procedures, areas of interest, and grantmaking activities of over 600 corporations.

Directory of Financial Aids for International Activities. 4th ed. Prepared by the Office of International Programs, University of Minnesota. Minneapolis, MN: University of Minnesota, 1985. Contains information on 455 individual awards for research, study, travel, and teaching abroad.

Directory of Grants in the Humanities, 1987. Phoenix, AZ: The Oryx Press, 1987. Lists approximately 2,000 funding sources in the humanities, including federal sources, state sources, university-sponsored programs, corporate, and foundation sources.

Directory of Research Grants, 1988. Phoenix, AZ: The Oryx Press, 1988. Lists over 6,000 funding sources including the federal government, foundations, and other private sector sources.

Federal Grants & Contracts Weekly. Arlington, VA: Capitol Publications, Inc. Published weekly; lists grant and contract announcements, RFPs and RFAs by the federal government of interest to the academic community.

Federal Register. Washington, DC: Superintendent of Documents, U.S. Government Printing Office. Published daily; includes public regulations and legal notices issued by federal agencies, as well as RFAs and RFPs.

Federal Research Report. Silver Spring, MD: Business Publishers, Inc. Published weekly; lists federal contract and grant opportunities.

The Foundation Directory. 11th ed. New York: The Foundation Center, 1987. Profiles 4,403 foundations, including over 700 corporate foundations.

Foundation Grants Index. 16th ed. New York: The Foundation Center, 1987. Identifies over 40,000 foundation grants of $5,000 or more awarded by 460 major U.S. foundations. The *Foundation Grants Index Bimonthly* is a bimonthly update of the *Foundation Grants Index*.

Foundation Grants to Individuals. 6th ed. New York: The Foundation Center, 1988. Lists foundation funding programs for individual applicants.

Funding for Anthropological Research. Karen Cantrell and Denise Wallen, eds. Phoenix, AZ: The Oryx Press, 1986. Lists over 700 sources of support for anthropological research, broadly defined.

The Grant Advisor. Arlington, VA: Toft Consulting. Published monthly; lists grant opportunity information on federal and nonfederal sources of support.

Grants and Fellowships of Interest to Historians. Thelma Schwartz, ed. Washington, DC: American Historical Association, 1986. Lists over 180 funding programs in support of historical projects.

Grants in the Humanities, A Scholar's Guide to Funding Sources. 2nd ed. William E. Coleman, ed. New York: Neal-Schuman Publishers, 1984. Lists 197 programs for scholars in the humanities.

Grants Magazine. New York: Plenum Publishing Corporation. Quarterly publication containing information on corporation, foundation, and government grants, and information on current funding trends and programs.

The Grants Register, 1987-1989. Roland Turner, ed. New York: St. Martin's Press, 1986. Lists support from international and national government agencies and private organizations including scholarships, fellowships, research grants, exchange programs, and study and travel grants.

Guide to Corporate Giving in the Arts 4. Robert A. Porter, ed. New York: ACA Books, 1987. Lists 505 corporations which support arts and arts organizations.

How to Get Money for Research. Mary Rubin and the Business and Professional Women's Foundation. Old Westbury, NY: The Feminist Press, 1983. Lists research funding opportunities for and about women at the pre- and postdoctoral levels.

Humanities. Washington, DC: Superintendent of Documents, U.S. Government Printing Office. A bimonthly review of NEH programs and deadlines.

The International Foundation Directory. 4th ed. H.V. Hodson, consultant ed. Detroit, MI: Gale Research Co., 1986. Lists 770 foundations worldwide (including the U.S.) which provide transnational service.

NSF Bulletin. Washington DC: National Science Foundation. Issued monthly (except July and August) and provides news about NSF programs, deadline dates, publications, meetings, and other sources of information.

National Data Book. 11th ed. New York: The Foundation Center, 1987. Lists names, addresses, principal officers, and fiscal data on approximately 24,000 U.S. foundations.

Source Book Profiles 1987. New York: The Foundation Center, 1987. Provides profiles and analyses of the grantmaking patterns and activities of the 1,000 largest U.S. foundations.

Taft Corporate Directory. Washington, DC: The Taft Group, Inc., 1985. Lists over 350 corporate foundations and profiles and analyzes their grantmaking activities. The *Corporate Giving Watch* provides monthly updates.

Taft Foundation Information System. Washington, DC: The Taft Group, Inc. Includes the *Taft Foundation Reporter* and twelve issues each of *Foundation Giving Watch* and *Foundation Updates*; profiles U.S. foundations and lists grantmaking activities.

GENERAL FUNDING

Online Databases

Budgetscope. Washington, DC: Data Resources, Inc. Computer searchable through Data Resources, Inc. Includes federal budget information.

CBD-Online. Silver Spring, MD: United Communications Group. The complete, online equivalent of the *Commerce Business Daily.*

DBD Plus. Greenwich, CT: DMS, Inc. Computer searchable through Data Resources, Inc. Provides contract information on federal government sources.

Federal Assistance Programs Retrieval System. Washington, DC: General Services Administration. Computer searchable through Control Data Corporation Business Information Services. Provides details on federal programs. Corresponds to the *Catalog of Federal Domestic Assistance.*

Federal Research Report. Silver Spring, MD: Business Publishers, Inc. Computer searchable through NewsNet. Includes information on federal contract and grant opportunities. Corresponds to *Federal Research Report* newsletter.

Foundation Directory. New York: The Foundation Center. Computer searchable through DIALOG Information Services, Inc. Includes profiles of grantmaking foundations with assets of $1,000,000 or more who have given $100,000 or more in the year of record. *The Foundation Directory* is the corresponding printed source.

Foundation Grants Index. New York: The Foundation Center. Computer searchable through DIALOG Information Services, Inc. Details grants of $5,000 and over awarded by major U.S. foundations. *Foundation Grants Index* and *Foundation Grants Bimonthly* are the corresponding printed sources.

Grants. Phoenix, AZ: The Oryx Press. Computer searchable through DIALOG Information Services, Inc. Includes information on grant sources in support of research and study in all fields. The *Directory of Research Grants* is the corresponding printed source.

Grants and Contracts Weekly/Grants and Contracts Alert. Arlington, VA: Capitol Publications, Inc. Computer searchable through NewsNet. Includes federal grant and contract funding information in the social sciences, education, and health. The corresponding printed sources are *Federal Grants & Contracts Weekly* and *Health Grants & Contracts Weekly.*

Illinois Researcher Information Service (IRIS). Prepared by Campus-wide Research Services Office. Urbana, IL: University of Illinois at Urbana-Champaign. Contains over 4,000 funding opportunities sponsored by federal agencies, private and corporate foundations, and other organizations which support research and scholarship activities. Identifies potential sponsors for faculty, staff, and graduate students' research, teaching, travel, equipment, advanced study, and other activities.

National Foundations. New York: The Foundation Center. Computer searchable through DIALOG Information Services, Inc. Lists 22,500 grantmaking foundations in the U.S., including those with total assets less than $1,000,000. The *National Data Book* is the corresponding printed material.

The Planned Giving Deskbook. 1st ed. Alden B. Tueller, J.D. Washington, DC: The Taft Group, 1988. A looseleaf volume, with an annual revision service, of planned-giving law and developments.

Research Monitor News. Washington, DC: National Information Service. Computer searchable through NewsNet. Includes funding information from the *Commerce Business Daily* and the *Federal Register*.

Sponsored Programs Information Network (SPIN). Albany, NY: The Research Foundation of SUNY. Lists funding opportunities (federal, nonfederal, and corporate) designed to assist faculty and administrators in the identification of external support for research, education, and development projects.

Denise Wallen is research development coordinator of the Office of Research at the University of New Mexico, Albuquerque. Karen Cantrell holds a doctorate in anthropology and teaches at the University of New Mexico, Albuquerque. They are coeditors of *Funding for Research, Study and Travel: Latin America and the Caribbean, Funding for Research, Study and Travel: The People's Republic of China,* and *Funding for Anthropological Research,* also published by The Oryx Press.